Günter Stemberger is Professor of
Jewish Studies, University of Vienna.

JEWS AND CHRISTIANS
IN THE HOLY LAND

JEWS AND CHRISTIANS IN THE HOLY LAND

PALESTINE IN THE FOURTH CENTURY

BY
GÜNTER STEMBERGER

TRANSLATED BY
RUTH TUSCHLING

T&T CLARK
EDINBURGH

T&T CLARK LTD
59 GEORGE STREET
EDINBURGH EH2 2LQ
SCOTLAND

www.tandtclark.co.uk

Copyright © T&T Clark Ltd, 2000

Authorised English Translation of *Juden und Christen im Heiligen Land*
© C. H. Beck'sche Verlagsbuchhandlung (Oscar Beck), München 1987,
and incorporating additional material by Günter Stemberger.

The publishers gratefully acknowledge the support of Inter Nationes, Bonn, in
the preparation of the English translation.

All rights reserved. No part of this publication may be reproduced, stored in a
retrieval system, or transmitted, in any form or by any means, electronic,
mechanical, photocopying, recording or otherwise, without the prior
permission of T&T Clark Ltd.

First published 2000

ISBN 0 567 08699 2

British Library Cataloguing-in-Publication Data
A catalogue record for this book is available for the British Library

Typeset by Fakenham Photosetting Limited, Fakenham, Norfolk
Printed and bound in Great Britain by Bookcraft Ltd, Avon

Contents

Abbreviations		vii
List of Maps		xi
Preface to the English Translation		xiii
Introduction		1
I	Administration, Economy, Population	6
II	The Jews of Palestine under Constantine	22
III	Church Building and Christianization	48
IV	Christian Pilgrimage	86
V	Synagogue Building	121
VI	The Revolt against Gallus	161
VII	Julian's Religious Policies and Palestine	185
VIII	The Samaritans	217
IX	The Jewish Patriarch	230
X	The Rabbinate	269
Prospect		298
Bibliography		317
Index of Passages Cited		323
Index of Names and Subjects		327
Index of Authors		332

Abbreviations

ANRW	*Aufstieg und Niedergang der römischen Welt*
AZ	Aboda Zara
BA	*Biblical Archaeologist*
BASOR	*Bulletin of the American Schools of Oriental Research*
BB	Baba Batra
BQ	Baba Qamma
Ber	Berakhot
Bik	Bikkurim
BJRL	*Bulletin of the John Rylands Library*
BSOAS	*Bulletin of the School of Oriental and African Studies*
CC	Corpus Christianorum
Chag	Chagiga
CIJ	*Corpus Inscriptionum Judaicarum*, ed. J.-B. Frey, Rome, I 1936 (repr. with intr. by B. Lifshitz, New York 1975), II 1952
CJust	Codex Justinianus
CSEL	Corpus Scriptorum Ecclesiasticorum Latinorum
CTh	Codex Theodosianus
DtnR	Deuteronomy Rabba
ed	Eduyot
EI	*Eretz Israel*
Er	Erubin
ESI	*Excavations and Surveys in Israel*
ExR	Exodus Rabba
GCS	Die griechischen christlichen Schriftsteller
GenR	Genesis Rabba (Th-A = J. Theodor/C. Albeck, *Midrash Bereshit Rabba. Critical Edition with Notes and Commentary*, Jerusalem ²1965)
Hor	Horayot
HUCA	*Hebrew Union College Annual*
IEJ	*Israel Exploration Journal*
j	Jerusalem Talmud
Jeb	Jebamot
JJS	*Journal of Jewish Studies*
JQR	*Jewish Quarterly Review*

JSS	*Journal of Semitic Studies*
Ket	Ketubbot
Kil	Kilayim
LA	*Studii Biblici Francescani Liber Annuus*
LamR	Lamentations Rabba (B. = S. Buber, *Midrash Echa Rabbati. Sammlung aggadischer Auslegungen der Klagelieder*, Vilna 1899, repr. Hildesheim 1967)
LevR	Leviticus Rabba (M. = M. Margulies, *Midrash Wayyikra Rabba*, 5 vols., Jerusalem 1953–60)
LRE	A. H. M. Jones, *The Later Roman Empire*, Oxford 1964
Meg	Megilla
MGWJ	*Monatsschrift für Geschichte und Wissenschaft des Judentums*
MidrPs	Midrash Psalms (B. = S. Buber, *Midrasch Tehillim*, Vilna 1892, repr. Jerusalem 1966)
MQ	Moed Qatan
MSh	Maaser Sheni
NEAE	*The New Encyclopedia of Archaeological Excavations in the Holy Land*, ed. E. Stern, 4 vols., Jerusalem 1993
Ned	Nedarim
PEQ	*Palestine Exploration Quarterly*
Pes	Pesachim
PesR	Pesiqta Rabbati (F. = M. Friedmann, *Pesikta Rabbati. Midrasch für den Fest-Cyclus und die ausgezeichneten Sabbathe*, Vienna 1880)
PG	Patrologia Graeca
PL	Patrologia Latina
PLRE	*The Prosopography of the Later Roman Empire.* Vol. I, ed. A. H. M. Jones, M. R. Martindale, J. Morris, Cambridge 1971; Vol. II, ed. J. R. Martindale, Cambridge 1980
PRK	Pesiqta de Rab Kahana (M. = B. Mandelbaum, *Pesiqta de Rab Kahana*, 2 vols., New York 1962)
Qid	Qiddushin
RAC	*Reallexikon für Antike und Christentum*
RB	*Revue Biblique*
REJ	*Revue des Etudes Juives*
RHPR	*Revue d'Histoire et de Philosphie Religieuses*
Sanh	Sanhedrin
SBLSP	Society of Biblical Literature, Seminar Papers
SC	Sources chrétiennes

Shab	Shabbat
Sheb	Shebiit
Sheq	Sheqalim
SongR	Song of Solomon Rabba
T	Tosefta
VigChr	*Vigiliae Christianae*
WCJS	World Congress of Jewish Studies
ZDPV	*Zeitschrift des deutschen Palästinavereins*
ZNW	*Zeitschrift für die neutestamentliche Wissenschaft*
ZPE	*Zeitschrift für Papyrologie und Epigiafik*

Maps

The political structure of Palestine in the fourth century 8

Church buildings in the fourth and early fifth centuries 66

Synagogue buildings in the fourth and early fifth centuries 146

Preface to the English Translation

My history of Palestine in the fourth century has been thoroughly updated for this English version. The German manuscript was completed in 1986, which does not seem that long ago. But the past decade has brought about a number of important developments regarding our knowledge of the Palestine of late antiquity. Much of my historical presentation is based on archaeology, which is a very lively field of research in present-day Israel. A number of churches and even more synagogues from this period – most important that of Sepphoris and several Samaritan synagogues – have been excavated in the last decade and several final publications now fully document earlier excavations. Important recent books on the rabbinate and the patriarchate, on Jewish–Christian traditions as well as on the history of monasticism in Palestine encouraged me to reconsider several aspects of my original presentation. Research goes on and new archaeological discoveries will without doubt continue to contribute to our knowledge of the history of the Holy Land; thus, every book presents only the knowledge of the day. But I do hope that the many revisions have improved the book and brought it up to date again. I am grateful to T&T Clark for their readiness to publish this English translation not only because it will make the book accessible to a much larger public than a book in German can reach nowadays, but above all because it gave me the opportunity to update the book. My thanks are also due to Professor William Horbury at whose suggestion the work was undertaken, and to Ruth Tuschling for her excellent translation.

Günter Stemberger
Vienna, August 1999

Introduction

'Judaism and Christianity remain, up to the present day, in many ways religions of the fourth century'.[1] This observation of J. Parkes may perhaps sound exaggerated; but the crucial importance of the fourth century for the development of Christianity is indisputable. For Judaism, too, with its changing fortunes, developments began during this period that were to determine the future of Jewish life in many ways. This is true both for the inner shape of the life of Jewish congregations and Jewish intellectual life, and for the relations of Judaism with the outside world. Since that period, these relations were largely shaped by the Christian laws of the period about the Jews, although not indeed as completely as has often been thought.

Two dates give the historical framework for the present account: 324 and 438. In the year 324, Constantine was victorious in the battle of Chrysopolis, on the Asian side of the Bosphorus opposite the later Constantinople, over Licinius, his rival for the imperial power in the Roman East. Thus he became sole ruler of the Roman Empire, and thus also the Edict of Milan, which had declared Christianity to be a permissible religion, became fully operative in the eastern half of the Empire also. In the year 438, with which our survey will end, Theodosius II published his great collection of laws, the Codex Theodosianus. This summarized rather more than a century of legal development and also included the law of 380 that elevated the Catholic form of Christianity to the official religion of the Empire. Within the sphere of Christianity, the development that began with the Council of Nicaea of 325 came to an end with the Council of Chalcedon of 451.

From a Jewish point of view also, at least with hindsight, the

---

[1] J. Parkes, *The Conflict of the Church and the Synagogue* 153; but see also the heading in J. Neusner, *Major Trends in Formative Judaism III*, Chico 1985, 77: 'The Fourth Century as the True First Century in the History of the Judaic and Christian West'.

year 324 was a decisive one: the Roman Empire's turning to Christianity set the course for the entire future development. The Codex Theodosianus of 438 fixed for ever the abolition of the central organ of Jewish leadership, the Patriarchate, which had taken place between 415 and 429. It was the end of an era, as is emphasized by the completion of the Palestinian Talmud around the same time. How definitive this break was, would again only be seen with hindsight.

Palestine was the centre of developments. Christians and Jews strove for this land; paganism too was still a force to be reckoned with here. Thus it is not only our lack of knowledge of the Diaspora Judaism of the period that recommends a concentration of the presentation on the Holy Land itself. Only here did Judaism have a starting-position from which a trial of strength with Christianity did not appear completely hopeless. And, as this study will show, Judaism did indeed come off surprisingly well in the clash for a long while.

Writing a history of the Jews of Palestine between Constantine and Theodosius II is only possible by taking into account the development of the other population groups in the land, and duly including Christians, pagans and Samaritans in the presentation. Naturally it was Christianity in particular against which the Jews of Palestine had to hold their own. We are not here primarily concerned with a history of Christian–Jewish relationships in Palestine between Constantine and Theodosius; nevertheless, we must give more scope to a presentation of developments within Christianity than is customary in a portrayal of Jewish history. Thus there are separate chapters on Christian church building and pilgrimage, whereby the focus of interest remains on Judaism, which comes under pressure from the increase in Christian institutions, which ultimately become its heirs. Jewish traditions have a determining influence on Palestinian Christianity to an extraordinary degree, as on much of Christian pilgrim tradition. May we see here signs of Jewish influence, or simply Christian usurpation of Biblical and Jewish tradition? Of course, the meeting point of both traditions would be Jewish Christianity. But had this still any significance in the fourth century? Such examples suffice to suggest that Jewish developments cannot be understood without their Christian counterparts.

The presentation of the Jewish history of Palestine in this

period customarily follows the Codex Theodosianus and the development of laws regarding the Jews deriving from it. Only a limited number of historical occurrences, such as the revolt against Gallus, and the attempted rebuilding of the Temple under Julian, complete the picture. However, is the Codex really a useful historical source? If the laws regarding the Jews are read in isolation and not within the context of legislation in general, we run the risk of reading out of them a more or less constant history of deterioration of the Jews' legal position. Yet legislation and political reality often do not correspond. The actual importance of a law is often only the result of a long process of development after the time of its promulgation. Laws of the fourth century were often only regionally valid and were unknown in wide stretches of the Empire. It was only through their incorporation in the Codex Theodosianus that they became general imperial laws; and even afterwards they were often not observed in practice.[2]

In order to get a clearer picture of the effectiveness of the laws, and thus to obtain a more accurate representation of the facts, we need as comprehensive an evaluation as possible of all the available sources. *Archaeology* in particular offers valuable information and opportunities for cross-checking; for this reason, the present account goes into the excavations of synagogues and churches of this period in some detail. However, this can only offer a snapshot of the current state of research, which is continually moving on, and moreover even archaeological facts first need to be interpreted, and are thus not such objective witnesses as is sometimes thought. But the results of excavations can also produce more concrete information about the history of the economy and population than the literary sources, which are seldom very helpful on such matters.

Among the *literary sources*, I attempt to limit myself as far as possible to contemporary and also geographically close texts. In the case of *rabbinic texts* this means that the Babylonian Talmud is only occasionally cited, and I also make use of later midrashim as little as possible. The principal source is the Palestinian Talmud, along with the early rabbinic Biblical commentaries, which were edited in Palestine towards the end of the period under discussion, particularly the midrashim on Genesis, Leviticus, the

---

[2] See B.S. Bacharach, *The Jewish Community*; J. Cohen, *Roman Imperial Policy*.

Song of Solomon and Lamentations. The experiences and statements attributed in these texts to Palestinian rabbis of the fourth and fifth generation, i.e. men of the fourth century, appear to me in general to reproduce reliably the situation and feelings of the time; although it cannot be denied that there are difficulties in checking this. Such attributions in later midrashim need to be treated with greater caution in view of the time difference.

As far as the *writings of the Church Fathers* are concerned, naturally those authors are to be preferred who lived in Palestine or its neighbour Syria during the period and may be treated as eyewitnesses: e.g. Eusebius (260/265–339/340), who was from 313 bishop of his home town of Caesarea, the provincial capital of Palestine; Epiphanius (315–403), who came from southern Judaea and was from 367 Bishop of Salamis on Cyprus, but retained an interest and involvement in developments in Palestine; Cyril, Bishop of Jerusalem between approximately 350 and 386, with intervals; and finally the scholar Jerome, who came from Dalmatia but spent decades in Bethlehem working on his Biblical studies (331/345–419). Also relevant are the reports of the early pilgrims to the Holy Land, like that of the anonymous Bordeaux Pilgrim, who visited Palestine in 333, or the unfortunately only partially extant text of Egeria, that doughty traveller, who came to Jerusalem about 380.

Finally, a number of *pagan authors* should be mentioned; occasionally they offer a less partial witness than the principal participants in the debate, the Christians and Jews. One is Julian 'the Apostate', Emperor 361–363, on whom the hopes of the traditional pagan educated classes were focused for a short while. Two Antiochenes should also be mentioned, Ammianus Marcellinus (*ca.* 330–395), a Latin historiographer, who in the suite of General Ursicinus gained an acquaintance with Palestine, and the great teacher of rhetoric Libanius (314–393), among whose teachers were two professors from Palestine, Ulpian of Ashkelon and Zenobius of Elusa. Among his pupils were not only John Chrysostom, but also a son of the Jewish Patriarch.

Certainly, even despite the use of all these and further sources, countless blanks remain on the map. But it should become sufficiently detailed and three-dimensional for us to correct a few misrepresentations of the period that have gained currency. Naturally, the present account is in continual dialogue with M. Avi-Yonah, even where this is not explicitly stated. His *The Jews of*

Palestine, which appeared in Hebrew in 1946 and later in German and English translations, has long since become a classic. As well as being one of the great archaeologists of Israel, Avi-Yonah had an outstanding knowledge of the written sources. We are today, despite our dependence on him, no longer able to agree with him on certain key points, not only because of the advances in Palestinian archaeology since his time, but especially because of certain basic assumptions of Jewish historiography, to which he was wedded and which are understandable in the light of the time of the book's production. It is fundamentally the concept of Jewish history as one of suffering and heroic resistance that made Avi-Yonah accept certain things as facts that do not stand up to more searching enquiry. Our discussion with him must of course include continual reviewing of the sources – significantly, Avi-Yonah did not offer any references for certain important dates such as the introduction of a fixed calendar, because they seemed to him so self-evident. In comparison to his beautifully crafted narrative, the reader will find here rather a discussion of many details, which only slowly come together to form a picture, and more question-marks than certain statements. For a new, justifiable narrative history of Palestine in early Byzantine times much work still needs to be done; but in the meantime the unlearning of earlier certainties is not a work to be despised.

I

Administration, Economy, Population

Before we turn to the details of the development of Palestine and of the various sectors of its population between Constantine and Theodosius, the external framework within which this development took place should be shown. Palestine's political geography, economic life and population distribution will be briefly sketched here, particularly with respect to the starting position at the beginning of the fourth century, but also anticipating some later developments.

1. Political and Military Administration

After the Emperor Hadrian had crushed the Bar Cochba revolt in 135, the Roman province of Judaea was called *Syria Palaestina*. Its capital was, as before, not Jerusalem but Caesarea. The province's area was significantly smaller than that of the modern state of Israel: in the south the Negeb was missing, in the north a sizeable coastal strip, roughly from Haifa, which belonged to the Phoenician province; on the other hand, the Golan Heights and a small strip east of the Jordan belonged to the province.

In his reform of the Empire, Diocletian subdivided many large provinces; the individual governors were not to become too powerful. The number of provinces was roughly doubled, which drew the following – surely unfair – remark from Lactantius: 'And in order that all might be filled with terror, even the provinces were cut into slices: many governors and countless officials weighed on the individual areas and almost on the individual cities.'[1]

---

[1] Lactantius, *De mortibus persecutorum* 7,4 (CSEL 27, 180).

Administration, Economy, Population

By contrast, in the course of this reform the province of Palestine gained significant territories, at some point after 284 that cannot be dated more precisely. The province of Arabia (in the area of the present country of Jordan) received in the north some parts of the province of Syria, namely Auranitis, Trachonitis and Batanaea. In exchange it ceded the areas south of the Arnon, on both sides of the Jordan, to the province of Palestine. Thus the Negeb and the Nabataean cities Eilat and Petra became part of Palestine. In Petra's case, this transfer is first attested in 307, in Eusebius' register of Biblical place-names, the *Onomasticon*. However, the fact that the calendar of Bostra was adopted in Auranitis in about 295 suggests that the boundaries were redrawn at about that date. Dora on the north coast of Palestine, first attested as a city of Palestine by the Bordeaux Pilgrim, could also have been transferred to that province at this early date.

The governor of the province of Palestine thus had a significantly greater territory to administer compared to the time before Diocletian. Accordingly, the respective office-bearers were given higher standing: Constantine classified Palestine, among others, as a consular province, in order to regain senators for service as governor.[2] On the other hand, Diocletian completed in many provinces a separation of the civil and military powers, which later became almost the general rule. The governor merely kept the civil authority, legislation and financial administration (for which previously a procurator had usually had the responsibility). The military command, including the administration of the *limes* or border area, belonged to a separate functionary with the title *Dux*, who usually had a significantly longer period of office than the provincial governor's stint of one or two years at most, which undoubtedly strengthened the former's position.

In the course of the fourth century, the province of Palestine was divided. It is customary to assume a first division in 358, relying on Libanius' *Letter* 337: it is assumed that at that time the south, which had been newly gained under Diocletian, was separated again and became a province of its own under the name *Palaestina Salutaris*. Its capital was probably at first the Nabataean city of Elusa in the Negeb, which was replaced in the fifth century by Petra.[3] Then, about 400, a division of the

---

[2] See Jones, *LRE* 106.373.
[3] Y. Dan, 'Palaestina Salutaris'.

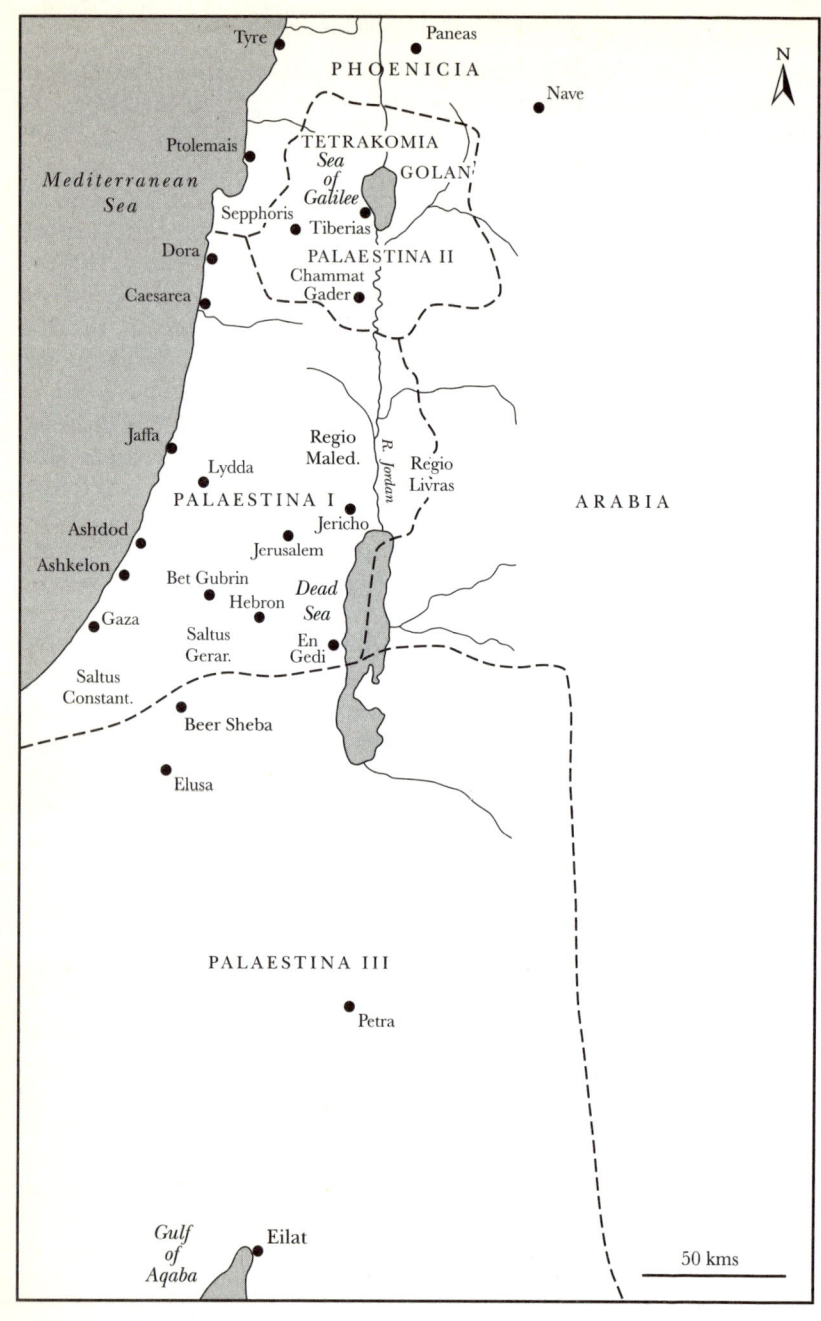

The political structure of Palestine in the fourth century

original territory of the province of Palestine into two parts is assumed: Judaea, Samaria and the coastal strip now formed the province of *Palaestina Prima*, whose capital remained Caesarea; Galilee, the Golan Heights and parts of the Decapolis formed the new province of *Palaestina Secunda* with its capital at Scythopolis, the old Beth Shean. The already independent *Palaestina Salutaris* now counted as *Palaestina Tertia*. However, there are also good arguments for the view that the province, having remained a unit until then, was only divided into three in 390, in a single operation.[4]

The subordinate level of administration to that of the province in the Palestine of this period was principally the *cities with their territories*. Even before this, the Roman administration had fostered the Hellenization of the country mainly by founding cities. Several such foundations are also attested for the time of Diocletian and Constantine: Diocletianopolis near Ashkelon and Maximianopolis in the territory of Caparcotna (Legio) belong in the reign of Diocletian. In the interest of the Christianization of the country, Constantine granted its own civic rights to the (mainly Christian) port of the pagan city of Gaza, under the name of Constantia Maiumas (also known as Neapolis). From the Jewish-dominated city of Diocaesarea (Sepphoris), he separated suburbs both for Helenopolis (near Nazareth, including Tabor) and for Naim (Come Nais). Thus the new foundations were without exception given territories that had previously belonged to other cities, for at the beginning of the fourth century Palestine was already mostly distributed into city territories. However, the cities continually lost more and more independence from the provincial administration, both regarding their tax jurisdiction (it was probably already Constantine who took their principal source of tax income, the *vectigalia*), and also regarding their judicial powers, of which they only retained traces, since nearly all cases were passed to the governor.[5]

Territories not belonging to cities were free of city jurisdiction and taxes. They were under a procurator, who answered directly to the provincial governor. Political reasons were often the cause of this form of administration, for example, in North-East Galilee

---

[4] This is argued by P. Mayerson, 'Libanius and the Administration of Palestine', *ZPE* 69 (1987) 251–60.

[5] See Jones, *LRE* 46.

with its mainly Jewish population, which apparently refused organization as a city for traditional and religious reasons. The territory was called *Tetrakomia* (the 'four villages'). At this period in the Roman Empire, village administration was relatively rare and existed in the imperial diocese of the Orient mainly in the provinces of Arabia, Palaestina Secunda and Tertia.[6] Sometimes there were also military reasons for a non-civic form of administration. For example, from the territory of Eleutheropolis (Beth Gubrin) in the south, the *Saltus Constantiniaces* and the *Saltus Gerariticus* were separated off; and the lower Jordan valley was divided into four *regiones*, the reasons for which were perhaps not only military, since a large area here was traditionally the property of the Roman emperor.

The *military* quota of the province of Palestine lay at two legions, since the time of Hadrian. The *Legio X Fretensis* was stationed in Aelia Capitolina, the former Jerusalem; the *Legio VI Ferrata* was quartered in Caparcotna near the old Megiddo. It was transferred to Damascus in the middle of the third century.[7] Whether it later returned to Palestine cannot be proved. It has been conjectured that the legion was transferred to Udruh, near Petra, in the late third or early fourth century, when that part of the province of Arabia supposedly came to Palestine.[8] However, the *Notitia Dignitatum*, a kind of official almanac of the Roman Empire, which was written *ca.* 420 and apparently survives unaltered as far as the eastern half of the empire is concerned, does not mention this legion, which must have been disbanded in the intervening period.

It is, however, certain that the Tenth Legion was transferred from Aelia Capitolina to Aila(th), today Eilat. This is usually dated to Diocletian's time, but could have happened somewhat earlier, under Aurelian.[9] Eusebius is our first witness to this important military alteration, in his *Onomasticon* under Ailat: 'At the furthest border of Palestine; there is the seat of the Roman legion with the title "The Tenth".' Jerome sees no need to

---

[6] Jones, *LRE* 713.
[7] See E. M. Smallwood, *The Jews under Roman Rule*, 498f.
[8] M. Speidel, *Roman Army Studies I*, Amsterdam 1984, 313 n. 11. S. T. Parker, *BASOR* 247 (1982) 25 n. 9, thinks this a plausible conjecture.
[9] On this, see D. F. Graf, 'The Saracens and the Defense of the Arabian Frontier', *BASOR* 229 (1978) 1–26, 19; B. Lifshitz, 'Légions romaines en Palestine', in *Hommages à M. Renard*, Brussels 1969, II, 458–69.

change anything in his Latin adaptation of the work towards the end of the century.[10]

The *Notitia Dignitatum* also mentions the Tenth Legion as still in Eilat. Most of the military bases are situated in the south, where the main weight of the military presence in Palestine lies in the fourth century. The *Limes Palaestinae* was also built to protect the south, probably under Diocletian.[11]

The background to this development was not only the fact that the Jewish population had long since come to terms with Roman rule. Thus unrest was unlikely in the interior of the province. But, from the side of the desert, the Arabian tribes were an increasing threat, less to the border than to the settlements within the southern region of the province; raids by Saracen robber bands penetrated as far as the neighbourhood of Jerusalem.[12]

Economic reasons also favoured the transfer of the military to the south. The constant difficulties with the Persian Empire made it seem advisable not to rely entirely on the traditional trade routes, which led through Persian territory, for trade with the east. In order to enable their circumvention by means of the sea route through the Red Sea, Eilat was fitted out as a trading port. From Eilat to Gaza or Ashkelon the goods had to be transported by land, and the military's task was to guarantee their safety.

As far as the overall strength of the troops stationed in Palestine is concerned, we must rely on conjecture. Certainly a legion no longer numbered 6,000 men, as under the principate, but probably between 1,000 and 3,000. In addition there were the auxiliary troops, about which Eusebius' *Onomasticon* and especially the later *Notitia Dignitatum* (Oriens 34) offer information. Moorish cavalry were stationed in Aelia Capitolina; halfway between Aelia and Jericho was the fort belonging to the *Cohors prima salutaris*, and at the Jordan itself – east of the present-day Allenby Bridge – the camp of the *Cohors secunda Cretensis*. These were the only units north of Hebron. A little south of Hebron there was a fort for a detachment of cavalry, *Equites*

---

[10] Eusebius, *Onomasticon* (GCS II/1, 6).
[11] See M. Gichon, 'Research on the Limes Palaestinae: A Stocktaking' in *Roman Frontier Studies*, Oxford 1979, 843–64; B. Isaac, *The Limits of Empire. The Roman Army in the East*, Oxford ²1992.
[12] P. Mayerson, 'The Saracens and the Limes', *BASOR* 262 (1986) 35–47; I. Shahîd, *Byzantium and the Arabs in the Fourth Century*, Washington, DC 1984, 284–329, 480f.

scutarii Illyriciani; the many other military posts were all situated in the original *Limes* strip between the Mediterranean and the Dead Sea (five bases) or even further south (approximately ten bases). Also under the command of the *Dux Palaestinae* were a series of forts in the Nabataean mountains east of the Jordan valley, which lie however outside our present concern. If we estimate these units of auxiliary troops at 500 to 1,000 men at most in each, we would arrive at a military occupation force of approximately 10,000 men; but the great uncertainty of the estimate must be stressed in this context.[13]

We also have little information on the recruitment of the troops. Apart from the (at least originally) Illyrian units, the *limitanei*, the border troops, were probably in general recruited locally. At least sporadically, Jews surely also served as soldiers, as is sufficiently attested by their later legal exclusion from military service. But usually they would probably have preferred the payment for a substitute (*aurum tironicum*), since they would otherwise have had difficulties keeping the sabbath and the dietary laws. The sons of soldiers generally also had to do military service, which must have contributed to a stronger sense of local loyalty among the troops. In peace-time, the military was occupied with building army camps and fortifications; road-building too, which by tradition was primarily oriented towards military interests, was chiefly the work of soldiers. However, agricultural work as military farmers was probably not yet done by soldiers at this period; this would rather have been a matter for the veterans.

2. The Economic Situation

(a) Currency, prices, taxes

The serious economic crisis that had hit the Roman Empire during the military anarchy of the third century naturally also made itself felt in Palestine, to its full extent. The astronomical rate of inflation led to a constant depreciation of the silver coinage; the striking of local bronze coins, a privilege exclusively

---

[13] For the figures see Jones, *LRE* 680–2, and M. P. Speidel, 'The Roman Army in Arabia', *ANRW* II 8, Berlin/New York 1977, 687–730, 725f. (reprinted in id., *Roman Army Studies* I). A list of military posts in Palestine is in F.-M. Abel, *Géographie* II, 178–84.

accorded to the cities, subsequently became too expensive and was abandoned. As a consequence, a money economy largely came to a standstill, at least in public life. Not only did soldiers and state officials receive the greater part of their income in kind; taxes too were increasingly replaced by payments in kind and services. Only from the end of the fourth century were state officials' salaries, military pay and taxes in kind gradually reconverted into payments in gold.[14]

Around 301 Diocletian attempted major economic reforms. In particular he reformed the money economy by introducing the gold standard, by which he probably only gave legal recognition to the *status quo*. At the same time he published an extensive catalogue of highest permitted prices. So far the evidence for this comes primarily from Asia Minor and is not necessarily suitable for application to Palestine, because there was considerable regional variation in the cost of living. Thus possibly the highest prices fixed in Diocletian's edict could be higher than the prices which had previously actually been effective in a province. Food prices and also wages, for example, were in Egypt only about half as high as in Palestine, and in Palestine only half as high as in Rome.

Reckoned in gold, prices around 300, when compared to those of the second century, show hardly any increase. However, this was no comfort to ordinary folk who had little to do with gold (coins). How much the situation had worsened in the third century for ordinary folk is shown by a saying of R. Levi in Cant.R. 2.5: 'Once, when money still existed, people eagerly listened to lectures on the Mishnah, Halakhah and Talmud. But now, since there is no money to be found and people are suffering in dire straits, they only want to hear words of blessing and consolation.'[15]

Diocletian's currency reform was not a success, because he could not strike enough gold coins to keep up the parity between the metals. Constantine was more successful in this regard, introducing the *solidus* (72 per pound of gold) and after 324 also striking new silver coinage (also 72 per pound). However, the *denarius* continued to be subject to severe inflation, and the return to a money economy was accomplished only gradually,

---

[14] See Jones, *LRE* 207f.
[15] D. Sperber, *Roman Palestine 200– 400. Money and Prices*, 126–8, 154.

particularly because of the constant fear of debasement of the coinage.[16]

Diocletian also attempted tax reforms. These are attested for Palestine by a series of boundary stones, which were set up by one Aelius Statutus during the time of the Tetrarchy in northeast Galilee, the Golan heights and the region of Damascus. He appears to have had an authority as tax official that went beyond the boundaries of the province, and was perhaps *censitor*, charged with the surveying of cultivable land. This may have become necessary when the previously *ad hoc* and unevenly levied *annona* was turned into a regular tax in kind.[17] Until that time, taxes in kind had been requisitioned as needed by means of extraordinary tax demands (*indictiones extraordinariae*); now these demands were intended to become clearer and more regular by calculating the requirements in advance.

(b) Agriculture

Although Palestine in the fourth century was largely divided into city territories, agriculture remained the basis of its economy. However, it had altered significantly due to the third-century crisis. The decades from the middle of the third to the early fourth century were a time of great periods of drought in Palestine, after which the climate cooled down again, bringing more rain.[18] These climatic changes are also attested by the fasts for rain which were declared with particular frequency by rabbis at this period. There are many mentions of these, e.g. jTaan II.1.65 a–b. For example, at 65 b R. Berechia is quoted: Once, even a thirteen-day fast for rain was unsuccessful; finally locusts even came and ate up the little that had grown. The consequences were many famines. We have evidence for these for the years 324 and 333, for example; in 350, Bishop Cyril of Jerusalem even sold church furnishings in order to buy food for the poor.[19]

---

[16] D. Sperber, *Money*, 96. The comment of R. Samuel b. R. Bun (jHor III,9,48c), quoted here, is however not necessarily to be understood as meaning that the possessor of gold can obtain credit, but the possessor of gold coins must pay cash. It may simply mean that it is easier to pay for one's daily needs with coins than with gold ingots.

[17] E. M. Smallwood, *The Jews under Roman Rule*, 535.

[18] E. Huntington, *Palestine and its Transformation*, London/New York 1911.

[19] Sozomen, *Church history* 4.25.3 (GCS 182).

This situation led to a decrease in population from the third century onwards. A significant migration to the cities also began, caused by the general increase in poverty and by the tax system, which was almost exclusively aimed at ownership of land and the yield of the harvest. The population of the cities paid almost no direct taxes, except the trade tax introduced under Constantine, the *collatio lustralis*, which, as the name indicates, was paid once every five years and was abolished again in the late fifth century due to the many complaints (from as early as 374 it no longer applied to rural craftsmen). Complaints about taxes were always customary. But the duties must have weighed particularly heavily on the country people in the late third century. In many cases, the produce was taken away from the farmers immediately after harvesting, as *annona* to supply the troops; during the time of the military emperors Palestine was repeatedly the scene of military campaigns. Quartering of soldiers and the duty to provide draught animals and workmen for the army (*angaria*) played a further part in the impoverishment of smallholders. In bad years it could happen that the entire harvest was taken away from the farmers and they themselves had to beg for bread in the city. This should perhaps be seen as the background to the rabbis' complaint about the Roman government in ExR 31.17: 'The governors, *duces* and eparchs march into the villages and rob and plunder, and when they return, they say: Bring us the poor, that we may take care of them!' Under these circumstances, the government was continually threatened with migration to the city unless taxes were lowered. But this was generally unsuccessful, as is shown by a story about Diocletian in Paneas, in the north of Palestine (jShebi IX.2.38 d).

Previously, family smallholdings had been typical for Palestine. But now the small farmers were increasingly disappearing, particularly because of extensive debts and the migration to the cities; large landowners profited from this situation. However, the possessions of the big landowners did not consist in continuous estates, as in other provinces, but usually in many small, widely scattered plots. To some extent, the previous farmers now worked the land as tenants, so that the original economic units were hardly changed; but partly the land simply lay fallow (the problem of the *agri deserti* existed elsewhere in the Roman empire and was repeatedly the subject of legislation). The previously customary system of small terraces collapsed on a large scale, and labour-intensive cultivation was replaced more and more by sheep farming.[20] The tenants' lack of interest, and even more the splintering of large estates into minuscule plots, also prevented the introduction of new methods which could have taken advantage of economies of scale. But since scattered property could also bring tax advantages, an important incentive towards uniting the estates was lacking.

In his comprehensive study of agriculture in Palestine between 200 and 400, D. Sperber finds that small family holdings had already disappeared almost entirely in the period between 300 and 350.[21] The rabbinic texts also now presuppose the exploitation of tenant farmers by the overseers (*epitropoi*) as the normal state of affairs in the villages (e.g. PRK, Aser Te'aser 2, M.161). From about 250, rabbinic preachers increasingly issue warnings about *patroni*, on whom the farmers became increasingly dependent.[22] Within this pattern of development, we notice however that the *colonatus*, a hereditary tie binding farmers to the soil, was only introduced in Palestine at a relatively late date, around 386 (CJust 11.51.1; in general as early as 332: CTh V.17.1). In the Negeb, at least, it appears even later not to have been customary.

But then, from the middle of the fourth century, a significant improvement of the agricultural situation makes itself felt. This is surely only in part due to the climatic changes already mentioned; in part the cause is probably an improved economic situation. A contemporary eyewitness is Ammianus Marcellinus, who writes in his *Res Gestae* XIV.8.11: 'The last (part) of Syria is Palestine, which extends over a wide territory and abounds in cultivated and well-kept land.' The approximately contemporary author of the *Expositio totius mundi*, like Ammianus a pagan, writes of Ashkelon and Gaza that they are 'outstanding cities with flourishing trade and abundance of everything, that export good wine to all Syria and Egypt' (§ 29)[23] – in Diocletian's maximum price edict there is no mention yet of wine export from Palestine. After listing the most important sites of the textile industry, among which the author names Scythopolis, Caesarea, Neapolis and Lydda, he adds

---

[20] D. Sperber, *Roman Palestine 200–400. The Land*, 63.
[21] D. Sperber, *The Land*, 136 n. 1.
[22] D. Sperber, *The Land*, 131.
[23] See also P. Mayerson, 'The Wine and Vineyards of Gaza in the Byzantine Period', *BASOR* 257 (1985) 75–80.

(§ 31): 'All the previously named famous cities are also fruitful in grain, wine and oil; they also have abundance of everything.' He then names for Jericho the Nicholas dates, pistachios and every kind of fruit.

3. The Population

Any attempt to estimate the population of a country or city in antiquity is extremely problematic, and its result unreliable. This is of course also true of Palestine. There is no study that considers this question specifically for the fourth century. However, there are several attempts for the first century and the time after the Bar Cochba revolt. M. Avi-Yonah estimates for Palestine, including the land east of the Jordan, in around 140 CE approximately 2.5 million inhabitants, of whom approximately 700,000 to 800,000 were Jews (as against 1.3 million before the revolt). In Galilee, so Avi-Yonah, they comprised about three-quarters of the population, in the coastal plain and beyond the Jordan about one quarter.[24]

While we may assume an increase in the population, and in particular a recovery of the Jewish share, in the decades under the Antonine and Severan emperors, which were a period of peace and security, on the other hand the crisis of the third century led to a decrease in population. Thus we might perhaps be entitled to apply Avi-Yonah's figures to the fourth century; but these premises are far too uncertain.

M. Broshi arrives at much lower figures for Palestine's heyday under Byzantine rule, which appear to be far more reliable, because of the criteria they are based on. Taking into account the water supply, the grain production and the population density in the cities, he calculates that Palestine west of the Jordan never passed the one million mark.[25] This figure, according to Broshi, is the maximum for the period around 600. We must take into consideration the fact that the significant drop in population

---

[24] M. Avi-Yonah, *The Jews of Palestine*, 19.
[25] M. Broshi, 'The Population'. Z. Safrai, *The Economy of Roman Palestine*, London 1994, 436ff., takes Broshi's estimate to be too low, but without himself giving concrete figures. See also id., *Godel ha-Okhlusia be-Eretz Yisrael ba-Tequfa ha-romit-bizantit*, in Y. Friedman et al. (eds.), *Hikrei Eretz* (*Festschrift* Y. Feliks), Ramat Gan 1997, 277–305.

because of the third-century crisis was only slowly made up, a fact that is also visible in the increased building activity of the fifth and sixth centuries. Thus we should probably not estimate the total population of Palestine west of the Jordan under Diocletian and Constantine as more than half a million.

Even more problematic is the distribution of this population figure to the individual groups of Jews, Samaritans, pagans and Christians. The *Christian population* of Palestine was certainly the smallest of these four groups. In his work on the martyrs of Palestine, Eusebius lists only 37 persons who were executed in the persecutions under Diocletian and afterwards until the year 311; there were also eight martyrs from Egypt. This low figure is surely not simply to be explained by lax implementation of the persecutory edicts by the provincial authorities. Furthermore, the fact that Palestine was represented by roughly fourteen bishops at the Council of Nicaea in 325, among them Eusebius of Caesarea and Macarius of Jerusalem, does not necessarily permit the conclusion that there were an equivalent number of significant Christian congregations in existence. The Christians were especially represented in the Hellenistic cities, but also in various villages in Judaea, mainly in the south, as may be seen from Eusebius' *Onomasticon*. However, archaeological evidence for the spread of Christianity before Constantine, e.g. church buildings, is only rarely available.

The *pagan population*, from which the Christian population had largely sprung, is principally to be found in the cities. Of the roughly twenty-five cities of Palestine west of the Jordan, only Tiberias and Sepphoris had a Jewish majority, and only Scythopolis, Caesarea and probably Lydda had significant Jewish communities. Aelia Capitolina – not only the city, but also its extensive territory, the three administrative areas of Herodion, Gophna and Oreine – was of course entirely forbidden to Jews, and, being a garrison town, remained largely pagan until Constantine. The same is probably true of Caesarea, as the seat of the provincial government. A further centre of the pagan population was the south with the coastal city of Gaza, where paganism remained very strong even as late as 400, and also the settlements of the Negeb, which was only Christianized at a late date. But we may assume a relatively numerous pagan population in Samaria also. Finally, the fact that pagans were also well represented outside the cities is a consequence, among other things, of the migration to the cities of the third century. Increasingly, land ownership came into the hands of non-Jews, which Jewish religious law opposed with increasing vehemence, but largely unsuccessfully. Roman officials and veterans gladly bought up the property of debt-ridden Jewish farmers; veterans received state funds and considerable tax relief for this purpose (CTh VII.20.3–4, from 320 and 325), which was probably a significant factor in these developments. Certainly in the early fourth century, most of the land in Palestine is already the property of non-Jews, as is suggested by a commentary on statements by R. Jochanan in jDemai II.1.22 c.

The *Samaritans* had spread ever further beyond Samaria proper since the middle of the second century. They founded communities in the coastal plain of Palestine, in Judaea and also in Galilee; even an extensive Samaritan diaspora came into being, whose congregations were scattered all over the Roman Empire. However, the source material for the Samaritans is particularly scanty, and their own chronicles are of quite late date. Thus we are forced to rely more on the (tendentious) accounts in rabbinic texts and the writings of the Church Fathers than would really be appropriate. It seems likely that the Samaritans, besides agriculture, engaged mainly in trade; in addition, service with the Roman authorities and the military seems to have attracted fairly large numbers. This probably explains their numbers in the provincial capital, Caesarea: according to Abba Mari, around the middle of the fourth century, Jews and non-Jews only outnumber the Samaritans in Caesarea when taken together (jDemai II.1.22 c). This may be an exaggeration, but that does not negate the importance of Samaritans for Caesarea. However, estimating the numerical strength of the Samaritans in the fourth century, 'the golden age of the Samaritans',[26] is again extremely difficult. M. Avi-Yonah has calculated their total numbers for the fifth to sixth centuries, the period of the great Samaritan rebellions against Byzantine rule, as about 300,000,[27] which is definitely much too high.

After the Bar Cochba revolt, the focus of the *Jewish population*

---

[26] H. G. Kippenberg, *Garizim und Synagoge*, 171.
[27] M. Avi-Yonah, 'The Samaritan Revolts against the Byzantine Empire', *EI* 4 (1956) 127–32 (Hebrew). Kippenberg, *Garizim und Synagoge*, 161, calls this 'a basically probable figure'.

was Galilee, with centres in Sepphoris and Tiberias. In addition, the community in Caesarea, where there was also a rabbinic school, must still have been significant. If we start from the synagogues for which we have archaeological evidence in the fourth century, there was a particular concentration in the region of Tiberias, in northern Galilee around Safed, in the neighbouring western Golan Heights. But also in Hauran (Nave, 45 km northeast of Tiberias) there is evidence for synagogues from this period. Some synagogue remains are also extant in the plain of Jezreel. In the south of Palestine, excavations of synagogues in the strip between En Gedi on the Dead Sea and Ashkelon witness to significant Jewish settlements, which are also known from literary testimonies, remarks in Eusebius' *Onomasticon* and rabbinic texts. Zoar too, at the southern end of the Dead Sea, had a Jewish community, which is attested archaeologically by several gravestones. However, it is questionable whether we may assume a Jewish majority in the coastal cities (at least together with the Samaritans), as Z. Safrai does. According to him, as well as Tiberias and Sepphoris, many other cities like Lydda, perhaps also Jericho, Emmaus and so on, had an absolute majority of Jews and Samaritans, and were thus run by Jews.[28] In the case of Lydda, a text in Eusebius' history of the martyrs of Palestine has caused some confusion: 'a large city in the land of Palestine, whose inhabitants are all Jews: in Aramaic it is called Lud, and in Greek it is known as Diocaesarea'. Diocaesarea is of course not Lydda, but Sepphoris! Is the name there in error, instead of Diospolis, or has the Semitic name been given wrongly?[29] However interesting it would be for us, the matter remains unclear. But at least the fact that the church was slow to gain a foothold in many cities is probably due less to a powerful Jewish population than to the persistence of pagan tradition and culture.

Bearing in mind all the caution that is necessary with regard to the sources, we are therefore justified in assuming for early fourth-century Palestine that the Jews were the largest population group, followed by the pagans, who were perhaps not far behind.

---

[28] Z. Safrai, *Gebulot*, 31f.
[29] The disputed text is extant only in the Syriac version (ed. W. Cureton 29). G. Alon, *The Jews in their Land*, 752, holds that Diocaesarea is a mistake for Diospolis, whereas e.g. S. Klein, *Sefer ha-Yishub,* 131, takes the clause about the Aramaic name to be a scribal gloss.

The number of Samaritans must have been significantly smaller, and the Christians came last. Naturally, these numbers were to change dramatically in the course of the fourth century, whereby the key movement was from the pagan to the Christian group, which also grew considerably through immigration. If it was already thought possible in the early fourth century that the majority of the land was owned by non-Jews, and if we take into consideration that the cities were in the majority non-Jewish, then it seems clear that after a century of Christianization we must certainly assume a sizeable non-Jewish majority in Palestine. Greater precision is unfortunately impossible.

II

The Jews of Palestine under Constantine

1. The Legal Position of Jews in 300

We must begin with some remarks on the legal situation before Constantine, in order to assess more easily the alterations of legal status for Jews in the fourth century. Of course, laws regarding Jews were each, in principle, valid for all Jews in the Roman Empire. But the extent to which they had an actual influence on the Jewish community in Palestine is a matter for individual investigation.

Information on the legal situation of Jews in the period between Antoninus Pius and Constantine is very scarce. Almost the only exception is the *Sentences* of Paulus, whose exact date in the third century is disputed: they were officially given legal force in the fourth century. In general we are forced to rely on conclusions based on the assumption that there was continuity in the legal situation.

Freedom of religion was almost universally settled by law of privilege in antiquity. This was true also for Jews, whose right 'to live according to their laws', as extensively documented by Josephus, was promised in countless Hellenistic decrees and then confirmed by Caesar. Since the Jews were not only recognized as a religious community, but also as a people, they also possessed a limited autonomy of government. The position of the patriarch as representative of the Jewish people was in certain respects, although with restrictions, comparable to that of a client king. Jurisdiction in lesser cases was also in the hands of Jewish authorities, if both parties were Jews or if a non-Jew voluntarily subjected himself to the Jewish court of arbitration. In cities where Jews were in the majority, such as Tiberias and Sepphoris, there was also the general civic jurisdiction, of which however only minimal traces remained in the fourth century, as mentioned above.

The awarding of *universal citizenship* by Caracalla's *Constitutio Antoniniana* of 212 should have had significant consequences for the Jews. As Roman citizens they would have been obliged to follow the common Roman law. But even after 212, Rome long maintained the local legal traditions. Thus the Jewish law of privilege surely remained generally valid for directly religious questions (e.g. on the question of circumcision). In addition, in Palestine the internal jurisdiction of the Jewish community remained in force until 398 for cases under civil law. Until the passing of the law CTh II.1.10, Jewish law applied, for example, in questions of property law not only when the parties were before a Jewish court, but also before the Roman court. The Jewish law of marriage also remained in force. Thus Jews were not affected by Diocletian's constitution of 285, which forbade bigamy, or by the ban on certain marriages, such as that between niece and maternal uncle, which was seen by Jews as an ideal union. Only in 393 were Jewish marriage customs forbidden, in a law addressed to the *Comes Orientis*: 'No Jew may retain his traditions in questions of marriage, neither contract marriages according to his law nor enter into several marriages at once' (CJust 1.9.7).[1] To what extent compliance with this law was enforced in practice remains an open question, as with other laws. Certainly a later Jewish collection of laws, the *Ma'asim libne Eretz Yisrael*, still assumes polygamy as a real possibility.

The award of Roman citizenship included access to *public office*, which became a key question in the legislation of the fourth and fifth centuries: 'The divine (Emperor Septimius) Severus and Antoninus (i.e. Caracalla) allow those who follow the Jewish religion to attain honourable office, but also lay the obligations on them, in so far as they do not offend against their religion.'[2]

---

[1] Cf. V. Colorni, *Legge ebraica e leggi locali*, Milan 1945, 104–12, *contra* J. Juster, *Les Juifs* II, 111ff., who argues that the Diaspora Jews also had their own jurisdiction in civil cases until 398. Cf. also A. M. Rabello, 'On the Relations between Diocletian and the Jews', 158f.

[2] Digests 50.2.3.3. Cf. also J. Juster, *Les Juifs* II, 243f. The Latin expression *superstitio*, rendered as 'religion', is not necessarily to be understood negatively, as 'superstition'. Cf. D. Grodzynski, 'Superstitio', *Revue des Etudes Anciennes* 76 (1974) 36–60, 50ff., according to which the expression is understood to mean, from the second century, the religion of minorities, and only gradually gains a negative connotation. In legal texts the expression only has an insulting undertone from the end of the third century. Cf. also A. Linder, *The Jews*, 105f.

The title is: 'On decurions'. But not only decurions, i.e. city councillors, are meant; rather these are named apparently as an example for all other public offices. It is questionable, however, to what extent Jews made use of this right. For very quickly, because of the burdens associated with it, it became a positive privilege not to have to serve on the city council, or *curia*.

Service in public administration and in the army were especially problematic for Jews, because in these cases participation in pagan sacrifices was often compulsory. According to rabbinic tradition (jAZ V.4.44 d), Diocletian issued a general command to offer libations, solely excepting the Jews.[3] It may probably be assumed that this exception only applied if they were not in public service or if they left it. The fact that the Samaritans did not take advantage of this possibility, that they did not make use of the Jewish privilege and preferred to offer the prescribed libations, gives the Talmud cause to describe Samaritan wine as libation wine, which is forbidden to Jews. However, it is not so sure whether the authorities would have allowed the Samaritans also the exceptional status conceded to the Jews. But it is probable that the final separation of the Samaritans from the Jews is connected with these events; we shall speak of this at greater length in a later chapter.

An important Jewish privilege was *circumcision*. They had long been exempted from its prohibition by an old law, the *lex Cornelia de sicariis et veneficis*; not until Hadrian was this exemption revoked and the Jews temporarily forbidden to circumcise. But Antoninus Pius allowed it again: 'By an edict of the divine Pius the Jews alone are permitted to circumcise their sons. But whoever performs this on someone who does not belong to that religion is liable to the punishment of one who castrates another.'[4]

The *Sentences* of Paulus confirm that this edict remained in force at a later date. Thus, by limiting circumcision to Jews, the conversion of men to Judaism was forbidden. The *Historia Augusta* (Sept. Sev. 17) confirms this, writing about Septimius Severus: 'He forbade becoming a Jew on pain of severe

---

[3] It is disputed whether this general obligation to offer libations belongs to Diocletian's time or should be dated to Maximian's persecution of 307: see A. M. Rabello, 'On the Relations', 150f., who prefers the year 303.

[4] Digests 48.8.11. A. M. Rabello, 'The Legal Condition', 700–3, concludes from the context in the Digests (slaves), that the primary concern is forbidding Jews to circumcise their non-Jewish slaves.

punishment.' It is again doubtful how strictly the law was obeyed. The rabbis, at least some of them, did on the one hand have a fairly negative attitude to converts. But on the other, it was a matter of principle not to be forbidden by the state to gain proselytes, which was seen to be an invasion of religious liberty. The legislation of the Codex Theodosianus bears witness to the constant struggle on this issue.

After the Jewish defeat in the revolt against Rome in 70 CE, a special tax was imposed on them, the *fiscus Judaicus*. There are no more references to this tax after the early third century. It seems reasonable to assume that it was abolished during the period of inflation in that century, when it was no longer worth collecting. We will return to this question in connection with Julian's policies.

The *Edict of Milan* of 313, whose text is preserved by Lactantius, was primarily intended to bring about the end of the persecution of Christians. But to this end, it announced complete freedom of religion:

> We thought that ... the reverence paid to the Divinity merited our first and chief attention. Our purpose is to grant both to the Christians and to all others full authority to follow whatever worship each man has desired; whereby whatsoever Divinity dwells in heaven may be benevolent and propitious to us, and to all who are placed under our authority.[5]

In the eastern Roman Empire the edict was initially without effect. Galerius, Caesar of the east and based in Antioch, in whose control Palestine lay, continued the persecution of Christians. He continued to do so as Augustus from 305, as did his nephew Maximin Daia, who was Caesar under him and then from 311 to 313 Augustus. Under Licinius, too, persecutions of Christians continued. Only after Constantine's victory over Licinius in 324 – a year later, the vanquished Licinius was executed – was Constantine as sole ruler able to promulgate the Edict of Milan in Nicomedia for the eastern Empire also.

The question remains to what extent this proclamation of general freedom of religion had an effect on the Jews. Theoretically, all their religiously motivated privileges would now be superfluous. In practice, subsequent Roman legislation shows

---

[5] Lactantius, *De mortibus persecutorum* 48.2 (CSEL 27, 229).

that the Jews continued to be seen as a special group, whose interests were to be ordered by special laws.

2. Membership of City Councils

During the period before his sole rule, Constantine only once had to deal with the Jews in a law – the law CTh XVI.8.1, traditionally dated to 315, which protects Jews who convert to Christianity, should probably be dated to 329.[6] So originally, the law was irrelevant to the Jews of Palestine. The text, dating from 11 December 321, is addressed to the city council of Cologne: 'By general law we allow all city senates (*ordinibus*) to appoint Jews to city councils. But in order that these, as a comfort, may retain a little of the old custom, we permit that two or three in each case may have the permanent privilege of not being burdened with any nominations (to particular duties)' (CTh XVI.8.3).

This text is the only extant evidence that Jews were once exempt from the *curia*; we may probably assume that this was only the case in the western Empire or an even smaller area. Once the status of a city councillor, a decurion, was seen as an honour and sought after; but because of the financial burdens associated with it, which were not only lifelong but hereditary, it had become an increasingly unloved duty, which people sought to avoid wherever possible.[7] The fact that Jews too attempted to escape this costly and laborious 'honour' is entirely understandable. Apparently they were indeed often successful, by pointing out that the sacrifices before council sessions were incompatible with their religion, as well as other religious problems. However, since the proclamation of religious liberty by Constantine, pagan sacrifices were no longer compulsory. Thus the special regulations in the Jews' favour could be cancelled and not replaced. For the city councils urgently needed all the available men (and especially their property!) in

---

[6] K. L. Noethlichs, *Die gesetzgeberischen Maßnahmen*, 26, now again defends the earlier date. Also K. D. Reichardt, 'Die Judengesetzgebung im Codex Theodosianus', *Kairos* 20 (1978) 16–39, 20. For the 329 date, see the reasoning in A. Linder, *The Jews*, 124–32; there also the earlier literature on the question.

[7] See W. Schubert, 'Die rechtliche Sonderstellung der Dekurionen (Kurialen) in der Kaisergesetzgebung des 4.–6. Jahrhunderts', *Zeitschrift der Savigny-Stiftung für Rechtsgeschichte* 86, Romanistische Abteilung (1969) 287–333.

order to be able to fulfil their duties. If one or two Jews in each case continued to be exempt from the burdens and duties of the *curia*, in memory of an earlier privilege, this was as a special favour. We do not know whether the Jewish community could itself nominate the privileged men. In any case, the law that abolishes the Jews' exemption from the *curia* is certainly not to be understood as an anti-Jewish measure, even though those concerned were certainly not overjoyed by it.

In a law dating from 29 November 330, Constantine settled anew the question of decurions, this time in a way that was also relevant for the eastern Empire and thus for Palestine:

> Those who have devoted themselves entirely to the synagogues of the Jews, to the patriarchs or the elders (*presbyteris*), and those who in the said religious community (*secta*)[8] themselves administer the law, shall remain exempt from all personal duties and those to be performed on behalf of the community (*tam personalibus quam civilibus muneribus*). Similarly, those who may already be decurions may not be designated for any public escort (*prosecutiones*), since such people may not for whatsoever reason be forced to leave the places where they are. But those who are in no way *curiales* shall obtain permanent immunity from the decurionate. (CTh XVI.8.2)

The law, addressed to the *Praefectus praetorio* Ablavius, basically puts the Jewish religious officials, as far as immunity from curial duties is concerned, on an equal footing with Christian and pagan clergy. Constantine initially allowed the clergy this immunity very liberally, which in the following period was taken advantage of accordingly and led to widespread difficulties in recruiting for the *curia*, and in consequence to constant attempts on the part of the legislature to limit this privilege. It is not certain whether, as S. Lieberman thinks,[9] the law simply continues and generalizes

---

[8] The fact that *secta* in this period is not yet understood negatively, as 'sect', is clearly shown by CTh XVI.2.5 of 323, which speaks of the clergy *catholicae sectae*. The previous passage *synagogis Iudaeorum patriarchis vel presbyteris* is translated by C. Pharr as 'to the synagogues of the Jews as patriarchs and priests', i.e. more narrowly than in the present translation, which includes all full-time Jewish religious officials, as does A. Linder's translation, *The Jews*, 134. See also. ibid., 135f., on the problem of defining *tam personalibus quam civilibus muneribus*, which overlap rather than complementing each other.

[9] S. Lieberman, *Palestine*, 359–64.

the exemption of ordained rabbis, which had been customary in Palestine since the third century, since we are ignorant of the legal basis for the Palestinian practice.

If the translation offered above is acceptable, then the group of people favoured by the law is quite generously defined. Exempt are all those who are employed full-time in the service of the synagogue, or in Jewish teaching or legislation, who are recognized by the patriarch or the presbyteri (in this context, *presbyteri* presumably means principally the rabbis connected with the patriarchal house, even though members of Jewish community councils in the Diaspora may be included in the term).[10] Whoever from this group is already member of a *curia* is to continue to serve on it, but need not undertake duties that involve absence from home (*prosecutiones*), and that could thus interfere with the performance of religious duties.

The law not only regulates the exemption of Jewish religious officials from the *curia*, but strengthens the position of the central authority of Judaism, the patriarchate, even though the elders are also mentioned as an alternative. Interpretations of the law that understand the patriarchs (plural) to be leaders of the Jewish communities in the individual provinces of the Empire, i.e. so-called 'little patriarchs', are untenable. The existence of 'little patriarchs' simply cannot be proved. Thus indirectly, although perhaps involuntarily, the law serves to support the cohesion of Judaism in the Roman Empire.

Only a few days after the promulgation of the above-mentioned law, on 1 December 330, a slightly different formulation of it was sent to the group in question, i.e. 'the priests, heads of the synagogue and synagogue fathers, and the others who serve there: We command that priests, heads of the synagogue and synagogue fathers, and the others who serve the synagogues, shall be free from all personal services (*ab omni corporali munere*)' (CTh XVI.8.4).

By comparison with the first text, we notice that the exemption here does not cover 'all personal duties and those to be performed on behalf of the community' in a general sense, but includes only concrete obligations to be fulfilled by those

---

[10] For the definition of *presbyteri* in this context, see M. Jacobs, *Die Institution*, 278. Thus the exemption is not only for religious officials recognized by the patriarch, as K. Strobel, 'Jüdisches Patriarchat', 66f., rightly stresses.

concerned. In this context this apparently means obligations that arise from membership of the *curia*. There is also a difference here in the persons addressed: patriarchate and presbyters are not mentioned, nor those whose full-time occupation is with the Jewish law; instead, more comprehensively, all who serve the synagogue (community). Perhaps we should assume an error in the formulation of the text of the law, if it here only names *munera corporalia*. This error could, according to A. Linder, have crept in when the exemption was extended from those who were already decurions to all synagogue officials.[11] However we are to understand the law, the extension of the favoured group of people represents an improvement on the past.

Unfortunately it is quite difficult to determine more precisely the identity of the Jewish officials named in these laws; for the organization of synagogue communities in the Roman Empire was anything but uniform, and the names of offices were also not uniform. The mention of 'priests' (*hiereis*) first in the list of addressees of the law is remarkable. The title 'priest' (*kohen, hiereus*) is often represented in Jewish inscriptions of the third and fourth century, but is generally to be understood as a mere honorific; whereas in the text of the law it is a question of functionaries of the Jewish community. Apparently the legislators use the expression 'priest' as a collective expression for all Jewish religious officials, who are to be granted privileges comparable to those of pagan and Christian priests.[12] In any case, the texts show a fairly broad exemption of Jewish religious officials; thus they could only be welcomed by the Jewish community, apart from Palestinian communities with a Jewish majority.

We cannot estimate in detail the meaning of these laws for Jewish communities in the Diaspora. We have too little information on the Diaspora at this period and, for example, do not know what the property status of Diaspora Jews was like: property, especially real estate, being of course an important qualification for curial status. At least we hear from inscriptions and papyri of Jewish city councillors in the second and third centuries in Asia Minor and in Egypt.[13]

In Palestine, the importance of the laws differed according to

---

[11] A. Linder, 'The Roman Imperial Government', 114f.
[12] A. Linder, 'The Roman Imperial Government', 122–4.
[13] A. Linder, 'The Roman Imperial Government', 113.

the region. Where the population had a Jewish majority, i.e. in the cities of Tiberias and Sepphoris, and perhaps also in Lydda, the participation of Jews in the city councils had been a matter of course since the time of Jehuda the Patriarch, around 200, at the latest. By contrast, in the cities with a pagan majority, especially on the coast, the small local Jewish communities had probably rather shunned participation in the city council, for religious reasons. Finally, a large proportion of the Jewish population of Galilee and the Golan was not affected at all by the question. They lived in a district not organized according to cities (although in political units like the Tetracomia there was also a certain degree of administrative autonomy[14]).

As early as the third century there are increasing numbers of complaints about curial duties in rabbinic texts also. A general complaint about conscription to the *curia*, relating not only to the Jews, is found in GenR 76.6 (Th-A 904): 'The wicked government, casting an evil glance at people's possessions, (says): N.N. is rich, let us make him *archōn*; N.N. is rich, let us make him *bouleutēs*', i.e. a member of the *curia*. The fact that specifically rich people were appointed to the *curia* was a natural consequence of the obligations of office, since the decurions were liable with their personal fortune for the city's tax assessment, and were also answerable for the cities' expenses. These had a steadily shrinking income since the emperors Constantine and Constantius confiscated civic landholdings (from 374 they were again permitted to keep one third of the income from these: CTh IV.13.7). The costs for maintaining public buildings, the water supply, the public baths (the heating of which represented a great burden), the repair of countless city walls in the fourth century, as well as the concern for police, market inspectors and charges for the public post system and so forth; all these greatly exceeded civic income and had to be guaranteed by payments and services on the part of the decurions.

Two sayings of R. Jochanan bar Nappacha in jMQ II.3.81 b should be seen in this context. The rabbi (who died in 279 according to a late source) thinks it entirely legitimate to free oneself from curial duties. He gives this strange advice: 'If they have named you for the city council [*boulē*], let the Jordan be your border'. Even on a half-holiday – the subject of the tractate – R.

---

[14] See Jones, *LRE* 713.

Jochanan thinks it legitimate to travel to the other side of the Jordan, in order to be out of reach for a specific duty in the *curia*. In this context he can hardly mean a long-term flight, that is from being nominated for the *curia* as such. Jochanan bar Nappacha, who lived in Tiberias, cannot however have meant his call to flee from curial duties to be for his home town in general: the overwhelming majority of the population of Tiberias was Jewish, as we have seen, and thus had a legitimate interest in taking the administration of their own 'capital' in hand. A pagan city council is hardly likely here.[15] Unless Jochanan is referring to other cities of Palestine, where non-Jews were in the majority, his advice is most readily understood as addressed to the rabbis. These had always fought for their immunity from curial duties, until the Roman law did in fact give it to them.

In the third century in Tiberias, a city council synagogue (*knishta de-bule*) is even attested. The expression probably does not simply mean, as would be possible, the place of assembly of the city council; for jTaan I.2.64 a speaks of the fact that R. Jirmeja preached there;[16] jSheq VII.2.50 c concerns the question whether a certain sausage that was found there is kosher, which is entirely possible even for a synagogue.

In jAZ III.13.43 b, R. Isaac b. R. Matna leans on R. Jochanan, until they come to the *tsalma de-bule*. G. A. Wewers translates: 'They came to the idol of Buli'.[17] But it is probably correct to see here the Greek word *boulē*, city council. If we are to assume a Jewish city council in Tiberias, an idol is hardly imaginable in front of its building, and the more neutral translation 'statue' is preferable.

However, we should also refer to jAZ IV.4.43 d, where R. Jochanan orders Bar Derosai to destroy the statues in the *demosin*; this seems to refer to the *dēmosion*, the public baths. We are told that Bar Derosai destroyed all the statues, with one exception; he left that one because he suspected that a Jew could have sacrificed before it. This does favour the possibility that there were images of gods in third-century Tiberias. But it seems more likely to refer to the rejection of plastic art, at least by the more conservative rabbis. Of course, the statues that were set up in the baths as decoration could always be understood as images of gods as well.

---

[15] A pagan city council in Tiberias is assumed by M. D. Judlewitz, *Tiberias* (Hebrew), Jerusalem 1950, 63.
[16] Y. Dan, *The City*, 73.
[17] *Talmud Yerushalmi. Avoda Zara*, tr. G. A. Wewers, Tübingen 1980, 123.

In jAZ III.1.42 c, we are told, with reference to the death of R. Jochanan, that the statues (*iqonion*, Greek *eikōn*) fell down, because none was as handsome as he. The anecdote attests both the existence of such statues in Tiberias at the time of R. Jochanan, and the continuing rejection of them by the rabbis. Whoever held literally to the Biblical prohibition of images could see every statue as an idol.

In a parallel passage to that quoted above, we are told that the *castellum* of Tiberias collapsed at the death of R. Jasa. This too points apparently to a pagan (military) presence in Tiberias,[18] but this need no longer have obtained at the time of the anecdote, and certainly tells us nothing about relative proportions. The *archōn* in Tiberias, mentioned in jBer II.8.5 c, who condemned a robber and a murderer to death, was definitely a non-Jew. But this is not the president of the city council, who was not entitled to impose the death sentence. Finally, epigraphic evidence for Jews on the city council of Tiberias should be mentioned, in the form of a sarcophagus from the third or fourth century, belonging to a certain Isidoros Bouleutes.[19]

Jewish city councillors in Sepphoris are frequently mentioned in rabbinic texts; however, this evidence also comes primarily from the third century. At one time the city councillors of Sepphoris hold a fast (jPea I.1.16 a); another time two groups in Sepphoris are mentioned as waiting on the Patriarch, the *buleuti* and the *paganaia*. It appears to mean the families of the decurions as opposed to the *pagani*, the country dwellers (jHor III.9.48 c; jShab XII.3.13 c). The second named group are probably the owners of estates and not simply the *plebs*.[20] JPes IV.1.30 c mentions a R. Simon Bouleuta.[21]

As has been mentioned earlier, the unpleasant duties of the city council caused people in general to seek exemption from this rank. Such attempts were often successful. If the civic system was

---

[18] On the more general question of *castra* in the Talmudic period, cf. S. S. Miller, *Studies*, 13–59.
[19] *CIJ* II 985; see A. Linder, 'The Roman Imperial Government', 111 n. 95.
[20] G. Alon, *Jews*, 471 f., n. 28, translates the expression as *plebs*. For the interpretation as landowners, cf. L. I. Levine, *The Jewish Patriarch*, 661.
[21] A. Büchler, *The Political and Social Leaders of the Jewish Community of Sepphoris in the Second and Third Centuries*, London (n.d.), 16, would like to explain him as a son or grandson of a city councillor, because rabbis constantly sought exemption from such duties.

to continue functioning at all, the legislature was forced from time to time to cancel all too generous exemption from the *curia*. For example, Constantine initially exempted all Christian clerics from curial duties (CTh XVI.2.1.2), but then was forced to issue a law against the flight of curial persons into the clerical state (CTh XVI.2.3). A continual to-ing and fro-ing in the relevant legislation documents the degree to which the Christian lobby was successful at the imperial court at a given time. Finally, in 398 the Emperor Arcadius forbade the ordination of people of curial status altogether (CTh IX.45.3). If such ordination had already taken place, lower-ranking clergy were returned to lay status. For subdeacons and upwards, the person concerned was forced to renounce two-thirds of his property in favour of his successor in the *curia* (possibly a relative). Other laws sought to bar further escape routes from the *curia*, for example, through the senate, office at the imperial court and so on, but all had little success.[22] In this context a case should be mentioned that concerns Palestine: On 1 March 363 the Emperor Julian, who was very concerned about the replenishing of the civic curias, issued a law addressed to the *Consularis Palaestinae* Leontius, which exempts a father of thirteen children from curial duties (CTh XII.1.55; XII.1.56 of 21 December 363 gives as a further ground for exemption ten years' military service).

In order to gain a better overview of the subject, relevant laws on the inclusion of Jews in city councils will be discussed here for the period after Constantine also. A law of the western Emperor Gratian, dated 18 April 383, significantly reduced the exemption of Jewish religious officials from the *curia*.

> Let the order be abolished, of which the people of the Jewish law boast, by which they are given immunity from the burdens of the curial state; since not even clerics are able to free themselves for religious office until they have performed everything they owe their country. Therefore whoever has truly dedicated himself to God must provide another, equipped with his property, to fulfil the duties for him. (CTh XII.1.99)

This law, promulgated in Milan and addressed to the *Praefectus praetorio* for Italy, is primarily aimed at western circumstances; it had hardly any impact in the east, specifically in Palestine, unless

---

[22] On its development see Jones, *LRE* 740ff.

after the promulgation of the Codex Theodosianus. But even in the west, it is not to be understood as a diminution of Jewish rights, but as a setting on an equal footing with the Christian clerics, who could free themselves from curial duties only by handing over their property before ordination.

In the eastern Empire, CTh XVI.8.13, dated 1 July 397, again confirms the exemption of Jewish religious officials from curial duties, in parallel with Christian clerics:

> Let the Jews keep to their ceremonies. We will emulate our predecessors in maintaining their privileges, by whose decree it was ordained that those who are subordinate to the power of the illustrious patriarchs, both the heads of the synagogue, fathers[23] and presbyters, and the others who are in the service (*sacramento*) of this religion, shall retain according to our gracious indication those privileges, which already render sacrosanct the clerics of the honourable Christian law. For this was also decreed, by divine counsel, by the holy Emperors Constantine and Constantius, Valentinian and Valens. Let them therefore be free of curial burdens and obey their laws.

Thus this law explicitly holds to the established legal tradition and puts Christian and Jewish religious officials on an equal footing in legal matters. Because the exemption is linked to subordination to the illustrious patriarch (of Tiberias), the central leadership of the Jews is strengthened at the same time.

Although impossible to prove, it could be that Jews in the western empire appealed to this law, in order to enjoy there also the advantages that it offered in comparison to Gratian's edict of 383. But if they did so, they were unsuccessful:

> We have been informed that in Apulia and Calabria countless city curias have been brought into difficulty, because there are people of Jewish belief (*superstitio*), who are of the opinion, based on some law that was passed in the eastern part of the empire, that they are exempt from the obligation to undertake public duties. Therefore we pronounce by authority that this law, if it indeed exists, is annulled; for it is clear that it is damaging to my part of the empire. All who in any way belong to the curia by right,

---

[23] One should probably read *patribusque* instead of *patriarchisque* (cf. CTh XVI.8.2).

irrespective of what religion (*superstitio*) they profess, shall be obliged to perform public services (*munia*). (CTh XII.1.158, dated 13 September 398)

Again, this is not an anti-Jewish edict (not only the Jewish religion is called *superstitio*!). Its primary focus is on the interests of the western half of the empire, which altogether wishes to curtail exemptions from curial duties as much as possible. It is typical that the west Roman authority does not even know the east Roman law, and does not take the trouble to verify the reference made to it. CTh XII.1.165, dated 30 December 399, repeats the principle: 'All Jews who are proven to be bound to belong to a city council are to be handed over to the city council.'

Altogether, the laws on the participation of Jews in city councils, which we have followed here far beyond the time of Constantine, do not show an anti-Jewish attitude on the part of the legislature, but only the constant struggle to keep the *curia* able to function. We do not see Jews in a worse position compared with Christian clerics.

3. Conversions

If a real religious policy indeed existed under Constantine, it had a much more solid basis in the question of conversions than in that of city councils. One could refer to ancient legal tradition. We have already mentioned the prohibition of circumcising non-Jews. In his work *Against Celsus*, Origen quotes Celsus as saying that Samaritans too are persecuted for their religion. He himself objects that 'the Sicarii are executed because of circumcision, as those who mutilate themselves contrary to established law, since this (i.e. circumcision) is only permitted to Jews.'[24] Thus at that time, the Samaritans must no longer have counted as Jews in the eyes of the law.

More important for the legal tradition are the *Sentences* of Paulus, which were given legal status in the year 328 by CTh I.4.2. Section V.22.3–4 must also have been adopted at that time, but it is often seen as a Christian forgery, and is thus not certain evidence:[25]

---

[24] Origen, *Contra Celsum* 2.13 (GCS 142).
[25] See H. Langenfeld, *Christianisierungspolitik*, 46 n. 110; G. de Bonfils, *Gli schiavi*, 134–7.

> Roman citizens who permit themselves or their slaves to be circumcised according to Jewish ritual are to have their possessions confiscated and be banished to an island in perpetuity; doctors (who perform such circumcisions) are to receive the death sentence. Jews who buy and circumcise slaves of other nationality shall be either deported or executed

apparently according to whether the condemned person belonged to the higher or lower rank. This differentiation of punishment is also attested in the *Digests* (48.8.3.5).

However, soon after the *Sentences* of Paulus were approved, Constantine himself intervened, without specifically mentioning circumcision:

> We wish to impress upon the Jews, their elders and the Patriarchs: according to this law, if someone should dare to attack with stones or other angry means another, who flees their pernicious sect (*feralem sectam*) and turns to the worship of God (as we understand currently happens), he shall immediately be consigned to the flames and be burned with all his accomplices. But if a man of the people joins their criminal sect (*nefariam sectam*) and takes part in their meetings (*conciliabulis*), he shall suffer the penalty he merits together with them. (CTh XVI.8.1)

As has been mentioned, this law is traditionally dated to 315, but ought more rightly to be dated to 329.[26] By comparison with the laws from the Codex Theodosianus which we have studied so far, this text shows strong anti-Jewish language, which one would not expect in a law. It appears that not only circumcision, but any form of joining the Jewish community, even taking part in their religious assemblies, is made a punishable offence. If this was indeed the law's intention, it was by no means successful in practice. Or does it only concern the involvement of non-Jews in violence against converts from Judaism to Christianity? The law's primary intention is to protect Jews who have converted to Christianity. It is likely that such cases gave rise to riots; evidence for this is provided by the story of Count Joseph in Epiphanius, which will be discussed below. However, executions are never

---

[26] M. Avi-Yonah, *Jews*, 174, dates the law even later, putting it under Constantius, in the year 339 (as O. Seeck, *Regesten*).

mentioned in this context; the mere threat of them must have been sufficient. It is also doubtful how common conversions of Jews to Christianity were at all – we will consider this later.

A much more important question in practice was that of slaves. The legal situation before Constantine is a matter of debate. According to some, Jews had always been forbidden to circumcise their slaves – the law that forbade the castration of slaves (*Digests* 48.8.6) having also been applied to circumcision;[27] others however dispute this legal equivalence. We have already discussed the difficulties of the relevant passage in the *Sentences* of Paulus. According to H. Langenfeld, a law that forbade the circumcision of slaves would have meant, for Jews that followed the Bible strictly, a blanket prohibition of slave ownership:

> Since such a prohibition would be scarcely possible in the social situation at the height of the Roman empire, and would certainly have provoked reactions that would have left some trace in the surviving sources, we may interpret the lack of such traces as confirmation that, according to Roman law until the time of the emperor Diocletian, the circumcision of slaves was not forbidden.[28]

In a law addressed to the *Praefectus praetorio* for Italy and Africa, Constantine decreed on 21 October 335: 'If a Jew has bought and circumcised a Christian slave or one belonging to any other religious community (*secta*), he may under no circumstances keep the circumcised person in slavery; rather, whoever suffers such a thing shall obtain the privilege of freedom' (CTh XVI.9.1).

Another part of the same law is preserved in CTh XVI.8.5. Again, the subject is the punishment of Jews who molest former fellow-Jews who have converted to Christianity. But the threatened punishment is not described in detail: 'It is not permitted to Jews to harass or otherwise frighten with wrongdoing persons who have changed from being Jews to Christians. The harassment is to be punished according to the severity (of the crime).' The common factor of the two parts of the law is clearly the change of religion.

The version of the text preserved in the Codex Theodosianus is

---

[27] J. Juster, *Les juifs* I, 269. Also E. E. Urbach, *Zion* 25 (1960) 167 n. 130, and G. de Bonfils, *Gli schiavi*, 21.
[28] H. Langenfeld, *Christianisierungspolitik*, 50. See also A. Linder, 'The Roman Imperial Government', 133.

supplemented by the fuller citation in the *Constitutiones Sirmondianae* 4 (dated 21 October 335, but only published 9 March 336 in Carthage):

> Some time ago a most salutary sanction of our constitution was promulgated, which we now make doubly noteworthy by the repetition of our law. If any Jew has acquired a Christian slave or one belonging to some other religious community, and has not shrunk from circumcising him, let the circumcised person, according to this decree, attain his freedom and enjoy its privileges. It is not right that a Jew who has circumcised a slave of this kind should keep him in slavery. We also order the following, by the same decree. If one of the Jews opens the gate to eternal life, dedicates himself to the sacred worship of God and confesses himself a Christian, he must not experience any harassment or molestation from the Jews. But if any Jew thinks he can frighten with any kind of wrongdoing a person who has changed from being a Jew to being a Christian, let the author of this ill-treatment be punished according to the severity of the crime.

The language of these constitutions, composed between 426 and 438 in Gaul or Africa, is in general of a more strongly ecclesiastical tenor than the general laws of the Codex Theodosianus.

In his *Life* of the Emperor Constantine, Eusebius attributes to him a law that forbade Jews from keeping slaves altogether: 'He also passed a law that no Christian might serve a Jew as a slave. For it was not right that those who had been ransomed by the Saviour should be subject to the murderers of the prophets and the Lord, under the yoke of slavery. If such a one were to be found, he might go free, and the Jew should be fined.'[29]

This section's insulting language towards Jews is completely unthinkable in a legal text of this period, and evidently represents Eusebius' own words.[30] The text's content is also difficult, for such a universal law of Constantine's is attested nowhere else. Either Eusebius has attributed to Constantine a law of 339, published by the Emperor Constantius (CTh XVI.9.2), or, what is more probable on chronological grounds, he has generalized from

---

[29] Eusebius, *Vita Constantini* IV.27.1 (GCS 130).
[30] Thus H. Langenfeld, *Christianisierungspolitik*, 75.

Constantine's decree emancipating from his Jewish owner a non-Jewish slave who has been circumcised.[31]

Equally not attested elsewhere is a law of Constantine's cited by CTh XVI.8.22, dated 415: 'If (a Jew) keeps Christian slaves, these are, according to Constantinian law, to be handed over to the church.'[32] Perhaps this 'quote' is based on Eusebius' biography of Constantine; in which case it must then have altered the biography so that a slave that had been circumcised by his Jewish owner did not simply go free, but was awarded to the church. In any case, XVI.9.2 is not concerned with the circumcision of Christian slaves, the prohibition of which would have been more likely to succeed than the blanket prohibition of the possession of Christian slaves. Such a prohibition of conversions (*Iudaica nota foedare*) of all non-Jewish slaves is then found in XVI.8.22. Turning back to Constantine's reliably attested slave law, we note that it does not prohibit Jews from owning Christian slaves, but simply the circumcision of the slaves – whether in accordance with older legal tradition, or for the sake of preserving slaves who were not already Jews from (forcible?) incorporation into the Jewish community. We ought perhaps also to note that the text of the law expressly mentions only the circumcision of slaves of non-Jewish background, which the Jew has bought. H. Langenfeld is of the opinion that slaves who already belonged to a Jew were not affected by the law, presumably on the assumption that they were all circumcised anyway. That would mean that the law did not alter the existing distribution of property, but simply forbade the circumcision of newly acquired slaves.[33]

Since we do not know the wider context, we cannot speak more precisely about the motivation for Constantine's slave law, although the humanitarian wish to protect the unfree from religious coercion suggests itself (which would not only have affected Jewish slave owners). Later legal developments, with their continual repetition of the prohibition of Jews' circumcising slaves, make it clear that this was a widespread and ineradicable practice. Ex. 12:44 was surely not the primary reason why Jewish

---

[31] Thus K. L. Noethlichs, *Die gesetzgeberischen Maßnahmen*, 39f.; G. de Bonfils, *Gli schiavi*, 42–8, 194f.

[32] For this translation of *mancipentur*, see H. Langenfeld, *Christianisierungspolitik*, 71f.

[33] H. Langenfeld, *Christianisierungspolitik*, 70.

slave owners were interested in the conversion of slaves. Because of the dietary laws, of course only a Jewish slave could be made full use of in the household and for handling food. However, female slaves were probably preferred for such work, whose conversion was performed by a simple immersion in water and was thus not verifiable. The sociological context of this problem thus remains fairly unclear.

4. Access to Jerusalem

After the suppression of the Bar Cochba revolt in 135, Jews were no longer allowed to enter Jerusalem – now named Aelia Capitolina. As Eusebius writes in his *Church History*, 'Since then, by Hadrian's law and edicts, the whole people was absolutely forbidden even to enter the country around Jerusalem, so that they could not even see their paternal home from a distance. This is the report of Ariston of Pella.'[34] Since then, so Eusebius continues, Jerusalem had had Gentile Christian bishops. This means that Jewish Christians, or probably circumcised people in general, were also excluded from Jerusalem. Hadrian's renaming of the city was so effective that it was possible for the old name of Jerusalem to be entirely forgotten. Thus we read in Eusebius that Firmilian, the Roman governor of Caesarea in 310, had ostensibly never heard the name Jerusalem.[35]

When Christian building work began in Jerusalem, the old prohibition was probably resumed and given a Christian reinterpretation. After the dedication of the Church of the Holy Sepulchre in 335 it was surely more rigorously enforced.[36] A statement in the pilgrimage report of the anonymous Bordeaux Pilgrim of 333 remains mysterious. It says of Jerusalem: 'Inside however, within the wall of Zion, one can see the place where David had a palace. And of seven synagogues that were here, only

---

[34] Eusebius, *Church history* IV.6.3 (GCS 9, 308).
[35] Eusebius, *The Martyrs of Palestine* 11.9f. (GCS 9,937f.).
[36] A report that Constantine himself renewed the prohibition is first found in the *Annals* of Eutychius (tenth century), and even here is missing in the oldest MS. The prohibition suited church interests in Jerusalem, and its bishops probably attempted to influence the provincial governors accordingly: O. Irshai, 'Constantine and the Jews: the prohibition against entering Jerusalem', *Zion* 60 (1995) 129–78 (Hebrew).

one remains; the others are ploughed and sown over, as the Prophet Isaiah said' (Isa. 1:8; cf. Mi. 3:12).[37]

Apparently this is a 'proof text' of Christian propaganda against Judaism, in whose history the prophecies of the prophets are fulfilled (both texts are combined by Eusebius and Cyril of Jerusalem as well).[38] It is also striking that sixty years later, in 392, Epiphanius mentions something similar, naturally independently of the anonymous Pilgrim: '... and seven synagogues that had stood alone like huts on Mount Sion, of which one remained until the time of Bishop Maximus and Emperor Constantine, like a tent in a vineyard, as it is written' (Isa. 1:8).[39]

Was the building that was shown to the Pilgrim really a synagogue? Even if one assumes that the law published under Hadrian, according to which Jews were not permitted to be in Jerusalem, was no longer kept so strictly in the course of time – an assumption that is supported by rabbinic texts – it nevertheless is surprising that Jews living there illegally should have openly constructed synagogues. It is also questionable for how long, if at all, Jews had free access to Jerusalem thanks to the religious liberty proclaimed by Constantine – a year after Constantine's victory over Licinius, preparatory work for the Church of the Holy Sepulchre was already beginning.

In the face of this uncertainty, H. Donner's attempt is understandable; he understands these 'synagogues' as Jewish-Christian churches, the one remaining one being the small church commemorating the meeting of the disciples after the Ascension – but Epiphanius distinguishes this from the remaining synagogue.[40] But this attempted solution is questionable, as is that of J. Wilkinson, that the words *una remansit* in the Pilgrim's report perhaps did not mean that the synagogue still stood, but simply that it outlasted the others.[41] Without further corroboration, we

---

[37] *Itinera Hierosolymitana*, CSEL 38, 22.
[38] Eusebius, *Demonstratio evangelica* VI.13.17 (GCS 23, 264f.); Cyril of Jerusalem, *Catechetical Lectures* 16.18 (PG 33, 944). Jerome interprets the passage Isa. 1:8 in the same sense in his *Commentary on Isaiah*: God has abandoned the Temple, the city has become deserted. 'It is not necessary to prove this with many words, especially not to us, who see Sion desolate, Jerusalem destroyed and the Temple torn down to its foundations' (CC 73, 14).
[39] Epiphanius, *De ponderibus et mensuris* 14 (PG 43, 261).
[40] H. Donner, *Pilgerfahrt*, 58 n. 91.
[41] J. Wilkinson, 'Christian Pilgrims', 87.

unfortunately cannot make any use of this solitary statement, and may not take it as proof for a Jewish presence in Jerusalem.

The fact that, even after its Christianization under Constantine, Jerusalem remained officially off limits for Jews, is attested by the Bordeaux Pilgrim among others. In connection with his visit to the Temple area, he writes of a pierced stone, 'to which the Jews come year by year, anoint it, wailing and sighing, tear their clothes and so depart.'[42] The Pilgrim is apparently speaking of the 9th Ab, the anniversary of the destruction of the Temple. On this day alone Jews were permitted to enter the city, so that their lamentation could attest for Christians the fulfilment of the prophecies. In his *Commentary on the Psalms*, written after 335, Eusebius writes on Ps. 59:15 ('evening by evening they return, they bark like dogs and run about the city') that the text has to do with the crimes of the Jews in Jerusalem against Jesus. Then the Romans came and fulfilled the prophetic statement. 'Since then, the entire Jewish people is forbidden to approach the places ... For this reason, still today they stand round about the hills, and go about in a circle from a distance.'[43]

We do not know how strictly this prohibition was observed in practice. M. Avi-Yonah at least sees in various rabbinic texts evidence for a renewal of Jewish pilgrimage to Jerusalem in the fourth and fifth Amoraic generation, that is, in the fourth century.[44] It was probably only observed in the city of Jerusalem, scarcely in the surrounding district belonging to the city. This is a reasonable deduction from Jerome's assertion that he associated with Jews in Bethlehem,[45] and perhaps also from Cyril of Jerusalem's warning to the catechumens to keep away from Jewish customs and ideas (which might also be a standard admonition with no concrete occasion).

On the Jewish side, naturally the claims to possession of Jerusalem and the Temple mount were maintained. That seems to follow also from GenR 79.7 (Th-A 945f.), on 33:19. Here Jacob buys from the men of Shechem the place where he had pitched his tent: '"And he bought the part of the field ..." R. Judan b.

---

[42] *Itinera Hierosolymitana*, CSEL 38, 22.
[43] Eusebius, on LXX Ps. 58 (PG 23, 541).
[44] M. Avi-Yonah, *Jews*, 164.
[45] See G. Stemberger, 'Hieronymus und die Juden seiner Zeit', in D.-A. Koch, H. Lichtenberger (eds.), *Begegnungen zwischen Christentum und Judentum in Antike und Mittelalter* (*Festschrift* H. Schreckenberg), Göttingen 1993, 347–64.

R. Simon said: that is one of three places regarding which the peoples of the world cannot accuse Israel, saying: they were stolen by you. These are: the cave of Machpelah, the Temple, and the grave of Joseph.'[46]

5. Constantine's General Attitude to the Jews

It is extremely difficult to deduce Constantine's personal attitude to the Jews from the surviving legal texts. Those laws regarding Jews that go back to him, as we have seen, put Jewish and Christian religious officials on an equal footing, as regards the key question of city councils. As regards the circumcision of non-Jews (including slaves?), Constantine keeps to current Roman legal tradition. Only CTh XVI.8.1 is striking in its strongly anti-Jewish language, describing Judaism as a 'pernicious' and 'criminal sect', and dismissing Jewish meetings as *conciliabula*. Is this a case of a spontaneous outburst of anger on the part of the emperor, in view of converts' being threatened by their former co-religionists? It would be surprising if an unsuitable expression, born from a moment of anger, had not been corrected during the editing process. Or does the language mirror the influence of Christian advisors?

Two further texts, found only in Eusebius, can now support the suggestion of church influence on this law's formulation (whose inclusion in the edition of the Codex Theodosianus a century later attests the changing attitude to Jews in the intervening period). These two laws also show clearly anti-Jewish language. Firstly, the law, attributed to Constantine, that Jews may not possess Christian slaves, in which the Jews are described, by way of justification, as 'murderers of the prophets' and 'murderers of the Lord'. Even more so, secondly, Constantine's Easter letter, quoted by Eusebius.[47] Constantine sent this text to all the provinces after the Council of Nicaea in 325, in order to achieve a uniform date of Easter, which should not coincide with the Jewish date:

---

[46] These proof texts follow: Gen. 23:15; 1 Chron. 21:25; Gen. 33:19. The name of the author, according to Midrash ha-Gadol on Gen. 33:19 (M. 522), is R. Jehuda b. R. Samuel.

[47] Eusebius, *Vita Constantini* III.18f. (GCS 90–92).

Above all it seems not fitting to keep this most holy feast in conjunction with the custom of the Jews, who have stained their hands with a nefarious crime, and, as tainted people, are rightly blinded in their souls ... Let nothing therefore be common to us and the most hated rabble of the Jews ... How then can they think rightly, who have lost their minds after that murder of our Lord and father? They do not follow any reasoning, but are carried away by animal urges, to which their innate madness drives them. Therefore they do not see the truth on this head also. The purity of your soul shall not appear to have anything in common with the customs of the worst of people, because of any similarity ... Let there be nothing in common with the people of those patricides and murderers of the Lord ...

In view of the absolutely proper language of Constantine's laws with regard to the Jews (with the exception of the isolated case of CTh XVI.8.1), it seems reasonable not necessarily to see in the strongly anti-Jewish wording of the Easter letter an expression of the emperor's own attitude, but rather to suspect the influence of his Christian advisors, in particular since it concerns an internal church announcement.[48]

A commonly expressed opinion in the past was that 'all the documents in the *Vita Constantini* are spurious, in that Constantine did not publish a single one of them in this form; but that is not yet to dismiss their content'.[49] Today this hypothesis finds few supporters. Apart from the argument that Eusebius did not write in such a poor style, there is now the fact that Papyrus London 878 documents a passage that was once equally disputed, for as early as the first half of the fourth century.[50] Even if we must reckon with the influence of Christian sermons on Constantine's manner of speaking in CTh XVI.8.1 'the tone [matches] perfectly well with Constantine's own style, which we know from edicts against heretics, and does not represent a unique and particular

---

[48] Thus M. Avi-Yonah, *Jews*, 165.
[49] O. Seeck, *Zeitschrift für Kirchengeschichte* 17 (1897) 58, quoted from F. Winkelmann, 'Zur Geschichte des Authentizitätsproblems der Vita Constantini', *Klio* 40 (1962) 187–243, 199; see also id. in the introduction to his edition of the text in GCS, LI n. 1.
[50] Eusebius, *Vita Constantini* II.26f. (GCS 59). See A. Ehrhardt, 'Constantine, Rome and the Rabbis', *BJRL* 42 (1959f.) 288–312, 305f.

severity only against Jews'.⁵¹ Thus arguments for a genuine Constantinian origin (or at least its possibility) are balanced against arguments that see church influence at work in the anti-Jewish expressions.

The fact that certainly not all of Constantine's laws are extant, and that the editors of the Codex Theodosianus often summarized or 'corrected' laws, makes it even more difficult to differentiate between Constantine's actual attitude to the Jews and the traditional legal style or ecclesiastical influence. This latter is naturally also at work in the laws themselves, with their 'non-technical language'⁵²

Certainly the laws that Constantine published brought no real deterioration for Jews, and in certain respects even strengthened their privileges. Is it right, in the face of this, to give undue weight to insulting expressions, and to see them as very important in paving the way for increasingly anti-Jewish attitudes? Or ought we not rather to imagine a Constantine who is not mealy-mouthed, particularly when speaking to the church, but in the exercise of his imperial authority is perfectly self-controlled, tradition-conscious and by no means anti-Jewish? The question whether Constantine actually even knew any Jews personally, not insignificant in this context, must also remain unanswered.

In any case, it would be wrong to describe Constantine as a particular enemy of the Jews. M. Avi-Yonah's sweeping judgement is also highly problematical, when he speaks of the end of tolerance towards the Jews from 324: 'The open hostility now displayed by the Roman authorities limited to a large extent the freedom of manoeuvre of the Jewish leaders. Even the smallest political force can exercise a certain pressure, ... The Jews now lost the freedom of choice, the basis of their political possibilities.'⁵³ On the contrary, it was precisely the laws regarding the exemption of Jews from city councils that caused a strengthening of the central leadership of the Palestinian Jews. We will return to this point in the chapter on the Patriarchate.

---

⁵¹ K. L. Noethlichs, *Die gesetzgeberischen Maßnahmen*, 38. See the equally harsh formulation of Constantine's edict against the heretics in Eusebius, *Vita Constantini* III.64 (GCS 117f.).

⁵² D. Grodzynski, 'Superstitio', *Revue des Etudes Anciennes* 76 (1974) 56, referring to E. Volterra, 'Quelques remarques sur le style des constitutions de Constantin', *Mélanges Lévy-Bruhl*, 1958, 325–34.

⁵³ M. Avi-Yonah, *Jews*, 159f.

It would be extremely interesting to be able to add something on the reaction of the people concerned, in particular the Jews of Palestine. A relevant text is a passage in a speech of John Chrysostom: 'Under Constantine they [= the Jews] attacked again. When the emperor became aware of their attack, he caused their ears to be cut off and so taught their body a parable of their disobedience; he caused them to be led about everywhere thus.'[54]

M. Avi-Yonah summarizes this text as follows: 'A revolt of the Jews was summarily suppressed.' His words are more careful elsewhere: 'Probably some zealot group attempted a coup-de-main in Jerusalem in order to keep Jerusalem from becoming a Christian city; their failure was immediate.'[55] The lone reference in Chrysostom, which is not supported by any other fourth-century source, neither a rabbinic text nor a non-Jewish author, does not suffice for such a statement. However, M. Avi-Yonah sees in MidrPs 5.6 (B.27 a) a rabbinic reaction to suppression under Constantine:[56]

> R. Jehuda interpreted (Ps. 5:2f.) with regard to the four empires. 'Hear my words' in Babel; 'give heed to my sighing' in Media; 'hear my loud cry' in Greece; '[my king and my God], for I plead with you' in Edom [= Rome].
>
> And why does [the Biblical text] say 'my king and my God' in the case of Edom? Rather the Israelites said before the Holy One, blessed be He: How many persecutions and evil edicts have they decided against us, in order to destroy your kingship and your rule among us; but we have not destroyed it, but on every single day we come to the prayer houses and schools, and there declare twice daily the kingship of your divinity and say, 'Hear, O Israel, the Lord your God is one God' [Dent. 6:4].

Then the previously Hebrew text continues in Aramaic: 'and you

---

[54] John Chrysostom, *Adv. Iudaeos* V.11 (PG 48, 900).
[55] M. Avi-Yonah, *Palaestina*, Munich 1974 (offprint from Pauly-Wissowa, supplementary volume XIII), 444. The second quote: *Jews*, 174. B. G. Nathanson, *The Fourth Century Jewish 'Revolt'*, 68, rightly sees in John Chrysostom the only independent source for a Jewish revolt under Constantine – later Byzantine chronicles depend on him – but she thinks it at least possible 'that there was some sort of modest uprising in Jerusalem'.
[56] M. Avi-Yonah, *Jews*, 165.

do your part and we do ours; for it is written, "my friend is for me and I am for him" [Song 2:16].'

It is extremely difficult to interpret this text with respect to a concrete situation. The complaint, that the Roman empire attempts everything in order to dissuade the Jews from their exclusive service of the God of Israel, is almost timeless, and may just as well express the Jews' total experience of centuries of Roman rule. This passage is certainly not a definite proof that the Jews of Palestine felt Constantine's rule to be particularly oppressive. Thus S. Lieberman stresses that there is no rabbinic complaint that Jews were forced to transgress their law under Constantine or Constantius.[57]

Even if Constantine's legislation is assessed differently, the fact remains to be explained that soon after him, for decades, hardly any laws were passed regarding Jews. R. L. Wilken concludes from this

> that Constantine's impact on the status of the Jews was less profound than is usually supposed. Even if there was a conscious effort under Constantine to restrict Jewish activity and to protect Christians from Jewish proselytization, that policy was not carried through in the years after his death. Indeed, one has the distinct impression that a great gulf lies between the time of Constantine and the age of Theodosius I ... Constantine was not the architect of Christian Europe.[58]

---

[57] S. Lieberman, *Palestine*, 324f.
[58] R. L. Wilken, *John Chrysostom*, 52.

III

Church Building and Christianization

The effects of laws on particular regions are always difficult to ascertain in detail, as we have seen. By contrast, the development of church building shows us very clearly the concrete changes which the legalization of Christianity brought in the eastern part of the Empire also. The churches for which we have archaeological, or at least literary, evidence, are also solid evidence for the expansion of Christianity in the Holy Land and for its regional distribution.

In the context of a general history of Palestine, one question of interest is how church building contributed to the economic development of the country and helped to secure jobs. The churches are also a visible proof of state support for the Christian faith, and thus can indeed influence the political atmosphere of the country. We must also ask to what extent the new church buildings represented an attraction for Christians from abroad, whether these came as pilgrims or long-term residents (see the next chapter). Finally, the building of churches could cause religious problems for Jews, just as the earlier case of building pagan temples brought up questions of 'idol worship', *'aboda zara*. These points show that the development of church building is not simply an aspect of Christian internal history, but naturally had an effect on the Jewish population of Palestine as well.

There were certainly Christian churches long before Constantine; but we have almost no archaeological evidence for them. We could hardly expect this; in general people surely built house churches, which did not differ externally from private dwellings. Even in the late fourth century this still seems to have been the case occasionally. This follows from a letter of Epiphanius of Salamis, preserved in Jerome's translation. Epiphanius writes that he once came, in the neighbourhood of

Church Building and Christianization

Bethel, 'to a village called Anablata. I saw in passing a lamp burning and asked what manner of place that was, and was told it was a church.'[1]

We may probably assume that the church in Caesarea, which Eusebius mentions for the time of Gallienus, was also simply a large house. Eusebius tells how the soldier Marinus was put on trial in Caesarea as a Christian. During the short period allowed him to think, he met the bishop Theoteknos, who led him into the church and gave him the choice between the gospel and the sword.[2] Only from after the persecution under Gallienus, until the middle of the reign of Diocletian, was there a blossoming of the Christian communities, who enjoyed the favour of the governors. In the following period, according to Eusebius, there were many assemblies in every city, 'and a remarkable confluence of people to the houses of prayer (*proseukteria*). Because of this, people were no longer content with the previous buildings (*oikodomēseis*), and erected in each city, from the ground up, extensive and large churches (*ekklēsiai*).'[3]

It is tempting to interpret the change in the text of Eusebius from *oikodomēseis* to *ekklēsiai* narrowly, and take it to mean the replacement of house churches by church buildings proper. But Eusebius changes his terminology; on the one hand, he already calls the church in Caesarea, mentioned above, an *ekklēsia*, while on the other, writing about the persecution since the eighteenth year of Diocletian, he says that he saw with his own eyes how the houses of prayer (*tōn men proseuktēriōn tous oikous*) were torn down from the roof to the foundations, and how the holy books were burnt in the market places.[4]

Since there is scarcely any archaeological evidence for the existence of pre-Constantinian churches in Palestine, the best guide for the spread of Christianity until the time of Constantine is the list of Palestinian bishops at the Council of Nicaea in 325. However, the tradition as to the names is not unanimous, since the records of the council are not extant and not even the exact numbers of participants are known. Only later tradition settled on the symbolic number 318, corresponding to Abraham's 318

---

[1] Jerome, *ep.* 51.9 (CSEL 54, 411).
[2] Eusebius, *Church history* VII.15 (GCS 9, 668–70).
[3] Eusebius, *Church history* VIII.1.5 (GCS 9, 738).
[4] Eusebius, *Church history* VIII.2.1 (GCS 9, 740).

servants in Genesis 14. The witness of the various manuscripts also conflicts regarding the list of Palestinian participants.[5]

Present in all the lists are the bishops of Caesarea, Nicopolis (Emmaus), Jamnia, Lydda, Eleutheropolis (Beth Gubrin), Ashkelon, Ashdod, Jericho and Scythopolis (Beth Shean). Jerusalem is of course a certainty, although it is missing from one list. The same is presumably also true of Sebaste and Neapolis. Strikingly, a bishop of Zabulon is named in all the lists (but there is also manuscript evidence for Gabalon, Diabulon and similar forms). If the traditional territory of the biblical tribe was meant, this would be the western Plain of Jezreel. However, the suggestion that this name refers to the large village of Kabul on the border of Galilee seems more plausible.[6] This could perhaps have served instead of a bishop's seat in central Galilee, which had largely resisted Christianity until that time. It is the only Palestinian bishop's seat which does not appear in later lists, and was apparently abandoned. Finally, in some lists Gaza, Aila and Maximianopolis also appear, and east of the Jordan Gadara and Capitolias. The northern cities of Ptolemais (Acco/Acre) and Paneas, also represented, did not form part of the ecclesiastical province of Palestine.

Within Palestine itself we thus have fourteen very well documented place names, as well as five less well attested ones. Particularly interesting in this context is the fact that no name is mentioned from the Tetrakomia, the principal area of Jewish settlement; for the territory of Palaestina Secunda, also an important Jewish centre, bishoprics are only named for the southern border (Maximianopolis and Scythopolis) and beyond the Jordan (Capitolias and Gadara); there is also Kabul, which is on the border and dubious. In part we must reckon with the addition of names to fit later circumstances – at the Council of Ephesus in 431, Juvenal of Jerusalem came with sixteen Palestinian bishops, that is, there had been hardly any change compared to the lists for Nicaea!

It must be stressed that a bishop's seat does not necessarily imply the existence of a large Christian congregation. This is

---

[5] Lists in J. D. Mansi, *Collectio Conciliorum II*, Florence 1759 (reprinted Paris 1901), 698; C. H. Turner (ed.), *Ecclesiae Occidentalis Monumenta Iuris Antiquissima 1.1*, Oxford 1899, 42ff.

[6] Z. Safrai, *Gebulot* 32; J. Geiger in Z. Baras et al. (eds.), *Eretz Israel I* 225; but for this remark see already F. M. Abel, *Géographie II*, 198 n. 5 and 287, referring to Josephus, *BJ* II.499, where Zabulon stands instead of Kabul.

particularly clear in the case of Gaza, where even at the end of the fourth century the Christian congregation was still very small in number. Some of the names may represent a programme of expansion rather than the actual state of affairs in 325. Thus the bishops' lists of Nicaea tell us more about the regional distribution of Christianity and its bases than about the numerical strength of the Christian communities. We may presumably assume the existence of Christian meeting-rooms in these places, but not necessarily the existence of actual churches.

1. Jerusalem before the Building Work under Constantine

We still have only very imperfect knowledge of the town plan of Aelia Capitolina. The new excavations in Jerusalem have brought little information on this subject, and what there is is hard to correlate with the literary evidence. M. Ben-Dov, one of those in charge of the Jerusalem excavations, emphasizes that the destruction of Jerusalem in 70 cannot have been as complete as Josephus describes.[7] Parts of the Temple reaching to a considerable height must have remained standing in Byzantine times; they were only destroyed in the Persian invasion of 614, when the Byzantine defenders barricaded themselves in it. This is the only possible explanation for the fact that many pieces of the Herodian temple have been excavated *above* the Byzantine layers, and that many parts of the Herodian Huldah Gate were used as building material in early Islamic buildings, but never in Byzantine buildings. Outside the Temple precinct, only towers from the fortifications of the royal palace remained standing, according to Josephus. Here also, M. Ben-Dov estimates that in reality a large part of the city's fortifications were preserved, as well as a number of houses, up to the second storey. By contrast, H. Geva assumes a complete destruction of the upper part of the city: 'it is hard to believe that any buildings remained which the tenth legion could rebuild and renew'.[8]

The archaeological remains of Aelia Capitolina are mainly represented by bricks with legions' stamps, which were often reused in Islamic buildings, as well as a few inscriptions (among

---

[7] M. Ben-Dov, *The Dig*, 186f.
[8] M. Ben-Dov, *The Dig*, 194f.; H. Geva, 'The Camp', 246.

others one of Hadrian, another with the name of Septimius Severus). The gate complex near the house of the Sisters of Zion in the Via Dolorosa, the so-called 'Ecce Homo arch', also stems from this period. The gate under the present Damascus Gate is usually counted as well,[9] but M. Ben-Dov rejects this. He attributes this gate to the Herodian period and doubts whether Aelia had a city wall at all; so far there are no archaeological traces of a fortification from this period.[10] If there were nevertheless city walls, remains of the wall from the time before 70 must have been reused for them. In the past it was thought that the present south wall of the old city was built along the line of the wall of Aelia; but here also, the excavations speak rather against it than otherwise, and the Bordeaux Pilgrim does not offer clearly positive evidence.[11]

The location of the legionary camp and the Capitol is of particular interest. The only definite evidence for the camp of the Legio X Fretensis is a burnt-out room (end of the third century) under an early Islamic palace, near the south-west corner of the Temple. Because of the finds, M. Ben-Dov takes it to be the room belonging to the priest of the troop stationed here to keep the Jews away from the Temple mount (statuettes and dice, perhaps for oracles).[12] There is no archaeological evidence for the customary assumption that the legionary camp was situated in the upper city, in the vicinity of the royal palace and Mount Zion. Were the legionary buildings so carefully dismantled, when the troops withdrew to Eilat, that not a single indication can be found of their presence? Or was there only a temporary camp, without walls, as H. Geva believes, corresponding to other examples in the region (e.g. Legio near Megiddo)?[13]

As regards the street plan, it was long thought that the orientation of Cardo and Decumanus, that is the north-south and east-west arteries of every planned Roman city, could still be traced in the present street grid, and was also attested in the mosaic map of Madaba in East Jordan (sixth century). According to this, the Cardo would have led from the Damascus Gate roughly to the present Zion Gate; the Decumanus would have

---

[9] E.g. N. Avigad, *Discovering Jerusalem*, 205.
[10] M. Ben-Dov, *The Dig*, 192; likewise H. Geva, 'The Camp', 251.
[11] M. Ben-Dov, *The Dig*, 194f.
[12] M. Ben-Dov, *The Dig*, 198f.
[13] H. Geva, 'The Camp', 251ff.

Church Building and Christianization

followed the line of King David Street from the Jaffa Gate, and would then have continued in 'Chain Street'.

However, the excavations of N. Avigad[14] now show that the northern part of the Cardo is Roman, but the southern part is Byzantine and does not simply renew a Roman construction. Therefore the present Jewish quarter was only inhabited after 324, presumably on the site which had previously been used by the Roman troops. Only when the Nea church was built under Justinian was the Roman Cardo extended towards the south. Thus only the northern part of the present old city was inhabited before Constantine; in the southern part were merely legionary buildings. We must also reckon with many open spaces in the whole city area: 'Roman Aelia was an insignificant provincial town ... Jerusalem was to rise to prominence only with the decline of pagan rule and the advent of Christianity as the official religion of the Roman Empire'.[15] After the departure of the legion at the end of the third century, which entailed the departure of families and other persons who earned their living from the troops, the city must have lost a large part of its population.

A further matter of disagreement is the location of the Capitol. This question also needs to be resolved with regard to the Constantinian building programme. B. Mazar writes: 'On the site of the Second Temple he (Hadrian) built a Capitoline temple with three cellae, dedicated to Jupiter, Juno and Minerva. He also had an equestrian statue of himself set up, and his successor Antoninus Pius (138–161) added a further statue.'[16]

Can this be correct? Then the Capitol would have been built in the middle of a field of ruins! And there are no reports from the fourth century that this complex of buildings was demolished or used for another purpose. B. Mazar himself refers to the fact that the Byzantine rulers left the Temple mount untouched as a heap of ruins, as a proof of the dissolution of Judaism's old ties to the holy place. He also understands an open space in the city's representation on the Madaba map, marked with brown mosaic stones, as the Temple mount.[17] Eusebius writes that in his time the stone blocks of the Temple were dragged away to build

---

[14] N. Avigad, *Discovering Jerusalem*, 225f.
[15] N. Avigad, *Discovering Jerusalem*, 207.
[16] B. Mazar, *Der Berg des Herrn*, 17.
[17] B. Mazar, *Der Berg des Herrn*, 24; 22.

theatres and other public buildings.[18] Is that conceivable – before Christianization! – right next to the Capitoline temple? Does it not rather suggest a place of ruins? This is probably also implied when John Chrysostom says, looking back to the attempted reconstruction of the Temple under Julian: 'The Jews began to expose the foundations by moving large amounts of earth to one side ... one can see the exposed foundations if one goes to Jerusalem today.'[19]

The fact that the Capitol would not be situated directly in the Forum, which is definitely near the later Church of the Holy Sepulchre, to the east of it, would not present a difficulty. However, the report of the building of the Church of the Holy Sepulchre appears to assume that this was built on the site of the Capitol. But if we suppose the shrine with three cellae in honour of the Capitoline triad, Jupiter, Juno and Minerva, to have been there (its importance is also attested by local coinage), should we then look for an additional shrine to Jupiter on the Temple mount?[20]

M. Ben-Dov is of the opinion that Hadrian intended to build a temple of Jupiter Capitolinus on the Temple mount, but that this temple apparently did not attain a respected position.[21] M. Stern offers a similar interpretation of a passage in Cassius Dio, *History of Rome* 69.12.1 (only extant in Xiphilinus' summary): 'In Jerusalem he (Hadrian) built a city to replace the one that was destroyed, which he called Aelia Capitolina, and in the place of the Temple of God he set another temple for Zeus. This caused a revolt that was not small and not short.' According to Stern, the time was simply not long enough for the building work to have progressed very far before the insurgents destroyed it all again.[22] However, the Dio text is not sufficient evidence for the erection of a temple of Jupiter on the Temple square itself (and not simply instead of the Jewish Temple).

The texts cited seem rather to suggest that the Temple square remained in ruins; the archaeological results to date do not prove

---

[18] Eusebius, *Demonstratio evangelica* VIII.3 (GCS 393).
[19] John Chrysostom, *Adversus Iudaeos* V.11 (PG 48, 901).
[20] Thus e.g. E. Otto, *Jerusalem – die Geschichte der heiligen Stadt*, Stuttgart 1980, 168–71.
[21] M. Ben-Dov, *The Dig* 191. B. Bagatti, 'Il "tempio di Gerusalemme" dal II all' VIII secolo', *Biblica* 43 (1962) 1–21, 14, also argues for a temple with three cellae on the Temple square. See also M. Avi-Yonah, *Jews*, 200.
[22] M. Stern, *Greek and Latin Authors* II, 396.

the existence of a Roman building on this site, which fact probably cannot simply be attributed to the preparations for building that took place under Julian. Presumably that square was only dominated by a statue of Hadrian, to which a further statue of Antoninus Pius was later added – the Bordeaux Pilgrim speaks of two statues of Hadrian,[23] whereas Jerome says, 'Where once the Temple and the worship of God were, a statue of Hadrian and an idol of Jupiter were erected.'[24] Neither mentions a temple.

A sermon of Cyril of Jerusalem, preached about 350, appears also to attest that the Temple square remained in ruins even after 324. In it he sees Mt. 24:2 confirmed, that not one stone of the Temple would remain on another: 'The Temple of the Jews, which is opposite you, is fallen.'[25]

2. The Church of the Holy Sepulchre in Jerusalem

As the place of Jesus' death, Jerusalem was of programmatic significance for the Christianization of the Roman Empire. It is, therefore, not surprising that, immediately after 324, plans were set in motion to uncover the grave of Jesus and to adorn it with suitable dignity, and that the emperor took a personal interest in the project. Until recently, as far as the history of the building and particularly the reconstruction of the Church of the Holy Sepulchre founded by Constantine are concerned, we were forced to rely almost exclusively on Eusebius' description in his biography of Constantine.[26] This text probably makes at least partial use of Eusebius' speech on the occasion of the dedication

---

[23] *Itinera Hierosolymitana*, CSEL 39, 22. A fragment of Origen's *Commentary on Matthew* on 24.15 (GCS 194), interprets the 'desolating sacrilege' as referring to the 'statue of Hadrian or Gaius' on the Temple square, while the other versions of the text only speak of the statue that Pilate erected in the Temple. See also J. Wilkinson, 'Christian Pilgrims' 78f., who postulates a temple of Jupiter in the north-west of the city, next to the temple of Venus, and who does not think in terms of a single temple to the triad. Also Bieberstein-Bloedhorn I 145. By contrast, S. Gibson, J. E. Taylor, *Beneath the Church of the Holy Sepulchre*, Jerusalem/London 1994, 68–71, suppose the capitol to have been in the area of the second forum, north of the Temple square.

[24] Jerome, *In Is.* I.2 (CC 73.33).

[25] Cyril of Jerusalem, *Catechetical Lectures* 10.11 (PG 33, 676f.; see *Catechetical Lectures* 15.15, PG 33, 889).

[26] Eusebius, *Vita Constantini* III.25–40 (GCS 89–95).

of the church. 'It is certainly the first-hand account of one who observed closely the building operations as they progressed, and who knew in detail the completed precinct.'[27] Nevertheless, the text is ambiguous on some points, omits a number of things we would want to know today, and thus has often led to contradictory reconstructions.

The complicated rights of ownership and use of the holy site, belonging to individual Christian denominations, prevented archaeological excavations for a long time. These could have provided information on disputed points. Equally, for a long time it was impossible to come to an agreement on the repairs which had become urgently necessary due to extensive damage caused by earthquakes, among other things. It was only from 1960 onwards that a general structural renovation of the holy place was undertaken. The archaeological investigations that were undertaken in this context allowed significant checks and supplementation of Eusebius' statements.[28]

According to Eusebius, the place which was traditionally regarded as the location of Jesus' grave was covered with earth and paved over by pagans: 'A gloomy chamber was built for an obscene deity, Aphrodite, and then shameful sacrifices were offered on unclean and accursed altars.' But, under Constantine, 'the buildings of error, together with all the statues and gods, were destroyed and torn down'. All the material of the demolished temple, and also the polluted earth, which was cleared away to a great depth, was carried far away, as Eusebius continues. Finally, against all expectation, the *martyrion* of the Resurrection, the burial cave, became visible.

A few decades later, Jerome makes a rather different statement. He writes that from Hadrian to Constantine 'at the place of the Resurrection an idol of Jupiter was worshipped, and on the rock of the Cross a marble statue of Venus, erected by the pagans'.[29] J. Wilkinson understands this as referring to the temple of the Capitoline triad and gives preference to Jerome's statement, since he knew Eusebius' work and presumably was consciously correcting him.[30]

---

[27] E. D. Hunt, *Holy Land Pilgrimage*, 10.
[28] C. Coüasnon, *The Church*; V. Corbo, *Il Santo Sepolcro*.
[29] Jerome, *ep.* 58.3 (CSEL 54, 531f.).
[30] J. Wilkinson, 'Christian Pilgrims', 82f.

Church Building and Christianization

The fact that the place of Jesus' grave must have been thought to be located in the centre of the city from an early period seems to be confirmed by Melito of Sardis, who visited Jerusalem between 160 and 170. In his Easter sermon he says: 'But the unjust murder of the Just One happened in the middle of the street, in the middle of the city, in the middle of the city before the face of all.'[31] Since this is quite contrary to the evidence of the New Testament, according to which Jesus suffered 'outside the gate' (Heb. 13:12), the contemporary localization must lie behind Melito's words. In any case, the location of the Church of the Holy Sepulchre on the site of the Hadrianic capitol, which itself lay directly on the forum of Aelia Capitolina (as mentioned by the pilgrim Egeria), seems certain.

The development of legends in the following decades adds at this period the Invention of the Cross by Helena.[32] The Bordeaux Pilgrim does not yet know of a relic of the Cross. Cyril of Jerusalem, however, says around 350 that 'the holy wood of the Cross is a witness [to Christ], which can be seen among us to this day and, thanks to those who have taken pieces from it in faith, now almost fills the whole earth'.[33] But Ambrosius is the first, in his sermon *On the death of Theodosius* on 25 February 395, to connect Helena with the Invention of the Cross. He already knows of the nails from the Cross which Helena sent to Constantine. According to Ambrosius, Constantine caused them to be set into his crown and the bridle of his horse, in accord with Zech. 14:20: 'On that day there shall be inscribed on the bells of the horses, "Holy to the Lord."'[34] The story spread very quickly, although it met with doubts from critical people such as Jerome: 'I heard from someone a story which, although dictated by a devout spirit, was nevertheless laughable: the nails from the Lord's cross, from which Emperor Constantine is said to have

---

[31] Melito of Sardis, *On the Pascha* (SC 123, 116).
[32] On this see S. Borgehammar, *How the Holy Cross was Found. From event to medieval legend*, Stockholm 1991; J. W. Drijvers, *Helena Augusta: The mother of Constantine the Great and the Legend of her finding the True Cross*, Leiden 1992.
[33] Cyril of Jerusalem, *Catechetical Lectures* 10.19 (PG 33, 685–7); cf. 4.10 (p. 469). P. W. L. Walker, *Holy City* 258–60, is of the opinion that Eusebius did not mention the wood of the Cross, which he knew about, as also Golgotha in general, for theological reasons.
[34] Ambrosius, *De obitu Theodosii*, CSEL 73, 40ff.

made his horse's bridle, are called "holy to the Lord". Whether that is to be accepted, I leave to the intelligence of the reader.'[35]

Particularly interesting, in our context, is the fact that Paulinus of Nola, a contemporary of Jerome's, already asserts that Jews assisted Helena in her search for the Cross of Christ:

> And so she sought out not only among the Christians men full of knowledge and holiness, but also the most experienced among the Jews as witnesses (*indices*; another reading is *iudices*, judges) of their own godlessness, of which the miserable wretches even boast. She called them and brought them together to Jerusalem, and was then given confirmation by the unanimous evidence of all ... The Cross of the Lord was thus covered through such long ages, hidden by the Jews at the time of the Passion, and not manifested to the heathen when they built the temple, when they heaped up earth, without doubt for this building. Did it not remain hidden by divine intervention, so that it might now be found, when it was sought for with pious intent?[36]

The church historian Sozomen also knows of Jewish participation in the Invention of the Cross, but doubts the story: The place of Jesus' Cross was laid bare 'as some say, because a man of the Hebrews, who dwell in the east, proved it from a writing of the fathers; but, as may more truthfully be thought, because God showed it by signs and dreams'. Then follows the story, also given by Socrates and Rufinus, that the place named was excavated, three crosses and the trilingual inscription of Jesus' Cross found, and how finally, in the presence of Macarius, the Bishop of Jerusalem, the true Cross of Christ was identified by miracles.[37]

Jews play an important part in the history of the finding of relics in the Holy Land, as we will see in the next chapter – not in reality, but from a Christian point of view. They are the indigenous witnesses who are able to make authentic statements about the time of Jesus and the occurrences of that time, and in fact must do so, against their own religious interests. Perhaps

---

[35] Jerome, *In Zech.* III.14.20 (CC 76A, 898).
[36] Paulinus of Nola, *ep.* 31.5f. (CSEL 29, 272f.).
[37] Sozomen, *Church history* II.1.4 (GCS 50, 48); Socrates, *Church history* I.17 (PG 67, 117–20); Rufinus, *Church history* X.7–8 (GCS 9, 969–71). On the role of Jews in the Invention of the Cross, see O. Limor, 'Christian Tradition', 34–43.

another motive is a contributing factor. While Eusebius still sees redemption concentrated in the grave and resurrection of Jesus, and the Cross is of no importance in his appreciation of the Church of the Holy Sepulchre, it apparently became an object of particular veneration, especially for converts from Judaism.[38] Bishop John of Jerusalem appears to have appointed Porphyrius, the exegete from Thessaloniki, later Bishop of Gaza, as first official guardian of the Cross, or *staurophylax*, in 392. In his sermon for the dedication of the church of Sion he calls Porphyrius 'an Israelite in whom there is no guile', a man who built an ark like Noah and went into it with his family. So Porphyrius was perhaps of Jewish descent.[39] If this suggestion is correct, it might indicate that converts from Judaism were rare in the Holy Land itself, but that they came from the other provinces of the Roman Empire; the expression 'a man of the Hebrews, who dwell in the east', which sounds odd coming from Sozomen, whose home was southern Palestine, would then make sense. We will return later to the problem of Jewish Christians in Palestine. It certainly seems not impossible that Jewish-Christian influence was at work in the development of veneration of the Cross; of course we cannot rule out the possibility that the role of Jews in general in the traditions of finding relics in the Holy Land owes its prominence particularly to this tradition.

In the further course of the legend of the Invention of the Cross, the building of the Church of the Holy Sepulchre was increasingly also attributed to Helena. However, she first travelled to Palestine in 327, when building had already begun. It seems probable that Macarius, Bishop of Jerusalem, took the initiative for this project at the Council of Nicaea, even though Eusebius,

---

[38] J. Vogt, 'Helena Augusta, das Kreuz und die Juden', *Saeculum* 27 (1976) 211–22. On the development of the legend of the Invention of the Cross, see E. D. Hunt, *Holy Land Pilgrimage*, 38–49 (literature). The anti-Jewish flavour of the legend is stressed by A. Linder, 'Judaism as a Focal Point in the Conflict between Judaism and Christianity' (Hebrew), in B. Z. Kedar (ed.) *Jerusalem in the Middle Ages. Selected Papers*, Jerusalem 1979, 5–26; 17ff. But see also Z. Rubin, 'The Church of the Holy Sepulchre and the Conflict between the Sees of Caesarea and Jerusalem', *The Jerusalem Cathedra* 2 (1982) 79–105, who is of the opinion that Eusebius intentionally suppresses the Invention of the Cross, or only gives a very veiled allusion to it, because of the role played in it by Macarius, Bishop of Jerusalem.

[39] See M. van Esbroeck, 'Jean II' 99, 112; 115–25: translation of the Armenian text.

in his biography of Constantine, describes it as entirely the emperor's initiative. He certainly had a strong interest in the Holy Land. Once, when he was a member of Diocletian's retinue, he had travelled in Palestine, and after his conversion to Christianity he even hoped to be baptized in the Jordan one day.[40]

Thus Constantine became enthusiastic about the project of the Church of the Holy Sepulchre, and gave the official order in a letter to Bishop Macarius to take care

> not only that a basilica should be built that was more beautiful than anywhere else, but that everything else should be of such a kind that all that was most beautiful in any and every city should be outdone by this foundation. As far as the walls and the ornament is concerned, know that Our friend Dracillian, who co-ordinates the duties of the noble governors, and the provincial governor have been entrusted by Us with their care. For my Piety has given order that master craftsmen, workmen and everything which your knowledge tells them is necessary for the building, are to be sent at once through their care. As regards the columns and the marble, write immediately to Us, once you have gained an overview, what you think is most precious and suitable, so that We may learn from your letter, how much and which are necessary, so that We may have them brought from all directions ... I would like to hear from you whether you think the ceiling of the basilica ought to be panelled or made in any other way. For if it is to be panelled, it can also be adorned with gold. Let your Holiness inform the above-named functionaries as quickly as possible, how many master craftsmen, workmen and how much money is necessary. Report to Me very swiftly not only regarding the marble and the columns, but also the panelling, if you think such to be more beautiful.[41]

The letter makes it clear enough that the building was a state project. That follows not only from the commissioning of Dracillian, who is attested for the year 326 as deputy *Praefectus praetorio*, but also from Constantine's appeal to the governors of the east, mentioned by Eusebius immediately before the letter,

---

[40] Eusebius, *Vita Constantini* I.19 (GCS 25); IV.62.2 (GCS 146).
[41] Eusebius, *Vita Constantini* III.31f. (GCS 98f.).

Church Building and Christianization

to give generously for the planned work, and also from his undertaking to see to the delivery of columns, marble and gold himself.

The architect engaged for the building was Zenobius; his name has given rise to the conjecture that he was perhaps a Syrian or Palestinian;[42] certainly he kept to the traditional eastern style of building. The grounds stretched roughly 132 m westwards from the Cardo Maximus with a width of roughly 43 m, giving an area of not quite 5700 m^2. From the Cardo, the entrance was through a ceremonial gate to the atrium, which the architect apparently based around the temple precinct of the Hadrianic capitol or the temple of Venus; he 'made use of the Hadrianic *temenos* as he found it, but panelled it with marble on the east side'.[43] Adjoining this was a five-aisled church, the 'Martyrium', which was *ca.* 58 m long and 40 m wide. The apse was at the west end – entirely contrary to tradition, but according to the traditional site of the grave of Jesus, west of the Cardo.

Thus the building was not of exceptional size, as one might be tempted to conclude from Constantine's letter; the available terrain was limited. Its worth lay in the decoration, for which the emperor was responsible, such as the enormous silver bowls above the twelve pillars of the *hemisphairion* (corresponding to the twelve apostles), which finished off the building, the polychrome marble incrustations and the gilded and coffered ceiling under the wooden roof, sheathed in lead.

On both sides of the church, an open walkway led to the inner courtyard with the rock of Calvary. At the western end of the complex was the Anastasis, the memorial of the Resurrection, which was entered from the courtyard by the eight gateways of the 46 m wide façade. The Anastasis was dominated by a domed rotunda more than ten metres in diameter, with twelve columns and six pillars; the rotunda itself was surrounded by a large semicircular structure with three apses. According to V. Corbo, the twelve columns are spoils from the Hadrianic building, a conclusion based on their unusually large diameter (up to 120 cm): 'Such massive columns are unthinkable in a Christian building, unless we assume reuse of material.' The twelve

---

[42] Thus J. W. Crowfoot, *Early Churches* 21.
[43] V. Corbo, *Il Santo Sepolcro* I, 117. The Hadrianic wall itself is composed of Herodian material.

columns, in his opinion, are the result of cutting six columns in half that originally decorated the façade of the Hadrianic capitol.⁴⁴

In view of Eusebius' explicit assertion that, when Jesus' grave was uncovered, all the defiled material of the temple was taken far away, reuse of building material from the pagan capitol is surprising, as is Constantine's promise to see personally to the provision of columns. On the other hand, Eusebius speaks of the general destruction of temples and idols under Constantine, when everything usable was taken off the statues, even the gilding was scraped off, before the sad remnants were handed back to the idol-worshippers.⁴⁵ His statement that the square was entirely cleared of pagan material before beginning with the new building should be understood programmatically: it symbolizes a completely new beginning and is not to be taken literally.

It seems that the Anastasis was from the beginning an integral part of the uniform plan of the complex; but technical difficulties probably delayed its completion. When the Bordeaux Pilgrim saw the complex in 333, building must still have been in progress, and it was not yet complete for the dedication of the Church of the Holy Sepulchre on 17 September 335, which was originally to have crowned the celebrations for the thirtieth anniversary of Constantine's reign. The dome above the grave of Christ was built only in the following decade; its existence is first presupposed in Cyril of Jerusalem's sermons around 350, when he says that the catechumens 'go into the sacred site of the Resurrection'.⁴⁶

Even without the emperor's actual presence, the dedication of the church was a clear demonstration of state support for the church. The bishops assembled at the Council of Tyre (the council which Constantine had already planned for 334 in Palestinian Caesarea had failed through Athanasius' obstinacy) were brought to Jerusalem for the dedication. An imperial notary, that is, a particular confidant of the emperor – even relatives of the emperor held this post! – was entrusted with the organization of the ceremony, and Eusebius, as the metropolitan of Palestine,

---

⁴⁴ V. Corbo, *Il Santo Sepolcro* I, 69f.
⁴⁵ Eusebius, *Vita Constantini* III.27 (GCS 96); III.32 (GCS 99); see *Oratio Tric.* VII.12–IX.8 (GCS 215–18).
⁴⁶ Cyril of Jerusalem, *Catechetical Lectures* 18.33 (PG 33, 1056). See C. Coüasnon, *The Church*, 15; E. D. Hunt, *Holy Land Pilgrimage*, 11.

gave the dedication speech, which is probably partly preserved in his biography of Constantine, as already mentioned.⁴⁷

The whole venture had a pronounced ideological slant, of course. This church building replaced the pagan centre of Jerusalem with a Christian one, as was stressed clearly enough by Eusebius in his description of the preparatory work. It is thus all the more surprising to find a different interpretation of the enterprise, viz. that of replacing the old Jerusalem:

> And so the new Jerusalem was built beside the saving Martyrium, opposite the one known from old time, which because of its defilement through the murder of God had been entirely laid waste, and so had paid the due punishment of its godless inhabitants. Thus opposite that one the emperor glorified the saving victory over death with rich and lavish generosity, so that this must be the completely new Jerusalem, announced through prophetic words of God, about which great and divinely inspired prophecies tell endless great things.⁴⁸

This interpretation is probably rather that of Eusebius than the emperor's. Constantine presumably thought of pagan sites being superseded by Christian ones. But how important was for him the replacing of the Old Covenant by the New, the Jewish Jerusalem by a Christian Jerusalem? In the previous chapter we discussed the fact that Jews were of no particular importance in Constantine's legislation. How important were they for him at all? Jerusalem was at that time a city without Jews, and the replacement of the old by the new Jerusalem not visible at all, in a literal sense. Yet it was Eusebius' interpretation that prevailed; for it was more useful for propaganda purposes than the idea of a pagan cult being displaced by a Christian cult, since paganism had to yield in the course of the following centuries, while Judaism remained as a continual challenge. For example,

---

⁴⁷ Eusebius, *Vita Constantini* IV.44f. (GCS 138f.); *Dedication speech* III.34ff. (GCS 99–101).
⁴⁸ Eusebius, *Vita Constantini* III.33 (GCS 99). P. W. L. Walker, *Holy City* 399f., emphasizes that in this work Eusebius uses the form *Hierusalem* only here, denoting the new, heavenly Jerusalem by contrast to the earthly city, which he always calls *Ierosolyma*. The Church of the Holy Sepulchre, and not the city as a whole, is for him as it were a symbol of the new Jerusalem. See 349–401 in general for Eusebius' critical attitude to Jerusalem.

Socrates also speaks of Helena as the woman 'who built the new Jerusalem opposite that old and deserted one'.[49]

3. Other Constantinian Buildings

Three further church buildings from the time of Constantine should be briefly mentioned here. Eusebius writes that the emperor's mother founded the Eleona church on the Mount of Olives during her stay in the Holy Land, and also the Church of the Nativity in Bethlehem. Constantine endowed both buildings with rich gifts. However, the Bordeaux Pilgrim attributes both directly to Constantine.[50]

The church on the Mount of Olives was built over a cave in which the risen Jesus was said to have taught his disciples about the end of the age. Veneration of this cave is attested for the early third century by the *Acts of John*.[51] In the Constantinian building, a portico led to an atrium with a large cistern; this led to the basilica itself, which measured *ca.* 30 x 18 m and had a mosaic floor.

The Church of the Nativity in Bethlehem was a basilica measuring *ca.* 28 × 28 m, with five aisles like the basilica of the Church of the Holy Sepulchre. Here too there was a mosaic floor; mosaics or paintings adorned the walls. Adjoining the nave was an octagonal *memoria* above the Cave of the Nativity, whose veneration in the second century is attested by the *Protevangelium of James*, and is probably also assumed by Justin's *Dialogue with Trypho*. Thus the complex in its entirety was closely related to the plan of the building in Jerusalem. In his anniversary speech for Constantine, Eusebius draws a parallel between all three buildings: 'three sites, venerated because of three mystic caves'.[52] Jerome writes of the Church of the Nativity: 'A grove of Tammuz, that is

---

[49] Socrates, *Church history* I.17 (PG 67, 121).
[50] Eusebius, *Vita Constantini* III.41–43 (GCS 101); *Itinera Hierosolymitana*, CSEL 38, 23–5.
[51] See J. Wilkinson, *Christian Pilgrims*, 84; cf. Eusebius, *Demonstratio evangelica* VI.18.23 (GCS 23, 278). On this, see P. W. L. Walker, *Holy City*, 202–13. J. E. Taylor, *Christians and the Holy Places*, Oxford 1993, 143–56, is of the opinion that the *Acts of John* do not prove the veneration of a specific cave on the Mount of Olives, but that rather the text led to the localization of a cave.
[52] Eusebius, *Oratio Tric.* IX, 17 (GCS 221). On the significance of the three caves in Eusebius' theology, see P. W. L. Walker, *Holy City* 184–94.

Adonis, overshadowed Bethlehem, and in the cave where once Christ cried as a little child, the lover of Venus was bewailed.'[53]

While the previously mentioned Constantinian church buildings were dedicated to sites of Christian remembrance, Mamre near Hebron is linked with an ancient Biblical tradition, the appearance of God, or of three angels, to Abraham (Gen. 18). Is this the reason for the fact that the bishops of Palestine paid no attention to Mamre, as Constantine underlines almost mockingly in his letter to Macarius of Jerusalem and all the bishops? He had to learn of the state of affairs there from his mother-in-law Eutropia.[54]

The sacred precinct of Mamre had been built up partly in the time of Herod, partly under Hadrian. The enclosure, which included the 'Oak of Abraham', his well and an open-air altar, had been venerated by pagans too from at least the time of Hadrian; they equated the angels with Hermes, messenger of the gods. At the fair which was held here, countless Jews were sold as slaves after the Bar Cochba revolt; it was still in existence centuries later and had a clearly pagan character. For the rabbis, this market was even more pagan than those of Gaza and Acco/Acre; it drew people even from abroad, as may be seen from finds of coins. Therefore they declared it to be forbidden to Jews (jAZ I.5.39 d), but this veto was apparently not adhered to.[55]

Constantine appointed Count Acacius to remove the pagan altar of sacrifice and the idols. The bishops of Palestine, together with those of Phoenicia, were to draw up a plan for a suitably worthy basilica. In the future, pagans were to be kept away from the enclosure, under threat of punishment. In the enclosure, a small church was built (rather more than 16 m long, but 20 m wide). The whole plan was forced to accommodate itself to the situation at the holy place: it had to take into account Abraham's

---

[53] Jerome, *ep.* 58.3 (CSEL 54, 532). P. Welten, 'Bethlehem und die Klage um Adonis', *ZDPV* 99 (1983), 189–203, does not regard this text as evidence for the distribution of the cult of Adonis, but simply a literary motif, suggested by Mt 2.18 and the weeping of Rachel. By contrast, J. E. Taylor, *Christians and the Holy Places*, 96–112, accepts the tradition of a pagan cult in Bethlehem, but doubts an early Christian veneration of the grotto of the Nativity (112: 'There is no evidence for the early Christian veneration of the Nativity Grotto in Bethlehem').

[54] Eusebius, *Vita Constantini* III.51–3 (GCS 105–7).

[55] See Z. Safrai, 'Fairs in the Land of Israel in the Mishna and Talmud Period' (Hebrew), *Zion* 49 (1984), 139–58.

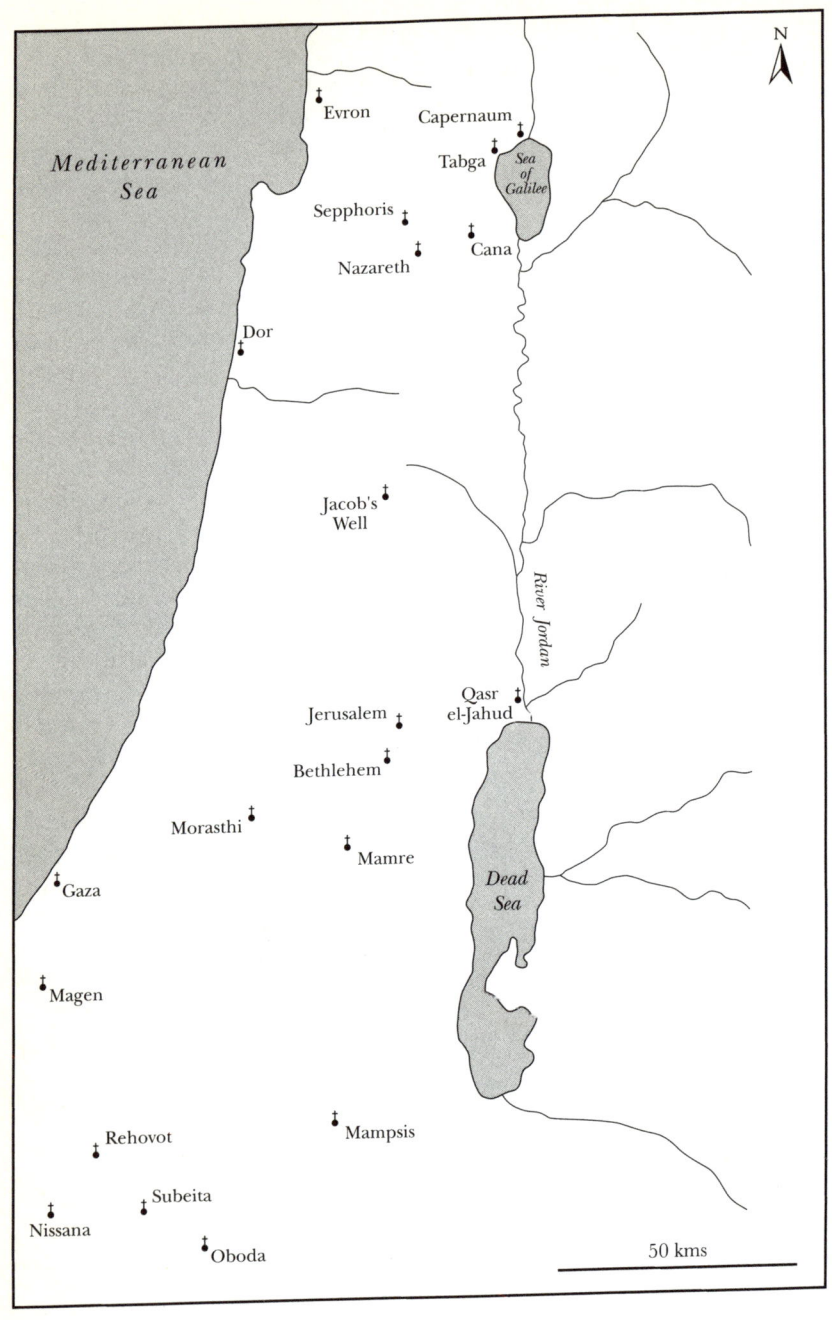

Church buildings in the fourth and early fifth centuries

Church Building and Christianization

well, also the site of the open-air altar, which dominated the open courtyard, and especially the oak of Abraham, which was still shown at the time of the building work, but must have died in the following decades, as follows from a comparison of Eusebius' *Onomasticon* with Jerome's reworking of it. Jerome corrects Eusebius' text in certain points, corresponding to the altered situation, e.g. saying of the oak of Abraham that it had been shown until the reign of Constantius, or of the monument to Abraham, that now there is a church on its site. Yet he retains the statement that the oak (or, in Jerome, its site) is the object of superstitious veneration on the part of all the pagans of the surrounding area. Thus the Christianization of the place of worship, which Constantine intended to achieve by building a church, appears to have been only partially successful because of the long tradition of Jewish and pagan worship. This also follows from the report of Sozomen, who came from near Gaza, and to whom we may attribute some knowledge of the true facts: At the yearly market, Jews, pagans and Christian unite for a festival; the Jews venerate Abraham, the pagans come because of the angels that appeared there; some pray to God, others set up idols on the altar and offer wine, incense and sacrificial animals, and throw votive gifts in Abraham's well.[56]

So all the Constantinian buildings, with the exception of the church on the Mount of Olives, replaced earlier pagan places of worship. They were all fairly small, built by local architects, and not comparable with the great architectural achievements of an earlier time, for example, that of Herod, and also not to be measured against the Constantinian buildings in Rome.[57] Palestine was still a small province, and Jerusalem not even its capital. The number of Christians in Palestine, too, was still probably quite small. Thus the small churches were fully adequate for normal liturgical needs, and the capacious open courtyards and enclosures in all of these complexes took into account the expected crowds of pilgrims.

---

[56] Eusebius, *Onomasticon*, GCS 11, 1.7; Sozomen, *Church history* II.4.2ff., GCS 50, 54f. The small finds during the excavations, among others from the Constantinian well, confirm these statements: E. Mader, *Mambre* (text), Freiburg 1957, 295f. and *passim*.

[57] J. W. Crowfoot, *Early Churches*, 160.

4. Archaeological Traces of Church Building in the Later Fourth Century

In the decades following Constantine's death Jerusalem remained the centre of Christianization and thus of church building.[58] At the grave of Lazarus in Bethany a church was built (34 × 17 m) with a coloured mosaic floor with a geometric pattern. Eusebius had written in his *Onomasticon* of Bethany that the place of Lazarus' grave was still shown. In Jerome's recension of his text, we read: '...whose grave is marked by the church now built there'. The pilgrim Egeria describes, around 380, a great ceremony that took place here, with people and clergy from Jerusalem participating. In the fifth century a new building replaced this church.

On the Mount of Olives, the rich Roman woman Poimnia (or Poimenia) founded the Church of the Ascension in the second half of the fourth century, a circular edifice 35 m in diameter, with walls almost 3 m thick. In the centre, above the rock, it was roofless and allowed one to look up to the sky.

Between 379 and 384 Theodosius I built the church of Gethsemane. The church of Sion, called 'Mother of all churches' from the middle of the fifth century, and from then on also associated with the Last Supper tradition, goes back to around 390 in its first phase of building.[59] A further large building (45 × 18 m) replaced a temple of Aesculapius at the Sheep Pool (*Probatica*) north of the Temple area at the beginning of the fifth century. Crosses in the mosaic floor might suggest a date before 427, when this was forbidden (CJust 1.8.1).[60]

At the traditional site of the feeding of the multitude by the Sea of Galilee, at et-Tabgha (= Heptapēgōn, 'seven springs'), a small chapel was built in the late fourth century (15.5 × 9.5 m). In the fifth century it was replaced by a larger building with a mosaic floor of the highest artistic quality, which suggests a rich donor.

---

[58] A. Ovadiah, *Corpus of the Byzantine Churches in the Holy Land*, Bonn 1970; A. Ovadiah, C. G. de Silva, 'Supplementum to the Corpus of the Byzantine Churches in the Holy Land', *Levant* 13 (1981), 200–61; 16 (1984), 129–64.

[59] M. van Esbroeck, 'Jean II', 111f., dates its dedication to 15 September 394.

[60] But the prohibition was not always observed, and should therefore be treated with caution as a criterium of date. See V. Tzaferis, 'Early Christian Churches at Magen', in Y. Tsafrir (ed.), *Ancient Churches Revealed*, Jerusalem 1993, 283–5; J. E. Taylor, *Christians and the Holy Places*, 240–3.

Church Building and Christianization 69

But the smaller building is already important evidence in our context, because it stands in the middle of Jewish territory. At this period, this can only be said otherwise of the house church at Capernaum, to be discussed at length later.[61]

The other churches for which we have archaeological evidence to date may be simply listed according to regions, in so far as they give evidence for the spread of Christian communities. In Judaea, apart from the monastic chapels in the Judaean desert, there are one or two buildings in the neighbourhood of Jericho. Qasr el Jahud by the Jordan is near the traditional site of the baptism of Jesus, and is named for John the Baptist. According to another tradition it lies opposite the place where the Israelites crossed the Jordan when entering the Promised Land, and is named for these Jews. Mary the Egyptian visited this site in the early fifth century. Capitals and a mosaic floor in the present-day crypt bear witness to the original chapel. The church of Ai, north of Jerusalem, was probably built at the beginning of the fifth century.

In the south of the country, the small church in honour of the prophet Micah, north of Beth Gubrin, was probably built in 385;[62] the oldest church at Magen is dated to around 400.[63] The earliest churches of the cities of the Negeb, whose heyday was in the two following centuries, were also built from the middle of the fourth century. The oldest of them is the eastern church of Mampsis; the local Christian congregation probably stemmed from the Roman garrison, as A. Negev concludes from the names in the church, which all point to Palestinian or Egyptian origin, but are never Arabian or Nabataean. The northern churches of Oboda, Subeita and Nissana are from this period, also probably both churches of Mampsis and the earliest church at Rehovot.[64]

On the Mediterranean coast, a church was built in Dor, south

---

[61] A. M. Schneider, *Die Brotvermehrungskirche von et-tabga am Genesarethsee und ihre Mosaiken*, Paderborn 1934; M. Avi-Yonah, 'Heptapegon', *NEAE* II, 614–16. For the dating see S. Loffreda, *LA* 20 (1970), 370–80.

[62] Jerome, *ep*. 108.14 (CSEL 55, 324), mentions this church.

[63] V. Tsaferis, 'An Early Christian Church Complex at Magen', *BASOR* 258 (1985), 1–15; id., 'Mosaics and Inscriptions from Magen', ibid., 17–32.

[64] A. Negev, 'The Churches of the Central Negev. An Archaeological Survey', *RB* 81 (1974), 400–22; see also the report of A. Negev and S. Margalit on new excavations at Subeita in *RB* 93 (1986), 267–9; A. Negev, *The Architecture of Mampsis. Final Report Vol. II: The Late Roman and Byzantine Periods*, Jerusalem 1988; Y. Tsafrir et al., *Excavations at Rehovot in the Negev. Vol. I: The North Church*, Jerusalem 1988, 14.

of Haifa, in the middle of the fourth century;[65] the church of Evron, near Acco/Acre, is dated to 415 by its mosaic inscription, and the church in the nearby Shave Zion is from the fourth or fifth century. In Samaria, at Jacob's Well, a church was built in the form of an equilateral cross of approximately 30 m in length.

By contrast, church building in Galilee begins remarkably late. Apart from the buildings in Tabgha and Capernaum by the Sea of Galilee, churches are built around 400 in Nazareth, on Mount Tabor, in Bardala in the Beth Shean valley and at Kafr el-Makr in western Galilee. Particularly interesting is the fact that church (and monastery) building advances as far as Tiberias, the seat of the Jewish Patriarch. For until the final decades of the fourth century the expanding Christian congregation had come into physical proximity with Judaism only in the south, where a number of towns in the strip between Gaza and En Gedi were entirely Jewish, according to Eusebius and even as late as Jerome (*Onomasticon*). So the period around 400 clearly brought a breakthrough of Christian material presence in Galilee, and a significant shift in the balance of power between Christians and Jews.

The archaeological evidence could probably be supplemented by many Byzantine church finds that cannot be precisely dated, and is also supported by contemporary literary references. In principle we must expect churches at the seat of every bishop; but not even in the ecclesiastical metropolis of Caesarea is there as yet any archaeological evidence for a church. In his revision of Eusebius' *Onomasticon*, Jerome mentions around 390 further churches at Bethel, at Jacob's Well in Sychar, and apparently assumes a church also at Sebaste, where he notes the relics of John the Baptist. Further remarks can be gleaned from the various pilgrim reports, also other texts by Epiphanius and Jerome.

The church building at Gaza, the as yet archaeologically unattested Eudoxiana, merits particular interest. It was built with money given by the Empress Eudoxia, after Bishop Porphyrius had decisively strengthened the situation of Christianity in that city from *ca*. 395, and in 402 had gained imperial support for the

---

[65] C. Dauphin, 'Dora-Dor: A Station for Pilgrims in the Byzantine Period on their Way to Jerusalem', in Y. Tsafrir (ed.), *Ancient Churches Revealed*, Jerusalem 1993, 90–97.

destruction of the pagan civic temple, the Marneion.⁶⁶ This discussion whether the church to be built on the site of the Marneion should be a domed rotunda, like the temple, or should follow a different plan, was decided by a letter from the empress, to which she appended a sketch with a cruciform ground plan. Under the direction of the architect Rufinus of Antioch, the building work was completed in five years, and the church was dedicated on Easter Sunday 407. Thanks to the generosity of the empress, who had donated two hundred pounds of gold and thirty-two columns, and had sent the necessary marble to Gaza, the church when completed was larger than all others at the time; some Christians in Gaza had rejected the spacious plans as too large for their little congregation. Until then there had been in Gaza only one small church dedicated to 'Peace' within the city itself, and an old church a considerable distance outside.⁶⁷

5. The Story of Count Joseph and Jewish Christianity

The principal literary evidence for Christianity's advance into the Jewish heartland of Galilee is Epiphanius of Salamis' story of Count Joseph.⁶⁸ It concerns a certain Joseph of Tiberias,

> who lived at the time of the blessed emperor Constantine the elder, and who obtained from this emperor the honour of the *comites* and received authority to build a church for Christ in Tiberias itself, also in Diocaesarea and in the other (towns). He had suffered much from the Jews before he became acquainted with the Emperor. This Joseph was numbered among their dignitaries. There are those whose

---

⁶⁶ Jerome compares the destruction of the Marneion at Gaza with that of the Serapeion in Alexandria, i.e. attributes the highest importance to it: *In Is.* 17.2f. (CC 73, 268); *ep.* 107.2 (CSEL 55, 292).

⁶⁷ Our detailed knowledge of the building of the great church in Gaza, which is comparable only with our information on the Church of the Holy Sepulchre, comes from the *Vita Porphyrii* of Mark the Deacon. The statement on the church's size is ibid., Chapter 92f. (pp. 71f.).

⁶⁸ Epiphanius, *Panarion* 30.4.1–12.9 (GCS 25, 338–48). I was not able to consult the dissertation of S. C. Goranson, *The Joseph of Tiberias Episode in Epiphanius: Studies in Jewish and Christian Relations*, Duke Univ. 1990. A brief analysis of the episode is also offered by T. C. G. Thornton, 'The Stories of Joseph of Tiberias', *VigChr* 44 (1990), 54–63.

(rank) is after the Patriarch, who are called apostles. They stand by the Patriarch and stay often with him without ceasing, by night as by day, in order to take counsel and to submit legal questions to him. The Patriarch at that time was called Hillel – for I believe that Joseph called him that, unless the intervening time deceives me ...

When the Patriarch lay dying, so Joseph told Epiphanius, he demanded to see the bishop who was nearest to Tiberias at that time (*plēsiochōron tēs Tiberieōn*), under the pretext that he was a doctor. He was baptized by him on his deathbed.[69]

According to Epiphanius, he heard this story from Joseph himself, who later settled in Beth Shean. At that time, Eusebius of Vercellae also lived in Joseph's house, whom Constantius had exiled there because of his orthodox faith. Joseph, who at that time was seventy years old or even older, was, solely because of his rank as count, not molested by the inhabitants of the city, who apart from himself were all Arians. Only one other orthodox Christian lived in the city, a young man of Jewish parentage, but he did not dare to come openly to Joseph.

Joseph is said also to have told how he looked through the keyhole into the Patriarch's room when the baptism was already over; but he understood what had happened and kept it to himself. The Patriarch gave the bishop a large gold piece, so that he should sacrifice for him. In the following days, the bishop visited the Patriarch several times in his guise as doctor, until he died.

Before his death the Patriarch entrusted his young son to Joseph and another man. Both of them initially conducted the business of the patriarchate together, since the new Patriarch was still a child. One day, Joseph opened a sealed treasure-house and found there a Gospel of John translated into Hebrew, also the Acts of the Apostles and the Hebrew original of the Gospel of Matthew. In the text there then follows a section on the immoral youth of the boy 'Jehuda, if I'm not mistaken', who chased girls together with his friends in the nearby bathing resort of Gadara.

When the young Patriarch had taken over the duties of office himself, Joseph once had to travel to Cilicia on his behalf, and to collect the tithes and firstfruits from all the Jewish communities.

---

[69] Epiphanius, *Panarion* 30.4.1–6 (GCS 25, 338f.).

On this journey he borrowed the gospels from a bishop, but was discovered studying them, taken into the synagogue, scourged, and, on a later occasion, even thrown into the River Cydnus. Finally he was baptized, met Constantine and was appointed Count by him.[70] He was also granted a wish, but only wished to 'build churches for Christ by imperial order in the cities and villages of the Jews. No-one had yet been able to found churches there, because neither Greek nor Samaritan nor Christian was found among them.' He names particularly Tiberias, Diocaesarea, Nazareth and Capernaum, where there were no non-Jews (literally 'foreigners', *alloethnon*). 'Thus Joseph received a letter and authority, together with the title, and came to Tiberias with letters permitting him to make use of state monies and himself be supported at state expense.'[71]

In Tiberias there was a large temple, the Hadrianeion, an unfinished building which the citizens would have liked to turn into a public baths. Joseph attempted to turn this building into a church. But he was prevented by the magic of the Jews and finally gave up, after having continued a large part of the temple (*naos*) and built a small church. Then he retired to Scythopolis, but also built churches in Diocaesarea and other towns.

I have summarized the whole text, although only a small part of it concerns the subject of church building, because its other aspects also are extremely interesting with regard to the development of Judaism in the fourth century. However, the text is full of difficulties. Occasionally the suggestion is made that Epiphanius was himself a Jewish convert, but there is no contemporary evidence for this.[72] However, if it is a fact, then Epiphanius might be pursuing his own interests in telling the story. In that

---

[70] Count (*comes*), previously only an unofficial description of the highest officials surrounding the emperor, became under Constantine an official rank in three classes, and replaced their previous titles in the case of some high-ranking officials. E.g. the *Comes Orientis* was set over the entire imperial diocese of the east. But, even early on, the title Count was also conferred as a mere honorific, which is presupposed here. See also Jones, *LRE* 104f.

[71] Epiphanius, *Panarion* 30.11.9–12.1 (GCS 25, 347).

[72] E.g. L. Lucas, *Zur Geschichte* 3, describes Epiphanius as a baptized Jew. B. Bagatti, *Alle origini della chiesa* II, 66, interprets Epiphanius' behaviour on his visit to the church at Anablata (see note 90), when he tears a curtain up because there is a sacred picture on it, as due to his rejection of pictures because of his Jewish origin. But this attitude is too widespread in the early church to warrant such a conclusion.

case, the stress on Joseph's orthodoxy is particularly striking, as the only orthodox person in the otherwise completely Arian Scythopolis. If we take into account the fact that Arians were often polemically called 'Jews' by their Catholic opponents, we might see here a conscious defence against the suspicion that Christians coming from Judaism should be suspected of the Arian heresy on principle.[73]

Let us assume for a moment the hypothesis that Epiphanius did in fact hear the story more or less as it stands from the aged Joseph in Scythopolis. The question then still remains to what extent his tale fits the facts. We must investigate the text in the light of three questions, that is: that of information on the patriarchate, to which we will return in a separate chapter, that of the conversion of Jews to Christianity, and finally that of church building in Galilee. The question of church building, our primary interest here, is of course inseparable from that of conversions.

Joseph's conversion should be dated to between 324 and 337, because of his meeting with Constantine that occurred shortly afterwards. His meeting with Epiphanius happened under Constantius, that is, before 361. Epiphanius finished the *Panarion*, in which he tells this tale, around 377. These dates, with the intervals of time between occurrence, telling and writing down of the story, already show that even with a more reliable author than Epiphanius there would be difficulties with the tradition.

---

[73] On this point, see R. Lorenz, *Arius judaizans? Untersuchungen zur dogmengeschichtlichen Einordnung des Arius*, Göttingen 1979, 224: 'The parallels between Arianism and Jewish thought that are treated in this work do not suffice to declare a positive dependence ... it is not improbable that heretical Jewish and Jewish Christian influences bore upon Lucian of Antioch and Arius.' Despite his nearness to Jewish thought, what was decisive was 'the fact that Arius started from Origenism'. This is what made the debate about Origen among Palestinian theologians of the late fourth and early fifth century so virulent. Epiphanius played a crucial role in this, as a radical opponent of Origen's teachings. On the dogmatic discussion in contemporary Palestine in general, see L. Perrone, *La chiesa di Palestina e le controverse cristologiche*, Brescia 1980. This, of course, does not yet clarify the actual behaviour of the Jews. Athanasius continually accuses the Jews of collaborating with his opponents; but a substantial part of this is polemic, and even if some of it may be true, we must not apply the situation in the diaspora to Palestine. L. Lucas' statement, *Zur Geschichte*, 28f., that apart from the anti-Jewish laws of the Arian Constantius, Jews and Arians always worked together, and that all the Church Fathers knew of this pact between Jews and Arians, is far too sweeping.

Church Building and Christianization

The text asserts, for the second quarter of the century, that only Jews lived in Tiberias, Diocaesarea, Nazareth and Capernaum. This statement can under no circumstances be taken literally; however, it surely gives a correct picture of the relative proportions of the population, except perhaps for Sepphoris. In Tiberias, a monastery is indeed only attested around 400; of course a Christian church would be possible earlier, but there is no evidence for one as yet. Only in the early fifth century do we find signs of a growing Christian congregation in Tiberias; at the Council of Ephesus, 431, it is represented by a bishop.[74]

But then where does the bishop come from in the story of Count Joseph? Is he entirely invented, or should we reckon with Jewish Christian communities in this area? Unfortunately the history of the Jewish Christians in the fourth century is unclear to a great extent, and much of the relevant literature is very tendentious.

At least the excavations at Capernaum appear to prove the existence of a Jewish Christian congregation there. Only one block away from the synagogue, an octagonal Christian room for worship has been uncovered, under which there was an older Christian place of worship, the so-called 'House of Peter'. The pilgrim Egeria, who was here shortly after 380, describes a house church: 'In Capernaum a church was made out of the house of the prince of the apostles, whose walls stand until today as they were. There the Lord healed the paralytic.'[75] Thus the octagon that has been excavated cannot have existed at that time. But the 'House of Peter' beneath it is much older. As the excavations have shown, it was renovated in the middle of the fourth century, when the small worship room received a multicoloured floor.

The excavator V. Corbo is of the opinion that this alteration 'was probably done by Joseph, the Count of Tiberias, for the Jewish

---

[74] Y. Zafrir, 'The Conflict between Christians and the Jews in the Tiberias Region in the Byzantine Period' (Hebrew), in *All the Land of Naphtali*, Jerusalem 1967, 79–90. On p. 84 he names Jerome's commentary on Isa. 9:1 (CC 73, 123) as evidence for the spread of Christianity in this region, but the text probably refers rather to the time of Jesus, as a historical interpretation, when, after initial successes of Christian preaching in the region around Zebulon and Naphtali, 'in recent times their faith was burdened, because most of the Jews remained in their error'.

[75] This report by Peter the Deacon is ascribed to Egeria among others: *Itinera Hierosolymitana* (CSEL 38, 112f.).

Christians of Capernaum'.⁷⁶ In this he follows E. Testa, who has edited the graffiti of this complex, and because of the context in Epiphanius (who speaks of the Ebionites, a Jewish Christian group, and says, 'One of these was Joseph'), sees Count Joseph as an Ebionite.⁷⁷ Unfortunately, Testa's interpretation is too imaginative to be taken seriously. According to him it was Joseph's task

> to penetrate into the Jewish Christian ghetto of the well-known rectangle Sepphoris, Nazareth, Tiberias and Capernaum, in order to build churches of Graeco-Roman type to the glory of Christ. A Gentile Christian had never yet succeeded in breaking into this ghetto ... Only he, a Hebrew by race, an Ebionite by religion, and united with the wider church ... could function as a bridge.⁷⁸

The 'Jews' who prevented Joseph from building a church in Tiberias, according to Epiphanius, are to be understood as Jewish Christians from the context, according to Testa; for they rely on magic, accept the judgement of God in holy water, and are only called sons of murderers of God, not murderers of God themselves, and finally confess that the only God protects the Christians.⁷⁹ With this interpretation, Testa has scarcely been faithful to the tendency of Epiphanius' text.

However, we should not doubt the existence of an early, and presumably Jewish Christian, congregation in Capernaum. This is suggested by fragments of Hebrew, Aramaic and Syriac writing, which were found together with much more numerous fragments of Greek on shards of plaster from the 'House of Peter'. However, E. Testa's reconstruction of texts, and his use of them for a theology of the Jewish Christians of Capernaum and the organization of their community, far exceeds what may be proved from the few extant letters.⁸⁰ Remnants of coloured flowers and other decorations on the plaster are even less suitable material for a reliable interpretation.

---

⁷⁶ V. Corbo, *Cafarnao* I, 72. J. E. Taylor, *Christians and the Holy Places*, 293, also attributes the alteration to Count Joseph, but doubts the continuous existence of a Jewish Christian congregation in Capernaum; believing that the veneration of the site only began in the fourth century.

⁷⁷ E. Testa, *I graffiti*, 87, n. 106. Testa is of the opinion that Joseph was introduced by an orthodox Ebionite teacher. But what is an orthodox Ebionite?

⁷⁸ E. Testa, *I graffiti* 87.

⁷⁹ E. Testa, *I graffiti* 87 n. 107.

⁸⁰ See the detailed review by J. F. Strange, *BASOR* 233 (1979), 64–9.

The church of Sepphoris has been thought to represent a further example of Joseph's church-building activity. The Byzantine church is situated over an older one, which Count Joseph is supposed to have built above a Jewish Christian centre of worship going back to the time before the recognition of Christianity, which has been thought to be discerned in a number of caves on the site of the church. The renovation of the church is attested by an early sixth-century inscription;[81] the Bishop Marcellinus mentioned in it, who was also present at the Jerusalem Synod of 518 (another bishop of Sepphoris was at the Council of Chalcedon, as early as 451), is said to have been 'the first Gentile Christian bishop of Diocaesarea'. Unfortunately, this interpretation also far exceeds what may actually be proved.[82]

The evidence is scarcely better in Nazareth. B. Bagatti, who directed the excavations here, sees early Christian remains under the basilica of the Annunciation and under the church of St. Joseph, but admits the difficulties inherent in a precise chronology. He assumes that the first building above the cave of the Annunciation was built in the second or third century and took the form of a synagogue. The grain silos hewn into the rock, which were used as early as the first century, served the Jewish Christians for baptisms, in his opinion. Graffiti also seem to him to confirm the presence of Jewish Christians.[83] However, so far the argument for such an interpretation of finds from the excavation is far from convincing. Particularly the tendency to attribute every cave that might once have been used for worship to Jewish Christians has no real foundation.[84]

[81] M. Avi-Yonah, 'A Sixth-Century Inscription from Sepphoris', *IEJ* 11 (1961), 184–7. His opinion that the results of the excavation should not be interpreted as a church at all, but rather as a Roman villa, and the so-called baptistery as a simple cellar, has now been confirmed by the new excavations: Z. Weiss, *NEAE* IV, 1327.

[82] F. Manns, 'Un centre judéo-chrétien important: Sepphoris', in id., *Essais sur le Judéo-Christianisme*, Jerusalem 1977, 165ff.; 179f. He bases his opinion on the excavation by L. Waterman, of which only the *Preliminary Report*, Michigan 1937, is published, and which has now been superseded by new excavations.

[83] B. Bagatti, *Alle origini della chiesa* I, 129–34; id., *Gli scavi di Nazaret* I, Jerusalem 1967.

[84] See the criticisms in J. E. Taylor, *Christians and the Holy Places*, 221–67. She discounts the Jewish Christian hypothesis, but thinks it 'very likely that the early church, the "House of Mary", was constructed by the convert Joseph of Tiberias' (267). However there is no literary evidence before the end of the fourth century.

The investigation of the history of Jewish Christianity must continue to rely primarily on the literary sources, since the interpretation of symbols is too precarious and leaves too much scope to the imagination.[85] However, the sources are largely only interested in the origins of Jewish Christianity, or in categorizing its individual groups in a family tree of heresies. Historically reliable evidence for so late a period as the fourth century is relatively rare; we must already ask in the case of Eusebius and Epiphanius to what extent they are actually describing the contemporary situation, and not simply repeating old traditions of the Church Fathers. Jerome offers slightly greater certainty, but even here, the individual descriptions of Jewish Christians are too imprecise for us to be able to differentiate with certainty between Judaizers (i.e. Gentile Christians who kept Jewish customs and laws) and Christians of Hebrew descent.[86]

The sermons with which Cyril of Jerusalem prepared his catechumens for baptism around 350 make it clear that the attraction of Jewish customs must still have been very strong. For example, in the fourth catechetical lecture he warns against the use of bandages (phylacteries?) in case of sickness, against observance of the sabbath and the food laws, and he also prepares his listeners for Jewish objections to Christian beliefs and tells them what they are to reply. Much seems related to traditional themes of baptismal sermons, often only repeated mechanically for tradition's sake. However, the fact that Jewish customs and ideas were still current in daily life may be gleaned from various remarks of Jerome's; and John Chrysostom's sermons in Antioch, in particular, show clearly how attractive Jewish traditions must have been in the Christian community.[87]

A remark made by the pilgrim Egeria about the Jerusalem liturgy might perhaps point to Jewish Christian members of the congregation. She writes that the population of the province of Palestine partly speaks Greek and partly Syriac, while parts are bilingual. The bishop, however, preaches only in Greek, even if he can speak Syriac, and for this reason a priest always offers a

---

[85] E. Testa, *Il Simbolismo*.
[86] On this, see esp. M. Simon, *Verus Israel* 277ff.
[87] R. W. Wilken, *John Chrysostom*, 73, is of the opinion that the rich fund of information on Jewish Christians and Judaizers in the late fourth century points to a new blossoming of Judaizing Christianity at this period, perhaps encouraged by Julian's plan to rebuild the Temple.

Church Building and Christianization

Syriac translation, so that all can understand the sermon. Eusebius reports something similar for the beginning of the century in Scythopolis, where Procopius served, among other things, as translator from Greek into Aramaic in the church.[88] Syriac and Aramaic here clearly mean the same thing. However, the language is not at all a clear signal of Jewish origin, but points rather to a rural setting, where Aramaic was not only spoken by Jews, but was simply the language of the country alongside Greek.

A further attempt to locate Jewish Christians in Jerusalem is connected with the Church of Zion. The arguments that have been advanced to date for the idea that in Jerusalem a Gentile Christian congregation, the majority, had its home at the Church of the Holy Sepulchre, while a Jewish Christian congregation centred on Mount Zion, represent no more than pointers.[89] Even should the suggestion be correct, the question remains where these Jewish Christians come from: are they a remnant of the old Jewish Christian communities in Palestine, Christians newly recruited from Judaism, Jewish Christians who have immigrated from the Diaspora or simply Judaizers, for whom Jerusalem would have had a particular attraction?

As far as the Jewish Christian groups in the strict sense are concerned, that is, Christians converted from Judaism (among whom we must also reckon pagans who come to Christianity via Judaism), we must ask whether they were perhaps groups which survived from an earlier period without significant gains of new members from outside. For there are strikingly few and isolated pieces of evidence in the fourth century for Jews who convert to Christianity. In Palestine, apart from Count Joseph and the young man whom Epiphanius mentions in connection with him, and a Jew mentioned later, who fails to convert simply for fear of his fellow-Jews, there is only Epiphanius himself (possibly, the

---

[88] *Itinera Hierosolymitana*, CSEL 38, 99. On Eusebius' witness in the Syriac version of his work on the martyrs of Palestine, see G. Fuks, *Scythopolis*, 145f. In the same work, Eusebius mentions how distressed Jews were during the persecution of 309 when they heard the Hebrew names of the Christians in the law court. On this see S. Lieberman in the *Festschrift* for S. W. Baron (Hebrew), Jerusalem 1974, 237.

[89] See in particular B. Bagatti, *Alle origini* I, 14–16. M. van Esbroeck, 'Jean II', sees the translation of the relics of St. Stephen to Jerusalem, the appointment of Porphyrius of Gaza as Staurophylax and the sermon for the dedication of the Church of Zion as conscious attempts to achieve agreement in the Jerusalem Church on Jewish traditions.

evidence is late) and perhaps the monk from whom Jerome learnt Hebrew in Syria.[90] But he could also come from Syria or East Jordan, where there is more evidence for Jewish Christians. It is striking that Eusebius mentions the Jewish Christian group of the Ebionites only in Coba near Damascus, in his *Onomasticon*, and that Epiphanius gives as homes of the Nazarenes Beroea near Aleppo (where Jerome had the *Gospel of the Hebrews* copied), Cochabe in Bashan and Pella in East Jordan.[91] Therefore it seems that there were no significant Jewish Christian communities left in Palestine itself, and the primary problem for the wider church was the attraction of Judaism for numbers of Gentile Christians.

There are no rabbinic texts for this period which may certainly be understood as referring to Jews converting to Christianity. Laws to protect Jews who have converted to Christianity need not necessarily refer to Palestine: Constantine's law CTh XVI.8.1, discussed above, was intended for Africa. Two laws from a later period should be mentioned, CTh IX.45.2 dated 17 June 397 and addressed to the *Praefectus Augustalis*, that is, intended for Egypt, and XVI.8.28 dated 8 April 426, addressed to the *Praefectus praetorio*. The first of these aims to prevent the acceptance of converts for dishonest motives: 'Jews who pretend to wish to join the Christian religion because of a crime or debts, in order to avoid punishment or the burden of debts by means of their flight into the church, are to be rejected and not received until they have paid all their debts or have cleared themselves of suspicion by proving their innocence.' According to this law, conversions were occasionally used as an escape from a creditor. Therefore, at least in some areas, there must have been a cancellation of debts associated with conversion – perhaps only vis-à-vis Jewish creditors? The churches' right of asylum may also have appeared attractive. The law aims to prevent this misuse of conversion to Christianity.

The later law ensures the right of inheritance of Jewish converts to Christianity: 'If the son, daughter or grandchild of a Jew or Samaritan, be they one person or several, should by dint of better

---

[90] Jerome, *ep.* 125, 12 (CSEL 55, 131). E. Testa, *Il Simbolismo*, 531, is of the opinion that this monk is definitely identical with Jerome's Hebrew teacher Bar Chanina, whose name Rufinus polemically alters to Barabbas (Jerome, *Contra Rufinum* I.13, CC 79, 12). But this is extremely unlikely.

[91] See B. Bagatti, *Alle origini* I, 29ff.; M. Simon, *Verus Israel*, 307f.; R. A. Pritz, *Nazarene Jewish Christianity*, Jerusalem/Leiden 1988.

judgement change from the darkness of their old superstition to the light of the Christian religion, then their parents, that is, father, mother, grandfather or grandmother, are not allowed to disinherit them, to pass them over unmentioned in their will or to leave them less than they would have received if there had been no will at all.' However, if a very serious crime against their parents or grandparents should be definitely proved against such a convert, they still receive a quarter of the inheritance they would otherwise receive (*Falcidiam debitae successionis*), 'for they appear to merit this at least in honour of the religion they have chosen. However, the punishment of the crimes remains, if these are proved.'

This late law, which represents clearly preferential financial treatment of converts and a serious invasion of the rights of the Jewish testators, is probably a reaction to complaints on the part of converts or their ecclesiastical patrons, and at the same time a conscious incentive towards further conversions. We do not know whether it achieved its objective. Nor can we say whether this law even fitted the circumstances in Palestine.

Conversions of Jews to Christianity are generally scarcely to be expected in uniformly Jewish areas of settlement. The social pressure which the community could exert there was too strong. Conversions are more likely to be found in the cities or the Diaspora. For example, Sozomen reports that in Constantinople (under Constantine?) countless Jews also converted to Christianity.[92]

The question remains to what extent it could still be expected of Jewish converts of this period that they should join a Jewish Christian congregation. Would they not rather attempt to make a radical break with their past? The Judaizers mentioned again and again, for example, in Jerome, are not automatically Jewish Christians. Pagans too, who converted to Christianity in Palestine, felt themselves often attracted to the Jewish parent religion of Christianity, and found a radical replacement of the old covenant unacceptable (Cyril of Jerusalem has to deal with heretics who wish to separate the Old Testament from the New!).[93]

---

[92] Sozomen, *Church history* II.3.7 (GCS 50, 52).
[93] Cyril of Jerusalem, *Catechetical Lectures* 7.6 (PG 33, 612).

6. The Economic Effect of Church Building

The church buildings should not only be studied from the point of view of religion. Such an extensive building programme also had economic consequences, especially since they were largely financed from abroad, by donations from the emperor or from nobles. What significance did this have for the local population?

The measurements of most of the churches can be verified, but it is very difficult to estimate the costs for building material and labour. In the face of the effusive descriptions of their magnificence in contemporary reports, we have already remarked on the relative smallness of the Constantinian church buildings in Palestine. For a long time it was thought that in the early period in Palestine, by contrast with other countries, conversion of temples to churches, or even the reuse of building material, was rejected; which does appear to follow from Eusebius. J. W. Crowfoot connected this with fear of demons.[94] However, the excavations in the Church of the Holy Sepulchre in Jerusalem have clearly proved that parts of the Hadrianic *temenos* of the Capitoline temple were reused. Equally, the church in Mamre was simply set on top of the platform of the older pagan and previously Jewish shrine, as E. Mader's excavations have shown. According to recent excavations, the church at Dor was also built on the foundations of a pagan temple.[95] The example of Gaza, cited in evidence by Crowfoot, cannot prove his hypothesis either.

Mark the Deacon writes in the *Vita Porphyrii* that the marble slabs from the pagan temple of Gaza were used to pave the square in front of the newly-built church, and that many women refused 'until today' to walk upon them (Chapter 76). But this refers to the pagan, not the Christian, population of Gaza! Mark writes explicitly that it was first discussed what should be done with the temple of Marnas – tear it down, burn it down, or 'to purify the site and sanctify it for a church of God' (Chapter 66). So this possibility was certainly entertained. A decision was brought about only by the words of a child inspired by God during the church service, namely that the inner temple should be burnt down to the foundations, since human sacrifice had taken place

---

[94] J. W. Crowfoot, *Early Churches*, 102.
[95] C. M. Dauphin, 'Dor, Byzantine Church, 1994', *IEJ* 47 (1997), 121–7.

there, but that the outer temple with its enclosure should be retained, and the site used to build a church.

Of course the costs of a building were significantly reduced if existing material could be used. It is however doubtful how often this may have been the case. In the north-east of the country basalt was available as building material, everywhere else limestone. Often hewn stones in two layers, with a core of rubble between, were used; the better stones were used for the outside, since the inner wall would be plastered or faced in any case. Marble had to be imported; it was partly already pre-worked and sculpted. Columns too were probably imported for the Constantinian buildings in general, although in the case of the Church of the Holy Sepulchre existing columns from the capitol were used to a certain extent. In Bethlehem there is no certain evidence for columns; pilasters could have been used instead. There is evidence that, as already mentioned, the columns were brought in by sea from abroad for the Eudoxiana in Gaza. The walls could be kept fairly thin, since they only needed to carry a wooden ceiling. For the Constantinian buildings cedar from the Lebanon was used, otherwise mostly local cypress or pine wood. It was only the increasing deforestation that made the stone ceilings and thus the solid walls of the Crusader buildings necessary.

As far as the interior decoration is concerned, there are no remains of any (possible) frescoes. Apart from panelling the walls with marble in the richer foundations, probably mosaics from local materials were a preferred choice. The mosaic artists probably initially came from abroad, perhaps from Syria; only later did local mosaic schools come into existence, near Gaza and Madaba.

What was the value of work done in the country itself? In the case of the great imperial foundations, we must surely reckon with a large amount of imported material, whose value did not benefit the country. Craftsmen resident in Palestine were probably hardly to be found; Jerusalem in particular was very thinly populated up to the middle of the fifth century.[96] Eusebius specifically mentions, with regard to the Church of the Holy Sepulchre, the master craftsmen and labourers from abroad.[97] Some probably stayed, swelling the numbers of inhabitants of Jerusalem and its

---

[96] M. Avi-Yonah, 'The Economics', 42 n. 14, citing Peter the Iberian.
[97] Eusebius, *Vita Constantini* III.32 (GCS 92f.).

surroundings. In addition, we must probably reckon with voluntary work on the part of the inhabitants. Mark the Deacon specifically mentions this in connection with the Eudoxiana in Gaza. All Christians there were called upon to report with tools. Together with the soldiers who had come to destroy the pagan temple, they walked in procession to the Marneion, cleared the building-site, dug out the pit, helped to transport the stones from the quarry and also the columns from the port. A contributory factor to the enthusiasm of the Christian population, whose bishop led the way in setting a good example, was the fact that he paid the workmen generously from the money provided by Eudoxia.[98]

We also know the time the construction of the Eudoxiana in Gaza took, namely five years. We know that the Church of the Holy Sepulchre was begun in 324 or 325 and dedicated in 335, but was not yet complete at that time. However, we have no other information on length of construction that might allow inferences regarding the economic effects of the projects.

As regards the maintenance costs of the buildings, we may assume that Constantine took care of these by means of donations, although no evidence survives. But he did give imperial estates for his Roman church buildings, including estates situated in the eastern provinces. Otherwise, we should think first in terms of donations from pilgrims, but caring for these again incurred expense.

The first phase of building after the Christianization of Palestine was characterized by imperial foundations; but the second phase, which began around the middle of the fourth century and lasted for approximately a hundred years, was largely made possible by private investments. The best-known donors are the rich women Poimenia, Paula, Eustochium and the older and younger Melania. In the early fifth century stupendous sums of money flowed into the country, brought by rich Roman families fleeing from the Goths and Vandals. Members of the imperial family like Eudokia also brought considerable sums.[99]

In consequence we must assume a significant stimulation of the

---

[98] Mark the Deacon, *Vita Porphyrii*, chapters 76–9; 84.
[99] M. Avi-Yonah, 'The Economics', 44, names the sum of one and a half million gold pieces, about ten tons of gold, which Eudokia is said to have spent in Jerusalem up to her death in the year 460. In Nicephorus this is the total sum which Eudokia provided for all her foundations; see E. D. Hunt, *Holy Land Pilgrimage*, 239.

Church Building and Christianization

Palestinian economy. But this probably only had a minimal and indirect effect on the Jews of the country. They were probably not employed as workmen for church building projects. At least the tight employment situation probably led to a slackening of competition for other jobs, even though roadbuilding remained a typically military affair, or was executed by forced labour. We unfortunately do not know either to what extent the Jewish population shared in providing the districts settled by Christians with agricultural produce. The trade relations of the Jewish agricultural regions in Galilee, at least, were primarily towards the north, to Tyre, as finds of coins at various excavations suggest.[100] Palestine's internal market in agricultural produce is not yet sufficiently researched, and the question whether the increased economic power of the country raised prices, and thus had a negative effect on the Jewish population, also cannot be answered.[101] The many synagogue buildings of the fourth century show that the economic power of the Jewish communities must have been considerable. But we cannot judge to what extent the stimulation of the economy by imported Christian capital was a factor.

---

[100] R. S. Hanson, *Tyrian Influence in the Upper Galilee*, Cambridge, Mass. 1980.
[101] Z. Safrai, *The Economy of Roman Palestine*, London 1994, 222–321, treats too long a period as a unit, and is thus of no help for our concerns.

IV

Christian Pilgrimage

When the Roman Empire turned to Christianity, this also encouraged pilgrimage to the Holy Land; conversely, the fact of pilgrimage was decisive in the development of a Christian Palestine.[1] Of course Christian pilgrims had travelled to the country long before Constantine; but pilgrimages only began on a large scale with the Christianization of the country. For example, as early as 315 Eusebius writes that Christians from all the corners of the world are coming on pilgrimage to Jerusalem and praying on the Mount of Olives, thereby stressing the contrast with the Jewish worship on the Temple mount opposite.[2]

As already mentioned, Constantine had himself once been to Palestine with Diocletian, and had originally intended to be baptized in the Jordan. He also wanted to link the dedication of the Church of the Holy Sepulchre in Jerusalem with the thirtieth anniversary of his own rule. Neither wish came to fulfilment. However, his mother Helena travelled to Palestine, as it were in place of Constantine, with full imperial pageantry,[3] and thereby made pilgrimage to the Holy Land socially acceptable, so to speak.

The improvements to the holy places in Constantine's time probably also contributed to the pilgrimage industry, quite apart from the official religious tourism in connection with the dedication festivals of various churches, to which bishops were brought repeatedly from far away, by means of the imperial post service.[4] As Ammianus Marcellinus laments (XXI.16.18), the

---

[1] On this, see especially H. Donner, *Pilgerfahrt*; E. D. Hunt, *Holy Land Pilgrimage*; P. Maraval, *Lieux saints*; J. Wilkinson, 'Christian Pilgrims'.
[2] Eusebius, *Demonstratio evangelica* VI.18.23 (GCS 23, 278).
[3] Eusebius, *Vita Constantini* III.44ff. (GCS 102–4).
[4] Eusebius, *Church history* X.3.1 (GCS 9, 860); *Vita Constantini* IV.43.2 (GCS 138).

imperial post service, the *cursus publicus*, was sometimes completely blocked by this. Edicts from various emperors had to be passed to free it again from this over-use and misappropriation.

Various pilgrim accounts attest that the holy places of Palestine exercised an enormous attraction on ordinary people also, who of course were not allowed to use the public post service.[5] Strikingly, all the early texts come from the west of the Empire. But pilgrimages from the eastern part of the Empire must have formed by far the majority. Jerome writes in a letter to Laeta of pilgrims from India, Persia and Ethiopia;[6] there are also many accounts of pilgrims from Syria, Egypt, Asia Minor and Armenia, from where crowds of pilgrims came again and again in closed groups.[7] But for people from these areas, a pilgrimage to Jerusalem was probably not such an unusual experience as for people from the west. Their accounts could be intended as handbooks for the preparation of further trips to Palestine, or – probably in most cases – could be read as a literary substitute for the journey itself.

For our purposes, the pilgrim reports are not only of interest as eyewitness accounts from fourth-century Palestine. They document the transformation of the religious landscape of Palestine in the course of the century; but they also make clear what pilgrims looked for in the Holy Land, what was shown to them and how it was explained. Of particular interest is the reactions of pilgrims to Palestinian Judaism, and their possible encounters with Jewish traditions.

It was a matter of great significance for the country and its population that many pilgrims settled there permanently. This contributed to the ethnic diversity of the Christian population of

---

[5] The early texts are collected in *Itinera Hierosolymitana* (CSEL 39; also in CC 175/6). Translations with commentary: H. Donner, *Pilgerfahrt*; J. Wilkinson, *Jerusalem Pilgrims before the Crusades*, Warminster 1977.

[6] Jerome, *ep.* 107.2.3 (CSEL 55, 292).

[7] M. E. Stone, 'Holy Land Pilgrimage of Armenians before the Arab Conquest', *RB* 93 (1986), 93–110: For example, Euthymius was visited, shortly after the foundation of his monastery in 428, by a group of 400 Armenian pilgrims! The first reliably attested Armenian pilgrim was Eutactus of Satala, who came to the Holy Land before 361 and there became infected with gnostic heresies. This shows the relevance of Cyril of Jerusalem's sixth *Catechetical Lecture*, with its urgent warning against the Manichees. See M. E. Stone, 'An Armenian Pilgrim to the Holy Land in the Early Byzantine Era', *Revue des Etudes Arméniennes* 17 (1985), 173–8.

the country, but also brought about conflict between the different Christian trends of the time. Jerome and his circle in Bethlehem, who clashed bitterly with the church in Jerusalem and the monks on the Mount of Olives, are the principal example. But we now turn to the three extant pilgrim accounts, that of the anonymous pilgrim from Bordeaux, that of Egeria, and that of Jerome's friends Paula and Eustochium.

1. The Anonymous Bordeaux Pilgrim

The oldest surviving account describes, briefly and soberly, the journey to Palestine of a pilgrim from Bordeaux. He set out from Constantinople for Palestine on 1.6.333, and returned there on 26.12. of the same year. If we allow a minimum of four months for the journey there and back, he can only have been in the Holy Land itself for two to three months at most.

H. Donner concludes from the report that the pilgrim was 'a baptized Jew from Bordeaux'.[8] By contrast, even earlier S. Klein proposed that the author was never in the Holy Land, but put together his book from three sources: a list of routes, a meagre Christian text with almost no information on the holy Christian sites, and (the biggest element) a collection of Jewish tales and traditions. The author owed his knowledge of this to a Jewish traveller in Bordeaux, who was not a scholar and not very precise.[9]

What should we believe about the Pilgrim's Jewish source or his Jewish origin? We must see it in connection with the repeated assertion that Christians made use of the help of Jewish guides.[10] If the Bordeaux Pilgrim entrusted himself to the guidance of such a Jewish tourist guide, we could well understand there being points of contact with Jewish tradition. However, the employment of Jewish guides is ruled out from the start in Jerusalem, to which, at least officially, Jews had no entry. Thus J. Wilkinson concluded specifically from the description of Jerusalem, with its mention of

---

[8] H. Donner, *Pilgerfahrt*, 29, 42.
[9] S. Klein, 'Sefer ha-Massa Itinerarium Burdig. al Eretz Israel', *Zion* 6 (1934), 12–38 (reprinted in *Me'asef Zion*, 2 volumes [= 1–6, 1926–1934], Jerusalem 1978).
[10] Thus M. Avi-Yonah, 'Economics', 45, who speaks of Jewish and Samaritan guides; in n. 37 he sees a general influence of Jewish guides in the early itineraries and the Madaba map.

the 'pinnacle of the Temple' and of the 'stone which the builders rejected' (Ps. 118:22f.), as also from the description of the 'pierced stone' which the Jews visit each year in order to lament there, that the Bordeaux Pilgrim had a Christian guide in Jerusalem.[11]

Let us examine the Bordeaux Pilgrim's route. From Constantinople he travels across the middle of Asia Minor to Ankara, then south to the Mediterranean, which he reaches at Adana, not leaving its coast until he arrives in the Holy Land. From Caesarea he goes into the interior to Neapolis, and via Bethel to Jerusalem. From there he takes excursions via Bethany to Jericho and the Dead Sea, where he visits the site of Jesus' baptism, and also via Bethlehem to Hebron. The return journey leads via Emmaus and Lydda back to Caesarea and from there to Constantinople. Jews are mentioned in his very brief text only in connection with the Temple square in Jerusalem, and Samaritans in Neapolis. According to his itinerary, he can only have encountered significant Jewish towns in the Vale of Jezreel, in the environs of Jericho and then again (perhaps) in Lydda.

What is striking in his description, and a reason for describing him as a Jewish Christian or supposing a Jewish source for his text, is the emphasis on Old Testament traditions, and individual Jewish-sounding motifs. Before his arrival in Palestine he mentions, among New Testament themes, only the fact that Paul came from Tarsus; for example, he says nothing about Antioch. On the other hand, even before reaching the provincial border of Palestine he mentions two reminders of Elijah: in Sidon, to which he transfers the story of the widow of Zarephath (1 Kgs 17:7–16), and in Sycaminus on Mount Carmel, where Elijah sacrificed (1 Kgs 18:19–40). In Caesarea he mentions the centurion Cornelius (Acts 10). He connects the story of Naboth's vineyard from 1 Kgs 21 with Jezreel at the eastern edge of the valley of the same name: 'There King Ahab sat and Elijah prophesied.' He also sees there 'the camp where David killed Goliath', which according to 1 Sam. 17 should be located at Socoh in the hill country of Judaea.

Between Scythopolis and Neapolis he comes to Asher with Job's estate: the Bible locates him in the (unknown) land of Uz. Speaking of Mount Gerizim, he says that according to the Samaritans Abraham offered the sacrifice there (Gen. 22); he also

---

[11] J. Wilkinson, 'Christian Pilgrims', 86.

mentions Joseph's grave in Shechem (Josh. 24:32), the rape of Dinah by the Amorites (Gen. 34), the well dug by Jacob, where Jesus spoke to the Samaritan woman (John 4, no Old Testament citation), and the tree that Jacob planted at Sychar.[12] Finally, at Bethar (= Bethel) he mentions the tradition of Jacob's dream (Gen. 28), but also connects it with the story of Jacob's wrestling with the angel (Gen. 32), located by the Bible east of the Jordan, and the story of the prophet killed by a lion (1 Kgs 13).

Apart from the selection of Biblical traditions which the Pilgrim thinks worth writing down, one would like to raise the question of underlying traditions and their sources in the case of locations that differ from the Bible, or where the Bible gives no precise location. Particularly mysterious is the location of the battle between David and Goliath, especially since Eusebius and Jerome still know of two villages called Socoh between Jerusalem and Eleutheropolis in their own day. The reason for diverging from the site given in 1 Kgs 17 could perhaps lie in the conflicting Biblical tradition (according to 2 Sam. 21:19, Elhanan kills Goliath near Gob). One might perhaps also postulate a general tendency to transfer important battles to the plain of Megiddo as the Biblical battlefield *par excellence*. However, to my knowledge there is no evidence for this either in the rabbinic or in the Christian tradition of interpretation.[13]

Job's location in Asher, not otherwise attested, is almost equally problematic. But this might be connected with the widespread Jewish tradition that Job was married to Jacob's daughter Dinah after the Amorites stole her from nearby Shechem. This tradition is attested as early as the first century by pseudo-Philo's 'Book of Biblical Antiquities' (8.8).[14] If Job was to be located in the

---

[12] In Sychar he also mentions a 'bath' (*balneum*), which H. Donner, *Pilgerfahrt*, 53, interprets as meaning 'baptismal pool'. By contrast, C. Nauerth, 'Pilgerstätten am Garizim in frühchristlicher Zeit', *Dielheimer Blätter zum Alten Testament* 20 (1984), 17–45, 21–3, takes the expression to mean simply a bath-house treated as a *locus sanctus*, perhaps a ritual bath (Miqve) of the Samaritans, which possibly should be connected with the synagogue foundations of Baba Rabba.

[13] S. Klein (n. 9), 14, connects the localization with the name of the River Jalud at the foot of the Gilead hills. It is possible that there is a folkloric association of Gilead with Goliath.

[14] On the rabbinic and patristic tradition of Job, see J. R. Baskin, *Pharaoh's Counsellors. Job, Jethro and Balaam in Rabbinic and Patristic Tradition*, Chico 1983, 7–43.

neighbourhood of Shechem, the tribe of Asher was an obvious candidate; it was proverbial for its wealth in the rabbinic tradition, and its daughters, like Job's, were the epitome of beauty (Job 42:12ff.; Gen. 49:20; also GenR 99.12, Th-A 1282). This could also go back to Jewish tradition, but cannot strictly be proved.

In Jerusalem itself, the Pilgrim begins his description with two pools near the Temple square, which Solomon is said to have constructed, and the Pool of Bethesda (John 5). Then he mentions a crypt where Solomon conjured up demons – a common motif in Jewish tradition – and the corner tower where Satan tempted Jesus (Mt. 4:5ff.). He also mentions the cornerstone 'which the builders rejected' (Ps. 118:22; Mt. 21:42), and many rooms under the corner tower, where Solomon had a palace.

> The room is still there where he sat and wrote Wisdom; the ceiling of this chamber is formed out of a single stone ... And in the building itself where the Temple was that Solomon built, there is to this day on the marble [floor] before the altar the spilt blood of Zechariah. The traces of the nails of the soldiers who killed him are also to be seen throughout the room, as if moulded in wax. There are also two statues of Hadrian there, and not far from the statues is a pierced stone, to which the Jews come every year, anoint it, lament with sighs, tear their clothes and then depart again. There is also the house of King Hezekiah of Judah ... a pool by the name of Siloam. It has a fourfold portico, and a further large pool is further out. This spring flows for six days and nights; on the seventh day is the sabbath, when it flows neither by day nor night.

He goes on, up Mount Zion to the house of Caiaphas the high priest, with the pillar where Jesus was scourged. 'Within the wall of Zion the place may be seen where David had his palace. Of the seven synagogues which were here, only one remains; the others are ploughed over and sown, as the Prophet Isaiah said.'[15]

From here he continues, past walls left standing from Pilate's praetorium, to the Church of the Holy Sepulchre (mentioned only briefly), and already leaves Jerusalem again, through the East Gate in the direction of the Mount of Olives. Outside the city he

---

[15] The translation is based on that of H. Donner, *Pilgerfahrt*, 54–8.

is shown the rock where Judas betrayed the Lord, the tree from which the children took the palm branches for Christ's entry into Jerusalem, and two graves, one supposedly belonging to the Prophet Isaiah, the other to Hezekiah, the Jewish king.

The relative importance attributed to the sights of the city is indeed striking. The fact that he begins his sightseeing in northeastern Jerusalem, above the Temple square, and only comes to the Church of the Holy Sepulchre at the end of his circuit, may be connected with his arrival from the north, on the road from Neapolis, but nevertheless seems rather strange. This is even more true of the comparatively short description of the Church of the Holy Sepulchre, as compared with the description of what he sees on the Temple square. It may be that he only describes the Church of the Holy Sepulchre briefly because the area was at least partly still a building-site, perhaps also because the tradition of this place of pilgrimage was still comparatively new. However, it is possible to detect a specific intention behind the emphasis on the Temple square, i.e. to stress that Judaism has now been superseded by Christianity.

In this context the statement about the blood of Zechariah (see Mt. 23:35; 2 Chron. 24:20f.) is of crucial importance. It is also very significant in rabbinic tradition.[16] The consequence of this murder, as of the rejection of Christ, the stone that was rejected but became the cornerstone, is the destruction of the Temple. But it is also the cause of the Roman rule, symbolized by the two statues of Hadrian (really one statue of Hadrian and one of Antoninus Pius). The 'building itself' in which the Pilgrim is shown the traces of blood could also remind one of the Roman rule, if we were in fact to think in terms of the Hadrianic temple of Jupiter, which, as we have seen, is not likely. We should probably assume that some walls of the Herodian Temple were still standing and were shown to the Pilgrim.[17]

The text may tacitly assume that, as a consequence of the murders of Zechariah and then Jesus, all that is left for the Jews is to lament and anoint the 'pierced stone'. What is presumably

---

[16] S. H. Blank, 'The Death of Zechariah in Rabbinic Tradition', *HUCA* 12–13 (1937f.), 327–46; M. McNamara, *The New Testament and the Palestinian Targum to the Pentateuch*, Rome 1966, 160–3.

[17] H. Donner, *Pilgerfahrt*, 55f., interprets the expression in the Bordeaux Pilgrim to mean the temple of Jupiter, of which remains at least should still have been visible in 333.

meant is the pierced rock of the altar, which according to rabbinic tradition is also the foundation-stone of the world. However, it is questionable whether at this period Jews would have entered the Temple square itself. If not, we would have to think of another stone, possibly at the 'Wailing Wall'. According to the dates of his journey it is entirely possible that the Pilgrim experienced the anniversary of the destruction of the Temple in Jerusalem,[18] and himself saw the lamenting Jews in the Temple square.

The importance of the blood of Zechariah for the Christian pilgrim tradition may be understood from Jerome's remarks, according to whom 'brothers of the simpler sort show red stones among the ruins of the Temple and the altar, or near the exit gates leading to Siloam, saying they are stained with the blood of Zechariah.' He himself does not believe this tradition; but 'we do not condemn the error, which stems from hatred of the Jews and pious belief.'[19] The anti-Jewish tendency of this statement for the faith is sufficiently clear.

Perhaps Hezekiah's palace is shown for the same reason in the immediate neighbourhood, as well as his grave, where he is pointedly called 'King of the Jews'. According to Jewish tradition Hezekiah is a messianic figure, as follows from the last words attributed to Jochanan ben Zakkai: 'Prepare a throne for Hezekiah, the King of Judah, who is to come' (Ber 28 b). The ruins of his palace and his grave could therefore point to disappointed Jewish messianic hopes. The same theme recurs on Mount Zion, where David once had his palace and where only one remains of the seven synagogues of old, the word of the prophet having been fulfilled in respect of the others, which are ploughed and sown (Isa. 1:8; Mi. 3:12).

The remarks concerning Solomon do not fit this context of Judaism being superseded by Christianity, nor does the strange remark on the Siloam spring which does not flow on the sabbath. Even if we are to imagine an intermittent spring that does not flow regularly, of course a regular ceasing on the sabbath is impossible, and during a long-term stay in Jerusalem the Pilgrim would of course have seen this. A most likely source is the

---

[18] According to the table in E. Mahler, *Handbuch*, 529, the 9th Ab 333 fell on 7th August.
[19] Jerome, *In Matt.* IV, on Mt. 23.35 (CC 77, 220).

tradition that, during the siege of Jerusalem under Hezekiah, because of Isaiah's prayers, water flowed from the spring only when Jews wanted to draw water, but not when the pagan besiegers came.[20] It is not far from there to the assumption that the spring kept the sabbath rest together with the Jews. Such a concept is clearly of Jewish and not Christian origin. It is interesting that even such a tradition which is more symbolic, but can easily be falsified by an observer in profane reality, was included in a pilgrim's tale.

Apart from these points, the description of Jerusalem as a whole does not give the impression of portraying Jewish or Jewish Christian interests. Rather, it reflects Christian propaganda connected with the Constantinian building programme in Jerusalem, that is, the assertion that the Jewish Jerusalem has been superseded by the Christian Jerusalem, just as Eusebius describes the Church of the Holy Sepulchre as the equivalent of the Temple and the new Jerusalem. Jewish traditions also noted by the Pilgrim do not rule out such an understanding of his sightseeing programme in Jerusalem; they only show the general strong attachment of the church of this period to the Old Testament, which it considered itself to have inherited legitimately from the Jews.

The Old Testament weighting of the narrative is also conspicuous in the Pilgrim's excursion to Jericho. Apart from Zacchaeus' tree (Lk. 19), he mentions Elisha's spring (2 Kgs 2:19–22), the house of Rahab the harlot (Josh. 2 and 6), the place where once the Ark of the Covenant stood, the twelve stones which the Israelites took out of the Jordan (Josh. 4:20), the place where Joshua circumcised the Israelites (Josh. 5), and finally, apart from the place of Jesus' baptism in the Jordan, the hill from which Elijah was taken up into heaven (2 Kgs 2).

From the detour to Bethlehem we should mention the interesting assertion that not far from the Constantinian Basilica of the Nativity 'there is the grave of Ezekiel, Asaph, Job, Isai, David and Solomon. If you descend, the above-mentioned names are written at the side in Hebrew letters.'[21] H. Donner comments on this passage that the Pilgrim meant the names of David's companions

---

[20] *Lives of the Prophets* 1.3. Text, translation and commentary in A. M. Schwemer, *Vitae Prophetarum* I, 96–158.
[21] *Itinera Hierosolymitana*, CSEL 38, 25.

in arms: 'Probably the Pilgrim misread the names of Asahel, Abishai and Joab (2 Sam. 2:18–32), perhaps because the inscription was already damaged.'[22] Of course this hypothesis presupposes that the Pilgrim was a Jewish Christian. However, even in the case of a converted Jew from Bordeaux, we cannot necessarily expect knowledge of Hebrew in the fourth century. We should rather assume that some grave or other with a Hebrew inscription was simply wrongly explained. In any case, this strange statement does not lead to the assumption of a Jewish background for the author or his source, even if we cannot explain it in detail, as with so many other statements in the pilgrim texts.

Apart from the polemical tendency in the description of Jerusalem, the emphasis on Old Testament traditions compared to the New probably springs from the fact that there was as yet no distinct Christian pilgrim tradition, and that the Christianity of the period was still strongly marked by the Old Testament in general.[23] This is probably also the reason for the fact that Christian Galilee has no place on the Pilgrim's itinerary. Does he perhaps fail to visit Galilee precisely because there there is no question of Judaism being superseded by Christianity, and because there are hardly any Christian sites to be visited?

J. Wilkinson rightly says: 'The Bordeaux pilgrim speaks of a Christian topography which existed almost without reference to Christian monuments.'[24] It is likely that the anonymous Pilgrim followed a standard programme. Does this go back to a pre-Constantinian tradition that was simply given a different emphasis by the new Christian propaganda? Unfortunately we lack the sources to be able to answer this question.

2. Egeria

In 1884 a pilgrim account was discovered that was probably written by an aristocratic nun from southwestern France or, more likely, Spanish Galicia. The Pilgrim was initially identified with Silv(an)ia, the stepsister of Rufinus of Aquileia, but this

---

[22] H. Donner, *Pilgerfahrt*, 63 n. 110; already also in J. Jeremias, *Heiligengräber*, 77ff.
[23] On this, see M. Simon, 'Les saints d'Israel dans la dévotion de l'Eglise ancienne', *RHPR* 34 (1954), 98–127; reprinted in id., *Recherches*, 154–80.
[24] J. Wilkinson, 'Christian Pilgrims', 88.

identification is no longer accepted today. H. Donner dates her journey to around 400, and justifies this with reference to the pilgrim's excursion to Job's grave at Carneas in southern Syria, saying that John Chrysostom appears not to know of this in the year 379, because in a sermon of that year he mentions only the ash-heap on which Job sat.[25] But we must remember how much that definitely existed is not mentioned elsewhere, e.g. in Jerome. Thus the argument is not very good evidence, and an earlier dating of Egeria's journey between 381 and 384 is probably more appropriate, especially in view of the fact that she mentions individual Syrian bishops as 'confessors', which indicates that they had experienced the persecutions.[26]

Unfortunately the sections on the West Bank and Jerusalem are missing from the description of Egeria's roughly four-year journey. The latter is more or less compensated for by the description of the Jerusalem liturgy in the second part of the work. For Galilee there are only scanty extracts in Peter the Deacon, whose *Liber de locis sanctis*, written 1137, adapts a work of the Venerable Bede, who in his turn is proved to have made use of Egeria. The pilgrim's name is transmitted in various forms apart from Egeria, as Aegeria, Aetheria and so on.

The account, as far as it is extant, seems to move in a world full of monks, priests, bishops and churches. Only in the case of Haran does Egeria remark explicitly that apart from the clergy only pagans live there. She always travels in company; monks and priests in particular always seem to have the time to join the pilgrims for a part of the way. In the Sinai desert and at the Gulf of Suez they also have a military escort, probably the usual Roman road patrol.

Everywhere monks are ready to show what pilgrims wish to see. Pilgrims seem already to be an everyday occurrence, and they can be led to a multitude of memorial sites. Every single sentence of the Bible is precisely located. This is particularly striking in the Sinai desert, where Egeria can simply and sweepingly refer her

---

[25] H. Donner, *Pilgerfahrt* 73f.; see 119 n. 125 on John Chrysostom's fifth homily (PG 49, 69) 'He appears to know nothing of a grave.' Already also in J. Jeremias, *Heiligengräber*, 102 n. 1.
[26] P. Devos, 'La date du voyage d'Egerie', *Analecta Bollandiana* 85 (1967), 165–97; also A. Baumstark, *Oriens Christianus* 1 (1911), 32–76. They are followed by, e.g. J. Wilkinson, *Egeria's Travels*, London 1971, 237–9, and P. Maraval, *Egérie. Journal de Voyage* (SC 296), Paris 1982, 38.

readers to the Pentateuch. A rock marks the site of the golden calf (Ex. 32:1–6); at the peak of Moses' mountain is a church, also on the neighbouring Mount Horeb, with Elijah's cave (1 Kgs 19:8f.), another at the burning bush (Ex. 3) etc. 'And so those saints always showed us every single place as we came to them, throughout the valley.'[27]

This orientation on the Old Testament seems reasonable in the case of the Sinai desert. But it also marks the other extant parts of the work: Abraham, Melchizedek, Moses, Job and Elijah are the centre of attention, whereas Christian objects of interest are mentioned almost only in passing. However, we cannot know whether the emphasis would be different if the work were preserved in its entirety.

The journey from Jerusalem to Mount Nebo, the place where Moses died, is also characteristic. It takes place after Egeria has returned from Egypt along the coast road through Palestine to 'Helia, that is Jerusalem'.[28] Of course she may have already described the Christian elements in the lost portion of the work; here certainly she only mentions Old Testament events: the place where Joshua led the Israelites across the Jordan (Josh. 3–4), the place where the tribes of Reuben and Gad, and the half-tribe of Manasseh, built an altar 'on that part of the bank where Jericho lies' (Josh. 22:10–34), the foundations of the Israelite camp at Livias beyond the Jordan (Num. 22:1 and *passim*) and so on. By contrast, Egeria does not even mention Jesus' baptism! H. Donner is of the opinion that this is because she locates John the Baptist at Aenon near Salim.[29] But this does not explain her silence, because she does not speak of Jesus' baptism in connection with that place – Aenon, the site of John the Baptist's work, is not equated with the site of Jesus' baptism (see John 3:23).

Egeria's visit to Sedima is of exceptional interest. She comes there on her journey to Carneas in the district of Ausitis, where she wishes to visit Job's grave: 'For I saw many holy monks who came from there to Jerusalem in order to see the holy places and to pray there. They told me details about those places and

---

[27] Egeria 5.1 (CSEL 38, 43). P. Maraval, *Lieux saints* 38, speaks of a 'localization that is Christian, or more precisely monastic, in origin; for the Christian population of the peninsula were largely monks in the fourth century.'

[28] Egeria 9.7 (CSEL 38, 50).

[29] H. Donner, *Pilgerfahrt*, 104 n. 85.

aroused the wish in me to take the trouble to travel to those places also.'[30]

Unfortunately Egeria does not say exactly where this village of Sedima is located. In any case, it is in the Jordan valley not far from Beth Shean, and is probably to be equated with the Salumias mentioned by Eusebius in the *Onomasticon*, which is identified with Tell Shalem (Tell er Radgha).[31] Egeria describes Sedima as an inhabited Tell: 'In this village, which is in the middle of a plain, there is a small hill in the centre, shaped like a large grave mound ... There on the height is a church, and down below, surrounding the small hill, massive old foundations are visible, and some heaps of ruins are also visible today in the village itself.'[32]

When she asks, Egeria is given the following explanation:

> That is the city of King Melchizedek, that used to be called Salem, which is why the village is now called Sedima, which is a corruption. For on the hill in the centre of the village you can see a building, a church. This church is called in the Greek language *opu* [?] Melchizedek. For this is the place where Melchizedek offered pure offerings to God, bread and wine, as it is written of him' (Gen. 14:18).[33]

The foundations surrounding the hill are explained to her as remains of Melchizedek's palace, where even today small pieces of silver and bronze may be found. Abraham returned after his victory over Chedorlaomer along the road leading from the Jordan through the village and met Melchizedek here. Then the priest who is acting as Egeria's guide makes a connection with the baptism of John in the same place. For this reason the candidates are still baptized in this spring at Easter, and then led in a torchlight procession to the church of Melchizedek.

This location of the Melchizedek tradition in the Jordan valley is contrary to the Jewish tradition, which unanimously refers Gen. 14:18 to Jerusalem = Salem. Josephus is already a witness to this (*Ant.* I.180; *BJ* VI.438); in rabbinic literature see e.g. GenR 43.6 (Th-A 420). By contrast, the Samaritan tradition referred the text

---

[30] Egeria 13.1 (CSEL 38, 55).
[31] Y. Tsafrir, L. di Segni, J. Green, *Tabula Imperii Romani. Iudaea Palestina*, Jerusalem 1994, 219f.
[32] Egeria 13.3 (CSEL 38, 56).
[33] Egeria 13.4 (CSEL 38, 56). The meaning of *opu* in this context is not clear.

to Shechem, as Eupolemus attests. This tradition may go back to Gen. 33:18: 'And Jacob came *shalem* to the city of Shechem in the land of Canaan.' Today *shalem* is generally understood as an adjective, 'safely', as in the Aramaic versions (the Samaritan Targum alone is ambiguous). But the Septuagint translates: 'And Jacob came to Salem, the city of the Shechemites, which is in the land of Canaan'; so also the Vulgate in its turn.

The fact that the tradition was not yet uniform in the fourth century is attested by texts in the Church Fathers. Eusebius, and Jerome following him,[34] follows the Septuagint of Gen. 33:18 with regard to Salem in Gen. 14:18, that is, they equate Salem, city of the Shechemites, with Shechem. 'But there is another village ...' There is a lacuna in the extant text of Eusebius; according to Jerome, it should be supplemented as follows: 'It is shown until today, west of Aelia, under that name; also, at the eighth milestone from Scythopolis a village in the plain is called Salumias.' Then Jerome quotes Josephus' equation of Salem with Jerusalem. Epiphanius also documents the confusion over this question: 'Salem is the name of a city about which everyone has a different opinion. Some say it is the [city] which today is called Jerusalem and sometimes also known as Jebus; others say there is a Salem in the plain of the Shechemites, opposite the place known today as Neapolis.'[35]

It is apparent from one of his letters that Jerome knows the pilgrim tradition of a Salem near Scythopolis. He writes that Salem is not, as Josephus and also some Christians believe, Jerusalem, a name put together from Greek and Hebrew, which would be an absurd mixture of languages. Rather, it is 'a small town near Scythopolis, which is called Salem to this day. There the palace of Melchizedek is shown, whose extensive ruins show the magnificence of the ancient building.' This is the same Salem as in Gen. 33:18. Jerome also remarks that Abraham pursued his enemies as far as Paneas; on his return journey he therefore could not have come to Jerusalem, which was out of his way, but rather precisely to a city in the neighbourhood of Shechem, the place where John baptized, Aenon near Salim (John 3:23).

The following remark in Jerome's letter is of interest: 'We learned this from the most learned men of that people, who

---

[34] Eusebius, *Onomasticon*, GCS 11/1, 152f.
[35] Epiphanius, *Panarion* 60.2.1 (GCS 31, 379).

however do not believe that the Holy Spirit or an angel was Melchizedek, but definitely describe him as a human being.'[36] So Jerome is quoting learned Jews. But the following addition, that they do not understand Melchizedek as the Holy Spirit or an angel, is strange as a remark about Jews, since it is all too self-evident. Does Jerome here mean Jewish Christians, who, by contrast with others, do not see Melchizedek as a heavenly saviour figure, as was the case in Qumran and also in Christian groups, following Heb. 7:3,[37] but rather stress that he is an earthly king?

Locating Melchizedek's palace would help to anchor Melchizedek in this world and thus to undermine his mythification. However, this alone would not yet be sufficient grounds to give up the pre-Christian location in Jerusalem, which had also now become a centre of Christian pilgrimage. Even the fact that, within the context of Gen. 14, a location in the Jordan valley is more logical, is not yet a sufficient reason for the transferral of the tradition. Its connection with John the Baptist suggests a Christian origin, which does not agree with the Jewish tradition. Is it possible to see here a pre-Constantinian, Jewish Christian local tradition, perhaps founded on a parallel between Melchizedek and John the Baptist, which began at a time when Jewish Christians also were forbidden to enter Jerusalem?

We can only ask the question without offering a satisfactory answer. However, what is significant in our context is the fact that Christian pilgrims preserve Old Testament traditions that do not agree with the Jewish tradition. So, in the case of Old Testament traditions, we must not think from the outset of Jewish tradition or even of Jewish guides. Rather, these texts have a life of their own within the Christian tradition. The same is probably true of many Moses and Elijah traditions, and also becomes clear in the case of Job, as Egeria continues her journey, leaving Palestine proper. We will return to this subject in connection with the discovery of graves.

---

[36] Jerome, *ep.* 73.7–9 (CSEL 55, 20f.).
[37] F. L. Horton, *The Melchizedek Tradition*, Cambridge 1976, 64–82, 90–113; M. Simon, 'Melchisédech dans la polémique entre juifs et chrétiens et dans la légende', *RHPR* 17 (1937), 58–93; reprinted in id., *Recherches* 101–26, 115–18. He takes this localization at the Jordan to be Samaritan, which I do not think to be very probable, since the Samaritans had their tradition of the village of Salem near Neapolis.

3. Paula and Eustochium

Paula, a rich Roman woman from the family of the Gracchi, undertook a journey to the Holy Land, together with her daughter Eustochium and a number of virgins, in the years 385 and 386, guided by her friend Jerome. She then settled together with her companions in Bethlehem. The journey is described in Paula's and Eustochium's letter to Marcella (probably written in 392 or 393, and preserved as letter 46 in the collection of *Letters* of Jerome); the journey is also reflected in Jerome's letter to Eustochium, a kind of memorial to Paula, who died in 404 (*ep.* 108).

H. Donner is of the opinion that Jerome 'turned the pilgrimage of his two friends into an educational journey, more or less what we would call today an academic field trip'.[38] He protests against the suggestion that the text is largely fiction. That is surely right; but neither is the journey a standard trip such as Egeria's journey was, if a vastly amplified one. The very specific interests of Jerome, the Biblical scholar, who was always particularly interested in Jewish traditions, made sure of that.

Coming from the north, the group travelled along the coast to Zarephath, where they commemorated Elijah and visited the tower in which he had lived (1 Kgs 17:8–24). Via the beach of Tyre, with its memories of St. Paul (Acts 21:5) they went on to Acco/Acre and to the plain of Megiddo, where long ago King Josiah fell (2 Kgs 23:29). From Dor the group arrived in Caesarea, where the house of Cornelius (Acts 10:1) was now a church; they also visited the house of Philip, and the room of his four prophetic daughters, in that city (Acts 21:8f.). The journey continues along the coast road to Lydda, where the healing of Aeneas and the resuscitation of Tabitha are mentioned (Acts 9:32ff.). In Jaffa the text only mentions Jonah and the legend of Andromeda, nothing from the New Testament. The remainder of the journey to Jerusalem via Emmaus is skimmed over in the text with scarcely more than a list of place-names and Biblical references, without mentioning sight-seeing.

In Jerusalem the group visits the site of the Cross and the grave of Jesus, the Church of Sion with the pillar of the scourging in its portico, and the site of the miracle of Pentecost. It is striking that the Temple square is not mentioned at all, nor are the pools of

[38] H. Donner, *Pilgerfahrt*, 140.

Bethesda and Siloam. The Mount of Olives, too, is only mentioned from a distance by Jerome: from Tekoa its golden cross can be seen, which not only commemorates Jesus' ascension, but reminds Jerome, who knows his Bible, of the rite of the red heifer (Num. 19). In particular, the Mount of Olives is for Jerome the place where Jewish worship is supplanted by Christianity, as Eusebius had read in Ezekiel before him: 'according to Ezekiel (10:19; 1:14–25) the cherubim leaving the Temple founded there the Church of the Lord'.[39]

The fact that Jerome has so little to say about Jerusalem, and does not describe the Mount of Olives in the context of a direct visit, probably has to do with the great tensions that separated Jerome and his community in Bethlehem from Bishop John in Jerusalem and the monks on the Mount of Olives. This is probably why he restricted the description of Jerusalem to the minimum.

After the women have distributed money to the poor in Jerusalem, the journey continues to Bethlehem, whose description is twice as detailed. The travellers visit the grave of Rachel, Mary's inn, the stable and the tower of Eder (Gen. 35:21). Then they continue towards Hebron, where the group remembers the Ethiopian eunuch (Acts 8) at Beth-Zur and the grapes of the spies in Eshcol (Num. 13:23).

At Mamre Paula stepped 'into Sarah's rooms, she saw Isaac's cradle and the traces of Abraham's oak'. Jerome explains Hebron was the city of the four men Abraham, Isaac, Jacob, and Adam the great: 'The Hebrews believe, according to the Book of Joshua (14:13–15), that he is buried there, although most think that the fourth is Caleb, whose monument is shown over to one side.'[40] Jerome also argues for Adam's burial at Hebron, and not on the hill of Golgotha, in his *Commentary on Matthew*, but in his letter 46.3 and in his commentary on Eph. 5:14 he adopts the Christian tradition that Adam is buried on Golgotha, directly under the Cross of Christ.[41]

From Hebron the group travels a few kilometres eastward to

---

[39] Jerome, *ep.* 108.12 (CSEL 55, 320); Eusebius, *Demonstratio Evangelica* VI.18.22f. (GCS 23, 278).

[40] Jerome, *ep.* 108.11 (CSEL 55, 319). [The point of Jerome's remark, and of the associated Jewish tradition, is that Kiriath Arba (Josh. 14:15) literally means 'the town of the four' – Editor]

[41] Jerome, *Comm. Matth.* 27.33 (CC 77, 270); *ep.* 46.3 (CSEL 54, 332); *Comm. Eph.* 5.14 (PL 26, 559).

the hill of Kafarbaruch, 'to which Abraham accompanied the Lord' (Gen. 18:16–19), from where there is a view to Sodom and Gomorrah. They then return through the home of the prophet Amos, Tekoa, towards Jerusalem. In Bethany the pilgrims view the grave of Lazarus and go on through Bethphage and Adommim to Jericho. Here too, apart from Zacchaeus' tree and the place where Jesus healed the blind man on the road, there are largely Old Testament memorials: the camp at Gilgal, the hill of the foreskins, the twelve stones from the Jordan. At the Jordan, apart from Jesus' baptism, Elijah and Elisha are of course remembered.

Through the Valley of Achor (Josh. 7:26) the journey continues to Bethel, near which the graves of Joshua and Eleazar the son of Aaron are mentioned, also the grave of Phineas in Gibeah. At Shiloh they see the ruined altar of the temple from the time before the Temple of Solomon, in Shechem the church at Jacob's Well, and nearby the graves of the twelve sons of Jacob according to Samaritan tradition.[42] At Sebaste they visit the graves of Elisha, Obadiah and John the Baptist; the text also mentions the cave there where Obadiah fed a hundred prophets with bread and water (1 Kgs 18:4).

One or two isolated New Testament reminders and even memorials have been added to those in the text of the anonymous Bordeaux Pilgrim; but the programme is still largely characterized by Old Testament memorials, whereby of course Jerome's Biblical scholarship plays an important role. Not every mention of a Biblical event means that there is actually something to see in connection with it. By comparison with the earlier text, a strikingly large number of graves of Old Testament characters has now become known. We will return to this point later.

The women in Jerome's circle have a particularly interesting programme in Galilee: 'She (Paula) hurried through Nazareth, the city of the Lord's childhood, Cana and Capernaum, the sites of his miracles, to the Sea of Galilee ... and to the desert, where many thousand people were fed with a few loaves ... She climbed Mount Tabor, where the Lord was transfigured.' From the summit she is shown Mount Hermon and the place where Barak conquered Sisera and his army (Judg. 4–5), the Brook Kishon

---

[42] Jerome, *ep.* 57.10 (CSEL 54, 522) also states that the sons of Jacob are not buried in Hebron but in Shechem.

and the city of Nain, where Jesus raised the son of the widow from the dead (Lk. 7:11ff.).[43]

Here Jerome interrupts his description: 'The day would end before I did, if I were to describe everything which the honourable Paula hurried through in her exceptional faith.' Thus he denies intending to give a detailed description of the journey. In view of the Christian interest of the sites in Galilee, the description is nevertheless extremely brief, although the programme seems fairly complete. Does Jerome take it for granted that these places are known, because he cannot offer any more that is new on Paula's piety in the context of her memorial letter, or are they less important to him? Or is there simply less that is worth seeing that can be recounted of these places? At his time the churches in Nazareth and Capernaum, at the site of the feeding of the five thousand and on Mount Tabor must already have existed. It is hard to draw conclusions from his silence – Jerome does not explicitly mention the Church of the Holy Sepulchre nor the church at Mamre. But the main focus of his description is clearly not in Galilee; overall, even there the Old Testament remains more important than the New.

Next Jerome describes the continuing journey to Egypt. At Socoh they come to Samson's spring (Judg. 15:14–19), at Morasthi (Moresheth) they go to Micah's grave, where a church already stands. After visiting the monks in Egypt the group returns by sea to Maiumas, the port of Gaza, and shortly afterwards settles in Bethlehem.[44]

To my knowledge, an accompaniment by a Jewish guide can at most be deduced from a single text of Jerome, and not certainly there. In the preface to his *Commentary on Nahum* Jerome writes: 'Elkosh is still today a little village in Galilee, small and barely showing the traces of old buildings by their ruins; nevertheless it is known to the Jews and was shown to me by a guide.'[45] Nahum's home is, even today, not definitely located. As well as a tradition in northern Galilee, there is another near Eleutheropolis,[46] also a later one near Mosul in Iraq. S. Klein believes 'it appears that a place near Capernaum is meant, and because of that place-name people also showed the place of Nahum, Elqoshi'.[47]

---

[43] Jerome, *ep.* 108.13 (CSEL 55, 323).
[44] Jerome, *ep.* 108.14 (CSEL 55, 324f.).
[45] Jerome, *Comm. Nah.*, Preface (CC 76 A, 526).
[46] See J. Jeremias, *Heiligengräber*, 33f.
[47] S. Klein, *Sefer ha-Jischub* I 5 n. on Elqosh.

If Jerome means this tradition, his remark would fit the context of his journey with Paula. Then one should also not assume another journey by Jerome, an aspect which is important for assessing his local knowledge. Thus J. Wilkinson suggests 'that the journey he undertook with her (Paula) was his only exploration of the Holy Land ... We must assume that his pilgrimage with Paula never took him further than Capernaum.'[48] Not even Paneas, the Caesarea Philippi of the New Testament, the location of Peter's confession of Jesus as the Messiah (Mt. 16:13–20), seems to have ever been seen by this so ecclesiastically-minded man, nor the other places of Jesus' ministry around the Sea of Galilee. Biblical reminders of the Old Testament thus remain at the forefront of Christian interest.

4. Old Testament Graves and Relics

The pilgrim accounts constantly mention graves which are visited and venerated. Strikingly, even in Jerome every single grave, with the exception of those of Jesus and John the Baptist, is attributed to an Old Testament figure. Only the graves of Stephen and James are added in the following years from the Christian tradition. This too confirms the one-sided Old Testament orientation of early pilgrimage to the Holy Land, and probably also of the spirituality of the local Palestinian church. A number of questions arise in this context: do these graves go back to Jewish tradition, are they found because of Jewish information, are there clashes between Christians and Jews in the fight for the possession of such sites?

Before we begin to consider these questions in detail, the additional question of veneration of relics, with its possible economic consequences, should be touched upon briefly. M. Avi-Yonah writes in his overview of the economy of Palestine in Byzantine times: 'Another source of income for Palestine was the export of relics. This involved in most cases rich compensation to the finder and to the local church. As regards the remains of Old Testament characters in particular, Palestine had what amounted to a monopoly.'[49]

---

[48] J. Wilkinson, 'L'apport de saint Jérôme à la topographie', *RB* 81 (1974), 245–57; 255f.

[49] M. Avi-Yonah, 'The Economics', 45.

E. D. Hunt is right to qualify this with the observation that, while trade in relics did have commercial potential for the Palestine of this period, its economic consequences in the Holy Land can hardly be proved.[50] There is no doubt that trade in relics already existed at this time. This is clear from the prohibition in CTh IX.17.7, dated 386: 'No one may transfer a corpse that is already buried to another place; no one may divide (the corpse) of a martyr, no one may trade (with it). Yet it is permitted, if a saint is buried at any place, to erect buildings in order to venerate him, which shall be called a martyrium.'

This law was not kept either, as the translations of various relics in the following years show. Many relics were taken to Constantinople in particular, for example those of the prophet Samuel. Jerome writes in 406, defending the veneration of relics to Vigilantius with reference to this case:

> Should then even the Emperor Arcadius be called ungodly, who caused the bones of the blessed Samuel to be translated from Judaea and Thrace, after a long time? Would all the bishops have to be thought not only ungodly, but also stupid, since they carried a completely worthless thing and loose ashes in silks and a golden vessel? Were the people of every church foolish, who processed out to meet the holy relics and received them with such joy as if they saw the prophet present and alive? ... Did they pray to Samuel and not to Christ, whose Levite and prophet Samuel was? You are casting suspicion on a dead man and thereby blaspheming God.[51]

In the year 415 the relics of the patriarch Joseph, which had been wrested from the Samaritans, were taken, also from Palestine, to Constantinople.[52]

Thus a certain amount of relics were definitely exported from Palestine. But this does not mean there was necessarily *trade* in relics in Palestine, for which we have no evidence. Even in the case of translations within Palestine, of which the translation of Stephen's relics to the church of Sion in Jerusalem was the most spectacular, ecclesiastical politics are rather the most prominent

---

[50] E. D. Hunt, *Holy Land Pilgrimage*, 135.
[51] Jerome, *Adv. Vigilantium* 5 (PL 23, 358f.).
[52] J. Jeremias, *Heiligengräber*, 33f.

feature. It is of course indisputable that the presence of important relics represented an additional attraction for pilgrims and thus could serve local commercial interests.

As regards the Old Testament figures, one must certainly assume the use of Jewish traditions, as in the case of the takeover of the tombs of the Maccabees at Antioch. However, it is hardly likely that Jews willingly passed on their own traditions regarding the tombs of Old Testament figures, because they would then have almost automatically lost those graves to the advancing Christian church. In Mt. 23:29 Jesus accuses the Pharisees of being the sons of murderers of the prophets, while 'you build tombs for the prophets and decorate the graves of the righteous'. But to what extent did such a veneration of prophets' tombs live on, so that it could be taken over by the Christians in the fourth century? The statement in a rabbinic text that a Biblical figure is buried at such and such a place, does not necessarily mean that a grave was known and venerated. We know of this principally in the case of the graves of the patriarchs at the cave of Machpelah in Hebron, of Rachel's tomb near Bethlehem and of the tombs of the sons of Jacob in Samaria. In the case of many other figures, however, whose graves appear in ever-increasing numbers from the late fourth century, Jewish tradition may only have been the occasion for Christians later putting it into concrete form.[53]

It is even less likely that Jews took part in trade in relics. The custom of secondary burial persisted for quite some time among Palestinian Jews, that is, despite the contrary injunctions of the purity laws people did not shrink from touching the remains of the dead; in Jad. IV.6 there is even a mention of people who make spoons from the bones of their parents! That would make something like 'veneration of relics' appear to be not impossible

---

[53] J. Jeremias, *Heiligengräber*, is much too sweeping in his reference to Jewish grave traditions from an early period. The fact that in scribal circles places were named as the site of the burial of Biblical figures, does not mean in itself that tombs actually existed and were venerated. The *Lives of the Prophets* of pseudo-Epiphanius probably goes back to various Jewish traditions, but the text itself should probably be understood as Christian, as D. Satran, *Biblical Prophets in Byzantine Palestine. Reassessing the Lives of the Prophets*, Leiden 1995. A. M. Schwemer, *Vitae Prophetarum*, offers a valuable commentary, but does not succeed in proving her hypothesis that the underlying text is a Pharisaic work of the first century.

even within Judaism.⁵⁴ However, apart from natural religious scruples, it must be pointed out that we have no evidence that Jews of this period ever took part in the discovery of Biblical figures and their relics.

Unfortunately a page is missing in Egeria's account before 16.5. This must have mentioned, among other things, a monk in the Syrian desert to whom the grave of Job was revealed in a vision. The extant text continues as follows: 'This holy monk and ascetic thought it necessary, after having spent so many years in the desert, to set off and go down to the city of Carneas, in order to admonish the bishop and priests of the day, according to what had been revealed to him, to dig at the spot he had been shown; as indeed took place.'⁵⁵ They dug at the place he indicated and found a cave, in which, after about a hundred metres, a stone was uncovered inscribed with the name Job. A tribune caused a church to be built, which was as yet unfinished when Egeria visited. H. Donner concluded that the building work had probably begun only a short time before.⁵⁶ But the building work could just as well have been interrupted much earlier, for unknown reasons. For example, P. Maraval dates this first case of 'inspired discovery' – apart from the description in the *Vita Constantini* of the discovery of the grave of Jesus – around 350, since in Egeria's time the tribune's name was apparently no longer remembered, and the event had happened under a previous bishop.⁵⁷ The discovery of the tombs of Stephen, Gamaliel and Nicodemus in Kephar Gamala in 415, told in the *Epistula Luciani*, followed exactly the same pattern.⁵⁸ Lucianus, priest of the church of Kephar Gamala near Jerusalem, tells how he was sleeping as usual in the baptistery of his church, and in a semi-waking state, as it were in ecstasy, he had the vision of an old bearded man in priestly clothes. He carried a golden staff in his

---

⁵⁴ L. Rothkrug, 'The "Odour of Sanctity" and the Hebrew Origins of Christian Relic Veneration', *Historical Reflections* 8 (1981), 95–142, is of no help for our purposes, despite its title.

⁵⁵ Egeria 16.5 (CSEL 38, 59). Translation based on H. Donner, *Pilgerfahrt*.

⁵⁶ H. Donner, *Pilgerfahrt*, 119 n. 105.

⁵⁷ P. Maraval, *Lieux saints*, 41.

⁵⁸ D. Vanderlinden, 'Revelatio Sancti Stephani' (BHZ 7850–7856), *Revue des Etudes Byzantines* 4 (1946), 178–217; critical edition 190–207. The customary text is found in PL 41, 807ff. See also J. Martin, 'Die revelatio S. Stephani und Verwandtes', *Historisches Jahrbuch* 77 (1958), 419–33. Sozomen, *Church history* IX.16.4 (GCS 50, 407) announces a description of this discovery, but the text breaks off before this.

hand and called him three times by name and commanded him, in Greek, to go to Aelia, i.e. Jerusalem, and to tell Bishop John: 'How long have we been locked in, and you do not open for us? And this, when we must reveal ourselves in the time of your priesthood! Open quickly for us the grave where our relics are neglected' (§ 2). The priest asked who he was and the man answers in §3: 'I am Gamaliel, who trained Paul the apostle of Christ and taught the law in Jerusalem. And he who is with me and lies in the eastern part of the grave, this is my Lord Stephen, who was stoned by the Jews and the high priests in Jerusalem because of belief in Christ.' The martyr's body had been left lying unburied, in order to be eaten by wild beasts. But he, Gamaliel, had caused the body to be taken secretly to his village Kephar Gamala ('which is translated as "Gamaliel's village"'), twenty miles from the city. There he caused him to be mourned for forty days and then buried in his grave. Next to him lay Nicodemus, who had been baptized. When they heard of it, the Jews removed him from his prominent position, excommunicated him and drove him out of the city. Gamaliel received him at his country estate, cared for him until his death and finally buried him beside Stephen. Also buried there was his son Abibas, who accepted baptism together with him. His wife Ethna and elder son Selemia, who did not want to become Christians, were buried at his wife's estate of Kephar Selemia.

In one version of the text (PL 41, 812), what follows is the discovery of his wife's grave, as confirmation of what Gamaliel has said. Then it is announced to Lucianus where he may find Stephen and those buried with him. 'You will find us on my property, which is now called in Syriac Delangabria or Debathalia, translated Property of the Men of God or the Warriors (of God).' In a further dream which urges haste – 'Do you not see what distress and drought there is in the whole world?' – Gamaliel gives directions for the identification of the coffins. The priest then tells John of Jerusalem his vision, and John claims for Jerusalem the protomartyr Stephen, 'who was the first to fight the wars of the Lord against the Jews'. Finally there follows the actual discovery of the grave.

What is striking in this discovery story, which exactly follows the literary genre of such stories,[59] is the prominent role of Gamaliel. Should we assume here a connection with Jewish Christian

---

[59] On this, see P. Maraval, *Lieux saints*, 43–7.

traditions and interests, as is occasionally asserted?[60] This is not impossible. But in order to be able to prove it, the role of Jewish witnesses, who played such an important part in the story of the Invention of the Cross, would need to be investigated on a wider basis.[61] Even if we should assume a Jewish Christian context, the question remains whether a tradition actually existed that saw Kephar Selemia as the grave of Gamaliel's elder son, and Kephar Gamala as the grave of Gamaliel himself.[62] For it is conceivable that the place-names were sufficient cause for the development of the legend, and that this was the occasion for inventing Selemia as a son of Gamaliel. If not only the story's motif comes from a Jewish Christian source, we should further ask whether the relics of Gamaliel and Nicodemus were then also venerated. Neither question can be answered.

E. D. Hunt also asks whether the story might not have a connection with the Patriarch Gamaliel, who in the same year 415 lost his *praefectura honoraria*.[63] Such an association cannot, of course, be entirely excluded, if the story was fixed in its extant form from the beginning, but cannot be proved. It would mean that the demotion of the most prominent Jew of the time raised associations with his ancestor of the same name, who plays a thoroughly positive role in the New Testament and is therefore suitable for Christian adoption. However, this role of the older Gamaliel is not new, and the discovery of Stephen's relics has a much more likely context in internal church affairs, particularly at the date given, than for us to think the conjunction of the degrading of one Gamaliel and the underlining of his ancestor's ecclesiastical role were more than coincidental.

Gamaliel's role in our story is comparable with his role in the *Gospel of Gamaliel*, where he serves as witness for the raising of a

---

[60] E.g. E. D. Hunt, *Holy Land Pilgrimage*, 215f.; in detail M. van Esbroeck, 'Jean II', who also stresses the analogy with the Invention of the Cross.

[61] Some of the traditions have now been investigated by O. Limor, 'Christian Tradition', but with the exception of the Invention of the Cross and the discovery of Stephen's grave they are all later than the period covered here.

[62] So E. D. Hunt, *Holy Land Pilgrimage*, 216. Two places are suggested for the location of Kephar Gamala, where these relics were found. One is about 25 km from Jerusalem on the road to Eleutheropolis, the second the same distance away, but northwest of Jerusalem and still in its territory. Only the second site fits all the other data: S. Mittmann, 'Chaphargam(ala) bei Heliopolis (Ba'albek)', *ZDPV* 91 (1975), 69–76; 71–3.

[63] E. D. Hunt, *Holy Land Pilgrimage*, 216.

dead man at Jesus' tomb.[64] In the *Gospel of Nicodemus*, preserved in the context of the *Acts of Pilate*,[65] Gamaliel also appears, but this time together with the high priests and scribes as one of Jesus' prosecutors, and later as a witness to the raising of dead men. Two sons of Simeon are raised from the dead by Jesus and are now in Arimathea. 'Then arose the chief priests Annas and Caiaphas, and Joseph and Nicodemus and Gamaliel and others with them, and went to Arimathaea and found the men of whom Joseph spoke.' They are brought to Jerusalem, into the synagogue, and the gates are barred. '... and the chief priests placed the Old Testament of the Jews in the midst and said to them: "We wish you to swear by the God of Israel and by Adonai and so speak the truth, how you arose and who raised you from the dead..."'[66] A second, Latin version of the text names three Galilean rabbis who watch Jesus' ascension and then report it.[67]

These and other texts in which Jews appear as witnesses would need to be systematically analysed for their picture of Jews. Until then it remains an open question whether Jewish Christian attitudes are indeed finding expression here, or whether simply Christian assertions about the time of Jesus are intended to be legitimated by mention of Jews who were contemporaries of Jesus. Certainly, in our story of the discovery of Stephen's relics, Gamaliel only appears as the legitimating witness, a figure as insubstantial as the Jewish witnesses to the Invention of the Cross of Jesus. There is certainly no mention of any veneration of Gamaliel's relics in this context; he has done his duty by giving evidence as a witness.

The internal church context of the discovery of the relics of

---

[64] See M.-A. van den Oudenrijn, *Gamaliel: Äthiopische Texte zur Pilatusliteratur*, Freiburg 1959. The work belongs in the category of Pilate literature and was probably written before the end of the fifth century, in Coptic. The work is written as devotional literature without a specific propagandistic aim, even though the 'hatred of Jews of this Christian writer, who chose as his "nom de plume" precisely one of the most famous rabbi's names of the past' (p. xxix), is conspicuous.

[65] The *Acts of Pilate* purport to be translated from the Hebrew. The Greek version is dated to 425, but could have older sources. The text attempts to lay the blame for Jesus' death on the Jews alone.

[66] *Gospel of Nicodemus* 17.1f.: E. Hennecke and W. Schneemelcher (eds.), *New Testament Apocrypha*, London 1963, vol. I, 471.

[67] Hennecke and Schneemelcher, *New Testament Apocrypha*, vol. I, 478. In vol. I, 462 § 14 the priest Phineës, the teacher Adas and the Levite Angaeus make their report.

Stephen and the others seems clear. It happens precisely at the time that the Synod of Lydda under the presidency of Bishop John acquits Pelagius, who had come under suspicion of heresy because he stressed the importance of human works against the traditional Christian doctrine of grace. If the discovery of the relics is intended to confirm the decision of the synod, although it did not formally accept the teaching Pelagius was accused of, that could certainly fit Jewish or Jewish Christian attitudes. Jewish witnesses would also fit in well, although they would tend to be rather embarrassing in questions of belief and religious practice.

The objection may of course be raised that according to the legend it was a *baptized* Jew, referring to attempts by Bishop John of Jerusalem to achieve a good relationship with the Jewish Christian minority in his congregation, as M. van Esbroeck thinks.[68] Since we have no knowledge of the importance and influence of Jewish Christian circles, or at least Judaizing groups, within the Christian church of Jerusalem, the role of Jews in these texts is hard to assess. Their function is uncertain, much remains unclear and open. Only a more comprehensive study of the texts could perhaps lead further. Perhaps it should be added, as not unimportant for the contemporary understanding of this story of the discovery of Stephen's relics with Gamaliel as witness, that in the year 418 the arrival of a relic of Stephen on the island of Minorca triggered the first large-scale forcible conversions of Jews.[69] Does the story perhaps have a stronger anti-Jewish potential than a present-day reader would like to believe?

In the same year as the relics of Stephen, the remains of the prophet Zechariah were found near Eleutheropolis, in Kephar Sacharia. Sozomen announces in his *Church history* that he will relate both of the discoveries – as a confirmation of the rule of

---

[68] M. van Esbroeck, 'Jean II', 125–34. At 101–5 he offers a translation of the Georgian tale of the martyrdom of Stephen, in which again Gamaliel buries his body.

[69] The only source is a letter of Severus of Minorca. A critical edition with extensive historical introduction is: *Severus of Minorca. Letter on the Conversion of the Jews*. Edited and translated by S. Bradbury, Oxford 1996; cf. F. Lotter, 'Die Zwangsbekehrung der Juden von Menorca um 418 im Rahmen der Entwicklung des Judenrechts in der Spätantike', *Historische Zeitschrift* 242 (1986), 291–326. More skeptical on the historical reliability of the text is G. Stemberger, 'Zwangstaufen von Juden im 4. bis 7. Jahrhundert – Mythos oder Wirklichkeit?' in C. Thoma et al. (eds.), *Judentum – Ausblicke und Einsichten* (*Festschrift* K. Schubert), Frankfurt 1993, 81–114, pp. 86–90.

Valentinian and Honorius by God –, but then tells only of the discovery of Zechariah's relics.[70] The prophet appears to a man in a dream and orders him to dig in a certain place. There he will find a double coffin, a container with water and two large, harmless snakes (snakes as guardians of graves are widespread in ancient mythology and also in rabbinic tradition!). The dig is successful: the prophet is found in priestly clothes, and at his feet the body of a child with a crown on his head. Priests and wise men are questioned as to the child, until Zechariah, abbot of the monastery near Gerar, accidentally discovers 'in an old Hebrew writing, not one used in the church' that it is the Jewish king Jehoash, who died soon after the prophet and was buried together with him. Here a Jewish witness is not necessary, because the Old Testament prophet himself appears and reveals the place of his burial; but the non-ecclesiastical ancient Hebrew writing has the same function.

Earlier, between 379 and 395,[71] the remains of the prophets Habakkuk and Micah were found according to a dream of Bishop Zebennos of Eleutheropolis;[72] a church was erected for Micah in Moresheth. The discovery of the relics of Samuel and Joseph, this latter taking over a Samaritan tradition, and not without resistance on the part of the Samaritans, has already been mentioned. For our purposes it must be stressed that living Jews never play the slightest part in all of these stories, even though Jewish localizations of the prophets which were taken over earlier must surely be significant. Jewish Christian influence cannot be ruled out, but remains unproven.

The export from Palestine of relics of Old Testament figures was probably rare at this early period; the translation of Samuel's relics to Constantinople is particularly well known. The most widespread relics from the Holy Land were not the remains of Biblical figures, but easily obtained and almost limitlessly available objects. Most important were pieces of the Holy Cross, which were already found all over the world at the beginning of the fifth century, whereby, as Paulinus of Nola remarks with wonder, the Holy Cross 'suffers no injury and remains as it were untouched'.[73]

---

[70] Sozomen, *Church history* IX.16f. (GCS 50, 407f.); cf. A. M. Schwemer, *Vitae Prophetarum* II, 172–5; 304f.

[71] P. Maraval, *Lieux saints*, 42. Cf. A. M. Schwemer, *Vitae Prophetarum* II, 30f.

[72] Sozomen, *Church history* VII.29.1–2 (GCS 50, 345).

[73] Paulinus of Nola, *ep.* 31.6 (CSEL 29, 274).

However, it did become necessary to guard the relic. Also popular was earth from the Holy Land.[74] For example, a martyrium in Tixter in Mauretania, dedicated in 359, possessed 'earth from the Promised Land, where Christ was born', as an inscription records. Augustine writes of a man called Hesperius, from near Hippo. While searching for help against damage caused by demons among his servants and animals, 'he hung up in his bedroom holy earth, brought by a friend from Jerusalem, where Christ was buried and rose on the third day, in order that he might not himself suffer damage'. When finally set free of the demons, he decided on the advice of Augustine and another bishop that the holy earth 'which he no longer wanted to keep in his bedroom, out of respect, should be buried elsewhere and become a place of prayer where Christians could come together to celebrate the liturgy'. Soon afterwards, Augustine continues, a lame young man who prayed at that place was healed.[75]

As well as earth from the Holy Land, particularly so-called *eulogiae*,[76] objects that had been brought into contact with the holy places, were brought back from Palestine as souvenirs. Above all, it was oil which had been brought to the Holy Sepulchre. Special little bottles were produced for this oil, which were often decorated with pictures of the pilgrim sites, which is why they are an important witness for the development of the holy places.

Altogether probably not much profit was to be made from the souvenir trade. What brought the profits was rather the general increase of tourism as a consequence of pilgrimage, and the gain principally went to the transport and hotel industries. Certainly a good deal of money also entered the country through pilgrims' donations; but the expenditure on providing for poor pilgrims must have been substantial. However the fact that the ultimate financial balance for the Holy Land was positive, especially for Jerusalem, follows from Jerome's (clearly polemically exaggerated) tirade against Bishop John of Jerusalem: 'you who overflow with riches and profit from the faith of the whole world'.[77]

---

[74] On this, see E. D. Hunt, *Holy Land Pilgrimage*, 129f.
[75] Augustine, *De civitate Dei* 22.8 (CC 48, 820).
[76] On this see A. Stuiber, *RAC* 6 (1966), 925ff.
[77] Jerome, *Contra Joannem Hier.* 14 (PL 23, 383).

5. The Monks

The emergence of monasticism in Palestine, which was of the greatest importance for the further religious development of the country, should be seen in close conjunction with the institution of pilgrimage.[78] Already before the pilgrimages attained large numbers, there existed in the south of the country settlements of monks that were independent of pilgrimage; here Hilarion, who came from Thavata near Gaza, began to live as a hermit near Gaza at the age of fifteen, after having been trained in Egypt, and years later founded a monastery, around 330. Epiphanius of Salamis, who was head of a monastery in Besanduk, near his home town of Eleutheropolis, probably belonged to his circle, until he was summoned to Cyprus as bishop. However, the majority of Palestinian monks were foreigners who had come as pilgrims to the Holy Land, given away their possessions there and remained as monks or nuns. Their centres were the Judaean desert, the area surrounding Jerusalem, the neighbourhood of Jericho, and also the Sinai desert (where the influence of Egyptian monastic culture was more clearly felt).

The first monk of Palestine is said to have been the Anatolian Chariton. He had suffered for the faith in Iconium before the end of the third century; then he went on pilgrimage to Jerusalem and settled as a hermit in a cave near the Fara spring, not far from the city. Some think this to have been around 275; however, his biography is so clearly characterized by the attempt to make Palestinian monasticism appear older than its beginnings in Egypt under Antony that the dates are scarcely reliable. But even if it was decades later, certainly the monasteries founded by him outside Jericho and near Herodion flourished in the fourth century.

However, the real increase of monasticism in Palestine began after Julian, when a regular Latin colony came into being on the Mount of Olives and in Bethlehem. Innocent from Rome, a high-ranking official under Constantius, settled as a monk on the Mount of Olives shortly after Julian's death. He was followed

---

[78] From the copious literature, see especially: Y. Hirschfeld, *The Judaean Desert Monasteries in the Byzantine Period*, New Haven/London 1992; J. Binns, *Ascetics and Ambassadors of Christ. The Monasteries of Palestine 314–631*, Oxford 1994; J. Patrich, *Sabas, Leader of Palestinian Monasticism. A Comparative Study in Eastern Monasticism, Fourth to Seventh Centuries*, Washington 1995.

shortly afterwards by Palladius from Galatia, who was later to write a history of the early monks. Another settler on the Mount of Olives, around 374, was Rufinus of Aquileia, who translated Eusebius' *Church history* into Latin. Next to his monastery Melania the Elder founded another for women. In 387, Paula and Eustochium came to Bethlehem with their companions and founded nunneries there, while Jerome built a monastery. Posidonius already had a monastery there, at the Shepherds' Fields; shortly after 380 he was joined by Germanus and John Cassian. Finally, in 417 Melania the Younger and her husband Pionius came to follow their monastic leanings on the Mount of Olives; Melania brought with her as private chaplain Gerontius, who later wrote her biography. These are only a few names from a constant stream of arrivals from the west, including many persons of the highest nobility and old-established wealth, who were able to afford the necessary investments for their monastic foundations.

The largely aristocratic monks with their intellectual leanings and literary ambitions stood in sharp contrast to the anti-intellectual tradition of the Syrian and Egyptian monks, which also characterized the indigenous Palestinian monasticism in the south of the country. Their attempts to interpret the Bible generally led them to adhere to the teachings of the great Palestinian exegete Origen, which smelt of heresy as far as the uneducated monks of southern Palestine, led by Epiphanius, were concerned. The resulting Origenist controversy was to split the Palestinian church for decades; since Jerome and his monks, surprisingly, took Epiphanius' part, the battle-lines ran right through the Latin colony.

The international composition of the Palestinian monastic community was also contributed to by many eastern immigrants, who mediated, so to speak, between the two groups. Armenians and Georgians, but also Cappadocians, played an important role in this respect. In 406 Euthymius, who came from Melitene in Lesser Armenia, had come to Wadi Fara as a monk. Later he settled with his friend Theoktistus at Wadi Mukellik by the Dead Sea, where he succeeded in converting an Arab tribe which had been expelled from Persia. Their sheikh, who took the baptismal name of Peter, was consecrated bishop of the tribe and was present as such at the council of Ephesus.[79] Euthymius

---

[79] See I. Shahîd, *Byzantium and the Arabs in the Fifth Century*, Washington 1989, 40–9; 180–4.

reorganized Palestinian monasticism and was thus instrumental in its later development under his pupil Sabas.

Euthymius' success in conversion was not at all an isolated case. While the Latin monks were scarcely concerned with pastoral work and lived more for study and contemplation, Hilarion, who had a great reputation for exorcizing demons, was already concerned for the Christianization of his home country. He appears to have had more success with the Bedouin tribes than with the pagan population of the cities. Another example is the monk Moses, who under Valens converted the Saracens to Christianity with their queen Mavia, becoming their bishop.[80] Christian mission, especially to the Bedouin tribes, was almost exclusively the work of the monks. But they also had great influence on the running of the Palestinian church in general; many of them became bishops. For example, Bishop John of Jerusalem was originally a monk, and also the later Bishop of Jerusalem, Juvenal. Porphyrius of Gaza was a hermit by the Jordan for years, before he settled in Jerusalem as a cobbler for reasons of health and soon became guardian of the Holy Cross and afterwards Bishop of Gaza. Three bishops (of Scythopolis, Jabneh and Madaba) also came from Euthymius' international monastic community – of the twelve first disciples four came from Melitene, three from Cappadocia, three from the Sinai, one from Antioch and only one from Palestine, from Tiberias. Thus the international character of the monastic community in Palestine had a decisive influence on the character of the church in general. The intellectual enrichment which it brought prevented from the outset the development of violent fanaticism such as characterized the uneducated monastic communities of Syria or Egypt. The pagan Eunapius complains contemptuously: 'Tyrannical power lay at that time in the hands of any man who wore a black robe and wanted to behave improperly in public.'[81]

Thus Palestinian monasticism was largely the product of the influx of pilgrims to the Holy Land. But its most famous representatives themselves became the object of countless pilgrims, who soon not only wanted to see in Palestine the holy places of

---

[80] On this I. Shahîd, *Byzantium and the Arabs in the Fourth Century*, Washington 1984, 138–201.

[81] Eunapius, *Vitae Sophistarum* VI.11.8. On the anti-intellectualism of the eastern monks, who made quite an ideal of it, see A. J. Festugière, *Ursprünge christlicher Frömmigkeit*, Freiburg 1963.

Biblical tradition, but also to meet the holy men in their monasteries. As was already clear from Egeria's pilgrim account, the monks gladly looked after the pilgrims and showed them the holy places, even inventing some themselves where there were not yet any.[82] More and more often, among the crowds of pilgrims were also monks from the other parts of the Roman Empire, for homelessness was an ascetic ideal at this period. For example, Gregory of Nyssa, who had in 381 himself been to the Holy Land, attempts in vain to discourage the Cappadocian monks from travelling to the Holy Land: 'If grace were greater in the sites of Jerusalem, there would be no sin among those who live there. But today there is no sin that men do not dare to practise there: fornication, adultery, theft, idolatry, poisoning, hatred, murder.'[83] The influx of travelling monks grew continually, special hostels had to be built for them at the holy places, and Jerome could only sigh, 'We are inundated with hordes of monks who hurry here from every corner of the world.'[84]

The numerical importance of the monastic movement is hard to estimate. However, by the end of the fourth century there must already have been thousands of monks. At the dedication of the church of Gaza in 408, according to the description in the *Vita Porphyrii*, every stranger who took part in the feast received a money donation of six obols, among them one thousand monks. Around 400, there are reports of about twenty monasteries on the Mount of Olives, with roughly eight hundred monks. We must also assume significant numbers in the monasteries of Bethlehem. The monks attempted to be autonomous, farming and working at ropemaking and plaiting, since these activities did not require too much concentration and did not disturb meditation. However, there were constant financial difficulties, especially in the intellectual Latin monastic settlement. For the monasteries felt themselves bound to take care of the poor pilgrims and provide hostels for them. Further, the charity of the rich pilgrims attracted crowds of professional beggars, who partly also became a burden on the monasteries. Thus it was a constant worry of Jerome's that Paula and Eustochium might spend their

---

[82] P. Maraval, *Lieux saints*, 60, even speaks of the 'caractère volontariste de la mise en place, à partir du IVe siècle, d'une géographie sacrée chrétienne'.
[83] Gregory of Nyssa, *ep.* 2.10, ed. G. Pasquali, Leiden 1959, 16.
[84] Jerome, *ep.* 66.14 (CSEL 54, 665).

enormous inheritance too quickly. It would then no longer have been possible to meet the monasteries' constant need of subsidies. So, despite the fact that it contributed to the success of the church in Palestine, the monastic life also brought a number of problems.

6. Criticism of Pilgrimage

It was not only the monastic movement that brought problems. Church and state propaganda for the holy places of Palestine continually swelled the numbers of pilgrims, so that they threatened to get out of control. A further increase was caused by the threat to the Roman west from the barbarian armies in the early fifth century. The refugees from the west were not pilgrims in the strict sense, but without the tradition of pilgrimage to the Holy Land that had grown up by now, surely so many of them would hardly have chosen precisely Palestine as their goal. Jerome writes as a witness of this movement when he describes how 'holy Bethlehem, to which once aristocrats of both sexes streamed with all their riches, now daily takes in beggars.' A little later he explains the delay to work on his *Commentary on Ezekiel* by the 'flight of the westerners and the overcrowding of the holy places', and the care for the poor that this entailed.[85] But if the influx was a heavy burden on the charitable institutions of the Holy Land, especially the monasteries, on the other hand a good deal of money belonging to rich refugees came into the country, so that overall the wealth and attractiveness of the country rather increased.

M. Avi-Yonah emphasizes that the enormous sums that came into the country with the pilgrims or refugees were largely unproductive. There was no unemployment, the population increased and with it demand for goods; the renewal of the walls increased security in the cities. However, in the long term the negative consequences of heavy dependence on foreign capital could not be ignored: they produced 'a quick economic boom, which was followed by a severe crisis'.[86]

---

[85] Jerome, *Comm. Ezek.*, Preface to Book 3 (CC 55, 91) and to Book 7 (CC 55, 277).
[86] M. Avi-Yonah, 'The Economics', 49.

Occasionally the impression arises that the movement soon alarmed those who had stood at the beginning. Along with the real pilgrims came many dubious characters, rich and poor. For example, Jerome writes around 394 of a rich pilgrim and the rumours she aroused: 'There was whispering about her age, dress, posture, walk, the carelessness in the choice of companions, the tasty banquets, the royal pomp of a Nero and the sexual relations of Sardanapalus.'[87] He writes to Paulinus of Nola around 395: 'If the sites of the Cross and Resurrection were not in a very famous city, in which there is a magistrate, a military garrison, whores, actors, clowns and everything that tends to occur in cities', then Jerusalem might be desirable. But 'people come here from all over the world. The city is full of people of every kind, and there is such a tumult of people of both sexes.'[88]

Jerome draws his conclusion: 'Having been in Jerusalem is not praiseworthy, but having lived virtuously in Jerusalem. That city, yes that one, is to be sought after, not the one that killed the prophets and spilt the blood of Christ, but the one that rejoices in the streams of water, that lies on a hill and cannot be hid.' The saintly Hilarion is an example to him: 'Although he came from Palestine and lived in Palestine, he saw Jerusalem only on a single day. He did not want to appear to be contemptuous of the holy places because of their nearness, nor to wish to lock God in a single place.'[89] If at the beginning of the movement the Christian Jerusalem could appear by contrast to the Jewish Jerusalem as the true promised city, it now appears that it is not here either, the goal of the search is still transcendent.

---

[87] Jerome, *ep*. 54.13 (CSEL 54, 479f.).
[88] Jerome, *ep*. 58.4 (CSEL 54, 533).
[89] Jerome, *ep*. 58.2f. (CSEL 54, 529–31).

V

Synagogue Building

The previous chapter could almost give the impression that no Jews lived in the Holy Land in the fourth century, or at least that the lives of Christians and Jews in Palestine were lived in completely separate areas. A very different impression is given by the letter with which the Synod of Jerusalem anwered a letter of the Patriarch Theophilus of Alexandria, around 400: Palestine is almost entirely free of heretics, apart from a few who adhere to the errors of Apollinarius (who taught in particular that in Jesus the Logos replaced the human soul, which seemed to detract from his true humanity).

> However, if only by means of the intercession of the saints we were not disturbed by the Jewish snakes, the unbelievable stupidity of the Samaritans and the quite openly godless deeds of the pagans, whose very numerous crowds completely close their ears to the truth of the sermons and, since they surround the flock of Christ like lions, cause us no little worry and trouble![1]

Thus around 400 Jews, Samaritans and pagans are still serious opponents of Christianity. Caution is therefore necessary in accepting the hypothesis of a swift Christianization of Palestine, as supported, for example, by H. Donner: 'In the decade between 325 and 335 the face of Palestine changed: it became a Christian country and Jerusalem a Christian city.'[2]

The continuing life of Samaritans and pagans in fourth-century Palestine will be discussed in later chapters. However, we have

---

[1] Jerome, *ep.* 93 (CSEL 55, 155). The letter of Theophilus is in Jerome as *ep.* 92.
[2] H. Donner, *Pilgerfahrt*, 29.

most evidence for the continuing life of Judaism. Here the synagogue finds will take the central place as archaeological evidence; for they can document indisputably the spread, life and economic power of the Jewish communities. The wealth of datable evidence, only the most important of which can be discussed in detail, naturally only includes a fraction of the synagogues that actually existed at the time. Many buildings for which we have archaeological evidence cannot be more precisely dated within the Byzantine period; even more synagogues must have vanished without trace in the course of the centuries; and year by year more synagogues are excavated. Thus the picture offered here can only represent a small section.

The greater part of the archaeological evidence for synagogues from the fourth and early fifth centuries is to be found in the regions of the north, the Tetrakomia and Gaulanitis, which were not organized in a city structure, and in the city territories of Tiberias, Sepphoris and Beth Gubrin (Eleutheropolis). However, we should surely also expect significant Jewish communities in the coastal areas, even if as yet there is little archaeological evidence.

Until very recently, the classical division of synagogues into three types appeared to be a secure basis for dating even buildings that otherwise offered no clues as to date. According to this, in the second to third centuries the Galilean synagogues were built in basilica style, with their façade oriented on Jerusalem; in the fourth century the 'broad house' type was built, largely in the south of the country; later, basilica buildings with an apse oriented on Jerusalem gained general acceptance. However, after the recent excavations of Capernaum, Meiron and so on, this division can no longer be maintained, and a dating can only be held to be proven when exact and detailed stratigraphic studies have been undertaken. Much greater regional differentiation than has previously been the case is also necessary. But as yet only a few synagogues have been thoroughly investigated, and the results published, in accordance with the new point of view.[3]

---

[3] For a general overview, see especially F. Hüttenmeister, *Die jüdischen Synagogen*; M. J. Chiat, *Handbook*; R. Hachlili, *Ancient Jewish Art*; D. Urman and P. V. M. Flesher, *Ancient Synagogues*.

1. Upper Galilee and the Golan

In Upper Galilee, the Tetrakomia of the period, the existence of approximately fifteen synagogue buildings can be proved for the fourth century. Several of them have been recently subjected to thorough archaeological examination.

(a) The village of *Meiron* in Upper Galilee possessed one of the largest Palestinian synagogues in the basilica style. At the highest point of the hill on which the village lies, the base for the synagogue was hewn out of the rock, which also formed the western wall of the building. The north and east walls were probably built with rough stones. Cut stone blocks were only used for the south-facing façade of the building, i.e. facing Jerusalem, which was fronted by a shallow portico with six columns. The synagogue hall itself had an interior measurement of 27.5 × 13.6 m, and was subdivided by two rows of eight columns each.

E. Meyers, the excavator, assumes that building work went on for decades; as well as local workmen, craftsmen and artists from further afield were probably employed.[4] The building was erected in the second half of the third or beginning of the fourth century, a time when the village expanded and its prosperity also grew, which was based principally on olive production and oil exports. The coins found in Meiron show that it traded mainly with Tyre, the most important import and export port of the eastern Mediterranean, or more generally with towns on the Mediterranean coast.[5] A large number of coins from Hippos, on the eastern side of the Sea of Galilee, show that Meiron was also in close trading contact with this town – although there are remarkably few coins from Jewish Tiberias. Perhaps Meiron obtained grain and fish from Hippos in exchange for its olives.

The fact that some people in Meiron achieved a certain degree of prosperity is shown, among other indications, by the 'patrician's house', so called by the excavators, a building with an upper storey and courtyard, as well as several rooms. Although it hardly has more room than a modern one- to two-apartment house, it stands out among the other village houses in Meiron.

---

[4] E. M. Meyers, *Meiron*.
[5] Meyers offers a correction of his hypothesis of Tyrian influence in Meiron in 'Galilean Regionalism: A Reappraisal', in W. S. Green (ed.), *Approaches to Ancient Judaism* V, Atlanta 1985, 115–31; see also D. Adan-Bayewitz, *Common Pottery in Roman Galilee. A Study of Local Trade*, Ramat Gan 1993, 244–7.

The high quality pottery ware and the relatively large number of glass vessels found in the house also speak for the sophisticated lifestyle of its inhabitants.

In a back room of the 'patrician's house', burnt food was discovered – grain, beans and walnuts. Since the jars it was found in showed no trace of burning, it must have been stored there when it was already burnt. But what reason could there have been for keeping charred food? M. Goodman interprets it as *heqdesh*, things devoted to the Temple (e.g. by a vow). At a time when the Temple no longer existed, such things had to be removed from human use by other means; so they were presumably burned deliberately and then stored in the jars.[6]

This may indicate a conservative religious attitude on the part of the inhabitants of the house. That is the interpretation of E. Meyers regarding the presence of a ritual bath or miqveh, and the burial customs at Meiron, especially the fact that there are many secondary burials and associated items, such as an unused inkwell (mentioned in Semachot 8.7 as a burial object for a dead bridegroom). However, it would be going too far to deduce from this that the rabbinate had a decisive influence here, since these are basic forms of popular religion which go back to the time before 70.

However, the picture of modest prosperity – during the final phase of the general economic crisis! – is dimmed by the bone findings in a large burial chamber near Meiron, which was in use throughout the Roman period until approximately 360. Here 197 people are buried, mostly as secondary burials. Thus the building is a kind of ossuary. Probably all the bodies belonged to a single extended family. Medical examination of the bones showed common skeletal anomalies, which suggests a group with a strong degree of in-breeding. Infant mortality was very high, at about 50 per cent. Iron and protein deficiencies are common, as is tooth decay, suggesting that bread represented the most significant part of the diet. Altogether the results point to frequent epidemics or poor living conditions.[7]

Of course the question remains to what extent it is legitimate to draw general conclusions from this burial-house regarding the

---

[6] M. Goodman in E. M. Meyers, *Meiron*, 71f. A very critical response is G. Foerster, *IEJ* 37 (1987), 267f.

[7] P. Smith and E. Bornemann in E. M. Meyers, *Meiron*, 118.

population of Meiron, or to make use of the results for a particular phase of its history, as E. Meyers does when he infers from it a cause for the decline of the village.

The decline of Meiron in the years around 360 to 365 is mysterious, given that at this time the neighbouring towns of Gush Halav and Teqoa continue to prosper. Initially E. Meyers and J. F. Strange adopted S. Lieberman's hypothesis, that the decline of Meiron was 'to be attributed to the harshness of the taxes imposed by the Roman provincial authorities, especially once inflation and its devaluing of local currencies forced them to go over to a system of taxation in kind. Without doubt olive oil and other products were delivered to the authorities in payment, calculated according to the total population, and also as supplies for the Roman army.' Thus smaller towns, despite an equally high production of olives, were less affected by the tax than larger ones. This finally led to a general decision to emigrate on the part of the inhabitants of Meiron.[8]

By contrast, in the final report of the excavations the authors suggest that the town was abandoned only gradually, and lived on even after 360, in a modest way. There were also, they say, additional factors that led to the abandoning of the settlement: the drought of 362/363, the local earthquake of May 363 and a further earthquake in 365 which had effects in the entire Mediterranean area. At that time the synagogue was severely damaged, or even destroyed: 'a population at the end of its tether was simply too poor and discouraged to repair it.'

This argument is not conclusive, since elsewhere in the report, as a result of a geological survey, it is stated that Meiron is not susceptible to earthquakes. A quake could only have caused superficial damage to plaster and rooftiles. Rather, the destruction of the synagogue is to be attributed to the fact that its roof was not kept in good repair after the inhabitants had left the village, and there was water and weather damage.[9] The interpretation of the protein and iron deficiencies in the skeletons as proof for the increase of sickness in economically difficult times, which is offered in this context,[10] is a questionable use of these results for a specific period, the last years of Meiron.

[8] E. M. Meyers, *Meiron*, 160.
[9] E. M. Meyers, *Meiron*, 17.
[10] E. M. Meyers, *Meiron*, 161.

Finally, the reference to the revolt against Gallus in 352 (see next chapter) is also only a conjecture. The revolt 'might very well have promoted sympathy for the rebels at a time of worsening relations with the Roman authorities and increasing pressure of taxation. Of course a conservative, free of images and fundamentally religious community would have welcomed the opportunity to escape a situation vis-a-vis the Roman authorities that could scarcely have improved.' But then E. Meyers writes, even about the last third of the century, after Julian (it was no accident that his Temple project followed the revolt against Gallus so immediately): 'A period in which Palestinian Judaism consolidated its communities and renewed their holy sites, as in Gush Halav or Capernaum ... Palestinian Judaism seems at this period to have been full of energy and self-confidence to a previously undreamt-of degree.'[11]

The attempt to explain the decline of Meiron leads to hypotheses that are mutually exclusive. The bone findings are not necessarily to be attributed precisely to the final phase of Meiron. Such high and one-sided taxation at this period would first require proof, especially since the conditions that caused the earlier above-average prosperity apparently had not changed. The earthquake explanation also remains confused, and the assertion of the community's religious conservatism would also need more definite proof.[12] Reference to the revolt against Gallus only introduces another unknown variable to the debate. Thus as regards the decline of Meiron more questions remain open than answers are offered. Perhaps an overall view together with other archaeological facts may lead to a more conclusive explanation.

(b) Meiron's neighbour, *Khirbet Shema'*, in rabbinic times probably Teqoa, was apparently a settlement that was closely linked with Meiron and dependent on it.[13] Only from the late

---

[11] E. M. Meyers, *Meiron*, 161.

[12] On the difficulty of the archaeological utilization of earthquakes, see K. W. Russell, 'The Earthquake Chronology'. He has no earthquake at all in his list for 365. He also stresses the difficulty of differentiating earthquake damage from that resulting from war action, for example, and thus of differentiating between the consequences of the revolt against Gallus and those of the earthquake of 363. We will encounter this difficulty in other cases also.

[13] E. Meyers, A. T. Kraabel and J. F. Strane, *Ancient Synagogue Excavations at Khirbet Shema', Upper Galilee, Israel 1970–1972*, Durham, NC, 1976, 15: 'a semi-detached satellite settlement of Meiron'; cf. E. Meyers, *NEAE* IV, 1359–61.

third century was it an independent town, and built its own synagogue. This was a 'broad house' synagogue, the first archaeologically established example of this building type in northern Palestine (later the synagogue of Nabratein offered another example). As mentioned above, this type of synagogue used to be thought characteristic of the south of the country. The synagogue was built into the hillside. It was entered from a platform on the western side. Inside, a stair led down to the main part of the prayer room, which measured 11 × 15 m and was divided by two rows of four columns each. Against its southern long wall was a podium (*bema*) for reading the Torah (perhaps only in the second phase of building).

Originally the synagogue was built in a mixed style; most of the walls were composed of roughly hewn stones, more carefully worked blocks were only rarely used. It has been suggested that the synagogue was destroyed in the earthquake of 306.[14] It was certainly rebuilt soon afterwards, on the same plan, but in a still simpler style. With the exception of a few cut stones around the northern gate, only undressed stone was used. Only the lower part of the western wall was cut from the living rock.

What is unique in this synagogue, which was probably destroyed in the earthquake of 419[15] – the latest coin found here dates from 408 – is the division of the interior, occasioned by the steepness of the terrain. On the west, or entrance, side, there is a gallery, from which a stair led down to the main room. Under the gallery was a small room, painted in colour, which served as a repository for the Torah shrine. From it there was access to a hardly larger room under the stairs, probably a genizah for Torah scrolls that were no longer in use. In the southeastern corner of the building there was a ritual bath, which was probably replaced in the second building phase by a larger miqveh outside the synagogue. Adjoining the synagogue to the north was another building, which is explained as a house of study (*beth ha-midrash*) and guest-house.

Altogether Teqoa gives the impression of being a simple Jewish village of a certain prosperity. This was probably based, as in Meiron, on the production of olives and oil, which was mainly

---

[14] The earthquake attested in Eusebius' *Chronicle* for Tyre and Sidon is dated only in PG. A date around 303 is more likely to be correct: K. W. Russell, 'The Earthquake Chronology', 42.

[15] On the earthquake of 419 see K. W. Russell, 'The Earthquake Chronology', 42f.

sold to Tyre or the Mediterranean coast in general, as the coins show here too. The fourth-century coins mostly come from Antioch – apparently minting had now ceased in Tyre; then towards the end of the fourth century coins from Alexandria increase. Since there are no coins from approximately 425 to the end of the fifth century, we must assume that the village was abandoned after the earthquake of 419 – still half a century after Meiron, the principal town. Here too the question remains of why it was abandoned and where the inhabitants went.

(c) About three and a half kilometres north of Meiron is the synagogue of *Safsaf*, which has not yet been investigated in detail. Since only a lintel stone from the third to fourth century has survived, the building cannot be identified as a synagogue with absolute certainty. However, the town of *Gush Halav*, about five kilometres north of Meiron, has been carefully investigated in recent years. The town is probably the old Gischala, home of John of Gischala, who led four hundred Zealots in the war against Rome and was an opponent of Josephus (*BJ* II 575, 585–590, 593f., 614–625; *Vita* 44f., 84–113, 122f., 132).

Gush Halav may have been the administrative centre of the Tetrakomia. Only isolated architectural fragments from the late second to early fourth centuries remain of the upper of its two synagogues; the lower synagogue was excavated by E. Meyers' team.[16] The building was erected after 250 in the basilica style. The main room measured approximately 14 × 11 m, and was subdivided by two rows of four columns each. Together with the porticos on the north, west and east sides the complex covered an area of about 306 m². The main entrance was on the south side, where the *bema* with the Torah shrine was also located. Behind a further entrance at the north-west a stair led downwards, which necessitated a gallery with two further columns, as in Teqoa. Only the southern façade was made of cut stone; the lower side of the lintel was adorned with an eagle relief.

In Gush Halav too, which lay on the road to Tyre, many Tyrian coins attest its economic orientation on that city. The synagogue was repeatedly destroyed in the fourth and fifth centuries –

---

[16] E. M. Meyers, C. Meyers and J. F. Strange, *Excavations at the Ancient Synagogue of Gush Halav*, Winona Lake 1990. E. Netzer, 'Review of the Synagogues at Gush Halav and Khirbet Shema' [Hebrew]', *EI* 25 (1996), 450–5, holds that the building phase described by Meyers as the second phase was in fact the only one, although there were several alterations.

presumably in the earthquakes of 306, 362–365 and 447. It was renovated each time, and only left in ruins after the great earthquake of 551 (Gush Halav lies on a fault line with its epicentre at Safed). The regular rebuilding points to lasting economic prosperity which continued long after Meiron and Teqoa were abandoned. Perhaps it was a relevant factor that the economy of Gush Halav was not only centred on olives, but also dairy farming, as the name of the place indicates. Fine late Roman ceramics from Cyprus, North Africa and Antioch, as well as a well-preserved mausoleum (second to fourth century) underline the impression of continuing prosperity.

(d) Approximately three kilometres north-west of Gush Halav is *Barʿam*, a village that also possessed two synagogues. They are usually dated to the third century because of their 'early Galilean' type. But according to more recent excavations, particularly in Capernaum, they could also come from a later period.[17] About four kilometres east of Gush Halav is the synagogue of *Dalton*, probably also from this period, and three and a half kilometres north of that is *Alma*, where synagogue inscriptions from the third century have been found. Finally, a little to the east of Alma, in *Khirbet Marus*, which is probably the Meroth mentioned in Josephus (*BJ* II.573), a synagogue has been excavated since 1981. Its first building phase dates from the end of the fourth or early fifth century. The synagogue, whose interior measurements are 11.4 × 17.9 m, was divided into three aisles by two rows of three pillars each. In front of the entrances on the south side was a portico and a large courtyard, which also surrounded the entire eastern long wall. The floor was of plaster and was only later replaced by a mosaic.[18]

Between Dalton and Safed is *Nabratein*, the Talmudic Kephar Nevoraia, whose synagogue has also been re-examined by E. Meyers' team.[19] The first synagogue was built here after the Bar Cochba Revolt. A larger synagogue was built on its site around

---

[17] R. Jacoby, *The Synagogues of Barʿam (Jerusalem Index of Jewish Art)*, Jerusalem 1987, gives as dates '3C?/5C?' respectively. N. Avigad, *NEAE* I, 147–9, still assumes the third century, without discussing it.

[18] Z. Ilan, 'The Synagogue and Study House at Meroth', in Urman and Flesher, *Ancient Synagogues* I, 256–88.

[19] E. M. Meyers, J. F. Strange and C. Meyers, 'Second Preliminary Report on the 1981 Excavations at en-Nabratein, Israel', *BASOR* 246 (1982), 35–54; idd., 'The Ark of Nabratein – A First Glance', *BA* 44 (1981), 237–43; E. M. Meyers, *NEAE* III, 1077–79.

250 (measuring approx. 11 × 14 m), containing, by the western *bema*, a Torah shrine supported by two leaping stone lions. The smaller, eastern *bema* was perhaps used for the priestly blessing. After the earthquake of 306 the synagogue had to be restored, whereby the lions from the Torah shrine were used as filler. In the middle of the fourth century, perhaps in the earthquake of 363, this synagogue too was destroyed. It was rebuilt only in the sixth century; the dedication inscription gives the date 564. The rebuilding was on a bigger scale: 11 × 17 m, with two rows of four columns each; the entrance was still situated in the south wall). This synagogue continued in use into the Islamic period. Architectural fragments found approximately 250 metres away from it could come from a further synagogue of the same period.

The fact that the synagogues of Meiron and Nabratein, and probably also the towns themselves (at least to a great extent), were abandoned after the earthquake of 363, may perhaps be explained by the remaining population's having transferred to the larger centre of Gush Halav, which continued to flourish for another two centuries after the earthquake. As far as Meiron is concerned, until the earthquake of 419 the neighbouring village of Teqoa was also a possible choice. Both villages are approximately an hour's walk away from Gush Halav; care of the olive groves did not require a regular presence, and could also be continued from a distance. However, after its destruction in the earthquake of 551 the synagogue of Gush Halav was not rebuilt; instead the synagogue of Nabratein was rebuilt, as the inscription documents. Such a direct association of the fate of these three towns must of course remain hypothetical, and could only be verified by more extensive investigations. In any event, the present stand of the excavations' findings resists any standardized explanations.

Altogether the analysis of the synagogue finds mentioned here, which may still be supplemented by others,[20] shows that in the fourth century rural Upper Galilee had a strongly Jewish population. Even taking the hilly terrain into account, the distance from one synagogue to the next is hardly ever greater than an hour's walk. The material expenditure on these

---

[20] Further synagogues are Sa'sa, about 4 km east of Gush Halav; perhaps Safed; Kephar Hanania, 9 km south-west of Safed: here there were perhaps even two synagogues, see Z. Ilan, *EI* 19 (1987), 184–6; 1 km west of it Beer Sheba; 3.5 km from that ar-Rama; and Jesud ha-Ma'ala on the south-western shore of Lake Hule (see A. Biran and Y. Shoham, *EI* 19 (1987), 199–207 [Hebrew]).

synagogue buildings is hard to estimate, and perhaps quite modest by today's standards. Nevertheless, E. Meyers' conclusion remains valid: 'The great flowering of Jewish culture in precisely this period (i.e. in post-Constantinian Palestine) – which is generally held to be a time of want and growing tension between Jews and Christians – appears to suggest that the restrictive legislation against Jews had a far more limited effect than had previously been thought.'[21]

(e) The same impression arises east of the Jordan, only a few kilometres from Nabratein and the other towns, in the *Golan Heights*. The results of the surveys to date, and of a few excavations, have recently been published.[22] However, the interpretation of the finds is still a matter of fierce controversy. About twenty-five sites have been definitively identified as synagogues by means of building remains, architectural fragments or inscriptions; but only a few have been systematically excavated. D. Urman is of the opinion that soon after the Bar Cochba Revolt Jews migrated to the Golan from Galilee, and that the growth of the Jewish communities was only briefly slowed by the effects of the Gallus revolt. According to him, the synagogues are to be dated to the third to sixth centuries. He relies for this mainly on the buildings' typology, rabbinic texts and a few inscriptions which name rabbis of the second and third centuries. By contrast, Z. U. Ma'oz and others believe that the immigration only began in the fourth century, and that the synagogues are to be dated from the middle of the fifth century, to which especially the ceramic and coin findings of the few excavated sites point, in their opinion.

Only the most important sites will be mentioned here, where at least the ground plan is known. Such is the case for *ed-Dikke*, on the east bank of the Jordan (three kilometres before it enters the Sea of Galilee). There was a brief excavation here in 1905; today the remains can no longer be seen on the surface, and new excavations have not yet taken place. The prayer room, measuring approx. 11 × 14 m, was divided into three aisles by two rows of four columns each. The datings vary between the third and fifth centuries.[23]

---

[21] E. Meyers, *Khirbet Shema'* (n. 13 above), 260.
[22] D. Urman, 'Public Structures and Jewish Communities in the Golan Heights', in Urman and Flesher, *Ancient Synagogues* II, 373–617; R. C. Gregg and D. Urman, *Jews, Pagans, and Christians*; Z. U. Ma'oz, *NEAE* II, 534–46.
[23] See the various hypotheses reported by Urman in Urman and Flesher II, 503–9; also Z. U. Ma'oz, *NEAE* II, 540f.

En Nashut was excavated in 1978. The building (interior measurements 10.45 × 9.35 m) was divided into three aisles by two rows of three columns. Benches lined three of the walls. The entrance was on the south side, to the left of which a podium for the Torah shrine is assumed to have existed. Because of the coins under the floor and the threshold, the excavator, Z. U. Ma'oz, takes the date of construction to be in the middle of the fifth century. D. Urman would prefer to interpret the findings as the renovation of an earlier synagogue (for which there are, however, no archaeological signs), and to see the excavated room, because of its small size, not as a prayer room but rather as a *beth midrash*.[24]

About two and a half kilometres south of En Nashut is *Qasrin*, whose particularly impressive synagogue (15.4 × 18 m; two rows of six columns each, a double row of basalt benches along all four walls) has repeatedly been the object of excavations since 1971. D. Urman, who led the first excavations, dates the earliest building to the third century. During renovations in the middle of the fourth century, according to Urman, the original simple earth floor was replaced by a mosaic floor, and a *bema* was erected against the south wall, which faced Jerusalem. The building complex was in use until the thirteenth century, with several renovations. By contrast, Z. U. Ma'oz, who led later excavations at Qasrin, assumes that the first synagogue was not built before the end of the fourth century, more likely in the fifth century. He also takes the first building to have been rather smaller (15.2 × 15.3 m); the complex was abandoned after the earthquake of 749, according to him, and only renovated in the thirteenth century as a mosque.[25]

These examples, to which others could be added, show clearly how contentious the dating is of the buildings which have been found to date. The later date appears to have the better arguments, but final clarification can only be expected when all the excavations in the Golan Heights are fully published.

---

[24] Z. U. Ma'oz, *NEAE* II, 412–14; D. T. Ariel, 'Coins from the Synagogue at 'En Nashut', *IEJ* 37 (1987), 147–57; D. Urman in Urman and Flesher II, 439–47.

[25] Z. U. Ma'oz, *NEAE* IV, 1219–22; D. Urman in Urman and Flesher II, 463–81. Urman, 'Jewish Inscriptions', 513, prefers to speak of Jewish public buildings, and only to use the name of synagogue in cases where this is clear (thus also in Urman and Flesher, *passim*). In Qasrin he assumes, following an inscription, that the room was used for religious community meals (p. 533).

However, it is an undisputed fact that in this region, which had very close links with the neighbouring Tetrakomia across the Jordan, there was already a significant Jewish settlement in the fourth century.[26]

2. Lower Galilee: The City Territories of Sepphoris and Scythopolis

(a) The Jewish centre in the territory of Sepphoris was for a long time *Beth Shearim*, 18 km southeast of Haifa.[27] The village was probably a royal possession as early as the Hasmonean period; certainly in the first century it was at the heart of the property of Berenice, Agrippa I's daughter (Josephus, *Vita* 119). Around 200, the Romans apparently gave it to Jehuda ha-Nasi as a state leasehold. The patriarch made the village into the seat of his administration (the 'Sanhedrin') and of the rabbinic school. And, although he had spent the last years of his life in Sepphoris, he was buried in Beth Shearim. Because of this, Beth Shearim became the preferred burial site for many Jews, as it were a replacement for the Mount of Olives, which they had not had access to for decades. Many Jews were buried here in the following century and a half, among them many from the Diaspora. The heyday of this place was in the first decades of the third century. From the beginning of the fourth century the

---

[26] See also C. M. Dauphin and J. J. Schonfield, 'Settlements of the Roman and Byzantine Periods on the Golan Heights, Preliminary Report on Three Seasons of Survey (1979–1981), *IEJ* 33 (1983), 189–206. Z. U. Ma'oz, 'Comments on Jewish and Christian Communities in Byzantine Palestine', *PEQ* 117 (1985), 59–68, concludes from various finds that the villages in the Golan Heights, and Palestine in general, by contrast to the cities, were inhabited exclusively either by Jews or Christians; according to this, the northwestern part of the Golan Heights was exclusively settled by Jews, while the Christian villages were in the south or north-east. But C. M. Dauphin, 'Jewish and Christian Communities in the Roman and Byzantine Gaulanitis: A Study of Evidence from Archaeological Surveys', *PEQ* 114 (1982), 129–42, interprets the evidence as showing Jews and Christians living together. R. C. Gregg and D. Urman, *Jews, Pagans and Christians*, 289–310, now also argue for this from the inscriptions in the Golan Heights.

[27] B. Mazar, *Beth She'arim I: The Catacombs I–IV*, Jerusalem ²1957; M. Schwabe and B. Lifshitz, *Beth She'arim II: The Greek Inscriptions*, Jerusalem 1967; N. Avigad, *Beth She'arim III: The Catacombs 12–23*, Jerusalem 1971 (all volumes in Hebrew).

quality of the buildings begins to decline. In the middle of the fourth century the town was destroyed; whether this should be ascribed to the revolt against Gallus, or to the earthquake of 363, is not certain.[28] To a small extent the catacombs continued in use to the sixth century.[29]

The synagogue of Beth Shearim measured 28 × 15 m, much larger than those mentioned so far. In addition, there was a 7 m wide forecourt and an extensive terrace in front of that. The building was erected in the basilica style of the early third century; the principal room, which was subdivided by two rows of eight columns each, had a raised *bema* against the rear wall. In the early fourth century, the central entrance was closed, probably to make room for a Torah niche. The building was composed of beautifully cut ashlar blocks and had a marble floor. The interior walls were painted in colour in the early fourth century, and marble panels with inscriptions were fastened on them, sixteen of them in Greek and only one in Hebrew.

Another large basilica (40 × 15 m) stood about 300 m west of the synagogue. It was built in the early third century and perhaps first served as the seat of the Patriarch's administration. However, it was later modified and then probably used as a private house in the fourth century. A large coin hoard was found in this house, mainly with coins of Constantine and Constantius; the newest coin was struck in 351. The ash layer above it shows that Beth Shearim was destroyed not long afterwards.

The 23 catacombs of Beth Shearim contain hundreds of graves. Their inscriptions are largely Greek, with only a few Hebrew inscriptions; Palmyrene and Aramaic inscriptions are also found. The bodies buried here come not only from Palestine, but from the whole Diaspora of the period: Syria, Phoenicia, Mesopotamia, Arabia, Asia Minor, North Africa and Europe. An exact analysis of which of these graves and inscriptions belong in the fourth century does not yet exist. It could offer valuable insights into relations with diaspora Jews of the period.

---

[28] K. W. Russell, 'The Earthquake Chronology', 51, sees B. Mazar's connection of the destruction of Beth Shearim with the revolt against Gallus as an example for the uncertainty of interpreting archaeological evidence if wars and earthquakes occur so close together. The layer of ash found at Beth Shearim could also point to a fire following an earthquake, as is often attested elsewhere.

[29] See F. Vitto, 'Byzantine Mosaics at Beth She'arim: New Evidence for the History of the Site', *Atiqot* 28 (1996), 115–46.

The decline of Beth Shearim began around the middle of the third century, and was presumably connected with the transfer of the patriarchate and its institutions to Tiberias. This probably explains why Beth Shearim never really recovered after the catastrophic fire; but it also shows that we cannot generalize from this case.

(b) *Sepphoris*, five kilometres north-west of Nazareth, with the Greek name Diocaesarea, must have been an important Jewish centre in the early third century, as the seat of the patriarch. Extensive excavations have been undertaken here since 1983. In 1993 a synagogue was discovered in the northern part of the town (20.7 × 8 m). A long, narrow nave (16 × 5.6 m) is separated from a single, very narrow side aisle to the north by a row of five columns. An entrance hall to the east opens onto the street at the side. Almost the entire west side of the main room is taken up by the platform for the Torah shrine. Mosaics cover the main and side aisle; in the latter they show geometric patterns containing Aramaic inscriptions to the donors, while in the main aisle figures are depicted. At the entrance a few remains apparently represent Gen. 18, the announcement of a son for Abraham. The sacrifice of Isaac (Gen. 22) follows, in two sections. The large central section shows the sun chariot surrounded by the zodiac, which is bordered by a Greek inscription to the donor, and the seasons. This is followed by two strips showing a motif that had hitherto been unknown in synagogue art, the sacrifices in the Temple (Num. 28), the table of the shewbread and a basket with the first fruits. In the section directly in front of the Torah shrine, two lions flank an inscription, largely destroyed. The explanatory texts in the mosaic are partly in Greek, partly in Hebrew. If the excavators' suggested date in the early fifth century is not setting the building in too early a period, this find just comes within the period we are considering here. In that case, it would be of the highest importance not only for Sepphoris, but for the history of synagogue art in general.[30]

---

[30] Preliminary publication in Z. Weiss and E. Netzer, *Promise and Redemption. A Synagogue Mosaic from Sepphoris*, Jerusalem 1996; a more detailed justification of the dating is still awaited. Cf. idd., 'Architectural Development of Sepphoris during the Roman and Byzantine Periods', in D. R. Edwards and C. T. McCollough (eds.), *Archaeology and the Galilee. Texts and Contexts in the Graeco-Roman and Byzantine Periods*, Atlanta 1997, 117–30, p. 127, according to which the synagogue 'is dated to the Byzantine period' without further precision. See also E. Netzer and Z. Weiss, *Zippori*, Jerusalem 1994.

Two synagogue inscriptions have been known for some time; both are in the medieval Church of St. Anne. An Aramaic mosaic inscription names R. Judan bar Tanchum (it is not certain whether some fragments found in the recent excavations stem from the same mosaic). More interesting is the Greek inscription on a door lintel of the church. I follow the readings and translation of B. Lifshitz for this inscription, who slightly corrects the earlier reading of M. Schwabe:[31]

> [Built] under the lawyer (*scholasticos*) Gelasios, the illustrious count, son of Count Aetios, and Juda, synagogue chairman of Sidon, by the efforts (?) of Severianus Afer, the illustrious synagogue chairman of Tyre.

Details remain unclear, such as the question whether the inscription proves the existence of synagogues in Sepphoris itself for Jews from Tyre and Sidon, as Lifshitz thinks, or only speaks of synagogue chairmen from these cities, who had a particular relationship with the synagogue congregation to whom the inscription belonged. We have already stressed the fact that Galilean communities had close relationships with Tyre. There is literary evidence for a number of synagogues in Sepphoris, for example, a synagogue of the Babylonians, a synagogue of the Jews from Gophna and probably also a synagogue of the Jews from Cappadocia (jShab VI. 8 a; jBer V.1.9 a: But what period does this evidence refer to?). The organization of local Jewish congregations according to their origins, with their own synagogues, was entirely customary in Palestine at this period, and Sepphoris was of course an important Jewish centre, although Epiphanius' assertion that no non-Jews were allowed there at all[32] is a gross exaggeration, as the excavations of recent years have clearly shown.

The titles used in the inscription are of particular interest, as they exclude a date after 438. For at that time Theodosius decreed in *Novella* 3.2 'that no Jew and no Samaritan[33] may attain

---

[31] B. Lifshitz, *Donateurs et fondateurs dans les synagogues juives*, Paris 1967, 60. He dates the inscription to the first half of the fourth century; by contrast, M. Schwabe, *Festschrift D. Yellin*, Jerusalem 1935, 112, dates it a century later, in the first half of the fifth century. On p. 110 he suggests a date between 400 and 420 on palaeographic grounds. See L. Roth-Gerson, *The Greek Inscriptions*, 105–9.

[32] Epiphanius, *Panarion* 30.11.9 (GCS 25, 347).

[33] After the word 'Samaritan' comes *neutra lege constantem*, which can only be

honour and rank, that no civic administration posts may be open to them, and none may even exercise the role of a defender [of the city].' A contemporary, polemical Christian text adds: 'A Jew may not be a count.'[34] A law was published in Rome in 404, according to which 'Jews and Samaritans who usurp the privileges of the *agentes in rebus* [secret service] must be excluded from any service.' If this law was also current in the eastern Empire (which is, however, not very likely), then the inscription would perhaps need to be dated even earlier.[35] After 438 the rank of *clarissimus*, which went with the title of count, must have become just as unthinkable for Jews as the function of a lawyer (*scholasticos*): this was granted by the state and was not a free profession in the strict sense. In 468 the Emperor Leo prohibited the *advocatio* for Jews.

On the other hand, the titles rule out a date before Diocletian; since the Jewish count named here is himself the son of a count, the earliest possible date of the inscription must be moved forward by some decades. The title of count sank in value in the course of time, but still remained a valuable honour, and the more so the earlier the inscription is to be dated. This is what makes this inscription so important for estimating the public standing of Jews in the fourth century. At the very least it appears to prove the existence of a well-established class of dignitaries in the Jewish community of Sepphoris, who had strong connections with Tyre.

(c) In the fourth century there is literary evidence for a synagogue in *Guphta de Tzipporin*, about three kilometres from

---

interpreted by altering the text, and is missing in the law's repetition in CJust 1.9.18. On various possible interpretations, see C. Pharr, *The Theodosian Code*, 489. Cf. A. Linder, *The Jews*, 335, who understands *lege* to mean religion, and translates: 'nor any one constant in either of these laws' (329).

[34] *Altercatio Ecclesiae et Synagogae*, PL 42, 1132 (mid-fifth century).

[35] J. Juster, *Les Juifs* II, 244f., takes the Jews to be excluded by this law from every form of public service – *militia armata, militia palatina, militia togata*. But since CTh XVI.8.24, published 418 in Ravenna, again forbids Jews employment as *agentes in rebus* and as *palatini*, while permitting those who are already employed to finish their careers, perhaps XVI.8.16 should be taken as referring to Samaritans alone, with the Scholia Vaticana (*Samaritanos Iudaeos*, 'Samaritan Jews'). But the law of 418 may also attest that the earlier law was without effect. A. Linder, *The Jews*, 222, sees XVI.8.16 only as a warning 'that Jews and Samaritans should be expelled from all State offices if they shall offend in connection with the privilege of the Executive Agents, but it is not a formal prohibition against Jews and Samaritans serving as Executive Agents'.

Sepphoris. In Nazareth, which according to Epiphanius was an exclusively Jewish town,[36] and which is also mentioned in the list of priestly classes discovered in Caesarea, B. Bagatti believes he has discovered two synagogues. Apart from the Jewish Christian synagogue under the Basilica of the Annunciation, mentioned in a previous chapter, he assumes a Jewish synagogue north-west of the Franciscan monastery, for which he takes some architectural fragments as evidence.[37] It is probably almost impossible, at least at present, to prove the existence of a 'Jewish Christian synagogue'; but the evidence is also too weak for the other synagogue.

The existence of a synagogue at *Cana* (Kafr Kanna, about six kilometres north-east of Nazareth) is, however, definite. The Catholic church in Cana has an Aramaic inscription that might come from the period that interests us. Here, too, Jewish Christians have been suggested.[38] Two kilometres south-west of Nazareth is *Jafia*, whose fortifications were once strengthened by Josephus (*BJ* II. 573, III.289–306). The synagogue which has been excavated there (almost 16 m wide, length debatable), on whose mosaic floor the zodiac or the twelve tribes of Israel were depicted, dates from the late third or early fourth century.[39] In *Kafr Misr*, seven kilometres south-east of Nazareth, a synagogue was excavated in 1984–87 (13.65 × 17.5 m, two rows of four columns each), whose beginning dates back to the third century. It was apparently severely damaged in an earthquake in the fourth century, and renovated soon after, when it received a mosaic floor with geometric and floral patterns, and a niche for the Torah shrine, later replaced by an apse.[40]

Half-way between Sepphoris and Tiberias, but belonging to the city territory of Sepphoris, is *Horvat 'Ammudim*; its synagogue was excavated in 1979.[41] The building, erected around 300 in the

---

[36] See n. 26, above.
[37] See Chap. IV, n. 83.
[38] B. Bagatti, *Alle origini* I, 135; in detail id., 'Antichità di Kh. Qana e di Kefr Kenna', *LA* 15 (1964f.), 251–92.
[39] See D. Barag, *NEAE* II, 659f.; R. Hachlili, *Ancient Jewish Art*, 295–7.
[40] A. Onn, 'The Ancient Synagogue at Kafr Misr', *Atiqot* 25 (1994), 117–34.
[41] L. I. Levine, 'Excavations at the Synagogue of Horvat 'Ammudim', *IEJ* 32 (1982), 1–12; D. Adan-Bayewitz, 'The Ceramics from the Synagogue of Horvat 'Ammudim and their Chronological Implications', *IEJ* 32 (1982), 13–31. D. Chen, *PEQ* 118 (1986), 135–7, sets the date of the building a generation later. On the inscriptions see J. Naveh, *EI* 20 (1989), 306f.

basilica style with a monumental southern façade, was comparatively large (the main room measured 14 × 22.5 m). It possessed a mosaic floor with geometric patterns, and coloured walls. This synagogue was in use throughout the fourth century; two Aramaic inscriptions and relief decoration have also been found there.

(d) We have significantly less evidence for synagogues from the city territory of *Scythopolis* (Beth Shean). A settled Jewish community was only organized there towards the end of the third century, and then began to build a synagogue. The question they put to R. Ammi in Tiberias, whether the stones of an old synagogue might be used for a new one (jMeg III.1.73 d), which was answered in the negative, perhaps referred to the synagogue which was destroyed in the revolt against Rome.[42]

There is archaeological evidence for two synagogues in Beth Shean. The earlier was built around 400 (measuring 17 × 14 m); later a 3 m wide narthex (vestibule) was built onto it; a third phase of building dates from around 600. A side room at the front was perhaps meant to take the Torah scrolls.[43] The basalt walls of this synagogue are almost a metre thick, thicker than those of the surrounding monasteries or of the nearby synagogue of Beth Alfa (sixth century). N. Zori takes this as proof that the synagogue was also used for defensive purposes.[44] If this were true, it might be interpreted as evidence for the fact that synagogues were endangered in Palestine too at this period (see later in this chapter on the relevant laws protecting synagogues); but this interpretation is far from proven.

Seven kilometres south of Beth Shean lies *Rehov*, whose synagogue was built in the early fourth century (17 × 19 m). It had three entrances on the north side, and an additional side entrance on the east side; two rows of limestone columns on basalt bases subdivided the room, which possessed a mosaic floor. After a fire around 400, the synagogue was largely rebuilt on the same ground plan. The new mosaic floor had geometric patterns, and the walls and columns were decorated in colour, with red

---

[42] G. Fuks, *Scythopolis*, 153.
[43] M. J. Chiat, *Handbook*, 128–32; id., 'Synagogue and Church Architecture in Byzantine Beit She'an', *Journal of Jewish Art* 8 (1980), 6–24.
[44] N. Zori, 'The Ancient Synagogue at Beth-Shean' (Hebrew), *EI* 8 (1967), 149–67, 167. However, wall thicknesses vary greatly, depending on the subsoil, material and roof (in Ma'oz Hayyim the walls are also 1 m thick!), and cannot be traced to a single cause.

stripes, triangles in several colours, stylized flowers, and so on. In a later phase of building a narthex was added, and the synagogue otherwise substantially altered. The famous Rehov halachic inscription dates from this last phase. In the seventh century the synagogue was destroyed and abandoned.[45]

In 1974, four and a half kilometres east of Beth Shean, the synagogue of *Ma'oz Hayyim* was discovered.[46] Its first phase of building dates from around 300. The prayer room (interior measurements 14 × 12.5 m) was subdivided by two times four pillars, its entrance was probably on the east side. The floor was composed of stone slabs. Against the south wall was a *bema* of unhewn stones, on which a wooden or stone Torah shrine probably stood. The excavator speaks cautiously of a public building which could be described as a synagogue. In its second phase it certainly was a synagogue. The first building was apparently not destroyed, but deliberately demolished around 400 to make way for a larger new building (16.5 × 14 m), which now received an apse and a geometrically patterned mosaic floor.[47] Later repairs to the mosaic are crude, and probably not the work of professionals. This could point to an economic decline on the part of the congregation. Such a decline is clearly visible in the synagogue's renovation around 600: only a very rough mosaic was laid, and wooden pillars were used instead of stone.

These three synagogues from the city territory of Scythopolis document a group of Jewish settlements that were able to exist into the Arab period, which in fact grew and were flourishing communities in the fifth to sixth centuries, when a number of further synagogues were built. This area, unlike Upper Galilee, was strongly Christianized at a relatively early date. But there is no evidence whatsoever that Jewish communities were displaced by Christian ones in the course of time; the synagogue finds from the following centuries indicate rather an increase in the Jewish communities in this region.

---

[45] F. Vitto, 'The Synagogue of Rehov', *IEJ* 30 (1980), 214–17.
[46] V. Tsaferis, 'The Ancient Synagogue at Ma'oz Hayyim', *IEJ* 32 (1982), 215–44; id., *NEAE* III, 946–8.
[47] Because of the apse, R. Hachlili, *Ancient Jewish Art*, 398, prefers to date this alteration to the late fifth century.

3. The Territory of Tiberias

Throughout the entire period under consideration, Tiberias was the seat of the patriarch. We should therefore expect a correspondingly dense pattern of Jewish settlement.[48] And indeed, apart from a few synagogues for which there is only literary evidence,[49] a number of buildings have been excavated or their existence proved by architectural remains, for example, *Cochav ha-Jarden* 22 km south of Tiberias, perhaps ancient Agrippina, *Tiberias* itself (both evidenced by inscriptions), and *Arbel* six kilometres north-west of Tiberias, whose synagogue (18.2 × 18.6 m) was built around 300.[50] The synagogues of Hammath Tiberias, Capernaum and Chorazin will now be considered in detail.

(a) *Chorazin* lies on a slight hill about four kilometres north of Capernaum. Eusebius writes of it that this Galilean town, for which Christ lamented in the Gospels, is now indeed deserted. Jerome repeats the assertion in his edition of the *Onomasticon* around 390: 'but now it is deserted.'[51]

The excavations seem to disprove these assertions of the Church Fathers. A large synagogue, built of basalt blocks (22.8 × 16.7 m) has been excavated, whose southern façade is richly ornamented with reliefs (four grape-gathering scenes, perhaps with Dionysian connotations, a head of Medusa etc.). The 'seat of Moses' is also very interesting. It is carved from a single block of basalt and has an Aramaic inscription.

When was this synagogue built? Z. Yeivin initially assumed a first phase in the second to fourth centuries; then, after partial destruction, that it was rebuilt in the fifth to sixth century.[52] However, on the basis of his own excavations in Capernaum,

---

[48] M. Avi-Yonah, 'The Foundation of Tiberias', *IEJ* I (1950f.), 160–9, 169, gives 0.8 km² as the city's area in the third century, and hence estimates a population of 30,000–40,000. M. Broshi, 'The Population', 5, is much more cautious. According to his criteria, even at the end of the Byzantine era, when population figures in Palestine reached an absolute peak, the numbers did not exceed approximately 12,000 inhabitants.

[49] Kafra near Tiberias, Serungin on the heights above it, and Kefar Hittaiya 8 km to the north-west: F. Hüttenmeister, *Synagogen*, 251f.; 390–2; 258f.

[50] See Z. Ilan, *IEJ* 39 (1989), 100–2.

[51] Eusebius, *Onomasticon* (GCS II/1, 174f.).

[52] Z. Yeivin, 'The Synagogue at Chorazein' (Hebrew), in *All the Land of Naphtali*, Jerusalem 1967, 135–8; id., 'Excavations at Khorazin' (Hebrew), *EI* 11 (1973), 144–57.

S. Loffreda doubted the early date of the first phase, saying that the synagogue could only have been built after Eusebius' text was written.⁵³ The first building should indeed be assigned an earlier date than was thought at first, since pottery finds also only begin in the third century in Chorazin. Yeivin himself stated, after new excavations in the northern part of the synagogue, whereby he found a coin of Diocletian and one of Maximinian (308) under the stone filler of the floor, that these coins 'indicate the earliest date for the foundation of the synagogue – the late 3rd or early 4th century CE.'⁵⁴ The older of the two coin hoards found in Chorazin appears to confirm this dating. Its oldest coin is from 134, from Gaza, but 90 per cent of its contents are coins from the period between 290 and 340; the latest coin may have been struck by the Empress Helena. This hoard was buried in the synagogue during its first phase.

No coins were found during the excavations from the period between 340 and 390. Y. Meshorer's explanation is that the site was deserted for some time after the revolt against Gallus. The second coin hoard comprises coins from a period from about 390 to the end of the fifth century. It was buried under the threshold of the synagogue; according to Yeivin this was at a time when the building was probably already partly destroyed, but still in use.⁵⁵

The results of the excavations are inconclusive. In theory both Eusebius and Jerome could be right. Then we would have to assume a synagogue that existed between approximately 320 and 350, and assume that rebuilding began in 390. However, the Church Fathers may have been more interested in confirming the New Testament, and may not have been over-particular about the facts. Did Eusebius ever go to Chorazin? If not, he could have been relying on older reports from the third century, when the site was in fact only thinly settled. Jerome in his turn appears to have been a very conservative editor of his source; there are other points on which he does not bring it entirely up to date. Did he himself go to Chorazin with Paula in 386, from Capernaum? It is

---

53 S. Loffreda, 'The Late Chronology', 37f.
54 Z. Yeivin, *ESI* 3 (1984), 67.
55 Y. Meshorer, 'Coins from the Excavations at Khorazin' (Hebrew), *EI* 11 (1973), 158–62. See also G. Kloetzli, 'Coins from Chorazin', *LA* 20 (1970), 359–69. Z. Yeivin, *NEAE* I, 304, no longer mentions the revolt against Gallus, but simply writes: 'The synagogue suffered some damage when the town was partially destroyed, probably in the early fourth century CE.'

possible. However, in his case too we must allow for the possibility of tendentious misrepresentation of the facts; not to mention his verdict that pilgrim guides' errors that stem from hatred of the Jews should not be condemned.[56]

Taking the revolt against Gallus into account in the explanation of the archaeological findings is also difficult. Did the revolt's effects even reach this far? It is just as questionable here as in the case of Meiron. The first synagogue could also have been destroyed in the earthquake of 363. Afterwards, the congregation of Chorazin could have joined with a neighbouring congregation for a few decades, until the synagogue was rebuilt after all. It is tempting to think of Capernaum, whose synagogue must have been far too large for the resident Jewish population there; but there is no evidence for this, and the Capernaum synagogue was probably still being built at that time.

Earlier excavations[57] found a basilica about two hundred metres west of the synagogue, whose remains have now vanished. It too could have been a synagogue. The fact that there are no coins from the time between the destruction and rebuilding of the first synagogue speaks against the possibility that this building took the place of the first, destroyed synagogue for a time. But the last word has not yet been spoken on this matter. Yeivin concludes from excavations in the village that the first two settlement phases of Chorazin – probably identical with the first two pottery phases, late third and fourth to fifth centuries – was the peak period of the place.

(b) *Capernaum* is the synagogue that played a significant part in the change in synagogue dating.[58] The principal room of the synagogue measures 24.4×18.65 m. It was subdivided by two rows of seven columns each; there were two further columns in the middle of the north side. The floor was composed of large stone slabs, the walls were covered with coloured stucco. Rich relief decoration adorned the outside, which was later partly damaged, perhaps intentionally by iconoclasts, Jews or more likely Muslims.[59] In front of the south façade there was a terrace

---

[56] See Chap. IV, n. 19.
[57] N. Makhauly and J. Ory in 1926: see M. J. Chiat, *Handbook*, 97.
[58] V. C. Corbo, *Cafarnao* I, 115–69; V. Corbo, S. Loffreda and A. Spijkerman, *La Sinagoga di Cafarnao dopo gli scavi del 1969*, Jerusalem 1970; S. Loffreda, 'The Late Chronology'; id., 'Le sinagoghe di Cafarnao', *Bibbia e Oriente* 26 (1984), 103–14.
[59] On the difficulties of the historical attribution of iconoclastic attacks, see D. Amit, 'Iconoclasm in Ancient Synagogues in Eretz Israel', *11th WCJS* (Jerusalem 1994), vol. I, 9–16.

over 3 m wide, and on the east side a closed colonnaded courtyard (20 × 11–13 m). The whole complex was built over what had been a residential quarter, on a basalt platform erected for the purpose.

In the past, the synagogue of Capernaum was thought to be a classic example of the 'early Galilean synagogue type'. However, the excavations since 1969 point to a late date. The principal argument for this is based on the coins found in the foundations of the synagogue, and even under the pillars. V. Corbo and S. Loffreda therefore assume that building only began around the middle of the fourth century, and that the synagogue was completed around the middle of the fifth century, when the floor was laid. The terrace and courtyard belong to the last phase of building, which however proceeded according to a uniform plan from the beginning. The synagogue was only destroyed after the Arab conquest, around 750 at the latest. Opponents of this late dating point to the style of decoration in the synagogue, which is said to belong to the third or early fourth century, and which was partly used again in the new synagogue.[60] However, there do not seem to be any clearly datable structural traces of a third-century synagogue to which these early decorative elements could belong. Many questions remain open, although the present state of our knowledge probably favours the later dating.

This synagogue complex is, beside the one at Beth Shearim, the richest Jewish building of the fourth century that has been excavated to date. Apart from the size of the buildings, the material used is impressive. The houses in the whole town are built of the local basalt stone; only the Christian octagon and the synagogue are made of hard white limestone, which was probably quarried some kilometres away near Tabgha, or in the hills north of Tell Oreime. Then there are the many sculptures which

---

[60] See M. Fischer, 'The Corinthian Capitals of the Capernaum Synagogue – A Late Roman Architectural Feature in Eretz-Israel' (Hebrew), *EI* 17 (1984), 305–11. He concludes from the capitals that the date falls in the second half of the third century. Cf. H. Bloedhorn, *Die Kapitelle der Synagoge von Kapernaum*, Wiesbaden 1988; Y. Tsafrir, 'The Synagogues at Capernaum and Meroth and the dating of the Galilean Synagogue', *The Roman and Byzantine Near East: Some Recent Archaeological Research (Journal of Roman Archaeology. Supplementary Series 14)*, (Ann Arbor 1995), 151–61. Tsafrir also stresses that in the filler under the floor of the synagogue, the later coins were always found in the upper layers, and in the lower layers older coins and pottery, which would be scarcely likely if the building work was carried out all at once.

adorned the outer walls of the synagogue. One could hardly imagine a greater contrast to the houses that have been excavated so far, which are all fairly humble.

As editor of the journal in which Loffreda justified his late dating of the synagogue, M. Avi-Yonah appended his own counter-arguments to Loffreda's article.[61] He particularly stresses the stylistic differences from the synagogue of Hammath Tiberias, which must have been built at approximately the same time, if the late dating of Capernaum is correct. He also states that the emperors Constantine and Constantius were too hostile to Jews for such a building to be conceivable in their time. Finally, the nearness of the synagogue to the Christian place of worship, the 'House of Peter', is significant: 'Such a state of affairs might be conceivable in our oecumenical age, but it seems almost impossible to imagine that it would have been allowed by the Byzantine authorities of the fourth century'; in particular since the entire decoration of the synagogue is on the outside, while other Byzantine synagogues are only decorated on the inside. M. Avi-Yonah finally leaves the matter unresolved.

However, rather than saying that the building of such a synagogue would be scarcely conceivable under the fourth-century emperors, we must probably accept a fourth-century dating as correct in view of the results of the excavations.[62] Rather, we need to correct our judgement of the effect of Constantine's and Constantius' policies regarding Jews on the Jews of Palestine. The close neighbourhood of church and synagogue also presents no great difficulty. This proximity would also exist in the case of an early dating of the synagogue – but with the difference that in the third century the state would certainly not have intervened in favour of the Christian congregation. We should also remember Pope Gregory the Great's decree – although it was issued for Italy and cannot be directly applied – that Jews were prohibited from erecting synagogues only where the noise of their worship might disturb Christian worship.[63]

---

[61] M. Avi-Yonah, *IEJ* 23 (1973), 43–5, quote p. 45.
[62] S. Loffreda, 'Vasi in vetro e in argilla trovati a Cafarnao nel 1984. Rapporto preliminare', *LA* 34 (1984), 385–408, emphasizes (p. 407) that the most recent excavations again offer confirmation of the late dating.
[63] Gregory the Great, *ep.* 1.10 (PL 77, 457). If the dating of the synagogue of Beth Jerach, 8 km south-east of the Sea of Galilee, is correct at around 500, this synagogue would have been built only 50 m away from an already existing church! See M. J. Chiat, *Handbook*, 305–7.

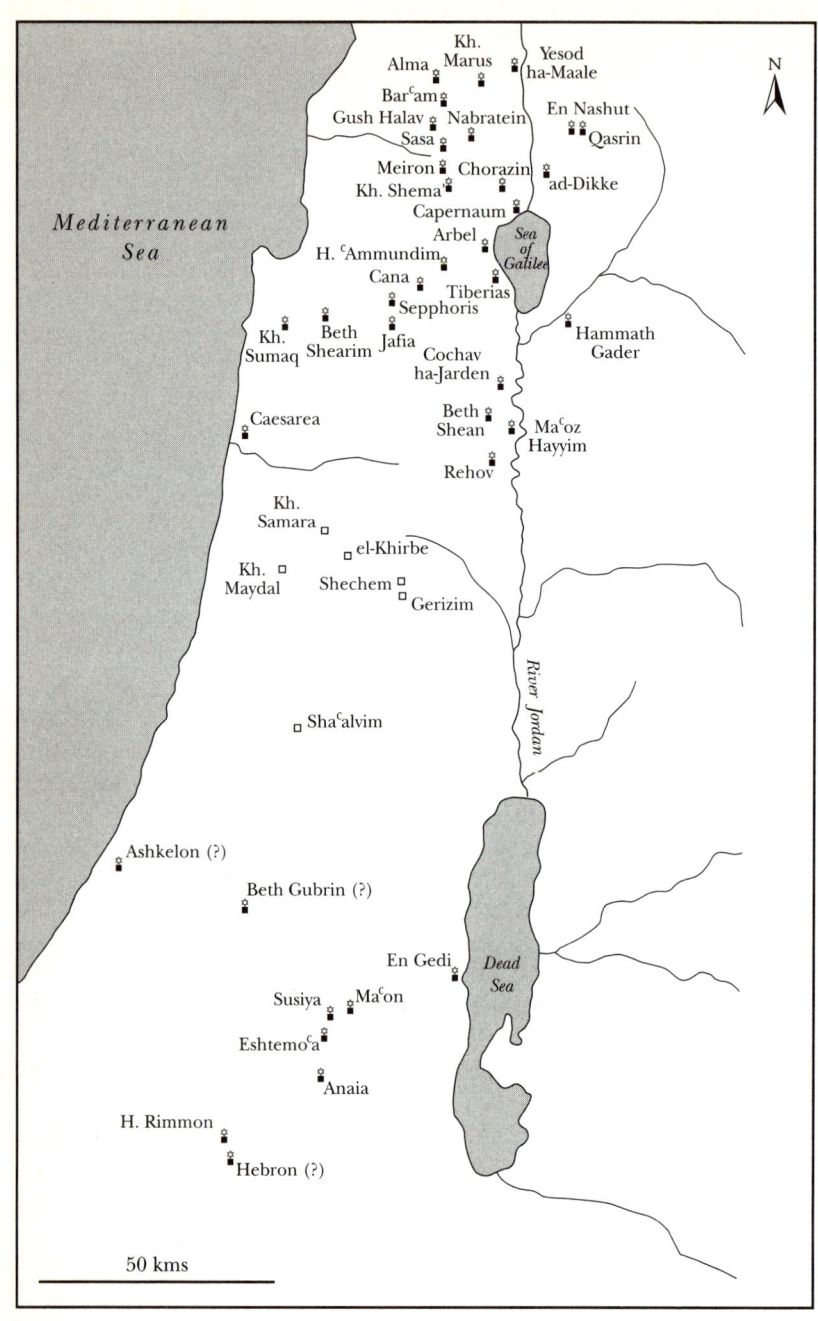

Synagogue buildings in the fourth and early fifth centuries

Finally, here in Capernaum the Jews were in the heart of their own territory; here they certainly resisted the advance of Christianity as far as they were able. There is no proof of oppression of the Jews of Palestine at this period, nor of any obstruction of synagogue building. Even if, as Yeivin assumes, the synagogue in neighbouring Chorazin was destroyed in the revolt against Gallus, the beginning of building work on the synagogue in Capernaum at almost exactly the same time would be surprising, but not inconceivable.

The problem remains of how the project was financed in this small and rather poor village. Two inscriptions are evidence for the donation of a column each by private donors: in a Greek inscription Herod, son of Monimos, and his son Justus, with their children, are named; an Aramaic inscription names as donor Halfai son of Zabdai son of Jochanan. Was the entire complex built on the basis of many such individual donations? We have no epigraphic evidence for this. Indeed, how large was the congregation?

V. Tzaferis, who has excavated the eastern part of Capernaum, belonging to the Greek Orthodox church, assumes on the basis of the synagogue the existence of a large and wealthy Jewish community which lived by trade, fishing and farming; and that, by contrast, the Christian church was a memorial, built under Christian ecclesiastical or political pressure, and did not presuppose the existence of a Christian congregation.[64] However, more recent excavations by S. Loffreda rule out such a hypothesis. In almost all of the residential dwellings at Capernaum that have been excavated to date, Byzantine pottery shards were found with the sign of the cross. Therefore S. Loffreda infers a largely if not exclusively Christian population in Capernaum, 'to the extent that the monumental synagogue was encircled on all sides by Christian neighbourhoods'.[65]

According to the finds published so far, it would be possible that as late as the fifth century there was a fairly rapid displacement of the Jewish community by the Christian

---

[64] V. Tzaferis, 'New Archaeological Evidence on Ancient Capernaum', *BA* 46 (1983), 198–204, 204. The part of Capernaum excavated by Tzaferis belongs to a later phase of settlement (seventh to eleventh centuries); id., *NEAE* I, 295f.

[65] See n. 62 above.

community. But that does not solve our problem. The possibility that the building was financed from outside might therefore suggest itself; but by whom and with what motive?

V. Corbo thinks 'of the Imperial Roman treasury at the time of Julian the Apostate'.[66] But this is scarcely conceivable. Are we to assume that Julian supported synagogues beside his project with the Temple in Jerusalem? But no sacrifices would have been offered there, which was his only interest. And even if he should have taken part in financing synagogues, why Capernaum in particular? Is it not more likely that help came from the house of the patriarch, which perhaps also owned property in the area? It is possible that the project represented a conscious strengthening of the Jewish congregation against Christianity when it attempted to spread here. This seems a more plausible motive for external financing than the religious politics of Julian, who only reigned for a few months. However, in this case we would expect epigraphic evidence which we unfortunately do not possess. Thus many puzzles remain unanswered. However, the synagogue of Capernaum represents a strong argument against a swift and continuous worsening of the situation of the Palestinian Jews in the fourth century.

(c) *Hammath Tiberias*, a little south of Tiberias, was (and is) a popular spa because of its hot springs. In the fourth century there were at least two synagogues there. One was excavated by N. Slouschz as early as 1920: it was a basalt building measuring 12 × 12 m with a courtyard of 12 × 8 m, built in the middle of the third century with a basalt floor, which was replaced during renovations in the fourth to fifth centuries by a mosaic floor. At that time the entrance, probably originally on the south side, was moved to the north. Unfortunately it is not possible to verify these details by new excavations.[67]

More thoroughly explored, and also much more important for our interests, is the synagogue by the hot springs after which the town is named, about 500 m south of the first. A synagogue was already built here around 230, which was in use until the end of the third century, or until the year 306 at the latest, the year of the earthquake. The second building is dated by M. Dothan[68] between Diocletian's visit to Palestine in 286 and Constantine's

---

[66] V. C. Corbo, *Cafarnao* I, 169.
[67] See M. J. Chiat, *Handbook*, 103–6.
[68] M. Dothan, *Hammath Tiberias*, 67.

death in 337. It was used throughout the fourth century, as coins (the latest in this layer dates from 395) and pottery (until the end of the fourth century) show. Dothan mentions a number of possible causes for the end of this synagogue. Perhaps it was destroyed in the earthquake of 419, perhaps also torn down by the congregation to make room for a larger new building (a basilica measuring 19 × 15 m, instead of an original 'broad house' measuring 15 × 13 m). But destruction by enemies of Judaism at the time of the emperors Honorius and Arcadius is not impossible, as indicated by the laws protecting synagogues since 393. In any case the synagogue must have been destroyed between 396 and 422, especially if the law of 423 against rebuilding of synagogues was actually implemented.

The fourth-century synagogue was distinguished by a magnificent mosaic floor, which covered a large part of the interior (over 100 m^2) and must have taken more than 2,000 manhours to lay. According to Dothan's reconstruction, the Torah shrine and the stair to the gallery lay on the south side. This floor is particularly important because of its zodiac mosaic and the Greek dedication, which mentions among the donors one Severus, who was closely connected with the house of the patriarch. Both will be treated in a later chapter in connection with the development of the patriarchate.

For our context it should be emphasized that the three phases of the synagogue correspond with developments elsewhere, and are evidence for the increasing prosperity and numerical size of the congregation. The fact that the fifth-century rebuilding no longer has any use for the zodiac mosaic points to a more conservative attitude on the part of the congregation. However, the individual arguments for dating brought forward by Dothan are somewhat doubtful; we will return to this point in connection with the patriarchate. In particular, we have no evidence for destruction of synagogues at the end of the fourth century in this region, and it is hardly likely in view of the fact that the synagogue was immediately rebuilt on a larger scale.[69]

---

[69] Cf. Z. Weiss in Y. Hirschfeld (ed.), *Tveriya me-Yissodah ad ha-Kibbush ha-Muslemi*, Jerusalem 1988, 38–43: the first synagogue was destroyed in the earthquake of 306 and rebuilt soon after, the second was destroyed by an earthquake in the second decade of the fifth century. There is no question of violent destruction here.

4. Synagogues in Southern Palestine

In his *Onomasticon* Eusebius mentions a number of towns around Eleutheropolis as Jewish settlements (and otherwise only Naarath, near Jericho): Anaia, which is a very large Jewish village in the Daroma, nine miles south of Hebron, also En Gedi by the Dead Sea, Zeif (Ziph) south of Hebron, Thalcha 16 miles from Eleutheropolis in the Daroma, Iettan 18 miles from Eleutheropolis, Eremmon 16 miles from Eleutheropolis in the Daroma, and Esthemo, a city of priests.[70] Jerome changed nothing here, which in this case is probably not because of his conservative editing or lack of knowledge, but apparently does reflect the facts, since in four of the towns named (and in Naaran) there is archaeological evidence for synagogues, all in the very extensive city territory of Eleutheropolis, the largest in Palestine.

(a) The synagogue of *En Gedi*[71] was built at the beginning of the third century and was an unequal rectangle of approximately 15.5 × 10 m, without columns. Around 300 it was extended by a narthex on the west side, separated from the hall by columns. Three rows of benches against the south wall and a mosaic floor belong to this phase of building. In the second half of the fifth century, the narthex was incorporated into the synagogue itself and a new narthex added. D. Barag suggests that the synagogue was destroyed in the persecutions of Jews under Justinian.

(b) *Eshtemo'a*, 15 km south of Hebron, had a synagogue in the form of a 'broad house' without columns (13.3 × 21.3 m), with a 4 m wide narthex. Niches in the north wall, i.e. in the direction of Jerusalem, indicate the direction of prayer; there was probably a mosaic floor. In 'Byzantine times' the area near the north wall of the synagogue was rebuilt (the ground plan remaining the same), and later the synagogue was turned into a mosque. The western wall is still standing to a height of 7 m.[72]

(c) *Anaia*, four kilometres south of Eshtemo'a, and corresponding to the Biblical Anim (Josh. 15.50), was excavated in 1988. The small synagogue (8.5 × 14.5 m), whose walls are still

---

[70] Eusebius, *Onomasticon* (GCS II/I, 26 and 82–106).
[71] D. Barag, Y. Porat and E. Netzer, 'En-Gedi' *RB* 79 (1972), 581–3; idd., *RB* 81 (1974), 96f.
[72] Z. Yeivin, 'The Synagogue at Eshtemoa' (Hebrew), *Qadmoniot* 5 (1972), 43–5; id., *NEAE* II, 423–6.

standing to a height of 3 m, had a floor of stone slabs. A *bema* against the north wall indicates the direction of Jerusalem. A vestibule on the east side had a mosaic floor; fragments of an inscription remain. The synagogue was built in the fourth century and remained in use to the seventh or eighth century, when it was turned into a mosque.[73]

(d) In *Susiya*, which is not mentioned in ancient texts, but perhaps corresponds to the Biblical Carmel (Josh. 15.55), a synagogue was built, probably in the early fourth century, which with several restorations and rebuildings continued in use until the ninth century. Its courtyard was turned into a mosque in the tenth century.[74] The building was a 'broad house' measuring 9 × 16 m, which also possessed a narthex; the mosaic floor could have shown a zodiac. The gallery on the west side was added later.

(e) 3 km south of Susiya lies *Ma'on*, whose synagogue was excavated in 1987–88. The small building (exterior measurements 10.5 × 15.5 m), dating from the late fourth or early fifth century, was entered by three doors from the east. There are remnants of a simple mosaic floor and of stone benches along the walls; in the narrow north wall there was probably a Torah niche. The synagogue was rebuilt in the sixth century and remained in use into the seventh century.[75]

(f) *Horvat Rimmon* received a synagogue in the second half of the third century, whose floor plan is not yet definitely identified; the building was probably a 'broad house' type. Remnants of capitals and reliefs show that it was richly decorated. The walls were painted in colour. Between the middle of the fourth and the middle of the sixth century, a new synagogue was built here and the whole complex surrounded with a wall (34 × 29.5 m). The walls are still standing to a height of 3 m. At the end of the sixth century a further synagogue was built.

Besides a coin hoard dating from as far as the early sixth

---

[73] See Z. Ilan and D. Amit, *ESI* 7–8 (1988f.), 6–8; D. Amit, 'Architectural Plans of Synagogues in the Southern Judean Hills and the 'Halakha', in Urman and Flesher, *Ancient Synagogues* I, 129–155; id., *NEAE* I, 62.

[74] Z. Yeivin, 'Inscribed Marble Fragments from the Khirbet Susiya Synagogue', *IEJ* 24 (1974), 201–9; id., 'Khirbet Susiya – The Bema and Synagogue Ornamentation', in R. Hachlili (ed.), *Ancient Synagogues*, 93–100; id., *NEAE* IV, 1117–21; A. Negev, 'A Town without History – Excavations at Horvat Susiya (Karmel) During 1984' (Hebrew), *Qadmoniot* 18 (1985), 100–5.

[75] Z. Ilan and D. Amit, *NEAE* III, 942–4; D. Amit in Urman and Flesher I, 133f.

century, 64 bronze coins (mainly third to the beginning of the fifth century) were found hidden in a hole in the wall of the second synagogue. This is firm evidence for continuous Jewish settlement over centuries, and probably also for the equation with Eremmon from the *Onomasticon*.

The size of the total complex is striking, given the small size of the synagogue itself (13.5 × 9.5 m in the sixth century). The coin hoards have not yet been interpreted. It is possible that the walls were built for defensive purposes. However, that would not necessarily indicate attacks against Jews by Christians in this region, but rather more generally the rising insecurity in this southern part of the country, because of the continual incursions of the Saracens. It is also possible that people wished for an open-air site, protected from the wind, for public functions – sandstorms increased markedly here in the later Byzantine period.[76]

(g) Two other synagogues in this region cannot be securely dated. In *Beth Gubrin* (Eleutheropolis) two Aramaic inscriptions were found which are dated between the fourth and sixth centuries. From *Ashkelon* we have two Greek and two Hebrew inscriptions. One of the Greek inscriptions dates from 709. In the Seleucid calendar this would be 397, and using the calendar of Ashkelon 604. The names in this inscription, Kyra Domna, daughter of Julia(n), and Kyros Com(modus), are also difficult. They are occasionally interpreted with reference to the imperial family, Julia and Commodus, but this is not compatible with the date.[77] Also very doubtful is evidence for synagogues in *Hebron* (fourth to sixth century) and *Khirbet Iocha* five kilometres north of Hebron (perhaps a church).

5. Other Synagogues

Apart from the two centres of Jewish settlement in Galilee and – to a lesser extent – in the south of the country, a number of other synagogues existed. The one in *Caesarea*, which was surely one of

---

[76] A. Kloner, 'The Synagogues at Horvat Rimmon', in R. Hachlili (ed.), *Ancient Synagogues*, 43–8; id., *NEAE* IV, 1284f.
[77] J. Naveh, *On Stone*, 89, accepts the later date; also B. Lifshitz, *Donateurs*, 55. Cf. L. Roth-Gerson, *The Greek Inscriptions*, 27.

several in that city, is worth special mention. It was built in the late third or early fourth century over a building from the Herodian period, which was later partly used as a water storage tank. The building was a kind of 'broad house' type (18 × 9 m), facing south, but with the entrance on the east side, towards the town. 3700 bronze coins were found in a projecting part of the wall, which perhaps served as a Torah shrine; most of them are of Constantius, a few of the Emperor Julian. That would fix about 355 as the earliest date at which the coins were hidden here. It is assumed that the synagogue was destroyed at about this time and rebuilt in the early fifth century, when a narthex was added.[78] Finds from the fourth-century building include lamp fragments with a menorah, three pieces of a Hebrew inscription on marble with the 24 priestly orders and a mosaic floor. Judging by the coin hoard, destruction in connection with the revolt against Gallus can be ruled out. Perhaps the earthquake of 363 was also felt here, or perhaps the destruction of the synagogue was due to some cause unknown to us.[79]

The synagogue of *Sumaqa*, on the southern side of Mt. Carmel not far from Beth Shearim, should also be mentioned here. The building is dated to the second half of the third century. It was a basilica with two rows of columns and a narthex (overall measurements 14.8 × 23.8 m). According to the excavators, the building was deliberately destroyed during the fourth or at the beginning

---

[78] M. Avi-Yonah and A. Negev, *IEJ* 13 (1963), 147.

[79] On the inscriptions see M. Avi-Yonah, *IEJ* 12 (1962), 137–9; J. Naveh, *On Stone*, 87f. M. Avi-Yonah, *NEAE* I, 279, dates the destruction of the first synagogue around 355; in the following period a covered drainage channel was built over it, and a new synagogue was built over that in 459 (a capital bears the monogram of the Consul Patricius). The heat-induced discolouration of the mosaics shows that the synagogue was finally destroyed by fire. A Greek inscription, which is dated 471, may come from a synagogue near Caesarea; L. di Segni, 'A Jewish Greek Inscription from the Vicinity of Caesarea Maritima', *Atiqot* 22 (1993), 133–6, refers this date to the calendar of Dora, which would correspond to the year 408/9 or 409/10. D. Barag, *Atiquot* 25 (1994), 179–81, takes the destruction of the Temple as his starting-point and arrives at 540/41; di Segni, ibid., 183–6, stands by her dating. However, W. Horbury, 'A Proselyte's *Heis Theos* Inscription near Caesarea', *PEQ* 129 (1997), 133–7, suggests taking the letters which are read as a date together with the previous letters, reading them not as an abbreviation for *presbyteros*, but together as a (misspelt) *proselytos*. He too understands the text to be a donor inscription, which would of course no longer be precisely datable.

of the fifth century, and rebuilt in the fifth century and then used into the seventh century. The details are uncertain, as is the question whether the building was always used as a synagogue. The reason for the destruction could 'stem from local disturbances or from political persecution by the Christian Byzantine rulers against the Jewish communities in Palestine. It is also possible that the Samaritan revolt ... was responsible.'[80] The first reason seems most plausible, especially thinking of fanatical hordes of monks, like those under Bar Sauma; but it would be surprising if that had left no trace at all in contemporary literature; there is absolutely no evidence for political persecutions of Jewish communities in this period; if the Samaritan revolts are considered, then the destruction would have to be dated much later. The excavators themselves lament the uncertainty of the entire reconstruction of the building's history, so that probably the reason (and date) of its destruction must remain an open question unless and until further discoveries are made.

6. Synagogues in Imperial Legislation

CTh VII.8.2, probably published in 373 in Trier, forbids quartering soldiers in synagogues, which are treated in this respect on a footing of equality with other religious buildings. Otherwise the only laws on synagogues in the Codex Theodosianus date from the end of the fourth century, and either protect them or restrict the building of new synagogues. During seventy years of Christian rule, synagogues were not the subject of legislation, apart from the text mentioned, and the exemption of Jews in the full-time employment of the synagogue from curial duties. The synagogue was simply a reality that was taken for granted by the legal recognition of the Jewish religion. This only changed as Christianity advanced ever further and became radicalized and increasingly intolerant in the period after Julian.

The destruction of the synagogue of Kallinikon on the Euphrates in 388 caused a stir throughout the empire, as did its rebuilding by order of the emperor at the expense of the

---

[80] S. Dar and Y. Mintzker, 'The Synagogue of Horvat Sumaqa, 1983–1993', in Urman and Flesher I, 157–65, quote 162f; see also S. Dar, *Sumaqua. A Jewish Village on the Carmel* (Hebrew), Tel Aviv 1998.

perpetrators, the Christian community, and also the resistance to it offered by Ambrose, Bishop of Milan.[81] However, CTh XVI.8.9, dated 19 September 393, clearly shows that this was not an isolated incident. The law was addressed to the supreme military commander of the eastern empire, Count Addeus: 'The Jewish religion is not forbidden by law. That is sufficiently clear. We are thus seriously concerned that in some places their meetings have been forbidden. Your sublime Greatness is to curb with suitable severity, on receipt of this order, the atrocities of those who take forbidden liberties under the cloak of Christian religion and attempt to destroy and plunder synagogues.'

This law appears to have been effective in the eastern empire. Not so in the west, where a new law was necessary four years later. In CTh XVI.8.12, dated 17 June 397, Arcadius addressed the *Praefectus praetorio* of Illyria: The governors are responsible for protecting Jews from attack and that 'they remain in their synagogues in their accustomed peace'. On 26 July 412, Honorius issued a further law at Ravenna (CTh XVI.8.20), addressed to the *Praefectus praetorio* John: '(Buildings) which are known to be used by Jews for their meetings, and which are described as synagogues, let no-one dare to desecrate or occupy; for all shall keep their own with rights undisturbed, without attacks on religion or worship.' There follows a reminder of the Jewish privilege not to be disturbed on the sabbath on the pretext of public business.

CTh XVI.8.21, dated 6 August 420, is again addressed to the *Praefectus praetorio* of Illyria.[82] The tone of this law towards the Jews is completely different, no longer neutral, but aggressive: 'Let no one, as long as he is innocent, be disparaged and subjected to attacks because he is a Jew, by whatever religion. Their synagogues and houses may not be burned down everywhere, nor wrongly damaged without any reason.' If someone is involved in some crime, that is a matter for the courts and not an excuse for private revenge. 'But as we wish care to be taken in this respect for the persons of Jews, so we also think it necessary to caution them that the Jews are not to become impudent and act rashly without

---

[81] Ambrose, *ep.* 40.6.18 (PL 16, 1103f.).
[82] The dating of the law is uncertain. Mommsen offers 412 as a possible date in his edition of the CTh; 418 has also been suggested. M. Avi-Yonah, *Jews*, 218, 230 n. 38, dates it with Seeck to 420, as does A. Linder, *The Jews*, 438f.

observing the proper deference towards the Christian religion, because of pride in the safety of their own religion.'

We do not know the precise occasion of this text, but there must have been several attacks in Illyria against Jews, their belongings and their places of worship. Although the law protects them against attacks 'without any reason', i.e. not absolutely, it is connected with a clear rebuke to the Jews that they should not dare to take liberties with regard to Christians.

The next law, CTh XVI.8.22, dated 20 October 415 and addressed to Aurelian, *Praefectus praetorio* of the eastern empire, will be considered in some detail in the chapter on the patriarchate, since it concerns the 'crime' of the patriarch Gamaliel. Among other things it states: 'From now on he may cause no more synagogues to be built, and if there are some in isolated places that can be pulled down without a disturbance, he is to do so.'

Does this mean that the building of new synagogues had been forbidden at an earlier time? Such a law has not been preserved, but should probably be assumed (see CTh XVI.8.25, 27, dated 423). Otherwise this paragraph would not describe one of Gamaliel's crimes and warn against its repetition, but rather it would represent a punitive restriction of his powers because of other, unspecified infringements. After the previously mentioned measures protecting synagogues, although they were finally only half-hearted, this is the first legislative restriction on synagogue building that is extant.

In the year 423 three laws follow each other within a short space of time, all addressed to the *Praefectus praetorio* Asclepiodotus. CTh XVI.8.25, dated 15 February, says:

> From now on, no synagogues of the Jews whatsoever may be simply taken away or burned down. And if, after publication of the law [i.e. CTh XVI.8.9 of 393] synagogues have been again forcibly dispossessed or claimed for churches or in any case sanctified for the holy mysteries, they are to be given sites on which they may build, according to the size of those which have been taken away. Votive gifts also, if any such have been taken away, are to be given back, in so far as they have not yet been dedicated for the holy mysteries. But if their honourable consecration does not permit their being returned, a suitable price should be given to the Jews

for them. No further synagogues may be built, but the old may remain in their present form.

There is no mention of compensation for synagogues that have been burned down; where synagogues have been consecrated as churches, only a corresponding piece of land is to be offered in replacement; apparently the Jewish community must bear the costs of rebuilding themselves. The final sentence forbids the building of new synagogues, unless these are simply to replace synagogues that have been taken away by Christians or burned down. It also appears to forbid alterations to existing synagogues.

The law CTh XVI.8.26, dated 9 April of the same year, was published after Jewish intervention. The condescending tone towards all non-Christians is striking:

> Our own and earlier decrees are known and published to all, by which we have set limits to the audacity of the detestable pagans, Jews and heretics. However, we are glad to take the opportunity to repeat the law, and wish the Jews to know: At their pitiful request we have decreed that those who, under the cloak of venerable Christianity, carelessly permit many things, shall cease to insult and persecute them, so that now and in the future no one may occupy their synagogues and no one set fire to them. The Jews themselves, however, shall be condemned to confiscation of their property and eternal exile if it comes to light that they have circumcised a person of our belief or have given the order to do so.

It is of course possible that the final threat of punishment against Jews who circumcise Christians or cause them to be circumcised gives an indication of the cause of the anti-Jewish violence against which the Jews have now asked the emperor for protection. But it is equally possible that the emperor promises the legal protection that has been asked for, but simultaneously, for no particular reason, perhaps on the insistence of ecclesiastical circles, puts the 'detestable' Jews in their place.

In CTh XVI.8.27, dated 8 June 423, Theodosius again returns to the subject.

> Let that which we have recently decreed regarding the Jews and their synagogues remain in force; let permission therefore never be given for new synagogues to be built,

but they should not have to fear that the old ones will be taken away from them.

Theodosius' third *novella* of 31 January 438 takes up and expands the prohibition of building new synagogues: 'No synagogue may be newly built. Permission to repair existing synagogues is only to be given if they are threatened with immediate collapse.'

These are the laws in the Codex Theodosianus regarding synagogues. A constant worsening of the situation is clearly to be seen. Not only does state protection for synagogues become more and more half-hearted; the obligation to compensate if synagogues are occupied or destroyed by Christians is continually lightened. The later laws are also increasingly restrictive on synagogue building, and threaten and insult Judaism. We may confidently assume that the church exercised particular pressure on the legislature on this point; we know this with certainty of Ambrose, but also of the Syrian Stylite Simeon, and can assume it in other cases. For our interests the question remains whether these laws also affected the synagogues in Palestine. CTh XVI.8.22 of 415, concerning the patriarch Gamaliel, is the only one of the laws cited which directly refers to Palestine. Did it have an effect on the actual life of the Jews in Palestine? The excavations to date seem to prove the contrary.

7. Some Conclusions

(a) The archaeological finds in Palestine confirm the spread of Jewish settlement known from literary sources: the centres are Galilee, the Golan Heights and a strip in the south, in the city territory of Eleutheropolis. In Judaea and Samaria, by contrast, there are hardly any synagogue finds, and in the coastal strip only Caesarea is certain for this period. If we may rely on the literary sources, new finds will complete this picture but not alter it substantially.

(b) The building types and furnishings of the synagogues are very varied. The inscriptions are often in Greek, but relatively often also in Hebrew or Aramaic. Some congregations must have been fairly rich. But, in contrast to the building of Christian churches, there is no epigraphic evidence for individual donors' giving an entire synagogue. Rather they donate individual columns, expanses of mosaic and so on.

(c) The history of the buildings hardly indicates a worsening in the situation of the Jews; in many cases three synagogues follow each other on the same site, each bigger than the last and continually altered. We do not know the reasons for the abandonment of Meiron and the temporary evacuation of Chorazin. In Beth Shearim the departure of the patriarch was probably responsible for the fact that in the second half of the fourth century no new building was undertaken. It is typical that a site for a synagogue, once chosen, was retained; this has halakhic reasons, but was also made possible by the situation. In the course of time, most of the synagogues were not only enlarged, but also more richly furnished. There is not a single example of the transformation of a synagogue into a church. An exception, but outside our period and area, is Gerasa, where in 530 a church was built over a synagogue of the fourth or fifth century. Here and there synagogues were later used as mosques.

(d) Deliberate destruction of a synagogue by hostile forces can nowhere be proven; even the cases of Beth Shearim and Sumaqa are inconclusive. Synagogues are more likely to have been destroyed by earthquakes, or had to make room for a new building. As regards the many coin hoards found to date, this would point to harassment by external enemies, flight without returning or death of the owners only if they were to cluster markedly at particular times. Many other reasons could be found to set up such a hiding-place for money and not to empty it later.

(e) Apart from in Capernaum, synagogues and churches do not seem to have stood in close proximity to each other anywhere in the fourth century. The closest proximity is found in the southern strip around Eleutheropolis, and should of course also be assumed in cities like Caesarea. Not until the fifth century, as a consequence of monastery building in Beth Shean and its surroundings, as in Tiberias and Jericho, was there a closer neighbourhood of synagogue and church.

(f) Thus in general we should assume peaceful coexistence of Jews and Christians in the fourth century, in largely separate spheres of life. It does not appear to have been necessary in Palestine to apply the laws protecting synagogues from the late fourth century. But the prohibition on building new synagogues or expanding existing ones does not appear to have been applied in the Jewish heartlands either, as the history of synagogue building in Palestine clearly shows. This is true despite the rebuke administered to the Patriarch in 415. The legislation regarding synagogues, like the Christian attacks which led to it, seems to have been principally a matter for the Diaspora.

VI

The Revolt against Gallus

In the previous chapter we several times came across the theory that the destruction of some Palestinian synagogues could have been a consequence of the revolt against Gallus shortly after 350. This is generally assumed for Beth Shearim, but is also accounted a possibility in the cases of Meiron and Chorazin. Since there is not sufficient evidence for the rising of the Palestinian Jews under Constantine which John Chrysostom reports (see pp. 46f.), the revolt under the Caesar Gallus would have been the first Jewish revolt against Rome since Bar Cochba. At the same time it would have been the first individual event of consequence in the history of Palestine for which there are reasonable witnesses since the Christianization of the Roman Empire. However, a more detailed assessment of the revolt – its exact date, extent and motives – is not at all certain. Scholars in the tradition of H. Graetz, who understand Jewish history as one of persecution and suffering, have combined the few notes in the Church Fathers, and a few rabbinic texts which cannot be precisely attributed, into a detailed history of a large revolt, as for example M. Avi-Yonah. In an understandable reaction, S. Lieberman places a very low value on the sources; according to him it was a relatively unimportant local affair, thus he represents the opposite extreme. Is an evaluation of the sources possible that does not simply represent a compromise for which there would be just as little historical justification?[1]

---

[1] A comprehensive survey, including the history of scholarship, is offered by B. G. Nathanson's dissertation. Before that the most detailed treatments are M. Avi-Yonah, *Jews*, 176–84, and S. Lieberman, 'Palestine', 366–444, 423f. B. Z. Luria, 'Zekher ha-Makkabim bime gezerot Ursiqinos', *Sinai* 46, vol. 90 (1981f.), 97–100, interprets too much from a passage in SongR and RuthR, which does not necessarily belong in this historical context. See also J. Geiger, *The Last Jewish Revolt*; id. in Z. Baras et al. (eds.), *Eretz Israel* I, 202–8; P. Schäfer, 'Der Aufstand'.

1. The Literary Sources

The oldest text which mentions this revolt is Sextus Aurelius Victor's *Liber de Caesaribus*, completed between 359 and 361. He was a pagan whose political career culminated in the post of Prefect of Rome in 388–389. After his description of how Magnentius sought to seize the imperial power, he writes: 'And meanwhile a revolt (*seditio*) of the Jews, who had raised Patricius against all law to a kind of royal position (*nefarie in regni speciem*), was suppressed' (42.11).

In his *Chronicon*, probably completed in Constantinople in 380, that is, before he settled in Bethlehem, where he could have obtained independent, detailed information, Jerome writes under the 282nd Olympiad and the 15th regnal year of Constantius (351–352): 'Gallus suppressed the Jews, who had killed soldiers by night and captured weapons for a revolt. Many thousand people were killed, even harmless children; and their cities of Diocaesarea, Tiberias and Diospolis, as well as countless villages, he gave over to the flames.'[2]

During his long stay in Palestine Jerome only mentioned the revolt once more, in his Daniel commentary of 407. There he adds no new facts, but combines the events with the subsequent developments, when he says that many Jews saw Julian as the 'little help' of Dan. 11:34: 'For after they had been oppressed by Gallus Caesar and had courageously endured much suffering in the oppression of their captivity, he (Julian) appeared as one who professed to love the Jews.'[3]

In the first half of the fifth century there is also the evidence of Socrates and of Sozomen, who is dependent on him. Socrates writes, after mentioning Magnentius' end: 'At the same time as these events there was another war in the east within the country. The Jews of Palestinian Diocaesarea arose in arms against the Romans and laid waste the area. But Constantius Gallus, whom the emperor had appointed Caesar and sent to the east, sent troops and overcame them. And he ordered them to raze their city of Diocaesarea to the ground.'[4] Although he was born in southern Palestine, Sozomen does not appear to have sought

---

[2] Jerome, *Chronicon* 282nd Olympiad, § 15 (GCS 47, 238).
[3] Jerome, *Comm. Dan.* 11.34 (CC 75 A, 924).
[4] Socrates, *Church history* II.33 (PG 67, 296 A).

additional information, but simply to have paraphrased Socrates: 'But the Jews of Diocaesarea laid waste Palestine and its surroundings; they had got hold of weapons and refused to obey the Romans. The Caesar Gallus, who was in Antioch, heard of this, sent troops and overcame them. And he laid waste Diocaesarea.'[5]

Finally there is the *Chronography* of Theophanes, from 810–814. He writes on the year 5843 since the creation of the world: 'In this year the Jews revolted around Palestine. And they killed many of the other peoples, Greeks and Samaritans. And they themselves, the entire people, were destroyed by the Roman army, and their city of Diocaesarea was obliterated.'[6] This is the earliest text that also mentions attacks on the local population by the insurgents; but strikingly he does not mention Christians alongside Greeks (Hellenes) and Samaritans.

Jewish texts that could be read as referring to the revolt against Gallus are scarce, if they can be found at all. PesR 8 (F. 29 b) is quoted repeatedly as the main source of evidence, commenting on Zeph. 1:10.[7] God answers Israel's question, when he will visit Jerusalem to drive out the worship of idols, as follows:

> As soon as I have done what is written above; 'On that day, says the Lord, a cry will be heard from the Fish Gate' – that is Acco, which lies in the lap of the fishes – 'and a wail from the Second Quarter' – that is Lydda, which was the second after Jerusalem; 'and a loud crash from the hills' – that is Sepphoris, which lies in the hills; 'wail, you inhabitants of the valley' – that is Tiberias, which lies deep down like a valley. The Holy One said, blessed be He, I have executed judgement on these four cities, which the heathen did to them. At the same hour 'I will search Jerusalem with lamps'.

It is indeed tempting to interpret the text as referring to the events under Gallus. The places named by Jerome are mentioned

---

[5] Sozomen, *Church history* IV.7.5 (GCS 50, 146).
[6] Theophanes Homologetes, *Chronography* for the year 5843 (PG 108, 140 C).
[7] E.g. H. Graetz, *Geschichte* IV, 394; he is followed by S. Dubnow, *Weltgeschichte* III, 219 n. 1, and M. Avi-Yonah, *Jews*, 179. More cautious are J. Geiger, 'The Last Jewish Revolt', 251, and B. G. Nathanson, *The Fourth Century Jewish 'Revolt'*, 182. P. Schäfer, 'Der Aufstand', 195, is completely against such an interpretation ('lacks any foundation'), following Z. Frankel, 'Der Aufstand', 151 n. 5, and S. Lieberman, 'Palestine', 338.

here also, with the addition of Acco. However, this was a city where the majority of the population was non-Jewish, and also fortified. M. Avi-Yonah suggests battles only in the vicinity of Acco;[8] but there is no other evidence for such battles.

There is no rabbinic name to help with the chronological classification of the text. The construction in the final, commenting speech of God is problematic. 'Which the heathen did to (in) them' seems to interrupt the rhythm of the text lamely. What is more, the sentence is ambiguous. How unclear the construction of the Hebrew text is may be seen in the different suggested translations for the final sentence. H. Graetz translates: 'I have executed judgement on these four cities by means of what the enemies have done to them.'[9] Thus he understands the fault that is being punished as having been committed in the cities; their judgement is executed by the action of their enemies. But W. Braude translates as follows: 'After I shall have executed judgement in those four places for that which idolaters wrought in them, then "I will search Jerusalem with lamps".'[10] The entire sentence is applied to the future, including the judgement on the cities which Graetz puts into the past. Braude comments on his translation as follows: God will proceed against the idolators in Jerusalem according to the tried and tested strategy of attacking armies, which, when they attack Palestine, only move in on Jerusalem at the end. Thus the translation differs according to the prior understanding, and influences its interpretation accordingly.

Are we to take the cities as the victims or the location of the heathen's acts ('what the heathen did *to* them' or '*in* them')? The second option is clearly preferable; otherwise God would not execute judgement on the cities, but *because* of them, because of the crimes of the heathen against these cities. Let us therefore assume that the divine judgement against the four cities mentioned was an action against the idolatry practised there. In that case the mention of the Jewish city of Tiberias is not entirely understandable; Sepphoris, being largely Jewish, and Lydda, also mentioned as a Jewish centre, do not fit very well either.

A further question has to do with the time of the judgement.

---

[8] M. Avi-Yonah, *Jews*, 180.
[9] See n. 7 above.
[10] W. G. Braude, *Pesikta Rabbati*, New Haven 1968, I 149.

Are we to understand that the judgement against the four cities has already been executed, so that only the purification of Jerusalem remains? Or is it simply a matter of a sequence of entirely eschatological events, of which the purification of Jerusalem is the final climax? If the text is to be interpreted with regard to events of the revolt against Gallus, then the first conclusion is preferable. For example, S. Dubnow speaks of this text as a sermon 'which speaks of a bloody judgement executed by the Romans against the Jews in four towns: Acco (Ptolemais), Lydda, Zippora and Tiberias'.[11] Then an eschatological act would already have occurred, and only the purification of Jerusalem would be still to come. Such an interpretation of historical events as the first act of the eschatological drama would only make sense if it were published very soon after those events; at a later date it would probably have been dropped as a historical misunderstanding. Even if we were to assume a date for our passage soon after 352 (for which there is no evidence), an unaltered adoption of the text into the much later body of the Pesiqta would be surprising, if the text is to be understood in this way.

Thus W. Braude's suggestion for understanding the text remains the most probable. Zeph. 1:10 is here commented on in the usual style of rabbinic interpretation, whereby the separate, partial statements are distributed to a number of important cities in Palestine. As for the choice of names, omitting Caesarea or even Scythopolis, the advances of enemy armies in the past may have provided the model; but to what extent could the preacher, centuries later, have still known about them? At least two of the names, Acco and Tiberias, could be read straight out of the Biblical text, and their mention is understandable as interpretation without any historical context. Lydda as the 'second' city could have come from a reinterpretation of the Greek name of the city, Diospolis, to Dispolis; then only one more Jewish centre remained to be found for a section of a verse, and Sepphoris was chosen.

If these considerations are correct, then the text does not speak of the suppression of a revolt, in fact it does not speak of a historical event at all; one is not even necessary as a model for

---

[11] S. Dubnow, *Weltgeschichte* III, 219 n. 1.

coming eschatological events. Topical Biblical interpretation is sufficient to understand the text.[12]

While the text quoted above cannot be ascribed to a fixed historical date, and no contemporary basis is necessary for its interpretation, there are a number of rabbinic statements which clearly belong in the period in question because of their mention of Ursicinus, the general under the command of the Caesar Gallus. For example, jMeg III.1.74 a says; 'Ursicinus burned a Torah scroll in Sennabris. R. Jona and R. Jose were asked: Is it permitted to read from this [damaged] book in public? He said: It is forbidden. Not that it was [truly] forbidden; rather, they should mourn and buy another [Torah scroll].'[13] The Talmud mentions an incident in Sepphoris from the same period: 'In the days of King Ursicinus, people from Sepphoris were wanted. They put plaster (*siplini*, Greek *splēnion*) on their noses and were not recognized. But finally they were denounced and all of them were captured by him' (jJeb XVI.2.15 c = jSota IX.3.23 c). GenR 31.16 (Th-A 283), where Ursicinus is not mentioned, but R. Huna roughly gives the chronological context, is thought to belong in this period. The text speaks of R. Huna staying in the caves of Tiberias on his flight from the Goths. We do not know whether this means Roman troops or perhaps the patriarch's Gothic bodyguard, which did proceed against rabbis, and thus this text is of no great help to us.

Other texts speak of supplying Ursicinus' soldiers. This illustrates the principle that in case of mortal danger the Biblical law may be broken, with very few exceptions: 'R. Jona and R. Jose permitted [the troops to be supplied] on the Sabbath because of Ursicinus. ... For he did not intend religious persecution, but only wanted hot bread to eat' (jShebi IV.2.35 a, also jSanh III.6.21 b). Thus it was not a situation in which it was necessary to confess one's faith by holding fast to an individual law. In jBetsa

---

[12] It is tempting to understand the phrase 'which the heathen did to (in) them' as a later gloss, in which case the object of judgement would not be Jewish guilt but the oppression of the Jews by the heathen. However, extreme caution is necessary if any alteration of a text is considered.

[13] Sennabris is on the Sea of Galilee. Z. Frankel, 'Der Aufstand', 150, wished to read Sinkaris instead of Sennabris – confusion of b and k is common in Hebrew manuscripts – and thus understood the text as referring to the inhabitants of the Roman fort of Singara in Mesopotamia, and the whole episode as belonging to Ursicinus' campaign against Persia.

I.6.60 c three rabbis give as a reason for their permission to deliver bread for Ursicinus on the Sabbath the fact that the community might need him in the future. jSanh III.6.21 b is probably to be understood in the same context: 'When Proclus came to Sepphoris, R. Mana permitted the bakers to go to market [on the Sabbath]. The rabbis of Naya [= Nave] permitted the baking of leavened bread at Pesach [for the soldiers]. It is usually assumed that Proclus was an officer of Ursicinus, but this assumption is not a necessary one.[14]

More evidence for Ursicinus is found in jBer V.1.9 a: 'R. Jona and R. Jose went to Antioch to Ursicinus. He saw them and rose up before them. People said to him: Do you rise up before these Jews? He answered, Upon your life, as I went into battle I saw their faces and was victorious.' At Joma 69 a, Alexander the Great says the same in an encounter with Jews. Legendary transferral is more likely from Ursicinus to the famous Alexander than the other way around, but it is more likely to be a 'wandering' story. In jBer, apart from Ursicinus, similar behaviour is ascribed to a Roman governor of Caesarea regarding R. Hanina and R. Jehoshua ben Levi, with the explanation: 'I saw their angel faces.'

When should this visit of the rabbis to Ursicinus be dated? It is usually thought to be an intervention after the revolt, which cannot be proved. But the anecdote could also refer to some other occasion, for example a visit to the Jewish community in Antioch. For even after the death of Gallus Ursicinus was again stationed in Antioch.[15]

Not a single one of the texts named above explicitly mentions

---

[14] S. Lieberman, 'Palestine', 352, prefers not to refer the text to the time of Gallus at all. R. Mana, he says, only became head of the rabbinic court in Sepphoris after the death of Gallus, perhaps even after Constantius. Unfortunately, we do not have the basis for such a chronological fixation as this either.

[15] For example, M. Avi-Yonah, *Jews*, 181, refers the journey of the two rabbis to an intervention immediately after the revolt. J. Geiger in Z. Baras et al. (eds.), *Eretz Israel* I, 206, while not specifying a time, assumes 'that they came to intervene with Ursicinus in some matter connected with the revolt, perhaps in favour of Jewish supporters of the revolt who were still in hiding and had not yet been punished.' Z. Frankel, 'Der Aufstand', 149, is of the opinion that the story dates from Ursicinus' second sojourn in the east in 359–360, and that under Gallus the rabbis would not have dared to travel to Antioch. This theory is just as unprovable as the hypothesis regarding Sennabris mentioned in n. 13 above. I was unable to consult R. Delmaire's article 'Le maître de la milice Ursicinus dans le Talmud de Jerusalem', in *Mélanges à la mémoire de M.-H. Prévost*, Paris 1982.

a Jewish revolt. On the one hand there are police actions for unspecified reasons in Sepphoris, possibly also in Tiberias, on the other everyday problems arising from the needs of the Roman troops stationed in or passing through Palestine. The incident with the Torah scroll in Sennabris is also hard to interpret without more details, but does not appear to have been particularly serious. The order of the Talmudic texts, which is by associated subjects, does not permit us to refer all the examples named for the necessity of supplying the troops to the same incidents. This has already been mentioned for the case of Proclus in Sepphoris, but neither can the decision of the rabbis of Nave be fixed more precisely; it could have happened at any time, and thus does not represent evidence for the extent of the revolt or its consequences so far east of the Jordan.[16] A more precise allocation of the rabbinic texts would be possible only if we were to succeed in reconstructing the course of events independently of them.

2. The Historical Context

Thus, at least in the present stage of our discussion, we do not have Jewish evidence for a revolt against Gallus Caesar. The non-Jewish texts also offer little concrete evidence. Perhaps a consideration of the historical context and the possible motives for a Jewish revolt may take us further.

The sources connect the events with the general unrest that was prevalent in the Roman empire around 350. In that year Magnentius revolted in Augustodunum (Autun) against Constans, Constantius' co-regent. Shortly afterwards, Constans was murdered near the Pyrenees, as he fled. Italy and Africa recognized Magnentius, making him *de facto* ruler of the west. Vetranio seized power in Illyricum, perhaps supported by Constantius, who wished to contain Magnentius. At the same

---

[16] Compared with my short description in *Die römische Herrschaft im Urteil der Juden*, Darmstadt 1983, 100–3, my assessment of the state of the evidence has become much more sceptical. P. Schäfer, 'Der Aufstand', 197, is of the opinion that if Naya should really mean Nave, then this would be an argument for the association of the Ursicinus text with the Persian campaign. But here too it may be objected that the connection with the previous Ursicinus text is simply editorial, and that the actual and chronological context remains unclear.

The Revolt against Gallus

time, the Empire was threatened by the Persians in the east. In the years 337, 346 and 350 Shapur II besieged Nisibis. His attacks were unsuccessful, as yet, but the next attack was only a matter of time.

In this situation Constantius appointed Gallus, his cousin (and brother-in-law), and like himself a grandson of Constantius I, to be Caesar of the east. Once the Persians had been pushed back for the time being, the emperor then had his hands free for his war against Magnentius (351–353) and for fighting off the Franks and Alemanni, who had invaded Gaul in 352.

S. Aurelius Victor makes the chronological interwovenness of events particularly clear, when he writes, immediately after a paragraph on the three-year war against Magnentius, '*And meanwhile* a revolt of the Jews ... was suppressed'. Directly after this he writes of the death of Gallus in 354. Jerome places his remarks on the revolt between Gallus' appointment in 351 and his execution of a number of noblemen in Antioch, in connection with the high treason trials of 353.

Judging by these authors, a date between 351 and 353 is possible, and each of these years has its supporters.[17] It is striking that Ammianus Marcellinus, who was in Ursicinus' suite from 353, and therefore in immediate proximity to Gallus in Antioch, does not mention the Jewish revolt against Gallus at all. This has been explained by pointing to Ammianus' own remarks at the end of his description of the high treason trial of 353: 'Gallus ... had many such things investigated. There is no point telling it in detail' (XIV.9.9). The revolt in Sepphoris, it has been said, was too unimportant to be mentioned.[18] Of course this is possible. But Ammianus' extant work begins with Book XIV and the year 353, and since it is in the form of annals, he could very well have written about a Jewish revolt in the lost portion. This would rule

---

[17] M. Avi-Yonah, *Jews*, 178, speaks of the revolt breaking out in June 351, i.e. at the beginning of the fifteenth year of Constantius; J. Geiger, 'The Last Jewish Revolt', 250, and P. Schäfer, 'Der Aufstand', 184, 198, prefer 351 but think 352 also possible; S. Lieberman, 'Palestine', 337, dates it to 352 or possibly 353.

[18] Thus S. Lieberman, 'Palestine', 340. Similarly R. C. Blockley, 'Constantius, Gallus and Julian as Caesars of Constantius II', *Latomus* 31 (1972), 433–69, p. 440: Ammianus passes over in his selection 'what are to him *minutiae*; and these include people whom the historian holds to be socially inferior'. But on p. 439 he also reckons with the possibility that the report of the revolt was in the lost portion of the work.

out the year 353;[19] thus we are left with the fifteenth regnal year of Constantius named by Jerome, or 351–352.

This period of general unrest in the empire, which entirely took up the emperor's attention in the west, could seem an opportune moment for a revolt in the east. In theory the pressing danger from the Persians could have encouraged people in Palestine who were thinking of revolting; for there are a number of texts in the Talmud according to which the Jews of Palestine were hoping for the foreign domination of the Romans to be overcome by the Persians. But on the other hand, the Persian peril meant some concentration of troops in the east, centred on Antioch, the seat of the Caesar. Therefore, unless the Persians attacked at the same time, a revolt in Palestine had little chance of success. Troops from Antioch could too quickly march south and deal with the situation.[20]

3. Possible Causes of a Revolt

(a) General discontent

Judging by the date, a long and carefully planned revolt is unlikely. It seems more possible that long-suppressed discontent suddenly broke out, without calculating the most favourable moment. For example, H. Graetz is of the opinion that 'the accumulated hardships which Judaea had suffered from the Christian emperors' gave the courage to revolt.[21] But in fact under Constantine and even Constantius, despite the harsher tone of the few of his laws that have to do with Jews, which will be covered later, the Jews of Palestine were certainly no worse off than before.[22]

---

[19] B. G. Nathanson, *The Fourth Century Jewish 'Revolt'*, 31.
[20] According to the Bordeaux Pilgrim, there were fourteen overnight stations of the imperial post service between Antioch and Caesarea; in emergencies, of course, troops could move more quickly.
[21] H. Graetz, *Geschichte* IV, 393.
[22] CTh XVI.8.1 is dated by M. Avi-Yonah, following O. Seeck, to 339, which gives Constantius a more negative balance (*Jews*, 174), but it is more likely to date from 329, i.e. under Constantine; see p. 26 above.

Nor can it be proved that Gallus' regency in the east gave cause for a revolt, even though Ammianus Marcellinus portrays Gallus in a very bad light. The extant portion of his work begins with a chapter on the cruelty of Gallus and his wife Constantina, the sister of Constantius. Ammianus describes her as a Fury who drove on the already raging Caesar and was no gentler than her husband in her thirst for human blood (XIV.1.2). He says that Gallus was constantly afraid of conspiracies and 'in his rage, like a lion fed with corpses, had many such cases investigated' (XIV.9.9).

Constantius intervened because of these abuses, and left Gallus only the palace and guard troops (Ammianus XIV.7.9). Overall command of the troops was taken over by the general (*magister militum*) Ursicinus, brought from Nisibis on the Persian border. But as soon as 354 Ursicinus was suspected of being unreliable and was called to the court at Milan. However, he was apparently indispensable because of his military prowess; so he was only posted to Gaul and later sent back east because of the threat posed by the Persians, to Nisibis, Amida and Antioch again, until he was finally dismissed in 360. The suspicious emperor had already executed Gallus in 354.

Ammianus was a loyal subordinate of Ursicinus. This attitude to Ursicinus, whose role at the side of the young Gallus had perhaps not been entirely honourable, could have coloured Ammianus' description of the Caesar. We should at least assume exaggeration in Gallus' negative traits: 'His years of exile had brutalized Gallus, but he was not the monster of cruelty, guilty of fearful crimes, which Ammianus portrays.'[23] However, Aurelius Victor confirms his character in essence. But however Gallus may have behaved towards those around him in the court at Antioch, it will hardly have affected the Jews of Palestine.

Gallus is never mentioned in rabbinic literature. But the Talmudic texts about Ursicinus, which are collected above (pp. 166ff.) have caused some to conjecture that he was responsible for the outbreak of the revolt. H. Graetz takes the incident in Sennabris on the Sea of Galilee, whereby a Torah scroll was damaged by fire, as grounds for this conclusion: 'But Ursicinus seems positively to have intended a religious persecution.'[24] This

---

[23] D. Bowder, *The Age of Constantine and Julian*, London 1978, 48.
[24] H. Graetz, *Geschichte* IV, 393.

is untenable. Ursicinus, one of the latest historical figures to be mentioned several times in the Palestinian Talmud, is characterized by the rabbis in a neutral or positive manner. The Talmud expressly denies the intention of religious persecution in connection with supplying the troops. Thus S. Dubnow's more general hypothesis, that molestation by Ursicinus' Roman troops was the cause of the revolt,[25] also cannot stand. The necessity of supplying the troops with fresh bread, even on the Sabbath and at Pesach, is clearly acknowledged by the rabbis; we need not assume that the ordinary Jewish population, or at least a part of it, was more radical than the rabbis on this point of religious law.

Whoever understands the Talmudic texts about Ursicinus as an explanation of the revolt is naturally forced to place the incidents mentioned there before the outbreak of unrest. More common is the hypothesis that they stem from a time of heavier Roman occupation after the revolt had been suppressed. Each is possible, but cannot be proved. Any increased stationing of troops could have occasioned the rabbinic decisions. Such a reinforcement of troops could perhaps also be connected with the march against the Persians;[26] but it should be remembered that this would have meant a march of several weeks to the disputed border near Nisibis. It is never explicitly stated in the texts that Ursicinus himself was in Palestine; even in the case of the incident in Sennabris, he is simply named as the commander responsible, according to the style of the rabbinic texts. Certainly these texts do not suffice to account for a possible revolt.

(b) Messianic unrest? A military coup?

Occasionally a Messianic explanation is offered for the revolt. However, there is no rabbinic evidence for increased Messianic hopes at this period, and there are also no Christian sources, which would certainly not have concealed such a connection. The single possible indication for it is S. Aurelius Victor's assertion that the rebelling Jews 'had raised Patricius against all law to a kind of royal position'. A Jewish 'king' could really only be understood in a Messianic sense.

---

[25] S. Dubnow, *Weltgeschichte* III, 218.
[26] P. Schäfer, 'Der Aufstand', 196f.

But who was this Patricius? Z. Frankel did not see it as a personal name, but as a title, thinking of an anonymous patrician.[27] This is not impossible, but unlikely. Even more questionable is the hypothesis that the Jewish patriarch is meant, whom the Jews elevated to be 'a kind of king', or whose usurpation of power was understood as a revolt and rebuffed by the authorities accordingly.[28]

Understanding Patricius as a proper name does not yet tell us anything about his origins. For example, the name Patricius is found in the synagogue inscription of Hammath Gader as the name of a donor, and also appears in rabbinic literature (e.g. in the form R. Patroqi in jJoma IV.4.41 d). It cannot therefore be ruled out that this Patricius was a Jew, although it equally cannot be proved.[29] S. Lieberman interprets the passage in Aurelius Victor as follows: 'The Jews (of Diocaesarea) raised a certain Patricius to royal power (perhaps with the help of the Roman garrison itself). This Patricius could have been a pagan officer, whom the Jews of Diocaesarea preferred to the extremely cruel Gallus, who, like the Emperor, was a devout Christian.'[30]

An argument in favour of Lieberman's interpretation could be that pretenders to the throne were common at this time. Beside the more well-known men in the west, there were also pretenders in Gallus' territory. Indeed, it was in order to investigate such charges that Ursicinus was called from Nisibis to Antioch in 353 (Ammianus Marcellinus XIV.9.1). Since we will shortly discuss the hypothesis that the revolt was started by textile manufacturers, it is of interest that the trial also concerned a royal gown that was discovered in Tyre: 'In Tyre, a secretly woven royal gown was reported. It was not clear by whom it had been ordered or for whose use it had been made.' In the course of the trial, 'the

---

[27] Z. Frankel, 'Der Aufstand', 147; J. Cohen, 'Roman Imperial Policy', 22 n. 160, also reckons with this possibility; B. S. Bachrach, 'The Jewish Community', 418, speaks of 'a Jew with the name or perhaps the title of Patricius'.

[28] Thus J. Seaver, *The Persecution of the Jews in the Roman Empire 300–438*, Lawrence, Kansas 1952, 13. He translates 'Patricius' as Patriarch, i.e. apparently assumes an error in the transmission of the text, for which there is no evidence. H. Mantel, *Studies*, 242, also understands the text as referring to the Patriarch.

[29] See J. Naveh, *On Stone and Mosaic*, 57f. J. Geiger in Z. Baras et al. (eds.), *Eretz Israel* I, 206, and P. Schäfer, 'Der Aufstand', 187, are too negative in their judgement, since they rely on *CIJ* alone.

[30] S. Lieberman, 'Palestine', 340.

employees of the purple dyeing works were tortured and confessed to having woven a small sleeveless gown.' A certain Maras was then produced, 'a deacon, as the Christians say'. A letter from this person to the manager of the weaving mill in Tyre is shown, wherein he is told to finish a certain work quickly. The deacon is tortured to death without confessing anything (Ammianus Marcellinus XIV.7.20; 9.7). There would indeed be possible links here between state textile workers and pretenders to the throne, but only in the purple dyeing industry. However, we do not know whether Jews were also employed in this industry. Of course the rabbis are also aware that purple is not permitted to private persons: In DtnR 1.7, R. Tanchuma bar Abba tells the parable of a king who hears a salesman crying purple for sale and calls him to him at once. There is epigraphic evidence for connections between Jews from Tyre and the congregation in Sepphoris, but this is far too little to be able to base a hypothesis on it.

A few years later, in 359, when Constantius had returned to Constantinople from Sirmium in order to strengthen the east after the Roman defeat at Amida, there were more high treason trials, this time in Scythopolis. Ammianus speaks of exaggerated accusations of high treason (*quaedam colorata laesae crimina maiestatis*: XIX.12.1). The notorious lawyer Paulus ('The Chain') was appointed to investigate them. Among other things, questions put to the oracle at Abydos in the Thebaid had been leaked to the prosecution and were now held to be incriminating material. Many accused, both noble and ordinary people, were brought in from all sides on the basis of slanderous accusations. 'A town in Palestine, Scythopolis, was chosen as the site of deadly punishments. It seemed more suitable than any others for two reasons, since it was out of the way and lay half-way between Antioch and Alexandria, from which places the great majority of the accused were brought to trial.'

In such a general political atmosphere, an attempt at revolt in Palestine as well is easily conceivable, and certainly suspicion could arise that such a plan existed. But may Aurelius Victor be interpreted in this sense? M. Avi-Yonah's objection to the expression, 'a kind of kingdom', may be countered by reference to the same description for Calocerus, who attempted to seize power in 334.[31] But how can Aurelius Victor describe such an

---

[31] M. Avi-Yonah, *Jews*, 178. The reference to Calocerus (S. Aurelius Victor, *Liber de Caesaribus* 41.1.1: *specie regni*) is made by J. Geiger, 'The Last Jewish Revolt', 253.

attempt, even if it was supported by Jews, as a 'Jewish revolt', without naming the pretender himself or his supporting army?

An even more serious objection to Lieberman's hypothesis now arises: Was there even a sufficiently strong garrison in Sepphoris to be able to dare to attempt a revolt with even a minimal chance of success? The *Notitia Dignitatum* does not mention a military unit in this city. A passage sometimes quoted in this context, *Oriens* XXXIV.28, mentions a cavalry unit in Sabure or Veterocaria. The name is occasionally corrected to the more well-known Sepphoris, but probably refers to a town in the south of Palestine.[32] Although jPes IV.9.31 b mentions that in the days of R. Mani there was a *numerus*, i.e. a Roman unit of troops, in Sepphoris levying recruits, it does not appear to have been stationed in the city, but to have come there especially for the recruitment.[33] The possibilty remains, of course, that in the course of concentrating troops to fight the Persians Sepphoris was also occupied by troops, although it was some distance from the border area. The passages quoted earlier on supplying the Roman troops on the sabbath and at Passover could argue in favour; but it could also simply be a case of such troops passing through. Thus the necessary conditions for a military coup in Sepphoris remain highly dubious.

Finally, we must return to Ammianus' silence on the matter. Even if he treated the revolt in the lost part of his work, at the latest in the context of the trials in Antioch or the trial in Scythopolis we would expect another mention of it. This would not be a case of false accusation, but there would have been military operations and a pretender who was known by name. The choice of Scythopolis as scene of the trial, near Sepphoris which would have been destroyed only a few years earlier in the Jewish revolt, would then have acted as a deterrent. It would have been something really worth mentioning compared with the trivialities reported by Ammianus, not something unimportant that could be omitted. Equally remarkable is the silence of John Chrysostom, who asserts the existence of a revolt under Constantine that is otherwise unknown, but says nothing about a revolt under Constantius. It is not likely that Chrysostom confused the names

---

[32] F.-M. Abel, *Géographie* II, 183.
[33] See S. S. Miller, *Studies*, 43f. M. Avi-Yonah's assertion that the unit in Sepphoris was of approximately the same size as the Moorish cavalry in Jerusalem, cannot be proved. Cf. B. Isaac, *The Limits of Empire. The Roman Army in the East*, Oxford ²1992, 434f.

of the emperors. Thus the hypothesis of a military coup with Jewish backing is just as untenable as that of a purely Jewish revolt with Messianic inspiration.

(c) A weavers' revolt?

Finally M. Avi-Yonah's hypothesis should be considered. He sees the fact that the three cities participating in the revolt, Sepphoris, Tiberias and Lydda, were famous for their weaving industry, as confirmation for the assumption that 'the principal motive of the revolt was an economic one, the result of the damage done to the Jewish textile manufacturers by the decrees of Constantius concerning slavery'.[34]

How important was the Palestinian textile industry? The most important centre was Scythopolis, which was one of the best places for the weaving industry in the whole of the Roman empire. In Diocletian's maximum price edict, this city's products are named in the first of the three categories of quality in every section – tunics, dalmatics, cloaks, hooded cloaks, towels and linen.[35] We should perhaps assume the existence of a state textile industry here, as A. H. M. Jones has concluded from CTh X.20.8 (see below).[36] In the Talmud R. Zera names as an example for luxury clothes 'fine fabrics that come from Beth Shean' (jKet VII.8.31 c). Elsewhere, he wishes to buy a small piece of material in Beth Shean at the Saturnalia (jAZ I.2.39 c).

Here the *Expositio totius mundi* should be mentioned, written under Constantius. In a kind of economic geography it mentions the following centres of the textile industry: 'In the linen [industry; but *linteamina* could perhaps mean the textile industry in general] there are the following: *Scythopolis*, Laodicea, Byblos, Tyre, Beirut, which send linen [or textiles] to the whole world, and are distinguished by every abundance. But also Sarepta and *Caesarea* and *Neapolis*, also *Lydda*, which [produce] well-dyed purple' (§ 31).

However, we should not assume a more than regional importance for these Palestinian textile towns, with the exception

---

[34] M. Avi-Yonah, *Jews*, 179.
[35] T. Mommsen, *Der Maximaltarif des Diokletian*, Berlin 1893, chapters 26–28. See also Y. Dan, *The City*, 199.
[36] Jones, *LRE*, 837.

The Revolt against Gallus

of Scythopolis and possibly the purple dyeing works. The Roman authorities and troops could not meet their needs from production within Palestine, and had to import uniforms from Egypt.[37]

As regards Jewish participation in textile production, we know of flax cultivation in Galilee (R. Hiyya in jMSh V.8.56 d; jTaan III.6.66 d on flax production). The processing of (sheep's) wool can also be taken for granted, and we know of individual rabbis who traded in silk. On the other hand, it should be pointed out that in Jewish society weavers and fullers were held in low esteem (TEd I.3: 'There is no lower craft than weaving'; TQid V.14 mentions a number of kinds of work, particularly from the textile industry, and speaks of these as low occupations). The extant rabbinic evidence for Jewish textile production appears to indicate small-scale cottage processing rather than industrial production.[38] The fact that R. Zera wishes to buy a piece of material at the Saturnalia market in Beth Shean, despite the fact that this leads to problems of 'idol worship', appears also to document the fact that especially fine fabrics, at least, were not available from Jewish producers. The hypothesis should therefore be questioned that there was significant Jewish participation in the textile industry, especially as regards large manufacturing concerns in which the use of slaves would perhaps have been decisive. We know little enough about the role of slaves in the textile industry of late antiquity, but even less about possible Jewish businesses. It is very doubtful whether these would have lost their competitiveness because of the prohibition of owning pagan slaves, since the products on offer were in any case too few.

The list of cities named for the revolt also appears problematic when compared with the list of known centres of the textile industry, if the hypothesis of a weavers' revolt is to be accepted. In particular, the absence of Scythopolis from the list of cities

---

[37] A. H. M. Jones, 'The Cloth Industry under the Roman Empire', *Economic History Review*, second series 13.2 (1960), quoted in B. G. Nathanson, *The Fourth Century Jewish 'Revolt'*, 224f.

[38] See the evidence in S. Krauss, *Talmudische Archäologie* I, Leipzig 1910, 127–90. Cf. Z. Safrai, *The Economy of Roman Palestine*, London and New York 1994, 155–61, on the linen industry in Palestine. However, his account ends in the middle of the fourth century. The evidence for Tiberias' position as a centre of flax cultivation is scarce. The assertion that 'the cultivation of flax became one of the major industries in the economy of Palestine, as well as one of its major exports' (161) should be modified, especially as regards the Jewish share in the industry.

involved in the revolt is remarkable. Of course it could be objected that Scythopolis had a non-Jewish majority at the time. But there was nevertheless an important Jewish community there, which has been documented by synagogue finds. If the revolt is to be derived from dissatisfaction in the Jewish textile industry because of the slave laws that impeded their work, this could equally be applied to the Samaritans. Why did their centre of Neapolis, which the *Expositio* also mentions as a well-known textile town, not take part in the revolt? Conversely, the revolted cities of Sepphoris and Tiberias, which Avi-Yonah incorporates in his explanation, are not documented as textile centres in this period.

Let us turn to Constantius' slave laws, which are said to have occasioned the revolt. In fact it is a single law, which the Codex Theodosianus preserves in two separate parts. Constantius published it on 13 August 339, addressed to Euagrius, at the time probably *Praefectus praetorio* of Italy.[39]

> If any Jew should believe that he may buy a slave belonging to another religion [*secta*] or nation, let the slave be immediately appropriated by the treasury. But if he has circumcised the slave, let him not only suffer the loss of the slave, but also the death penalty. But if a Jew does not shrink from buying slaves that belong to the honourable faith, all [the slaves] that are found in his possession shall be taken away immediately, and no time may be lost before he loses possession of those who are Christians. (CTh XVI.9.2)

The second part of the same law is preserved in CTh XVI.8.6:

> Furthermore: as for women which Jews have brought into the society of their shame and which were previously in our

---

[39] The text does not mention a title for Euagrius. According to *PLRE* I, 284f., Euagrius was last *Praefectus praetorio* in 336 (–). The list of dignitaries in the appendix does not mention a *Praefectus praetorio* for 339. This would lead to the assumption of an earlier date for the law, especially since the MSS read Constantine instead of Constantius. For the hypothesis that Euagrius was *Praefectus praetorio* of Italy in 339, see K. L. Noethlichs, *Die gesetzgeberischen Maßnahmen*, 46, and the literature offered in his notes pp. 273f. According to him, the law should be ascribed to Constantine II rather than Constantius; thus also A. Linder, *The Jews*, 144–51; but G. de Bonfils, *Gli schiavi*, 125–42, again defends the ascription to Constantius, who could well have intervened by means of laws in his brother Constans' sphere; but the principal target, according to him, were probably the Jews in the great cities of the east (133).

The Revolt against Gallus

textile manufacturing industry [*gynaeceum*], it is decreed: they must be returned to the imperial textile manufacturing industry. This shall be the rule for the future: they may not join Christian women to their shame, and if they do it nevertheless, they shall suffer the death penalty.

No other relevant laws were published before the revolt against Gallus. Compared to earlier laws, CTh XVI.9.2 plus 8.6 does indeed represent greater stringency, because it forbids the purchase and not only the circumcision of non-Jewish slaves by Jews. Women are also explicitly mentioned. The terminology of the law does not make it clear whether mixed marriages between Jews and state textile employees are meant, or simply the conversion and enticing away of such women. Mixed marriages also involved the conversion of the woman to Judaism, and the question of women from the *gynaeceum* is closely related to the slave question, since the employees of this institution were more or less state slaves.[40]

B. S. Bachrach attempted a reconstruction of the events that led to this law. During the short interregnum after Constantine's death, 'a band of Jewish missionaries illegally invaded an imperial factory where wool was woven for the production of military and civil service uniforms. The missionaries vigorously preached and proselytized among the female Christian workers who had been assigned there.... Following their conversion to Judaism, the women refused to work in the government factory, but remained in the area and practiced their new religion.'[41] Their refusal to work was for religious reasons, because mixed fibres were also produced in the state factories, which were forbidden by the Jewish law. Bachrach takes Euagrius to be the *Praefectus praetorio* of Oriens, and therefore locates the events in Antioch.[42]

This reconstruction has only a very tenuous basis. It cannot be proved that Euagrius was *Praefectus praetorio* of Oriens in 339; nor is there evidence for a *gynaeceum* in Antioch; finally it is very unlikely that whole groups of Jewish missionaries could hold

---

[40] Jones, *LRE*, 836f.
[41] B. S. Bachrach, 'The Jewish Community', 408.
[42] B. S. Bachrach, 'The Jewish Community', 412 n. 48. K. L. Noethlichs, *Die gesetzgeberischen Maßnahmen*, 48, thinks of a state weaving factory in North Africa, specifically Carthage; all the concrete occasions for laws relating to weaving come from North Africa (n. 286).

missions in a state factory without being disturbed, and thus entice away valuable workers who were bound to their work for life by law. It is more than unlikely that in the case of such action, two years would have gone by before an intervention was finally resolved on. Further, such heavy-handed missionary attempts on the part of Jews are unknown in this period.

If we may assume Euagrius to have been in Italy in 339, as is generally done, the actual target of the law is surely to be found in the west, even if it may have affected individual Jewish textile producers in Palestine. Lists of *gynaecea* are only extant for the western empire; but of course such factories must have existed in the east as well. The occasion for the law were probably isolated cases in which state textile workers joined a Jewish business and also converted to Judaism. It may also have happened that converts married into a Jewish business. It is hardly possible to separate the two cases as regards the text of the law; both are equally forbidden as far as the legislature is concerned. In order to safeguard the economic interests of the state, the law stresses and intensifies religious directions.

Here we should briefly also consider CTh X.20.8. The law was published on 16 February 374 in Antioch and addressed to the finance minister (*Comes sacrarum largitionum*) Tatian:

> By the Kalends of August, those who, as it is said, retain linen weavers (*linteones*) must return them to their original situations. Otherwise let them know that for their persistence in such a great presumption they will be fined five pounds of gold each per person. No lesser punishment is promised to those who in future attempt to take on linen workers [*linyfos*] from Scythopolis who are subject to the public duty.

Apparently the law differentiates between state slaves in the manufacturing industry (*linteones*) and free linen workers in Scythopolis who were obliged to deliver raw material (yarn or half-finished cloth). This law does not absolutely prove that there was a *gynaeceum* in Scythopolis;[43] but it is clear evidence for an intervention in the (Jewish?) textile industry of Palestine. However, it occurred only after the events under Gallus, and was also not unusual for the time. If similar interventions occurred

---

[43] Y. Dan, *The City*, 196–8.

earlier, which then led to the revolt, it would be surprising that Beth Shean was not involved. But as an explanation for the revolt under Gallus the law is too late, while Constantius' law is too early. If this indeed occasioned the revolt, the time lapse between law and revolt would be surprising.

Thus the hypothesis of a revolt started particularly by Jewish textile manufacturers cannot be proved:[44] We know nothing of a significant Jewish textile industry in Palestine. State intervention, such as the prohibition for Jews of owning non-Jewish slaves, did not occur in the years before the revolt. In any case it cannot be proved that such interventions would have impaired the competitiveness of Jewish businesses, because the market was far too receptive for that.

Apart from the slave law of 339, Constantius did not pass a law respecting Jews that can be securely dated before the revolt. CTh XVI.8.7, dated 3 July 353, is probably too late: 'If, after the publication of this honourable law, anyone converts from Christianity to Judaism and joins the sacrilegious band (*sacrilegis coetibus*), We order that, if the accusation is proved, their property be forfeited to the treasury.' Basically this merely repeats the customary law that predated Christianity, which threatened a Roman citizen who allowed himself to be circumcised with the loss of his possessions and exile. But the text of this law forbids conversions to Judaism in general, that is, also those of women. Such prohibitions are not new; thus the law offers no plausible grounds for the revolt, even if it is chronologically prior to it. Thus our search for clear motives for such a Jewish revolt has remained fruitless.

4. Extent and Course of the Revolt?

Our examination has not so far yielded any information that might confirm and supplement the literary sources Aurelius Victor, Jerome and Socrates. But archaeological evidence that has been utilized for the revolt is also dubious. So far there is no archaeological evidence for the assertion that during the fighting Diocaesarea, Tiberias, Diospolis and many other cities were burned down. Not even in Sepphoris, which was the main sufferer, was the destruction very extensive. For as early as 374, as

---

[44] Thus B. G. Nathanson, *The Fourth Century Jewish 'Revolt'*, 227: it is unlikely that economic factors were a significant cause of the revolt.

Theodoret of Cyrrhus reports, eleven orthodox Egyptian bishops 'were exiled in a city called Diocaesarea, inhabited by Jews, the murderers of the Lord'[45] by the Arian emperor Valens. Thus the complete destruction of the city two decades before can scarcely be assumed. Much less is this a possibility for Tiberias, the most important rabbinic centre. There are neither archaeological grounds for this nor indications in rabbinic literature. Nor do we have evidence for Lydda/Diospolis. One indication might be, however, the fact that after the middle of the fourth century rabbinic sources cease to mention the Jewish academy 'of the south'.[46] But only a few decades later a synod of bishops took place in that city, which was also the home of a Jewish teacher of Jerome's: life apparently continued there. Did Jerome perhaps generalize from his information about Jewish unrest in Palestine, and simply give the names of the most important Jewish centres as well as the 'countless villages'? Socrates and Sozomen (who is dependent on him) only mention Sepphoris/Diocaesarea.

How are we to assess Jerome's assertion that countless villages were destroyed in the course of the revolt? M. Avi-Yonah points to traces of burning from this period in Sepphoris, and to the destruction of Beth Shearim. In three cities and fifteen villages (in Galilee, the western Plain of Jezreel and in the coastal plain) no Jewish inhabitants are mentioned after the revolt.[47] Unfortunately he does not offer evidence for this statement. B. G. Nathanson gives the following summary of her survey of possible archaeological evidence of destruction during the revolt: 'The following towns and villages were at least partially destroyed or

---

[45] Theodoret of Cyrrhus, *Church history* IV.19 (GCS 44, 259f.). Despite extensive excavations in Sepphoris, there is as yet no evidence of traces of destruction that may with absolute certainty be ascribed to the suppression of this revolt. See Z. Weiss and E. Netzer, *Qadmoniot* 30 (1997), 10.

[46] Z. Frankel, 'Der Aufstand', 146. He transfers the whole revolt to the south of Palestine. Ursicinus, he says, need not have been at the site of the revolt in person; 'a legion under a subordinate would probably have sufficed to reduce the cities, Lydda among them, to ashes and to turn the country into a wilderness.' (147).

[47] M. Avi-Yonah, *Jews*, 180. B. S. Bachrach, 'The Jewish Community', 418f., follows Avi-Yonah in his summary of events and adds details for which, however, there is no evidence. In Sepphoris, J. F. Strange and T. R. W. Longstaff associate a house which was destroyed by fire in the fourth century with the revolt: *RB* 93 (1986), 253. Not so the Israeli archaeologists who have excavated next door; see n. 45 above.

abandoned as a result of events to do with the Gallus revolt: Diocaesarea/Sepphoris, Beth Shearim, Chorazin and possibly Capernaum in Lower Galilee; Meiron and Nabratein in the Tetrakomia, and Tell el Juhadar in Gaulanitis.'[48] She concludes from this that the revolt spread over a wide geographical area, but was local and selective in character, and should rather be regarded as 'a number of very serious and destructive local disturbances'.[49]

It is surely correct not to deduce a revolutionary movement encompassing the entire region from isolated instances of destruction scattered widely across the region in this period. But the list cited goes much too far. Not every instance of destruction from this period can be connected with a revolt against Gallus. Quite apart from the earthquake of 363, there can have been many other reasons, by no means all of them military, for the destruction of buildings. But if we were to assume extensive effects of the revolt, Nathanson's hypothesis of a series of locally separate disturbances (roughly similar to the race riots of the sixties in the United States) seems to fit the archaeological evidence to date, which shows life going on undisturbed in many places in the region, better than the hypothesis of a comprehensive revolt.

Certainly the 'revolt against Gallus' cannot be entirely interpreted away. The literary witnesses, S. Aurelius Victor, Jerome and Socrates, who are probably independent of each other, should be taken seriously. However, we do not know to what extent their respective statements are historically reliable when they do not overlap with the other texts. Aurelius Victor, in particular, should be taken seriously as a witness. He speaks of *seditio*, which could perhaps also describe smaller instances of unrest. Thus, instead of a full-grown revolt, we should speak of Jewish terrorist activity; its

---

[48] B. G. Nathanson, *The Fourth Century Jewish 'Revolt'*, 161. The difficulties associated with this list may be seen in her remarks on p. 163: Tell el Jukhadar (in the Golan Heights) cannot with certainty be described as a Jewish settlement; the destruction of two large buildings and the coin finds, however, do suggest participation in the Gallus revolt, from which the existence of Jewish inhabitants could be deduced. This is a completely untenable circular argument. The excavator, D. Urman, thinks it proven that the town participated in the revolt against Gallus, Gregg and Urman, 146. By contrast, Z. U. Ma'oz, *NEAE* II, 521–3, ascribes the destruction to the earthquake of 363.

[49] B. G. Nathanson, *The Fourth Century Jewish 'Revolt'*, 164.

consequence was Roman intimidatory action, which Ursicinus' soldiers were involved in. Since Ursicinus himself was not involved in these actions, Ammianus did not need to mention him. We may probably assume Diocaesarea as the centre or place of origin of such unrest; it is the first or only name mentioned everywhere (except in Aurelius Victor). It is also not unlikely that weapons were looted from a Roman unit of troops. Since we have no evidence for Diocaesarea as a garrison town in this period, it was probably only a small unit, perhaps travelling through. It, or individual units on guard duty, could easily be overcome by 'terrorists'. Perhaps unrest spread to the surrounding country; in any case it was suppressed by the government without difficulty. The thousands of dead mentioned by Jerome would then be a gloating exaggeration, common in Christian authors. There is no evidence for H. Graetz' assumption that the revolt was so extensive that Constantius had to send Gallus new legions; this belongs to the legends of Jewish persecution and resistance.[50]

---

[50] H. Graetz, *Geschichte* IV, 393.

VII

Julian's Religious Policies and Palestine

A decade after the unrest under Gallus, the tables appeared to be turned again for the Jews of Palestine, and the religious development of the whole empire appeared to be on the threshold of a decisive change. From the viewpoint of later Christian historiography, 313 and the Edict of Milan was the turning-point, with the Christianization of the Roman empire then only a matter of time. But this was by no means an inevitable development, as Julian's reign shows.

Julian, Gallus' half-brother and cousin of the emperor Constantius, was in power for less than two years. After the death of Constantius he became sole ruler in November 361; he died on 26 June 363 as a result of a wound received in the Persian campaign. But these few months showed that the victory of Christianity was not a foregone conclusion. It was a shock from which Christian theologians did not recover for a long time. In a work written as late as 379, John Chrysostom reckons with the possibility that pagan rulers might again come to power;[1] in the western Empire, usurpers could hope to succeed, even in the early fifth century, with the support of the pagan population.

Despite Julian's failure, his attempt to reassert traditional paganism, Hellenism, against Christianity in the Empire has lost nothing of its fascination. How would history have continued if Julian had succeeded? Endless books have attempted to plumb the depths of this emperor.[2] Here we are simply concerned with

---

[1] John Chrysostom, *On the Enemies of the Monastic Life* 2.9 (PG 47, 344). See R. L. Wilken, *John Chrysostom*, 31.

[2] From the extensive literature on Julian, the older studies by J. Bidez, *La vie de l'empereur Julien*, Paris 1930, and J. Geffcken, *Kaiser Julianus*, Leipzig 1914, should be mentioned. Newer literature: G. W. Bowersock, *Julian*, and R.

a small section of the question, namely the effect of Julian's religious policies in Palestine. What response was aroused in Palestine by the revival of Hellenistic religion and the cancellation of the privileges previously afforded to Christianity? How did Julian behave towards the Jews, and how should we judge his project of rebuilding the Temple in Jerusalem?

1. The Survival of 'Paganism' in Palestine

The letter from the Jerusalem Synod, around 400, to the Patriarch Theophilus of Alexandria has already been quoted in an earlier chapter. In it, the bishops not only complain of problems with Jews and Samaritans, but also about 'the quite openly godless deeds of the pagans', whose very numerous crowds close their ears to Christian preaching and endanger the Christian faith of the members of the congregation (p. 121). Decades after the death of Julian, and years after the prohibition of pagan forms of worship by Theodosius in 391 (CTh X.10.10), traditional paganism was apparently still a factor to be taken seriously, in Palestine as elsewhere.

Fourth-century 'paganism' should not, however, be equated with the multitude of cults of classical Graeco-Roman religious history. Classical polytheism had long since been replaced by a basically monotheistic syncretism, whether the deity that was venerated was Zeus or Helios, Mithras or Isis. It was a Hellenistic, philosophical religion of Neoplatonic character that lived on especially in educated circles. The ideas of simple country folk continued to be determined by different forms of folk religion, superstition and magic.

Of course it would be extremely interesting if we were able to offer more precise details on paganism in Julian's day. M. Avi-Yonah estimates that approximately 30 to 40 per cent of the population of the empire were Christians at that time.[3] Of course there were enormous regional differences. Generally speaking, the eastern Empire was more strongly Christianized than the west, and cities more so than the countryside. Constantine had

---

Browning, *The Emperor Julian*. For Julian's relationship with the Jews, J. Vogt, *Kaiser Julian*, remains the classic study.

[3] M. Avi-Yonah, *Jews*, 186.

confiscated the property of pagan temples, and in one or two instances had ordered the destruction of temples by the troops, for example in Phoenicia the temple of Aphrodite in Aphaka and the temple of Venus in Heliopolis.[4] But it was not until Constantius that more severe measures were undertaken against the pagan cults. In CTh XVI.10.2, dated 341, he states laconically: 'Let superstition cease, let the madness of sacrifice be abolished'; for the abolition of sacrifice he referred to an earlier law of Constantine's. But then, in CTh XVI.10.3, dated 346, he had to take the temple buildings of Rome under his protection: 'Although all superstition must be entirely obliterated, we nevertheless wish that temples situated outside the city walls should remain intact and unharmed'; apparently Christians had attempted to destroy temple buildings that stood unprotected in the open countryside. In 346 (or 354?) Constantius ordered the universal closure of all temples, and prohibited entering them or offering sacrifice (CTh X.10.4). Finally, in 356, he threatened anyone with the death penalty 'of whom it is known that they offer sacrifice or worship idols' (CTh XVI.10.6).

It is generally true to say of fourth-century anti-pagan religious policies that they were not very effective, especially since the civil servants often offered passive resistance.[5] Nevertheless, Constantius' actions represented a serious threat to the traditionally pagan population, and the relief that arose when Julian came to the throne is very understandable.

Julian was very aware of the weaknesses of traditional Hellenism. He attempted to overcome them by imitating Christian models. Among other things, he endeavoured to raise moral standards among pagan priests, and to overcome their complete disorganization by introducing a strict hierarchy. As supreme high priest of the empire he appointed high priests for the individual provinces. He appointed such a high priest for the province of Palestine too, as may be seen from the correspondence of Libanius.[6]

---

[4] Eusebius, *Vita Constantini* III.54f., 58 (GCS 108f., 111).
[5] See Jones, *LRE*, 407, where he says generally of the late Roman empire: 'Its religious persecutions were very inefficient'; thus paganism was still quite openly practised in some districts as late as two centuries after its official prohibition. See also *LRE*, 938ff., and F. R. Trombley, *Hellenic Religion and Christianization c. 370–529*, 2 vols., Leiden 1993–4.
[6] See M. Schwabe, 'Chapters on Hellenistic Palestine'.

In a letter from the autumn of 364, Libanius calls the addressee, Lemmatius (according to other MSS., Clematius), 'a priest whom the gods too would rightly honour', and asks him to intervene on behalf of Acacius, a professor of rhetoric in Caesarea (*ep.* 1283). However, the letter appears not to have arrived. Thus at the end of 364 a further letter (*ep.* 1307) follows, carried by the young lawyer Paionius who intended to settle in Palestine. Lemmatius is to exercise his influence for him too: 'Indeed for you it is an easy matter, who are great in every respect, both because of your background and because of your eloquence and your other duties, of which the greatest is the presidency over the priests, whereby you honour the gods and maintain the cities. For they spend most of their time in the temples and around the altars, under your leadership, and obtain for the city the protection of the gods – and I know of no better than this.'

M. Schwabe takes Lemmatius to be the high priest, who exercised other administrative functions also, according to Julian's ideal, and managed to persuade the Hellenes – uncharacteristically, and probably following Christian practice – to spend most of their time in the temples. We should then conclude from the letter that about fifteen months after Julian's death – knowledge of which must have reached Palestine at the end of July or the beginning of August – Lemmatius was still in office. (Sacrifices were only forbidden in 371 and 372, during the trial of the Hellenes on suspicion of magic; at this time Julian's teacher, the magician Maximus of Ephesus, was also condemned to death.) Shortly after Libanius wrote his letter, Lemmatius was dismissed and taken prisoner, and his property confiscated. But in the summer of 365 the Emperor Valens pardoned him again; shortly afterwards he was fully rehabilitated and reappointed to the high priesthood.[7]

What basis could Lemmatius rely on as high priest? His seat was surely in the provincial capital of Caesarea. Temples must also have existed there, as may be inferred from the letter quoted above, although there is as yet almost no archaeological evidence. Only a temple of Mithras has been excavated to date, which was used in the late third and early fourth century. Otherwise there is only a sixth-century inscription which speaks of renovations in the

---

[7] Thus M. Schwabe, 'Chapters on Hellenistic Palestine', based on Libanius, *ep.* 1503, 1504, 1526 and 1458.

Hadrianeion. In theory this could prove the survival of a pagan cult in Caesarea even at this late date; but it is more likely that the building had meanwhile found a different use.[8] A series of literary sources from Josephus to Eusebius clearly show that Caesarea possessed a number of temples. What happened to them after 324? Julian ordered that temples which had been turned into churches by Christians were to be given back. But this probably only covered a few cases, because in the fourth century people were generally still reluctant to take over pagan temples for Christian worship, for fear of demons.[9] There is no certain evidence for it in Palestine. The church of Dora is built on the foundations of a pagan temple that was destroyed by fire. But it is still unclear whether the destruction should be attributed to Christians, who then used the site for a church, or whether a longer interval of time should not be assumed between the two buildings. It is also unclear whether the first church building should be attributed to the period before Julian, or not rather to the end of the fourth century.[10] Temples that had been closed were now reopened,[11] and the building of new temples was encouraged. But in Julian's short reign it was impossible to implement his orders successfully. However, Lemmatius must have had temples at his disposal in Caesarea.

Evidence for pagan cults in Palestine in the fourth century comes mainly from the south of the country. In Elusa the shrine of Venus was still of great importance in the middle of the fourth century, as may be seen from the *Life* of Hilarion the monk by Jerome:

> On the way to the desert of Kadesh ... he came with a vast crowd of monks to Elusa, just on the day when the yearly festival had gathered the whole populace of the city in the temple of Venus. For they worship her because of the

---

[8] L. I. Levine, *Roman Caesarea. An Archaeological-Topographical Study*, Jerusalem 1975, 21f.

[9] R. P. Hanson, 'The Transformation of Pagan Temples into Churches in the Early Christian Centuries', *JSS* 23 (1978), 257–67.

[10] C. Dauphin, *IEJ* 47 (1997), 120–7, points to the destruction and transformation into a church of the Marneion in Gaza, in 402, as a direct parallel (125); we must await the full publication of the results for a clear picture.

[11] Several coins of Julian found in the temple of Zeus on Mt. Gerizim suggest that this temple was again in use: Y. Magen, 'Mount Gerizim and the Samaritans', in F. Manns and E. Aliata (eds.), *Early Christianity in Context*, 91–148, p. 127.

morning star, which the people of the Saracens worship. Because of its situation, the city itself is to a great extent semi-barbarian.[12]

However, other statements about Elusa in the fourth century show it as by no means a semi-barbarian village in the desert; but it was largely pagan, and probably also formed an attraction for the Bedouin who participated in the cult of Venus.[13]

As already mentioned, Jerome and Sozomen offer evidence that pagans still venerated Abraham in Mamre in the fourth and fifth centuries. But, thanks to Mark the Deacon's *Vita Porphyrii*, our fullest information is for Gaza and its cults. As late as 400 the city still possessed eight temples to the gods: Helios, Aphrodite, Apollo, Kore and Hecate were worshipped, there was a Heroon and a Tycheion, a temple for the Fortune-goddess of the city. But the principal temple was the Marneion: Marnas, who was worshipped there, was equated with the Cretan Zeus. There were also still many statues of the gods in private houses.[14]

In the north of the country, the Roman temple of Qedesh was excavated in 1981–84, which dates from the second or third century and perhaps only collapsed in the earthquake of 363.[15] Finally, Phoenicia should be mentioned, which bordered Palestine to the north and had many temples; pagans were still very numerous among the population, especially around Heliopolis/Baalbek. But indications for the continuation of pagan cults were also found in the new excavation at Beth Shean, where an altar to Dionysus perhaps still stood in the centre of the city's basilica in 363,[16] and also in the house of the Nile festival in Sepphoris, with its magnificent mosaics.

It is no coincidence that the three cities of Palestine that were

---

[12] Jerome, *Vita Hilarionis* (PL 23, 42).

[13] On this, see P. Mayerson, 'The City of Elusa'.

[14] Mark the Deacon, *Vita Porphyrii* 64. For Gaza, see also G. Downey, 'Gaza', *RAC* 8 (1972), 1123–34; R. Van Dam, 'From Paganism to Christianity at Late Antique Gaza', *Viator* 16 (1985), 1–20.

[15] A. Ovadiah, M. Fisher, I. Roll and G. Solar, 'The Roman Temple at Qedesh in Upper Galilee' (Hebrew), *Qadmoniot* 15 (1982), 121–5, also *IEJ* 33 (1983), 254; idd., *NEAE* III, 857–9; M. Fisher et al., *The Roman Temple at Kedesh (Upper Galilee)*, Tel Aviv 1984.

[16] L. Di Segni, G. Foerster and Y. Tsafrir, 'A Decorated Altar Dedicated to Dionysos, the "Founder", from Beth-Shean (Nysa-Scythopolis)' (Hebrew), *EI* 25 (1996), 336–50.

most open to pagan cults, Caesarea, Gaza and Elusa, each also had a school of rhetoric.[17] These, the most important institutions of higher education of the time, which produced many civil servants, among others, remained pagan in character throughout the fourth century. This was true both of the subject matter, which continued to be drawn exclusively from the classical Greek authors, and of the teaching staff. It may be clearly seen in the correspondence of the greatest rhetor of the age, Libanius the pagan. His own teacher Zenobius came from Elusa, the administrative centre of the province of Palaestina Salutaris.[18] The school of rhetoric in Gaza, which Libanius praised, became one of the most important schools in the empire in the fifth and sixth centuries. Finally, Libanius praises Caesarea because of the good salaries paid to its rhetors: for this reason, one rhetor preferred Caesarea to Antioch, he says.[19] There was probably also another school of rhetoric in Ashkelon,[20] about whose pagan inhabitants R. Pinchas bar Hama knew some anecdotes (e.g. LamR on 1.11).

Since the schools of rhetoric were such bastions of paganism, Julian's prohibiting Christians to teach there is understandable; it gave rise to very bitter polemic on the part of the Christians. However, Christians were not prohibited from attending these schools; but they lost interest in the schools of rhetoric because of their by now militant pagan orientation. It should be added that at this time no organized Christian system of education existed yet, and that almost all the important Christian leaders of the day had come from such schools of rhetoric.[21]

Since the schools of rhetoric with their pagan character educated a large proportion of the higher civil service, and the church in any case, for moral reasons, did not encourage the baptized to embrace either the civil service or a military career, it is understandable that pagans continued, long after the Christianization of the empire, to play a significant part in administration

---

[17] A. H. M. Jones, 'The Social Background of the Struggle between Paganism and Christianity', in A. Momigliano (ed.), *The Conflict between Paganism and Christianity in the Fourth Century*, Oxford 1963, 17–37, 32: 'In the East the pagan opposition was never a serious political force. It was in both senses of the word academic. The leaders of paganism were almost all professors ...'
[18] P. Mayerson, 'The City of Elusa', 248f.
[19] Libanius, *Or.* 31.42. L. I. Levine, *Caesarea*, 59.
[20] Y. Dan, *The City*, 158.
[21] See R. Browning, *The Emperor Julian*, 169–74.

and the military.[22] In general we rarely have any information on the religious affiliation of civil servants, but we do know of a number of pagan governors in Palestine. Not only Leontius, governor of Palaestina (Salutaris?) under Julian (362– 363), was a pagan (and continued his career after Julian's death), but also Priscianus, who trained as a rhetor in Antioch and was governor of Palestine in the year 364, and Proculus, who was governor of Palestine before 382 and rose to be *Comes Orientis* in 383. Proculus is praised in an inscription for the celebration of a pagan cult in Heliopolis. Another pagan is Siburius, governor in 390, and probably also Bacurius, who was *Dux Palaestinae* between 378 and 394, despite the fact that Rufinus, whom he visited several times on the Mount of Olives, portrays him as a Christian. Libanius (*ep.* 1060) certainly saw him as a pagan; altogether we know of the pagan affiliation of almost all of these civil servants from the letters of Libanius. We lack a comparable source for the later period; but we may be sure that the situation did not change very quickly.[23]

Paganism remained a force to be reckoned with in the middle of the fourth century and even later. This may also be seen in the Palestinian Talmud. When the Talmud comments on the Mishnah tractate on idol-worship (*Aboda Zara*) and fourth-century masters take an active part in the discussion, this is not merely due to the fact that, from a Jewish point of view, the Christian Roman Empire seamlessly continued the tradition of the pagan empire, and that both were to be seen as a unit, theologically speaking. This is one aspect but does not explain the text as a whole. Neither is it simply a matter of backward-looking interest, as is often the case with works of commentary. Although not in the Jewish heartland of Upper Galilee itself, at its fringes towards Phoenicia, and particularly in the south, Judaism still shared a border with pagan life.[24]

The baptismal catechetical lectures given by Cyril of Jerusalem

---

[22] Jones, *LRE*, 983f.
[23] The material is in *PRLE* I. See also R. von Haehling, *Die Religionszugehörigkeit der hohen Amtsträger des Römischen Reiches seit Constantius I. Alleinherrschaft bis zum Ende der Theodosianischen Dynastie*, Bonn 1978.
[24] For possible concrete evidence of paganism in this period, see A. Ovadiah and S. Mucznik, 'Orpheus from Jerusalem – Pagan or Christian Image?' *The Jerusalem Cathedra* 1 (1981), 152–66 (the authors hold to a pagan provenance in the fourth or early fifth century; only later did the statue receive a Christian reinterpretation; M. Hengel, *Achilleus in Jerusalem*, Heidelberg 1982, 50f.

around 350 also give a picture of the continuing reality of paganism in Palestine. In the introductory lecture he draws the baptismal candidates' attention to the fact that they need to learn how to treat pagans. He warns them against eating food offered to idols (IV.28) and mentions the pagan objections to the resurrection of the body (XVIII.2). It is certainly striking that, compared with the warnings against Jews, Samaritans, Manichees and heretics in general, those against pagans take up very little space. This is surely connected with the special situation of Jerusalem. Through the Constantinian building programme Jerusalem had become the Christian city *par excellence*, and apparently the pagan peril was not felt so acutely there as elsewhere. However, it would not be right to see the catechetical lectures as simply taking over elements from stock preaching of an earlier age: paganism was still a force to be reckoned with.

It is probably no accident that in his description of the province of Palestine the pagan Ammianus Marcellinus stresses particularly those cities that are still largely pagan, and only mentions the Christian centre, Jerusalem, in connection with its capture by Pompey. He writes that the province 'also has a number of excellent cities, none inferior to the others, but all competing with each other for the prize: Caesarea, which Herod built in honour of the Princeps Octavian, and Eleutheropolis and Neapolis, also Ashkelon and Gaza, built long ago' (XIV.8.11). The *Expositio totius mundi*, also written by a pagan, leaves Jerusalem out altogether, probably because the city is now Christian, but also because it is of no particular economic significance. The author describes Caesarea (§ 26), Ashkelon and Gaza (§ 29), Neapolis, Scythopolis and Eleutheropolis (§ 30). He mentions Lydda because of its purple dyeing industry, and Jericho because of its pistachios and dates (§ 31). He also thinks Caesarea worth mentioning because of its circus and the pantomimes that come from there; Gaza is particularly noted for good readers (*auditores*, those whom you actually hear), but also wrestlers and free-style fighters (*pammacharii*); Ashkelon is noted for wrestlers. All this fits much better in a pagan than a Christian context. Finally, the general picture is rounded off by the fact that Libanius mentions in his correspondence Elusa, Gaza, Ashkelon and Caesarea among the cities of Palestine, that is, the sites of pagan schools of rhetoric.

The reports of anti-Christian riots under Julian should also be seen against the background of a living pagan culture in Palestine. Ambrose principally mentions Jews: 'I could mention how many basilicas belonging to the church were burned down by Jews during the reign of Julian. Two in Damascus, one of which has only just been restored ... the other basilica is still a heap of ruins. The basilicas in Gaza, Ashkelon, Beirut and in almost all of those cities were set on fire ... The basilica in Alexandria was also set on fire by pagans and Jews ...'[25] In individual cases, like Alexandria, Jews probably were involved in these riots. But Ambrose is deliberately generalizing: his work is intended to prevent the rebuilding at Christian expense of the synagogue of Kallinikon on the Euphrates, which was set on fire by Christians. This is why he asserts that the Jews behaved much worse and never paid compensation. In general it was doubtless the pagans who turned against the Christians.

As regards Gaza, Sozomen writes that Julian joined Maiuma to Gaza again, the harbour which under Constantine, because of its Christian population, was separated from Gaza and raised to the status of an independent city under the name of Constantia.[26] Three brothers were arrested on the charge of damaging temples and taking advantage of the moment to denigrate Hellenistic religion. The furious mob lynched the three men and burned their bodies outside the city. The provincial governor had the ringleaders arrested for the sake of law and order, but was disciplined by Julian because of it. His action was not necessary 'simply because they took revenge on a few Galileans for the many wrongs which they had done both to them and the gods'.[27] The accusation of partisan justice, harsh towards Christians and sparing pagans, is also to be found in Gregory of Nazianzus, in his fourth speech against Julian, where again Gaza is mentioned first, before Heliopolis and Syrian Arethusa, because of its anti-Christian riots.[28]

Ashkelon's support for Julian may be seen in the inscription on a milestone found there, dated 362/363: 'One God. Be victorious, Julian!'[29] It, too, was the site of anti-Christian rioting, as Theodoret notes in his *Church history*[30]: as in Gaza, the pagans are

[25] Ambrose, *ep.* 40.15 (PL 16.1154).
[26] Sozomen, *Church history* V.3.6f. (GCS 50, 196).
[27] Sozomen, *Church history* V.9 (GCS 50, 204–6).
[28] Gregory of Nazianzus, *Speeches against Julian* 4.93 and 4.86 (SC 309, 235; 218).
[29] M. Avi-Yonah, *QDAP* 10 (1944), 160f.
[30] Theodoret, *Church history* III.7 (GCS 19.182).

said to have committed atrocities against priests and consecrated virgins.

In the centre of Samaria, Sebaste, pagans are said to have defiled the relics of John the Baptist, as Philostorgius stresses in his *Church history*, completed between 425 and 433,[31] and as Rufinus describes at length. The latter also tells that, despite the fact that the relics were burned and the ashes strewn on the fields, part of the bones was saved in a miraculous manner. Indeed, soon after Julian's time the relics of the Baptist were again venerated in Sebaste.[32]

In the most northerly part of Galilee that already belonged to Phoenicia lay Paneas (Caesarea Philippi), which was the scene of an incident. Eusebius tells that he himself saw, at the house said to belong to the woman suffering from a haemorrhage whom Jesus healed (Mt. 9: 20), a bronze statue on a high stone pedestal, representing Jesus and the woman kneeling before him asking to be healed.[33] This may possibly be a reinterpretation of a pagan statue. However, under Julian the pagan population of the city pulled down the statue (now only a statue of Christ is mentioned, which the healed woman is said to have endowed), and in its place put up a statue of Julian; however this was soon struck by lightning.[34]

As with the cases previously described, our interest here is not so much in the historicity of the details in these sensationalist or miracle-seeking reports, but only in the undoubted fact of anti-Christian rioting in these places. There must still have been a correspondingly numerous pagan population at this time; having been frustrated by the Christian community's vigorous action against them under Constantius, they made use of the changed balance of power and supported Julian.

A Latin inscription, excavated near Kibbutz Ma'ayan Baruch in the upper Jordan valley (eight kilometres from Paneas), also offers evidence for support for Julian in this region: 'To the liberator of the Roman world, the restorer of temples, the renewer of curia and community, the destroyer of the barbarians, our Lord Julian ... by the Phoenician community for benefac-

---

[31] Philostorgius, *Church history* VII.4 (GCS 21, 80).
[32] Rufinus, *Church history* XI.28 (GCS 9, 1033f.).
[33] Eusebius, *Church history* VII.18 (GCS 9, 672).
[34] Sozomen, *Church history* V.21.1–4 (GCS 50, 227f.); Philostorgius, *Church history* VII.3 (GCS 21, 78f.).

tions received.' From an eastern point of view, the barbarians are the Persians; thus the inscription appears to date from 363, when the first messages of success from Julian's Persian campaign were received. It appears to be a tribute to the ruler who was soon expected to return victorious.[35]

Julian's sudden death meant an end to state promotion of pagan religion. But his short reign showed clearly how strong the pagan elements still were. It was wise not to enter into a trial of strength, particularly since Christianity was by no means united in the dispute over Arian teaching. Thus there were initially isolated trials of pagan priests, as in the case of Lemmatius shows, quoted above. But soon paganism was tolerated again, and pagans continued to be able to rise to high public office. As late as the year 388 Libanius was able to write as follows to Theodosius (*De templis* 7): 'We must not weep for that of which we have been deprived, but rather count ourselves fortunate for what you have conceded. For you, you have neither caused the temples to be closed nor forbidden attendance at them. You have banned from the temples neither fire, nor incense, nor the other olfactory sacrifices.'

CTh XVI.10.7 of 381 is a reminder of the prohibition of sacrifices and oracles. But only in 391 did Theodosius' open war against paganism begin – perhaps due to Ambrose's influence. In a series of laws (CTh X.10.10ff.) not only were every form of sacrifice and of scrutiny of the future forbidden, but at the same time the judges and other civil servants threatened with punishment if they did not execute these laws or if they themselves visited temples in order to sacrifice or consult the oracles there. CTh XVI.10.16, dated 399, orders the destruction of temples in isolated spots, and XVI.10.25, dated 435, orders the general destruction of temples. CTh XVI.10.21, dated 416, excludes pagans from any public office. However, none of these laws was very effective. Pagans continued to occupy the highest civil posts, and it remained possible to practise the pagan cults, if the authorities were only bribed appropriately.[36]

---

[35] A. Negev, 'The Inscription of the Emperor Julian at Ma'ayan Barukh, *IEJ* 19 (1969), 170–3. Negev thinks it possible that the inscription was erected in the local temple, or in another temple among the many Roman religious sites in the region. For the dating and interpretation I follow G. W. Bowersock, *Julian*, 123f.

[36] See Jones, *LRE* 399. On the survival of paganism in this period, see also the collection edited by A. Momigliano mentioned in n. 17 above.

This is the background against which Mark the Deacon's report should be seen, in his biography of Porphyrius of Gaza for the period around 400. The city's administration still lay firmly in the hands of the pagans; indeed, 'when the adherents of idolatry saw that the Christians became numerous, they turned savage and did not permit them to exercise public office, but treated them like bad fellow-citizens' (§ 32). Bishop Porphyrius sent Mark the Deacon to Constantinople to obtain the destruction of the temples in which forbidden sacrifices were still being performed. He also gave him a letter to John Chrysostom, but received only a letter from the emperor to the effect that 'the temples of the city of Gaza are to be closed, and may no longer give oracles.' (§ 26.) Its success was apparently not very great. A new attempt on the matter in 400 won the support of the Empress Eudoxia; but the emperor is said to have answered simply: 'I know that this city is full of idols. But it pays its taxes faithfully. If we suddenly frighten it, they will flee and we will lose this revenue.' (§ 33.)[37] Not until the occasion of the birth of Theodosius II, when permission was cunningly obtained from the emperor, were the temples of Gaza finally destroyed in 402 by the troops and the Christian congregation of the city (§ 49ff.). But years later the city council was apparently still pagan. In 407 there were riots in which seven Christians were killed, many were wounded and the bishop had to flee over the rooftops of the city, until finally the governor restored order (§ 95–99).

The destruction of the Marneion must have made a tremendous impression. Jerome places it on an equal footing with the destruction of the Serapeion in Alexandria: 'Already the Egyptian Serapis has become Christian; Marnas in Gaza mourns in captivity and is constantly trembling for the destruction of the temple.'[38] Elsewhere he says: 'By the destruction of idol-worship the gospel is built up. We see it fulfilled in our day. The Serapeion in

---

[37] H. Grégoire and M.-A. Kugener, *Marc le Diacre, Vie de Porphyre*, Paris 1930, refer in their introduction to the text to the parallel between this explanation and Justinian's *novella* 103. They think it not impossible that the latter is the source for the expression in the *Vita Porphyrii* (XLIIIf.). They assume that the *Vita* was reworked and given legendary embellishments in the sixth to seventh century.

[38] Jerome, *ep.* 107.2 (CSEL 55, 292).

Alexandria and the temple of Marnas in Gaza have become churches of the Lord.'[39]

It sounds like a final dismissal of the battle against paganism when, in 423, Theodosius begins a law against the pagans with the words: 'The pagans that still exist – although we believe that there are none left – ...' (CTh XVI.10.22). The emperor was to find that he was mistaken. Paganism lived on for a long time, and in Palestine too it was far from being dead.

2. Julian and Judaism

We do not know whether Julian had ever met Jews before he ascended the throne. His knowledge of Judaism came primarily from the Bible, from the writings of Eusebius of Caesarea and ecclesiastical polemics against Judaism. After he turned to the pagan tradition, he also read the opinions of the Neoplatonists, as represented especially by Porphyrius and Iamblichus. Julian's study of Judaism was closely connected with his critical examination of Christianity. That is why his most important remarks on the matter are found in his work 'Against the Galileans', of whose seven books, however, only excerpts from three are extant, preserved in Cyril of Alexandria.[40] There are also various remarks in his letters, the most important of which is the possibly spurious *Letter to the Jews*.[41]

Although Julian's opinions on Judaism generally concur with those of his Neoplatonist predecessors, they are of particular significance in so far as he alone was in a position to translate them into political reality. Theologically speaking Julian had to deny Judaism's strict monotheism and also its claim to divine

---

[39] Jerome, *Comm. Isa.* 17.2f. (CC 73, 268). Sozomen, *Church history* VII.15.11 (GCS 50, 321), after describing the destruction of the Serapeion, also writes of the destruction of temples in the provinces of Arabia, Palestine and Phoenicia.

[40] A critical edition of the excerpts is C. J. Neumann, *Iuliani Imperatoris Librorum Contra Christianos Quae Supersunt*, Leipzig 1880. A new edition is promised for SC.

[41] From the literature on the subject of Julian and Judaism, see especially M. Adler, 'The Emperor Julian'; C. Aziza, 'Julien et le Judaisme', in R. Braun and J. Richer (eds.), *L'empereur Julien. De l'histoire à la légende*, Paris 1978; Y. (H.) Lewy, 'Julian the Apostate'; M. Stern, *Greek and Latin Authors* II, 502–72; J. Vogt, *Kaiser Julian*.

election, against which he points out the small historical achievements of the Jews and their history of suffering.

On the other hand, Julian also found support for his polytheism in the Bible, and was able to find positive aspects to the Jewish concept of God:

> Although I am – by the Gods! – one of those who avoid celebrating feasts together with the Jews, yet I always worship the God of Abraham, Isaac and Jacob, who were themselves Chaldees from a holy people experienced in dealings with God, and who learnt to practise circumcision when they sojourned in Egypt as strangers. And they worshipped the God who was well-disposed towards me and those who worship him as Abraham worshipped him; for he is a very great and mighty god.

Elsewhere he calls the Jews 'godfearing in a certain sense, for they worship a god who is truly extremely powerful and good, and rules the visible world. I know well that we worship him too under other names ... However, they err on one point in that, despite worshipping this god most, they do not also worship the other gods.'[42] In his *Letter to the Jews* – if the text is authentic – Julian speaks of the Jewish God as 'the greatest of all and the god who created the world [the Demiurge], who condescended to crown me with his spotless right hand'. Thus for Julian the Jewish God is simply the national god of the Jews, but he has a high rank in the pantheon as the Demiurge. He appears to equate him with Zeus-Helios-Serapis, which means that in Julian's eyes Moses must have falsified the true picture of God.[43]

Positive aspects of Judaism, as far as Julian was concerned, were its faithfulness to the commandments and customs, in particular as regarded circumcision and the food laws. In the letter to Theodore quoted above, Julian contrasts Jewish zeal with the pagans' carelessness in their veneration of the gods: 'Those who adhere to the teachings of the Jewish religion are so passionate in its favour that they would even suffer death for it; they would rather endure the most bitter want and hunger than taste pork or

---

[42] Julian, *Contra Galileos* 354 A, B, and *ep.* 89 a to Theodore. Every text of Julian's is quoted here according to the collection in M. Stern, *Greek and Latin Authors*.

[43] For a full discussion, see Y. (H.) Lewy, 'Julian the Apostate'.

any meat that has not been immediately expressed [of blood].' Julian probably had the opportunity to see such things in Antioch, where he prepared for his campaign against the Persians. We may assume that the large Jewish community in Antioch was sympathetic to Julian because his attitude promised them greater freedom. Then again, by supporting the Jewish community Julian was able to annoy the Christians. In addition, it was to his advantage to know that the Jews were on his side, and thus to obtain if not support, then benevolent neutrality on the part of the numerous Jews of Mesopotamia during his Persian campaign.

This is the context in which the disputed *Letter* to the Jewish community should be read. It used previously to be understood as a Jewish forgery from around 400, arguing from the style, which is similar to the Septuagint, and from the content. However, the Biblical style of the letter is not surprising, since it is addressed to Jews by an emperor who was well versed in the Septuagint. Neither is it surprising that Julian countered the oppressive taxation of the Jews, since he, as emperor, worked to lighten taxes in general, while at the same time endeavouring to collect them more efficiently. However, it is very doubtful whether the text is speaking of the special Jewish tax introduced by Vespasian, the *fiscus Iudaicus*, for this tax probably came to an end in the third century. However, special taxes on individual regions, towns or sections of the population were not unusual at the time. Certainly Sozomen, writing around 450, already knows of a letter of Julian 'to the Patriarchs and their leaders and the people itself, that they might pray for him and his government.'[44] There are therefore no unanswerable objections to recognizing the letter as authentic, and this opinion has now largely gained acceptance.[45]

> Julian to the community of the Jews. More even than in the past, the yoke of servitude has become most galling to you because you were subjected to unannounced demands for payment, and were forced to deliver an inestimable amount of gold to the treasury. I have seen much of this with my own eyes, and learnt of even more when I found

---

[44] Sozomen, *Church history* V.22.1 (GCS 50, 229).
[45] A comprehensive argument for the authenticity of the letter is given especially by Y. (H.) Lewy, *Studies in Jewish Hellenism* (Hebrew), Jerusalem ²1969, 248–54 (reprinted from *Zion* 6, 1940f.). This section is not in the English translation of his paper. See also M. Stern, *Greek and Latin Authors* II, 508–10.

the lists that were kept against you. I have also prevented a tax that was to have been demanded of you, and forced this impious crime to be stopped. And I put into the fire the lists that were kept in my archives against you, so that no-one may be able in future to bring such accusations of impiety against you ...

The Jewish patriarch is to give up his messenger tax also, so that the Jews may be able to pray to their God for Julian's government with a mind free of cares. 'You must do this so that, when I have successfully completed the Persian war, I may rebuild and found the holy city of Jerusalem by my personal efforts, which you have wished to see inhabited by yourselves again for many years now, and so that you and I may give honour to the Almighty there.'[46]

Thus the letter not only mentions tax relief, apparently after the previous imposition of special taxes on religious grounds (the 'accusation of impiety' of which the letter speaks), but also announces that after the Persian war Julian intends to ensure that Jerusalem is again inhabited by Jews. Indeed, he himself intends to go on pilgrimage to Jerusalem – a reversal of the pilgrimages with Christian motivation on the part of members of the imperial family – and there to worship their God together with the Jews. At first sight this promise seems surprising. But Jerome, in his *Commentary on Daniel* 11.34 mentioned earlier, also writes that the Jews saw in Julian the 'little help' of the Biblical text, since he appeared 'as one who professed to love the Jews and promised to sacrifice in their Temple' (see p. 162).

3. The Reconstruction of the Temple[47]

At least as much as his return to traditional paganism, Julian's attempt to have the Jewish Temple in Jerusalem rebuilt must have been a serious blow to the Christian church. Jesus' prophecy over the Temple 'Truly, I say to you, there will not be left here one stone upon another, that will not be thrown down' (Mt. 24:2),

---

[46] Text in M. Stern, *Greek and Latin Authors* II, 559f.
[47] Apart from the literature mentioned in n. 41 above, see especially G. W. Bowersock, *Julian* 88–90, 120–2; S. P. Brock, 'The Rebuilding'; id., 'A Letter'; C. R. Phillips, 'Julian's Rebuilding'. I was not able to consult D. B. Levenson, *A Source- and Tradition-Critical Study of the Stories of Julian's Attempt to Rebuild the Jerusalem Temple*, Diss. Harvard 1979.

combined with Dan. 9:27 on the 'desolating sacrilege' that would be seen in the holy place (quoted in Mt. 24:15), had long been an important argument in the dispute against Judaism. The fact that the Temple had not been rebuilt after 70 was seen as a confirmation of Jesus' prophecy and as proof that Judaism had now been replaced by Christianity. Therefore a rebuilding of the Temple would be understood as a refutation of Jesus' words and thus of Christianity as a whole.[48] Christians were all the more relieved when Julian's attempt was unsuccessful.

The affair became a standard topic in disputes with Judaism and Jewish appeals to the continued validity of the revealed law of the Bible: if there was no Temple, a large number of the laws could no longer be kept. The loss of the Temple was a sign from God that the Old Covenant had been replaced by the New. The importance of this subject for polemic led to the story of the attempted rebuilding being retold again and again. It was embellished with legendary features to such an extent that it is almost impossible today to ascertain the actual course of events.

The surviving sources are almost exclusively Christian. Only two isolated quotations survive from Julian himself that mention the attempt to rebuild the Temple. In addition there is, in all probability, the *Letter* to the Jewish community discussed above, from which we may infer a further letter to the Jewish Patriarch. Julian probably also notified the governor of Palestine officially and asked for his co-operation, as Constantine did for the building of the Church of the Holy Sepulchre, which must in some sense have served Julian as a model.[49] The only surviving pagan description of the affair is that of Ammianus, who accompanied Julian on his Persian campaign: even in his report the events are given a miraculous interpretation.

On the Christian side the first descriptions were written in the year of the attempted rebuilding, immediately after Julian's death. These are Ephrem's Syriac hymns against Julian and the two denunciatory speeches of Gregory of Nazianzus against Julian (counted as his fourth and fifth speeches, perhaps written in spring 364). John Chrysostom treats the matter extensively in the fifth of his eight speeches against Julian (386); Ambrose mentions it in a letter of 388.

---

[48] A full discussion is in R. L. Wilken, *John Chrysostom*, 130–60.
[49] Thus M. Avi-Yonah, *Jews*, 195.

Conspicuous by its absence from the early sources is any mention by the contemporary bishop of Jerusalem, Cyril. Early in the fifth century a man who was well acquainted with the situation wrote a letter using Cyril's name; the Syriac version of this has been edited by S. P. Brock. In the first half of the fifth century every church historian describes the events, with ever-increasing additional detail.[50] Naturally later church writings return to the subject again and again, but no new information may be expected here; their only interest is from the point of view of the history of tradition. There is not a single authenticated Jewish source to set against the plethora of Christian texts.

From whom did the initiative for the rebuilding of the Temple come? Among the early sources John Chrysostom is the first to state that, in reply to Julian's question as to why they offered no sacrifices, the Jews answered that they were only permitted to do so in Jerusalem, and asked permission to rebuild the Temple.[51] The Syriac Julian novel then amplifies the subject in an anti-Jewish polemic: a Jewish embassy, led by the high priest, is said to have come to Julian in Tarsus and presented him with a throne adorned with seven gods, to have eaten unclean food, sacrificed to the gods and finally asked permission to rebuild the Temple.[52]

The other texts state that Julian arrived at the idea independently. He must have known very well from the Septuagint that Jews were not permitted to sacrifice outside Jerusalem. In his work *Against the Galileans* he mentions it explicitly. On the other hand, we cannot simply ignore John Chrysostom's statement; he experienced Julian's stay of some months in Antioch as a fourteen-year-old, and could presumably remember the news of court affairs that was current in the city. The most likely hypothesis is that Julian formed the plan independently but let its feasibility be tested by having enquiries made in the Jewish community, whether in Antioch or with the patriarch in Tiberias itself, before granting an audience to a Jewish delegation and

---

[50] Rufinus, *Church history* X.38–40 (GCS 9, 997f.); Philostorgius, *Church history* VII.9 (GCS 21, 95–100, 235f.); Socrates, *Church history* III.20 (PG 67, 429–32); Sozomen, *Church history* V.22 (GCS 50, 229–32); Theodoret, *Church history* III.20.1–8 (GCS 44, 198–200).

[51] John Chrysostom, *Oratio contra Iudaeos* 5.11 (PG 48, 900), and *De S. Babyla* 22 (PG 50, 568). Rufinus and Socrates likewise.

[52] The text, which was probably written in Edessa in the early sixth century, is edited by J. G. Hoffmann, *Julianos der Abtrünnige*, Leiden 1880, 108–16.

permitting them to present the imperial plan as their own wishes.⁵³

There are several possible motives for Julian's project; perhaps a number of them combined at the same time, in varying degrees. The most important is his strong personal interest in sacrifices. It is clear from his own works, but also in John Chrysostom and particularly Socrates: 'Julian enjoyed the blood of the sacrifices so much that he would have thought it damaging if others did not also offer sacrifice. But as he found only a few such people, he sent to the Jews and wished to know why they did not offer sacrifices, since the law of Moses ordained it.' On hearing the reply that they might only do so in the Temple in Jerusalem, 'he ordered that the Temple of Solomon should be speedily rebuilt'.⁵⁴ The Jews were to take part in the universal cult for the good of the empire; that left only the Christians as outsiders who did not pray for the good of the government.

A further motive is Julian's reverence for the received traditions of the peoples contained within the Roman empire. He could only honour the fact that the Jews had clung to their customs despite persecution and misfortune. This is still perceptible in Gregory of Nazianzus' version; but he speaks of hypocrisy and states that the Jews' preferential treatment was only for the sake of annoying the Christians:

> After he had exhausted all other means (against the Christians) ... he finally also let loose the tribe of the Jews against us. He made use of their old volatility and their long-standing hatred of ourselves for his own plans. He supposedly read the will of God in their books and mysteries: now was the time for them to return to their own country, to rebuild the Temple and to renew the power of their fathers' customs. And he hid his true intentions behind a screen of pretended benevolence.⁵⁵

From the point of view of Christian polemics, this passage of Gregory stresses the rebuilding of the Temple and the return of the Jews to their country. This surely takes up Jewish expectations, be they simply general expectations or those given concrete shape under Julian. Did Julian himself intend this, and perhaps have a

---

⁵³ Thus M. Avi-Yonah, *Jews*, 192.
⁵⁴ Socrates, *Church history*, III.20 (PG 67, 429).
⁵⁵ Gregory of Nazianzus, *Or.* 5.3 (SC 309, 298).

political end in view with the abolition of the Jewish Diaspora? Was part of his plan something like a Jewish temple state centred on Jerusalem? His intention, mentioned in the letter to the Jewish community, to take part in the rebuilding and refoundation of Jerusalem after the war, might point in this direction. Did he also intend to drive the Christians out of Jerusalem? We cannot answer any of these questions. But it would suit Julian's religious politics if he were to set territorial limits to the Jewish religion, which he only found acceptable in certain aspects, as a national religion. However, it would certainly be going too far to describe him as a proto-Zionist for this reason.

A connection with the Persian campaign may be most clearly seen in Ammianus. While Julian made intensive preparations for the campaign, he always divided his attentions, and wished to leave a memorial for himself through great works, which was why he intended to renew the once important Temple in Jerusalem with extravagant funds (XXIII.1). The large numbers of Jews in the Persian empire were surely worth a sympathetic gesture if he could thereby gain their support during his projected campaign. There is in fact a Persian source according to which thousands of Jews were killed by the Persians because they wanted to travel to Jerusalem for the rebuilding of the Temple.[56]

From a Christian point of view Julian's primary motive was to refute Jesus' (and Daniel's) prophecy about the lasting destruction of the Temple. Julian was of course aware of this argument and, beside his other reasons for the rebuilding, was surely glad, to have an occasion to provoke the Christians. From his own standpoint it was natural that Ammianus should omit this motive; but the Christian texts are unanimous on this head. It is already implicit in Gregory of Nazianzus, and clear in Ephrem the Syrian: Since Julian wished to give the lie to Daniel (9:27), he was given over to judgement at Babylon and condemned – thus here too the Persian campaign is taken together with the rebuilding of the Temple, but from a different standpoint.[57]

---

[56] G. Widengren, 'The Status of the Jews in the Sassanian Empire', *Iranica Antiqua* 1 (1961), 132f. J. Vogt, *Kaiser Julian*, 49f., is of the opinion that the Persian campaign was not important as a motive, since according to Ammianus XXIV.29ff. the Persian Jews resisted Julian fiercely. Pirisabora, Birtha and Maiozamalcha, which had a strong Jewish population, were burned down or exterminated.

[57] Ephrem, *Hymni contra Julianum* I.20.

Such an argument would affect the Church in Jerusalem in particular. Only a few years earlier, its bishop Cyril had referred to Mt. 24:2 in one of his baptismal catecheses, as a statement about the lasting destruction of the Temple, and equated it with the collapse of the walls of Jericho.[58] However, we surprisingly have no knowledge of a reaction on Cyril's part to the attempted reconstruction of the Temple. Only Rufinus and Socrates mention that, during the preparations for building, Cyril reminded his hearers of Daniel's prophecy, confirmed by Jesus in the Gospels, that 'there will not be left here one stone upon another'.[59] The letter attributed to Cyril and published by S. P. Brock apparently attempts to fill a gap here: 'The punishment of our Lord is certain, and his judgement, that he gave over the city of those who crucified, is sure.'[60]

It is normally assumed that Julian planned his project as a conscious parallel to and reversal of the building of the Church of the Holy Sepulchre by Constantine. There is no direct evidence for this. However, parallels do exist: Julian planned the building, just as Constantine did before him, as a state project. The foundation of a Christian Jerusalem by Constantine would thereby be annulled, and the city revert to being the centre of Judaism. As is to be expected with a state project, the manner of proceeding was surely the same in both cases. The decision was communicated to the religious (and political) representatives of the group concerned – by Constantine's letter to the bishop of Jerusalem, by Julian's letter to the patriarch. A senior civil servant was appointed to oversee the work – in the case of the Temple project the Antiochene Alypius, who had previously been governor in Britain. The provincial governor was informed of the plan and ordered to support it. The imperial treasury provided substantial funds, which were to be augmented by private contributions. Just as Constantine originally intended to be present at the dedication of the Church of the Holy Sepulchre, so Julian planned to offer sacrifice in Jerusalem after the Persian campaign. Finally, just as after the building of the Church of the Holy Sepulchre Jerusalem was to belong exclusively to the

---

[58] Cyril of Jerusalem, *Catechetical Lectures* 10.11 (PG 33, 676f.).
[59] Rufinus, *Church history* X.38 (GCS 9, 997f.); Socrates, *Church history* III.20 (PG 67, 429).
[60] S. P. Brock, 'A Letter', 269, translation p. 274.

Christians, so presumably after the renewal of the Temple Julian intended to drive the Christians out of the city, leaving a Jewish monopoly. This seems to be Socrates' meaning when he writes that the Jews set to work; 'but they frightened the Christians and threatened to do as much to them as they themselves had once suffered from the Romans'.[61]

What was the Jewish reaction to Julian's plans? There is not a single text in rabbinic literature that indisputably speaks of this project. W. Bacher thought to have found a supporter of the plan in R. Acha, a contemporary of Julian's.[62] In jMSh V.2.56 a, R. Acha interprets R. Jose ben Halafta's statement in the Mishnah, 'when the Temple is rebuilt there will be a return to the old order', as follows: 'This means that the Temple will be built before the kingdom of the House of David.' Thus the restoration of the Temple would precede the messianic restoration of the Davidic rule. This statement may indeed be understood as support, but may also be intended much more generally. The same is true of R. Acha's statement in jTaan II.1.65 a that the second (or last) Temple did not have five things that were in the first Temple. This could be a justification for building the Temple, even if for the moment it does not exhibit all the qualities of its Solomonic model. But the sentence could also be primarily a historical statement, a judgement on the deterioration of the second Temple period compared to the time when a Jewish kingdom still existed.

R. Judan, another contemporary, has a statement in MidrPs 18.36 (B. 81 b) which has been understood as supporting Julian: 'Salvation comes to this people not in a moment, but little by little'; since Israel was at present in great affliction it could not endure salvation in a moment. This too could be meant as a call

---

[61] Socrates, *Church history* III.20 (PG 67, 429). M. Avi-Yonah, *Jews*, 192, takes it for a certainty that Julian's plan 'seems to have involved the return of Jerusalem and its territory to the Jews and the consequent re-erection in Palestine of an autonomous Jewish entity.' But this must remain a mere conjecture.

[62] W. Bacher, 'Statements of a Contemporary of the Emperor Julian on the Rebuilding of the Temple', *JQR* 5 (1898), 168–72; id., *Die Agada* III, 111–13. He is followed, for example, by M. Avi-Yonah, *Jews*, 197. S. Lieberman, 'The Martyrs of Caesarea', *Annuaire de l'Institut de philologie et d'histoire orientales et slaves* 7 (1939–44), 395–446, 412ff., sees a story about R. Acha in QohR 9.8 as showing other rabbis rejecting Acha's support. But his argument falls short of proof.

to see even imperfect improvements as preparations for the messianic salvation, which would include support for Julian. But this is not certain.

M. Avi-Yonah points to R. Acha's statement, according to which the mention of salvation in the seventh section of the Eighteen Benedictions means that Israel would only attain salvation in a seventh [sabbath] year (jBer II.4.4 d – 5 a). The year 362–363, according to Avi-Yonah, was in fact a sabbath year.[63] This reckoning is true from the point of view of the present-day Jewish calendar; but it is not certain whether the sabbath year was uniformly calculated at that time. Certainly the four tomb inscriptions from Zoar on the Dead Sea, which give the year of death both as the year since the destruction of the Temple and as the year in the sabbath cycle, cannot be reconciled with each other.[64] Even if 362–363 was in fact a sabbath year, this would not be conclusive proof, since the correlation of the sabbath with eschatological salvation was traditional. It is of course possible that Julian's appearance gave a new urgency to certain speculations; but these existed throughout the rabbinic period.

If the rabbinate has left no definite witness to Julian's intentions, we may certainly assume that the patriarchate was against the plan, in its own interest. If it had been brought to fruition, a high priest would again have taken over the leadership of the Jewish people – unless a double leadership were planned, as in the time of the Herodian dynasty, because his alleged Davidic descent could have legitimated the patriarch as a secular prince. The abolition of the messenger tax, suggested by Julian, cannot have been welcome to the patriarchate either. It remains a purely hypothetical suggestion that Julian consoled the patriarch for the loss of these revenues with the title of *illustris*, the highest rank in the senatorial order.[65]

As far as the rabbinate is concerned, it was probably in general

---

[63] M. Avi-Yonah, *Jews*, 198.
[64] On the difficulties of calculating the sabbatical year, see E. Mahler, *Handbuch* 410ff.; B. Z. Wacholder, 'The Calendar of Sabbatical Cycles during the Second Temple and the Early Rabbinic Period', *HUCA* 44 (1973), 153–96 (according to his table, the sabbath year did not fall until 363–4!). On the grave inscriptions at Zoar, see J. Naveh, 'Another Aramaic Tombstone from Zoar', *HUCA* 56 (1985), 103–16, and M. Assis, *HUCA* 49 (1978), Hebrew section 5–13.
[65] This is the opinion of M. Avi-Yonah, *Jews*, 195 and 206 n. 32.

very sceptical of the project, because it had its own interests to defend against the priests, who would come to the fore again if the project were successful. Where tithes and first fruits were still paid, they generally went to the rabbis rather than to the priests, who no longer functioned. Furthermore, for too long the rabbis had sought to restrain any immediate expectation of restoration, so that they were unlikely to succumb to it hastily themselves. In particular it must have caused difficulty that an eschatological event such as the rebuilding of the Temple should be set in motion by a non-Jew, unless this were affirmed by recalling the example of Cyrus, which Julian himself, who knew his Bible, must have been conscious of.

The ordinary Jewish population probably reacted with much greater spontaneity, especially the congregations of the eastern Diaspora. Gregory of Nazianzus writes that as soon as Julian persuaded the Jews of his plan, they 'set to work with great energy and enthusiasm. Their admirers even say that every one of their wives not only took off their personal jewellery in order to help the work and those who were busy about it, but even carried out the earth (from the Temple building) in their skirts, without sparing their beautiful clothes or delicate limbs; for they believed they were carrying out a religious work, and that everything else was to be despised in comparison with this undertaking.'[66] Ephrem the Syrian writes of the mad enthusiasm of the Jews, who blew the ram's horn and rejoiced; according to Rufinus the Jews became arrogant, believing that the days of the prophets had come and molesting the Christians; many set off in the direction of Jerusalem.[67]

The correctness of these statements should not be doubted. An inscription, discovered recently on the Western (or 'Wailing') Wall, is dated by B. Mazar to the fourth century, and interpreted as a relic of Julian's project: 'When you see it, your heart will rejoice and your bones will sprout like green grass' (Isa. 66:13f., slightly altered).[68] Unfortunately such exact dating of inscriptions is impossible from a palaeographic point of view. This inscription could theoretically have been written in some other context;

---

[66] Gregory of Nazianzus, *Oratio* 5.4 (SC 309, 298–300).
[67] Ephrem, *Hymni contra Julianum* I.16,19; II.2. However, both texts are general, not referring directly to the building of the Temple; Rufinus, *Church history* X. 38 (GCS 9, 997).
[68] B. Mazar, *Der Berg des Herrn*, 88.

however, at what other time could Jews stay in Jerusalem long enough to carve such an inscription in the stone, even if it were hastily done? If we are not to assume a date in 362–363, we would have to go back at least as far as the beginning of the fourth century, or perhaps Eudokia's sojourn in Jerusalem in the fifth century. Thus a date in Julian's time has at least a very high degree of probability.[69] We may assume that a large proportion of the ordinary Jewish population, especially in the Diaspora, was delighted with Julian's plan. Even if the emperor had little detailed knowledge of the organization of Jewish self-administration (which is scarcely likely) he would probably not have relied on a positive reaction on the part of the patriarchate, but directly on the ordinary Jews. These latter did indeed take part, while the patriarch and the rabbinate exercised restraint.

The course of events must be fitted into the period between 19 July 362, when Julian arrived in Antioch, and 5 March 363, when he set out on his campaign against the Persians, or at the latest soon after 26 June 363, the day he died. The statement in the Syriac Julian novel should not be taken seriously, according to which a Jewish delegation travelled to meet him in Tarsus, i.e. asked permission to build the Temple even before his arrival in Antioch.

We may perhaps assume the following: Firstly, that Julian met a large Jewish community for the first time in Antioch, and only there was able to test the feasibility of realizing a plan he may have already formed previously. Secondly, that it was perhaps his disappointment over the Antiochenes' lack of enthusiasm for his programme of Hellenization that finally prompted him to favour the Jews in a special way. In that case we should probably take it that a couple of weeks elapsed after his arrival in Antioch before the emperor made his decision public. It is also a matter of course that a certain period of time was necessary for the news to spread, for building material to be prepared and suitable construction workers and Jewish volunteers to be collected. Since the period of

---

[69] R. Jonas, 'Titus (Flavius Vespasian) and (Flavius Claudius) Julian: Two Gem Portraits from the Jerusalem Area', *PEQ* 103 (1971), 9–12, describes a medallion with Julian's portrait, ostensibly found in the Jerusalem area; but stylistically it does not belong to the east. However, it is not permissible to make use of this find in judging the Jewish reaction, as does J. Geiger in Z. Baras et al. (eds.), *Eretz Israel* I, 214. Not only is the location where it was found not proven, but also its Jewish provenance.

winter rains was not very suitable for large-scale construction works, work at the site can only have begun in mid-February or late March of 363 at the earliest.

M. Adler was of the opinion that actual construction was never begun at all, and that the report of the miraculous interruption of the work was solely due to a tendentious assertion on the part of Gregory of Nazianzus, who was followed by all other authors, including the pagan Ammianus.[70] That is completely untenable, although it is clear that Christian propaganda made full use of the story and added miraculous exaggerations. But even Ammianus believes that the interruption of the work is due to not entirely natural causes; there is no doubt that he is not dependent on Gregory for this.

After the necessary building materials were collected, preliminary work began in the Temple grounds themselves, surely including the preparation of the foundations. All the Christian texts, beginning with Gregory of Nazianzus, certainly mention corresponding excavations. Near the 'Wailing Wall' an early Byzantine house has been excavated that was destroyed by fire. The latest coins found under the layer of rubble and ash come from Julian's time. B. Mazar concludes: 'The Constantinian structures near the Western Wall may have been destroyed by Jews, who, encouraged by Julian, began preparations for the reconstruction of the Temple.'[71] It is certainly conceivable that in the course of such work, buildings in the immediate vicinity of the Temple that were hindering access were pulled down. But would Christian propaganda have missed the opportunity for pointing out such a work of destruction? In the face of silence from our sources, the destruction of the building in the great earthquake of 363 seems more probable.[72]

However, then a disaster caused work to be abandoned. Ammianus writes: 'And when this Alypius was energetically taking

---

[70] M. Adler, 'The Emperor Julian'. C. R. Phillips, 'Julian's Rebuilding', 167f., believes that Ammianus, John Chrysostom and Ambrose all somehow gained knowledge of Alypius' official report, while Gregory of Nazianzus was too far from the events and the centres of political power, and relied instead on folk tradition, which then also became the basis of the Syriac reports.

[71] B. Mazar, 'The Archaeological Excavations near the Temple Mount' in: *Jerusalem Revealed. Archaeology in the Holy City 1968–1974*, Jerusalem 1975, 38.

[72] Thus K. W. Russell, 'The Earthquake of May 19, A.D. 363', *BASOR* 238 (1980), 47–64, 56.

care of this matter, and the provincial governor was assisting, frightening balls of fire broke out repeatedly near the foundations, burned a number of workmen and rendered the place inaccessible. In this manner the work that had been begun stopped, because the element constantly prevented it' (XXIII.1).

For the pagan Ammianus the disaster was an omen which should have warned Julian, who was otherwise so observant of signs, against the Persian campaign.[73] Christian interpretation naturally saw the event very differently, understanding it as divine punishment for those who wished to prove a Biblical prophecy false. The story could not fail to be given legendary embellishment. The two texts that were written in the year after the event are already noteworthy in this respect. Ephrem speaks in his second hymn against Julian of an earthquake which God produced to convict pagans of error, and which destroyed whole cities.

> But Jerusalem was to put the cursed crucifiers, who dared to decide and attempt the rebuilding of the ruins, the work of their sins, most especially in the wrong ... Jerusalem quaked when it saw that its destroyers returned to disturb its peace. It begged the Almighty for help against them, and was heard. He gave order to the storms, and they blew; he beckoned to the earthquakes, and they came, to the lightnings, and they flashed, to the air, and it was darkened, to the walls, and they collapsed, to the gates, and they opened. Fire broke out and consumed the scribes who had read in Daniel that the destruction was to last for ever. They had read it, but learnt nothing from it; thus they were taught by their miserable end.[74]

Poetic language resists a strictly historical interpretation; but Ephrem certainly insists that all the elements combine to prevent the refutation of the Daniel passage.

In his satirical speech on Julian, Gregory of Nazianzus gives much more detail. The Jews who were occupied in cleaning the Temple foundations were suddenly driven away by a terrible storm, accompanied by an earthquake. They wanted to flee for

---

[73] C. R. Phillips, 'Julian's Rebuilding', 168.
[74] Ephrem, *Hymni contra Julianum* II.18–20. Translation by S. Euringer in *Bibliothek der Kirchenväter* 37, Kempten 1919, 235f.

shelter into a nearby temple, but as they attempted to enter, fire burst from the sanctuary, killing some and maiming others. A shining cross also appeared in the sky. As a consequence of these events, many Jews went to the priests and were baptized.[75]

The text itself states that he makes use of different reports that do not agree in all particulars; his rhetorical freedom should also be noted. His remark on the flight of the Jews into 'one of the nearby temples' (*ti tōn plesiōn hierōn*) is striking. What is Gregory thinking of? There had probably not been any pagan temples in Jerusalem since Constantine's time. The letter attributed to Cyril of Jerusalem speaks of a synagogue, or rather the place in which the Jewish synagogue usually met (§ 7). Of course there was no time to build a synagogue in Julian's short reign; but it is entirely possible that an existing building was used for the synagogue service. Some think of a Christian church to which the Jews had fled for protection and were beaten off by force by the Christians. It is also possible that it refers to a still standing or already rebuilt section within the Temple precinct; for Rufinus, Philostorgius and Theodoret speak of a colonnade whose collapse killed Jews who had sought shelter there.

The story of the cross of light in the sky reminds us not only of Constantine's vision, but also of a letter from Cyril of Jerusalem to Constantius, in which he reports the appearance of a cross of light over Golgotha in 351.[76] Later authors speak of shining or black crosses that appeared on the clothes of the Jews and could not be removed in any way (Rufinus, Socrates, Theodoret). It is a reasonable assumption that the tradition about 351 was simply incorporated into the episode of the rebuilding of the Temple. The reports of it appear to combine and condense various traditions, in order to demonstrate the chronological unity of the action of the Jews and their punishment, together with its heavenly corroboration. It is typical that the baptism of the converted Jews is mentioned immediately afterwards, without the customary long preparation that preceded baptism.

The fifth-century descriptions continually expand the story. All the texts stress that immediately after the building material was provided, after the foundations were uncovered and all the preparations had been made for laying the foundation stone, a

---

[75] Gregory of Nazianzus, *Oratio* 5.4 (SC 309, 298ff.).
[76] Cyril of Jerusalem, *Letter to Constantius* (PG 33, 1165ff.).

storm broke out, an earthquake followed and fire broke out of the foundations. The details are unimportant, as is the expansion of the story to three miracles that caused the conversion of many Jews or made them resist the truth still more. In each version we simply see a case of religious bias dressed up as narrative, with little historical value.

The letter about these events attributed to Cyril is the most interesting. He alone mentions that many Christians also died in the earthquake, and offers a list of Palestinian towns affected by the earthquake. This clearly makes use of historical memories belonging to a man familiar with the situation in Palestine. The text is also interesting because it dates the events to Monday the 19th Iyyar, after a severe storm had prevented the laying of the foundation stone on the previous day. This 18th Iyyar (18 May 363) was the half-holiday of Lag ba-Omer, which could have been purposely chosen as an auspicious day for beginning work.[77] However, the evidence for this festival all comes from a later period, so that the dating should be approached with caution. The fact that the correct day of the week is given for the date shows that this must be a fairly early tradition,[78] but it could simply have referred to the earthquake, and only later have been combined with the abandoning of the building of the Temple.

G. W. Bowersock argued against such a late dating of the failure of Julian's project. However, his principal arguments were aimed against the even later dating of the disaster proposed by M. Avi-Yonah, who deduced 27 May 363 from an Abyssinian menology and a Syriac chronicle of 724.[79] The synaxary only mentions the Temple project for the period before 27.5.; the Syriac text mentions the earthquake in the month of Iyyar, but not the Temple; here, the earthquake is rather a punishment for the supporters of Julian's paganism. According to Bowersock, the

---

[77] S. P. Brock, 'A Letter', 268, 279f.; id., 'The Rebuilding', 104. He assumes that this half-holiday originated in the events of 363. This seems quite unlikely, since the project failed.

[78] G. W. Bowersock, *Julian*, 122, disagrees. He sees this Syriac text as an ancient forgery by someone who knew the Syriac tradition well but had no direct knowledge of Jerusalem. The tradition of a late date for the abandonment of the Temple project developed in the east, according to Bowersock, and then could have induced John the Lydian to date a fragmentary letter of Julian's on the building of the Temple during the Persian campaign.

[79] M. Avi-Yonah, *Jews*, 200.

project to rebuild the Temple was abandoned even before Julian set off on the Persian campaign. John the Lydian dates Julian's words, 'With all eagerness I am building the temple of the highest god', to the time 'when he marched out against the Persians'; but, according to Bowersock, this need not mean the campaign itself, but could simply refer to the time after he left Constantinople. Nor should Julian's words in *Letter* 89 to Theodore from Antioch, that he himself had intended (*dienoēthēn*) to build the Temple, be understood to mean that he intended to do so some time in the future. Bowersock takes as a positive argument, in favour of his early dating of the abandonment of the project, the context in Ammianus' description, who portrays Julian afterwards, 'during those days', as still in Antioch.[80]

The arguments for an early date are not conclusive. One could also cite Theodoret of Cyrrhus, who ends his description of the failed attempt with the remark that Julian hardened his heart, as Pharaoh once did, when he heard of it.[81] But this remark is just as theologically motivated as the interest of other authors in creating a causal connection between the failure of the Persian campaign and the 'godless' Temple project, which they stress by telescoping the chronological sequence of events, including the earthquake. But if the later date of the project's failure is correct, it would mean that Julian did not live to hear of it; a report from Alypius could hardly have reached him before his sudden death.

Thus the precise dates are not certain, nor is the connection with the great earthquake of May 363, since the early texts do not yet mention it in this context, except Gregory of Nazianzus, who may already be combining two chronologically separate events. Ammianus, Ambrose and John Chrysostom agree in mentioning only a fire that led to the abandonment of the undertaking.[82] This suggests that an unexplained and mysterious fire interrupted the project; perhaps only weeks later the great earthquake occurred, which together with Julian's death meant the definitive end of the attempted rebuilding. As far as Christian interpretation was

---

[80] G. W. Bowersock, *Julian*, 120–2. He did not yet know Brock's longer article (*A Letter*). The quotations from Julian's letters: M. Stern, *Greek and Latin Authors* II, 568f., 553.
[81] Theodoret of Cyrrhus, *Church history* III.20.8 (GCS 44, 200).
[82] Ambrose, *ep.* 40.12 (PL 16, 1152); John Chrysostom, *Contra Iudaeos et Gentiles* (PG 48, 835); *Adv. Iudaeos* V.11 (PG 48, 900f.).

concerned, it was all part of a single event, and could therefore be represented as a chronological unity.

M. Avi-Yonah sums up as follows: 'The news of the death of Julian provoked in southern Palestine a Christian reaction, which led to the destruction of most of the Jewish communities in the *Darom.*'[83] This unfounded assertion cannot stand scrutiny. Jewish villages in the south of the country may have suffered damage at this time; but this should be seen as a consequence of the great earthquake, which according to the list of towns in Ps.-Cyril's letter affected large areas of the country. Anti-Jewish disturbances are of course not impossible in Palestine after the failure of the Temple project and Julian's death, but there is no evidence for them. The uncertainty of what would follow after his death probably prevented rash reactions, and at least until 364 the governor of Palestine was a pagan. Most of all, however, in the critical situation of summer 363, affecting the whole empire, the authorities could not risk slackening their control. It is altogether unlikely that Christians could have destroyed entire villages belonging to Jews undisturbed. Whatever damage the earthquake did in these villages, Jerome attests them as Jewish villages at the end of the century; the rich synagogue buildings, in the south of the country too, prove that their vitality was able to survive even Christian rule.

---

[83] M. Avi-Yonah, *Jews*, 209.

VIII

The Samaritans

Following the description of events in Palestine under Gallus and Julian, we now turn to the fourth section of the population after Jews, Christians and pagans. The Samaritans are usually not mentioned at all, or only in passing, in accounts of the history of Palestine in the fourth century. The reason is that, in contrast to Jewish and Christian history, there are few documents for the development of the Samaritan community in that period, despite the fact that the fourth century is generally held to be the Samaritans' heyday. Jewish and Christian sources speak of Samaritans at most in passing; the Samaritan texts themselves are late, without exception, and great caution is necessary when making use of them for historical purposes. Archaeological information is also relatively scarce and hard to date. Only recently, since 1990, have several undoubtedly Samaritan synagogues been excavated which may be securely dated to the fourth century. Nevertheless, in order to gain a full picture of contemporary Palestine, the importance of the Samaritans must be borne in mind.

This chapter attempts to relate the reports of the Samaritan chronicles with data that is otherwise historically verified. I shall make most use of the so-called 'Chronicle II', the portion of which relating to the third and fourth centuries has been edited, translated and commented on by J. M. Cohen. He dates this work, described by J. Macdonald as 'the best and most exact of all chronicles',[1] to the fourteenth century.[2] It would therefore be

---

[1] J. Macdonald, *The Theology*, 44. More sceptical is P. Stenhouse, 'Samaritan Chronicles', in A. D. Crown (ed.), *The Samaritans*, 218–65; id. in A. D. Crown et al. (eds.), *A Companion*, 50–53.
[2] J. M. Cohen, *A Samaritan Chronicle*, 177.

roughly contemporary with the Arabic chronicler Abu'l Fath, who wrote in 1355 and used as his principal sources the Tolida and the Arabic Book of Joshua.[3] The *Second Chronicle* largely agrees in content both with Abu'l Fath and with the other chronicles.

As rabbinic texts show, the Samaritans spread from the second century onwards beyond the boundaries of their original home of Samaria. R. Abbahu, head of a rabbinic school in Caesarea around 300, says, 'Thirteen villages were mingled with Samaritans in the days of persecution' (jQid IV.1.65 d; jJeb VIII.3.9 d). Thus he connects the spreading of the Samaritans with the consequences of the Bar Cochba revolt, which is entirely plausible. Initially at least, the Samaritans appear to have lived in relative harmony with the Jewish population, as is shown by the context from which the above quote is taken, in marriage law, i.e. it assumes the possibility of mixed marriages.

Life together with Samaritans is also assumed by TPes II.3 (L. 145): 'Unleavened bread from Samaritans is permitted, and the Pesach duty is fulfilled by it. But R. Leazar forbids it, since they are not experts in the precise regulations of unleavened bread. Rabban Simeon ben Gamaliel says: every law which the Samaritans have retained, they keep more strictly than the Jews.'[4] Thus religious sharing was possible in many, although not all, areas of life, and in comparison with the New Testament period we must assume a considerable improvement in relationships between the two religious communities.

Not until Diocletian's time did the break come, according to rabbinic tradition. Apparently a key question was whether Samaritan wine was religiously acceptable or whether, as with pagan wine, there was a fear that it was intended for libations in honour of idols. The Palestinian Talmud attributes to R. Abbahu the decisive initiative in declaring Samaritan wine to be suspect (jAZ V.4.44 d).

---

[3] J. Bowman, *Samaritanische Probleme*, 25. E. Vilmar produced a Latin translation with commentary, together with an edition of the Arabic text, *Abdulfathi Annales Samaritani*, Gotha 1865. An English translation with notes is *The Kitab al-Tarikh of Abu Fath. Translated with notes by P. Stenhouse*, Sydney 1985 (with new chapter divisions).

[4] Archaeological evidence for a high degree of correspondence with Jewish halakhah in the matter of ritual purification is offered by the Miqvaot excavated in Qedumim. See Y. Magen, 'The Ritual Baths (Miqva'ot) at Qedumim and the Observance of Ritual Purity Among the Samaritans', in F. Manns and E. Aliata (eds.), *Early Christianity in Context*, 181–92.

The text first tells of R. Simeon b. Eleazar (end of the second century): in a Samaritan city he asked a scribe for a sealed jug of wine; apparently he was already suspicious of wine in an open jug, but not in a sealed one. However, the Samaritan repeatedly directed him to the spring in front of him; that is, if he had religious scruples, he should not drink any Samaritan wine at all. The anecdote ends with the sentence: 'Already the Samaritans were corrupted.'

The following story, about Simeon's contemporary R. Yishmael b. R. Jose, is intended to confirm this judgement. R. Yishmael accuses the Samaritans in Neapolis: 'I see that you do not worship this mountain (i.e Mt. Gerizim), but statues under it. For it is written, "And Jacob hid them (the idols) under the tree near Shechem" (Gen. 35.4).' But then the rabbi suspects that the Samaritans may kill him because of his accusation, and flees early in the morning (cf. GenR 81.3, Th-A 974).

If here, as early as the end of the second century, the Samaritans are accused of breaking with Biblical monotheism, this may go back to earlier, traditional polemic. The fact that since the middle of the second century a temple of Jupiter had stood on the Samaritans' holy mountain could only strengthen such polemic. But perhaps there was indeed a certain openness for pagan forms of expression among the Samaritans of this period. For example, M. Avi-Yonah draws this conclusion from the pagan images on the coins of the city of Neapolis after the Bar Cochba revolt.[5] However, the Samaritan population of Neapolis should not be held responsible for the images on the coins. They probably simply indicate an increase in the numbers and influence of the pagan population. Yet the Samaritan chronicles also appear to assume a certain degree of assimilation among the Samaritans of this period, under pressure of religious persecution. This might be an appropriate context for a remark by Epiphanius that the inhabitants of Neapolis sacrificed to Kore, supposedly because she was the daughter of Jephtha who was once sacrificed to God.[6] However, in the context of jAZ V.4, the editor may also be interested in finding earlier roots for the final

---

[5] M. Avi-Yonah, 'The Samaritans in the Roman and Byzantine Periods' (Hebrew), in *Eretz Shomron*, Jerusalem 1973, 34–7.

[6] Epiphanius, *Panarion* 78.23.6 (GCS 37, 473), referring to Judg. 11:29ff. H. G. Kippenberg, *Garizim und Synagoge*, 102, stresses that this can hardly be a Samaritan tradition.

break which was apparently forced by R. Abbahu in particular, as the continuation of the text shows:

> R. Abbahu forbade their wine, according to R. Hiyya and R. Assi and R. Ammi. They climbed the royal mountain [the Samaritan Mount Ephraim] and saw a pagan [Samaritan?] who was suspect on account of their wine. They came and told him [the rabbi] so. He answered: And [should we] not [forbid their wine] even because of a pretext?
>
> And others said: One sabbath evening there was no wine in all Samaria. By the end of the sabbath there was plenty, which had been brought by the Romans and which the Samaritans had accepted from them.
>
> And others said: When King Diocletian came here, he decreed the following: All peoples must offer libations except the Jews. And the Samaritans offered libations. And their wine was [suspected by the Jews of being tainted with idol-sacrifice and therefore] forbidden.
>
> And others said: They have something like a dove and offer libations to it.

The story with its three alternative explanations shows that already by the time the Palestinian Talmud was compiled, it was no longer clear why exactly the Samaritan wine had come under suspicion of not being religiously irreproachable. All that was unanimously retained was the fact itself and its connection with Abbahu of Caesarea.

The first two versions of the explanation accuse the Samaritans of receiving wine from non-Jews, of having no religious scruples about it and thus of coming under suspicion of idolatry themselves. This accusation is made explicit by the third explanation, according to which the Samaritans were forced to offer pagan libations under Diocletian. The fourth explanation is the most radical, according to which the cult on Mt. Gerizim itself includes libations for the image of a bird, an accusation which has apparently also been reflected in Samaritan legend.[7]

If we are to look for a single explanation, the order published under Diocletian that civil servants and soldiers had to demonstrate their loyalty to the Roman state with a libation seems the

---

[7] J. M. Cohen, *A Samaritan Chronicle*, 200–4, connects this rabbinic accusation with the Samaritan story of the bronze bird.

most probable. Another statement by R. Abbahu is evidence for the fact that very many Samaritans were occupied in the administration of Cacsarea: 'The majority of the administration or occupying force (*taxis*) of Caesarea is Samaritan, and thus, in the case of pagan festivals, to be treated like the pagans themselves who are celebrating the feast' (jAZ I.2.39 c). This means that on those days Jews were not permitted to have any business or social contact with them; otherwise they themselves would come under suspicion of idolatry. Abbahu here apparently treats Samaritans as counting as pagans, a radical position which did not become generally accepted, even later.

It surely happened repeatedly that Samaritan civil servants or soldiers accepted the duty to sacrifice as a religiously insignificant gesture. However, this need not necessarily have been an occasion for Jews to renounce all fellowship with Samaritans. We can no longer decide what really lay behind the decision, whether simple competitiveness because of the increasing Samaritan population,[8] or truly religious reservations. But the fact remains, as the continuation of jAZ V.4 shows: 'The Samaritans of Caesarea asked R. Abbahu: "Your fathers supplied themselves with our [food]. Why do you not supply yourselves from what is ours?" He answered them: Your fathers did not corrupt their deeds. You have corrupted your deeds.' Therefore the Samaritans should now be regarded as pagans. It is only a logical conclusion when then R. Jakob bar Acha (*ca.* 300) says in the name of R. Hanina: 'It is permissible to lend at interest to the Samaritans of Caesarea.' They no longer count as fellow-tribesmen, and the prohibition of usury among Jews does not apply to them.

The fact that Diocletian treated Jews and Samaritans differently in his religious policy appears to go back to older Roman political practice. Antoninus Pius' rescript, according to which, after Hadrian's blanket prohibition of circumcision, only the Jews were again permitted to circumcise, appears to have been interpreted very strictly, at least periodically. The Samaritan chronicles do in fact assert that the Samaritan religion was persecuted by the Roman emperors of the third century, and that circumcision was forbidden. They say that the prohibition was still in force at the time of the birth of the great reformer Baba Rabba, and that

---

[8] Thus G. Alon, *The Jews in their Land in the Talmudic Age* II, Jerusalem 1984, 745.

towards the end of the third century they were even forbidden to climb Mt. Gerizim.

This is the period in which the great Samaritan reformer was at work, Baba Rabba, the 'Great Gate' (probably a title of honour rather than his real name). Despite the fact that emperors of the early third century are mentioned in connection with his story, he is normally dated to the first half of the fourth century.[9] J. M. Cohen attempts a more precise dating, assuming that Baba Rabba was born around 288 and appeared in public between 308 and 328.[10] The following section summarizes the salient points in the *Second Chronicle* (paragraph divisions according to J. M. Cohen).

Baba Rabba, the oldest son of the Samaritan High Priest Netanael, is said to have incited people to resist the Romans, who had long persecuted the Samaritans and forbidden circumcision (§ 1–2). His first step was to reopen all the Samaritan synagogues that had been closed by the enemy, and institute the few elders and wise men who had survived the persecutions to teach the Torah and care for the synagogues in their towns (§ 4).[11] A group of seven men, three priests and four laymen from the tribe of Joseph, formed the new leadership; however, many priests initially resisted Baba Rabba and were replaced by laymen. The seven men were intended to be responsible for decisions relating to religious law, teaching and the courts in their several districts, as well as taking over the leadership of the community in general (§ 5).

Furthermore, Baba Rabba is said to have built eight stone synagogues, apparently all in the Samaritan heartland. Overlapping to a certain extent with the distribution of areas to the seven leaders, the districts of Israel were now divided into eleven regions for the priests (in accordance with the distribution of the land to the eleven tribes of Israel – the twelfth tribe, Levi, did not receive its own land). Baba Rabba distributed all the regions from Gaza to Tyre, and eastward to the Jordan (§ 9). This is surely a

---

[9] J. A. Montgomery, *The Samaritans*, 102: 'All the sure data refers his life to the middle of the IVth Century; probably he flourished under the eastern co-emperor Constantius.'

[10] J. M. Cohen, *A Samaritan Chronicle*, 225f. The arguments published here do not suffice for such a precise dating – I was unable to consult Cohen's typescript dissertation.

[11] J. Bowman, *Samaritanische Probleme*, 36, suggests that it was Baba Rabba who first introduced the synagogue as an institution among the Samaritans.

literary fiction, or rather a symbolic claiming of all Israel, according to the original Biblical distribution of the land; but that should not be thought to imply a total absence of Samaritan settlements in the individual regions.

Since the Romans prevented the Samaritans from keeping the religous law, they rose in revolt together at the new moon of the seventh month against their oppressors (§ 11). Baba Rabba gathered troops against the approaching Roman army, and kept back the taxes that had previously been paid to Rome. He was helped in his resistance against Roman rule by the fact that the Chaldaean king, that is, probably the king of Persia, was fighting a war against the Roman emperor ('King Alexander') at that time. At the same time there were also plundering raids by Arabs whom Baba Rabba was able to drive off, so that the surrounding rulers supported him (§ 14).

Since the Romans were unsuccessful against Baba Rabba, they incited the Jews to wage war on him, promising as a reward the permission to rebuild the Temple (§ 15). As a result, the Jewish elders formed a conspiracy against Baba Rabba, who was in the habit of spending the sabbath at the synagogue of Nemara. But a Jewish woman whose friend was a Samaritan woman betrayed the plan to her, and so Baba Rabba was warned (§ 16). Despite the failure of the attack the emperor Gordian permitted the Jews to rebuild their Temple, but a whirlwind frustrated the attempt (§ 17).

Subsequently Baba Rabba sent his nephew Levi to Constantinople. He was to study Roman customs there, which was to enable him to overcome the Roman bronze bird which was set up on the border with Mt. Gerizim and cried *Ibriyyos*, 'Hebrew', every time a Samaritan approached, betraying him to the Roman sentries.

Thirteen years later, having risen unrecognized to the highest honours in Constantinople, Levi returned to Palestine with a great escort and climbed Mt. Gerizim. The bronze bird immediately reported the presence of a Hebrew. Levi made the Roman soldiers search for a Samaritan on the mountain, but they were unsuccessful. So Levi was able to order the destruction of the bird which had 'gone mad' (§ 18f.). This was followed by battles between Baba and the Romans, in which Baba was successful. They finally offered peace and enticed Baba to Constantinople. There he remained in honourable captivity under 'King Philip' and was finally buried by the Romans with a magnificent state funeral.

This, in brief, is the novelistic content of the Chronicle. Its actual historical basis would be of great interest to us. Baba Rabba undoubtedly existed and implemented reforms among his people, the Samaritans. However, it is extremely difficult to fit the rest into the chronological framework of known events.

Let us begin with the many names of Roman emperors in the Samaritan Chronicle. Hardly a single one is known in Jewish sources. Were the Samaritans considerably more interested in the political history of their times than the Jews? Or did they augment their rather novelistic historical traditions with historical material during the Middle Ages? This question is of decisive importance when judging the reliability of Samaritan historical traditions. Unfortunately, we cannot answer it here. The fact is that the story of Baba Rabba cannot be made to correspond with the dates of the Roman emperors mentioned as his contemporaries.[12] It is much more easily understood in the context of the fourth century. Not only the fact that Baba Rabba spends his final years in Constantinople fits this alternative,[13] but also the great synchronism in § 10 which dates Baba Rabba's first appearance:

> And he appeared in the year 4600 since the creation of the world, which is the year 1806 since the entrance of the Israelites into the land of Canaan ... the year 1005 since the arrival of the Samaritans from the first exile. This exile was Nebuchadnezzar's exile ... the year 655 since the appearance of King Alexander, king of the whole world, which is the year 308 since the appearance of Jesus the son of Mary.

It would be very interesting to learn when and with what material this synchronism was put together; but we must be content with the fact that it points to the early fourth century. It would also fit

---

[12] P. Stenhouse (see n. 3 above), notes 732, 876, 949, prefers to date Baba Rabba to the early third century, i.e. he accepts the names of emperors, but must also accept other anachronisms. Cf. id., 'Fourth-Century Date for Baba Rabba Re-examined', *New Samaritan Studies* III–IV (*Festschrift* G. D. Sixdenier), Sydney 1995, 317–26. B. Hall and A. D. Crown, A. D. Crown (ed.), *The Samaritans*, 49ff. and 55f., also argue in favour of the third century.

[13] J. M. Cohen, *A Samaritan Chronicle*, 226f., rejects the historicity of the stay in Constantinople.

that in Baba Rabba's time the Persian king waged war against the Romans, although this would also correspond with many other periods of the third and later centuries. Nor are invasions by Arabs in the fourth century a rarity. Finally, the detail that the Jews received permission to build the Temple for their actions against Baba Rabba fits best with memories of the attempt to rebuild the Jerusalem Temple under Julian. The explanation that a whirlwind scattered the materials which were lying ready, after all the preparations for building had been completed, is also found in the traditions of the Church Fathers on the subject. The increasing enmity between Jews and Samaritans could have led to the formation of a tradition according to which their own misfortune was attributed to the enemy, and the traitor was first rewarded for his action, before God's intervention prevented it after all.

However, the most serious difficulty in fitting Baba Rabba into a historical context is presented by his military activity. There is no evidence for this outside the Samaritan tradition. But since within this tradition chronologically widely separate events are telescoped together in other cases also, it is possible that the Samaritan revolts of the late fifth and early sixth century have been backdated to the time of Baba Rabba. Another possibility is that Samaritans took part in the unrest under Gallus. However, non-Samaritan evidence for this is again lacking, and such participation would have to have been hugely exaggerated in the Samaritan Chronicles, since, as we saw, the extent of this unrest was fairly small. Finally, we should perhaps also take note of the isolated remark concerning a Jewish revolt against Constantine; but the combination of Baba's story with the later Samaritan revolts remains the most likely explanation. We may certainly exclude the possibility of extensive military activity on the part of Baba Rabba in the fourth century, on lack of evidence.

On the other hand, it is certainly possible that Samaritans were involved in ending the cult of Jupiter on Mt. Gerizim. According to the *Life* by Peter the Iberian, Pomnia, a Roman woman, threw down the idol on Mt. Gerizim.[14] But there may have been

---

[14] H.-G. Kippenberg, *Garizim und Synagoge*, 100. Coins from the fourth century (Diocletian to Julian), found around the Roman temple on Mt. Gerizim, point to a thriving life that breaks off sharply after Julian. See R. J. Bull, *RB* 75 (1968), 238–43; Y. Magen (Ch. VII, n. 11).

attempts by the Samaritans to win back their holy mountain even before this; Baba Rabba's reforming activity might belong in this context, but his reorganization of Samaritan administration can only have been short-lived.

In the decades after Baba Rabba the most important texts of the Samaritan liturgy were written, the Defter with its oldest hymns (the Durran), which are attributed to Amram Dara, one of the seven leaders appointed by Baba Rabba. Amram's son Marqa wrote the greatest religious work of the Samaritan tradition, Memar Marqa.[15]

The fact that from the late fourth century the Samaritans are put on an equal footing with the Jews in the laws of the Codex Theodosianus also speaks for a revival of the Samaritan community. For in the time of pagan Rome they had not shared the privilege of a permitted religion with the Jews (see CTh XIII.5.18, dated 390; CTh XVI.8.16, dated 404: this law excludes Jews and Samaritans from certain civil service careers; CTh XVI.8.28, dated 426, secures the inheritance rights of Jews and Samaritans who convert to Christianity; novella 3, dated 438, excludes pagans, Jews and Samaritans, and also heretics, from all public office. These are all negative laws, but the fact that Samaritans are now named separately shows that they were recognized as a separate group).[16] Finally, the fact that the Samaritans were strong enough to sustain several revolts against the might of the Byzantine state in the fifth and sixth centuries is a sufficient sign that previously they had experienced a long period of flourishing growth.

Archaeological finds represent concrete evidence for the spread of Samaritans in the fourth century, in particular the synagogues which have recently been excavated. As yet no archaeological proof of the existence of the eight synagogues attributed to Baba Rabba has been forthcoming; but several synagogues from this period are now known in the Samaritan heartland.[17]

---

[15] J. Macdonald, *The Theology* 42, describes Memar Marqa as 'by far the most important Samaritan document after the Pentateuch.'

[16] However, the rarity of mentions of Samaritans in laws, compared with Jews, remains noticeable, as does the complete failure to mention any leader of the Samaritan community or any other institution of leadership. J. A. Montgomery's suggestion that every law about Jews also includes Samaritans may be correct, but cannot be proved.

[17] Y. Magen, 'Samaritan Synagogues', *Early Christianity in Context*, 193–230; id., 'Mount Gerizim and the Samaritans', ibid. 91–148, esp. 108f., 129; id., *NEAE* IV, 1424–27.

In Khirbet Samara, on the road from Nablus to Tulkarm, a synagogue orientated on Mt. Gerizim was built in the fourth century over a Roman building, making use of its remains (the synagogue measures 12.7 × 16.4 m, with a 3.4 m wide narthex attached). At its western end is a semicircular atrium. The interior walls are lined with stone benches; the floor is adorned with a mosaic with complex geometrical motifs, a Torah shrine, various plants, a candelabrum flanked by vessels, and two empty birdcages. The apse in the east wall was added later. The building was damaged in the Samaritan revolts and repaired in the early Arab period.

Only a few kilometres away, near Sebaste, is the synagogue of el-Khirbe, which like that of Kh. Samara is constructed from recycled building material from a Roman building. The massive longitudinal walls of the hall (exterior measurement 14 × 12 m) supported a barrel vault. Here too stone benches lined the walls; the mosaic floor, besides a pattern of interlocking circles, has a Greek donor inscription, below which the table for the shewbread can be seen, flanked by a menorah and Torah shrine. The complex also boasts a large atrium and side rooms; it was also destroyed in the Samaritan revolts and only restored in the Arab period.

Another synagogue is in Zur Natan (= Kh. Maydal), which has been excavated since 1989. It was built in the fourth to fifth century. This building, also orientated on Mt. Gerizim, follows the same pattern (stone benches, mosaic floor). In the sixth century the building was turned into a church: a narthex and apse were added. But in the Arab period Samaritans appear to have taken possession of the complex again.[18]

Near the al Hadra mosque in Nablus (Huzn Ya'aqub) the foundations of a synagogue have been excavated, from which the decalogue inscription and the inscription with the words of creation, both built into the wall of the mosque, probably come. The synagogue should probably be dated to the fourth century. A stone relief with a Torah shrine, discovered in 1941 in Kafr Fahma, which was originally regarded as the remains of a Jewish synagogue, is also probably to be attributed to a Samaritan building.

Finally, remains were also found on Mt. Gerizim itself.

---

[18] See E. Ayalon et al., *ESI* 16 (1997), 82.

However, it is not certain whether the building with a mosaic floor, discovered near the temple of Zeus, was a synagogue. A Samaritan presence in the fourth century around the Byzantine church, which stands on the site of the Samaritan Temple, is however clearly proven by a number of Greek inscriptions. All these synagogues share the following characteristics: their orientation on Mt. Gerizim, where possible with a clear view of the mountain, a single-aisled hall without pillars, and a stricter observation of the prohibition of images by comparison with Jewish synagogues. Animals and human beings are not to be seen on Samaritan mosaics. The inscriptions are all in Greek; those in Samaritan script perhaps only come from a later phase.[19]

Before these new excavations, architectural remains were known from only two synagogues, both outside Samaria and dating from the late fourth or early fifth century. Salbit (Hebrew Sha'alvim, 12 kilometres south-east of Ramla) was excavated in 1949. The building measures 15.4 × 8 m and has a mosaic floor. In its centre is a circle with a mountain, presumably Mt. Gerizim, which the building is orientated on, and a Greek inscription; two other Samaritan inscriptions are written at the edge of the mosaic.[20] The second synagogue is in Beth Shean, where the mosaic floor of a three-aisled basilica (14.2 × 17 m) has an inscription in Samaritan script as well as three Greek inscriptions. However, it is not entirely clear whether this was a purely Samaritan synagogue or whether the building was used by Jews and Samaritans together in some form of co-operation.[21]

G. Reeg also mentions in this context the three-aisled synagogue that was found in 1975 in front of the Haaretz museum in Tel Aviv, and whose mosaic floor preserves two Greek inscriptions

---

[19] See L. Di Segni, 'The Greek Inscriptions in the Samaritan Synagogue at El Khirbe with Some Considerations on the Function of the Samaritan Synagogue in the Late Roman Period', in F. Manns and E. Aliata (eds.), *Early Christianity in Context*, 231–9; Y. Magen, ibid., 219f., 228f; L. Di Segni, 'The Church of Mary Theotokos on Mt. Gerizim: The Inscriptions' in G. C. Bottini et al. (eds), *Christian Archaeology in the Holy Land. New Discoveries (Festschrift V. Corbo)*, Jerusalem 1990, 343–350.

[20] G. Reeg, *Die samaritanischen Synagogen*, 635–7.

[21] G. Reeg, *Die samaritanischen Synagogen*, 571–5; G. Foerster, *NEAE* I, 234. It should be noted that the Samaritan inscription (in the Greek language!) comes from a late stage of the building, and that thus an attribution of the building to Samaritans as early as 400 is not certain. On the inscription most recently J. Naveh, *IEJ* 31 (1981), 220–2.

and a Samaritan-Aramaic inscription.[22] However, this building, which the excavator regarded as a Samaritan church,[23] was only built towards the end of the Byzantine period.

These architectural remains are joined by a few Samaritan inscriptions which could belong to the period under consideration (unless the existence of Samaritan script is taken to be altogether a sign of a later date). They probably also generally come from synagogues. Mostly they contain the Ten Commandments, but also other Biblical passages. Some evidence comes from the centre of Samaria, for example, two inscriptions from Shechem, where the synagogue is said to have been built in the middle of the fourth century by Aqbon, Baba Rabba's brother and high priest after him. Nearby is Balata, where Epiphanius attests the existence of a synagogue,[24] and where a Decalogue inscription was found. A door lintel with a Decalogue inscription comes from Beth al-Ma', a little west of Shechem; finally, the inscriptions from Huzn Ya'aqub (Helqat ha-Sade) with the Decalogue and the words of creation, mentioned above, come from the same area. A Samaritan inscription from the neighbourhood of Gaza, where Eusebius attests the presence of Samaritans,[25] could also belong in the fourth century, as also a number of Samaritan lamps, among them a lamp with a Samaritan inscription from Caesarea, where a bronze bracelet with a Samaritan inscription had been found earlier.[26]

All this information is still very meagre, and does not afford anything like a complete picture of the development of the Samaritans in the period under consideration. But the finds of recent years allow us to hope that further discoveries may be reckoned with, which will be easier to categorize on the basis of what is already known. Apparently the Samaritan revolts of the fifth and sixth centuries did not, as had previously been feared, lead to such thoroughgoing destruction that any traces of Samaritan culture were lost for ever.

---

[22] G. Reeg, *Die samaritanischen Synagogen*, 631f.
[23] H. Kaplan, 'A Samaritan Church on the Premises of "Museum Haaretz"' (Hebrew), *Qadmoniot* 11 (1978), 78–80. The hypothesis of its being a Samaritan church was attacked immediately, most recently by Y. Tsafrir, 'A New Reading of the Samaritan Inscription from Tel Qasile', *IEJ* 31 (1981), 223–6. Further literature ibid.
[24] Epiphanius, *Panarion* 80.1.6 (GCS 37, 485).
[25] Eusebius, *De martyribus Palaestinae* 8.10 (GCS 9, 927).
[26] See I. Ben-Zvi, 'A Lamp with a Samaritan Inscription', *IEJ* 11 (1961), 139–42. For further literature see V. Sussman in A. D. Crown et al. (eds.), *A Companion*, 32f.

IX

The Jewish Patriarch

The institution of the Jewish patriarchate has been mentioned several times in preceding chapters. From the late second century this institution was, for the Roman government, the recognized representative of the Jewish people in Palestine, and even in the whole Roman empire. This position of leadership, which had grown out of the rabbinic movement, was hereditary in the family of Jehuda the Patriarch, editor of the Mishnah, for as far as we are able to trace it. This family went back to Hillel, the ancestor of the rabbinic movement, and ultimately to David, which underlines its political and almost messianic aspirations.

In view of the importance of the patriarchate, it is surprising that there is only very scanty evidence for its history, and that it has only recently been the subject of detailed research.[1] Apart from a very few passages in the Church Fathers, our documents for the second and third centuries are purely rabbinic, and therefore reflect the party interests of the rabbinate within Judaism. In the fourth century, by contrast, rabbinic evidence is very rare. Instead we have inscriptions, passages in the Church Fathers, isolated pagan texts and above all the laws of the Codex Theodosianus; in other words largely non-Jewish sources, which again pursue particular interests.

The reason for the one-sidedness of the individual sources of material surely lies in a change in the office itself. The patriarchate developed from an inner-Jewish institution of leadership, which gradually gained recognition from the state, to an office

---

[1] See esp. M. Jacobs, *Die Institution*; D. Goodblatt, *The Monarchic Principle*; L. I. Levine, 'The Status of the Patriarch in the Third and Fourth Centuries: Sources and Methodology', *JJS* 47 (1996), 1–32. From the older literature esp. H. Mantel, *Studies*, 175–253; L. I. Levine, 'The Jewish Patriarch'; H. Zucker, *Studien*, 148–72.

that was increasingly orientated outward, and whose influence on rabbinic religious discussion decreased accordingly. The texts of the relevant laws have been studied several times with regard to the development of the patriarchate in the fourth century; naturally all other possible information should be included to gain a more rounded picture of developments.

The synagogue of Hammath Tiberias, discussed in a previous chapter, with its inscriptions and zodiac mosaic, may serve as a point of departure for our description. The mosaic floor of Hammath Tiberias shows several donor inscriptions. The largest is formed of nine squares with a total of eight names. The only part of this inscription which takes in two squares, and is thereby marked as particularly important, reads as follows: 'Severos, the protégé (*threptos*) of the most illustrious (*lamprotatōn*) Patriarchs, made it. Blessing on him. Amen.' The second half of this text, beginning with the word 'Patriarchs' is in the dead centre of the inscription. This brings out the text, as does the closing formula: the 'Amen' concludes the entire inscription, as it were (the other parts of the inscription end with 'long may he live', 'may he be saved', or without a final wish). Severos is also mentioned in another inscription in the synagogue, here again with the title 'protégé of the most illustrious Patriarchs'. Here too he is being blessed for completing something, together with Ioullos (= Hillel), who is described as the one responsible for the synagogue (*pronoētēs*). This Hillel also appears in the large inscription, as he who 'full of responsibility (*pronoumenos*) completed everything'.[2]

The expression 'patriarch(s)' is otherwise attested in Jewish inscriptions only in the Diaspora. In an inscription on a column of the synagogue of Stobi in Macedonia[3] the donor (Cl.) Tiberius Polycharmos reserves to himself certain rooms in the complex of buildings. If anyone alters his orders, 'let him give the patriarch twenty-five myriads of denarii'.

The inscription is dated at the beginning with the Greek letters TIA. J.-B. Frey referred this to the Macedonian calendar and thus

---

[2] On the inscriptions see M. Dothan, *Hammath Tiberias*, 57–60; B. Lifshitz, *Donateurs*, 61–6; id., *ZDPV* 78 (1962), 180–4.

[3] Text in *CIJ* I, 505 (No. 694); see B. Lifshitz in the Prolegomena to the new edition of *CIJ* I, 76f.; id., *Donateurs*, 18. For an analysis of the text see M. Hengel, 'Die Synagogeninschrift von Stobi', *ZNW* 57 (1966), 45–183 (reprinted with appendix by H. Bloedhorn in M. Hengel, *Judaica et Hellenistica. Kleine Schriften* I, Tübingen 1996, 90–130).

determined a date of AD 165. Consequently he took the patriarch to be 'some provincial official particularly responsible for raising and administering monies intended for the religious treasury'.[4] At this early date, according to Frey, there was scarcely any influence on the part of the patriarch of Palestine to be expected in the Diaspora, if the institution existed yet at all in a legally recognized form.

However, the date may also be taken to refer to some other of the calendars that were in use concurrently at this period. The enormous sum of money mentioned in the text indicates a time of high inflation, and therefore the inscription is today usually assigned a later date. 264 is a possible date, even more probably 281, a date at which the recognition of the Palestinian patriarch in the rest of the Roman empire is already a distinct possibility.[5]

B. Lifshitz explains the inscription's instructions with reference to Roman law, under which the authorities disliked seeing corporations or congregations with continually changing membership as owners of land or buildings. This, he says, caused the donor to grant ownership of the building not directly to the congregation, but to the Jewish patriarch or perhaps a provincial dignitary with the same title, by a legal fiction; similarly fines were also to be paid to him.[6] The only difficulty with this explanation is the assumption of Jewish dignitaries in the provinces who also bore the title of patriarch; there is no evidence for such a conjecture. The existence of 'lesser patriarchs' cannot be proved.[7]

Patriarchs in the plural, as at Hammath Tiberias, are mentioned in two funerary inscriptions from the Diaspora. A Latin inscription from Catania, dated to 383, runs as follows: 'I, Aurelius Samuel ... beseech you by the honour of the patriarchs; I also beseech you by the Law which the Lord gave to the Jews: let no one open the grave and lay another body on our bones! But if

---

[4] J.-B. Frey, *CIJ* I, 507; also p. cx.
[5] F. M. Heichelheim, cited by B. Lifshitz in the Prolegomena to *CIJ* I, 76. Such a date is confirmed by the more recent excavations, during which two further inscriptions with the name of Polycharmos were found in the third-century synagogue: H. Bloedhorn (n. 3 above), 125f. M. Jacobs, *Die Institution*, 264f., prefers to date the inscription even later, to Constantine's time.
[6] B. Lifshitz, Prolegomena to *CIJ* I, 77.
[7] M. Dothan, *Hammath Tiberias*, 59, applies the text to 'lesser patriarchs'. J. Juster, *Les juifs* I, 402–5, attempts to offer evidence for 'lesser patriarchs'.

anyone should open it, let him give the treasury (as punishment) ten pounds of silver.'

The funerary inscription from Argos, which bears no exact date, is closely related: 'I, Aurelios Ioses, implore the great and divine powers, the [powers] of God and the powers of the law, and the honour of the patriarchs and the honour of the ethnarchs, and the honour of the scholars and the honour of the [synagogue] service which is offered to God every day ...': let no-one destroy this grave.[8]

In both cases J.-B. Frey refers the expression 'patriarchs' to the Biblical patriarchs.[9] By contrast, B. Lifshitz states: 'But the expression *timē* [honour], which is scarcely appropriate for the Biblical patriarchs, well reflects the Jewish people's deeply-felt reverence for its spiritual leaders'.[10] The sequence 'patriarchs, ethnarchs, scholars' in the Argos inscription does indeed appears to point to dignitaries; but the sequence closes with the '(synagogue) service', which *timē* is also applied to, which weakens Lifshitz's argument.

It would be easier to decide how we are to interpret the inscriptions if we knew more about the foreign connections of the Palestinian patriarch. But rabbinic texts are very selective, particularly in their comments on the patriarchate. However, the date of the Catania inscription does at least point to a period in which the patriarch demonstrably also collected his tax in Italy. Thus a reference to the Palestinian patriarch cannot be excluded for any of the three inscriptions, although it cannot be strictly proved either. The plural 'patriarchs' presents no difficulty: it may refer to the family or the court of the patriarch, as it surely does in the Hammath Tiberias inscription, where one of the donors is given

---

[8] *CIJ* I, 466 (no. 650) and 519 (no. 719). For the Catania inscription see also D. Noy, *Jewish Inscriptions of Western Europe* I, Cambridge 1993, 187–92 (no. 145).

[9] J.-B. Frey, *CIJ* I, 467, explains this with the observation that they are named before the Law. However, he then qualifies it with reference to the Argos inscription and its context. Then on p. 519 he does assume a reference to the Biblical patriarchs in the Argos inscription. Regarding the Catania inscription, Frey quotes G. Libertini's interpretation, that the patriarchs are the leaders of the Jewish Diaspora. M. Dothan, *Hammath Tiberias*, 59, follows Frey in referring 'patriarchs' in both inscriptions to the Biblical patriarchs. M. Jacobs, *Die Institution*, 234f., also thinks this likely, while D. Noy, *Jewish Inscriptions*, 191, takes the Catania inscription to refer to the Jewish patriarch.

[10] B. Lifshitz, *Donateurs*, 65.

particular prominence because of his close relationship with the patriarchate.

1. Title and Official Position

The Hammath Tiberias inscription describes the patriarch as *lamprotatos*, which corresponds to the Latin *clarissimus*. This title was introduced in the third century for members of the senatorial order, and was given to the heads of certain highly placed administrative departments in Constantine's time. In the late fourth century, the order of *clarissimi* was subdivided into three ranks: simple *clarissimi*, above them the *spectabiles*, in the highest rank the *clarissimi et illustres*. As is often the case with honorifics, in the course of the Byzantine period they experienced a certain inflation and thus loss of value. At the end of the fourth century, ordinary provincial governors already bear the title of *clarissimi*; finally in the sixth century senators dropped the title *clarissimus* altogether. However, in the period presently under discussion this stage had not yet been reached: thus the use of such titles for the Jewish patriarchs could be an important indication of their position within the Roman empire.[11]

In Jewish inscriptions we find the title *lamprotatos* in Beth Shearim, where a grave inscription commemorates the most illustrious synagogue president of Beirut; in this case the expression could simply be used as a mark of honour rather than a title. Not so in the two other instances, the inscription from the synagogue at Sepphoris, quoted above (p. 135) and a funerary inscription from Shiqmona near Haifa; in each case the person thus titled is also described as *comes*.[12] In the case of the inscription from Hammath Tiberias, it would again be possible to assume that *lamprotatos* is used simply as a mark of honour – this question is bound up with the matter of the exact date of the inscription. However, it is more likely that an imperial title is intended here, for official state texts also use this title for the patriarch (although these are doubtless later). If Julian's letter to the Jews is authentic it would represent the earliest official evidence for such a

---

[11] For the titles see P. Koch, *Die byzantinischen Beamtentitel*, Jena 1903; Jones, *LRE*, 142f., 378, 525–9.

[12] M. Schwabe and B. Lifshitz, *Beth She'arim* II, Jerusalem 1967, no. 164; *CIJ* II, 114 (no. 883).

classification: Julian says that he has already written to 'Brother Julos (= Hillel), the most honourable patriarch'. The Greek expression *aidesimōtatos*, used here, was equivalent to *lamprotatos* in the late fourth century. Perhaps it is no accident that, after the end of the Jewish Patriarchate, the bishop of Jerusalem was given the title of patriarch with the same honorific *aidesimōtatos*, at the Council of Chalcedon.

The Codex Theodosianus is the first to give definite and incontrovertible evidence for the titles of the patriarch. CTh XVI.8.8, dated 392, calls the patriarchs *viri clarissimi et illustres*, i.e. it classes them in the highest senatorial rank, equal to a *Praefectus praetorio*, the highest-ranking civil servant in the empire. CTh XVI.8.11, dated 396, and XVI.8.13, dated 397, also call the patriarch *illustris*. The fact that CTh XVI.8.15, dated 404, describes patriarchs as *spectabiles*, i.e. classes them only in the middle group, does not necessarily represent a demotion. Perhaps the patriarch of the time was still young, and did not automatically and immediately attain the highest rank at his accession.[13] He certainly seems to have reached it later; this follows from CTh XVI.8.22, dated 415, where the privileges (*codicilli*) of an honorary prefect are taken from the patriarch by way of punishment.

Thus all the attested official examples of the Jewish patriarch's titles of rank come from the period between 392 and 415, with the possible addition of Julian's letter of 362/363. In other words, the official state recognition of the Jewish leadership was at its highest just at the time when Christianity had already gained the position of the state religion, a truly remarkable state of affairs. The only two earlier laws to mention the patriarch, CTh XVI.8.1 and 2 of 315 (more probably 329) and 321, that is, both from Constantine's time, give no titles. It does not necessarily follow that the patriarchs did not yet have an official rank, for Constantine's laws have not been preserved verbatim. Yet it remains extraordinary that the explicit evidence for the titles is so late.

If it were the case that the emperor Theodosius I was the first to honour the Jewish patriarchs with the highest rank, this would flatly contradict the widespread assumption of a constant

---

[13] Thus A. Linder, *The Jews*, 221, but he also mentions the possibility either that the patriarch was demoted by way of punishment, or that *spectabilis* and *illustris* were used interchangeably.

deterioration in the Jews' position since the Christianization of the Roman empire. For this reason any evidence that could prove that such titles were given before his time is of the greatest importance. If the expression *lamprotatos* in the Hammath Tiberias inscription is used as an official title of the patriarch, this inscription would represent the earliest evidence. Hence the particular interest in as exact a dating as possible for it.

In dating the stage of building of the synagogue from which the inscription comes, M. Dothan argues precisely from its use of the title. According to Dothan, if Julian had conferred the title on the patriarch he would have boasted of it, and Constantius is also an unlikely contender in view of the insulting references to Jews in his laws. The only remaining possible candidates are Constantine or, more likely, Diocletian, who had a good relationship with the Jews and perhaps wanted to strengthen them in their polemics against the Christians by the conferral of this title. Thus the synagogue could have been built even before the end of the reign of Diocletian; but if the previous building was not destroyed until the earthquake of 306, the time of Galerius, that bitter enemy of the Christians, or Constantine is a possibility.[14]

Even though the chronological context for the building of the synagogue can be approximated by archaeological means, this more precise dating is positively bizarre, in that it attempts to determine the unknown date of building by means of something even less known, the time when the title was conferred. Dothan also contradicts his own early dating of the mosaic; for according to him the zodiac with the sun-god in the centre was produced 'approximately a century after R. Yohanan approved the decoration walls with paintings and apparently shortly before the ruling in which R. Abun did not object (לא מיחא) to figurative mosaics'. The traditional date for the death of Johanan is 279.[15] Moreover, Dothan's early date is not compatible with his interpretation of the zodiac mosaic as a calendar picture, in connection with the

---

[14] M. Dothan, *Hammath Tiberias*, 58f., 67. In *NEAE* II, 575, he dates this stage of the synagogue to the fourth century, based on its floors, coins and lamps. The dating of the Hammath Tiberias zodiac to the 'mid-third century C.E.' by Z. Weiss and E. Netzer, 'Architectural Development of Sepphoris During the Roman and Byzantine Periods', D. R. Edwards and C. T. McCollough, *Archaeology and the Galilee*, Atlanta 1997, 117–33, p. 122, is presumably an oversight.

[15] M. Dothan, *Hammath Tiberias*, 68.

announcement of the fixed calendar: according to tradition this occurred in 358. Thus the mosaic unfortunately does not offer a secure basis for an early dating of the title *lamprotatos*, unless the precise date of the mosaic can be determined apart from the title.

We should not accept the common assumption that the raising of the Jewish patriarchate to senatorial rank, and even to its highest honour as *illustris*, would no longer have been possible under the Christian emperors. Laws and other evidence point in quite the contrary direction. L. I. Levine stresses that the office of patriarch only attained its zenith in Christian Rome: 'With the backing of Christian emperors, extensive leverage was once again added to religious authority. From all indications the last century of the Patriarchate, which coincided with the advent of Byzantine rule, was one of the most flourishing in the history of the office.'[16]

We will consider this statement further in the following section on the political influence of the patriarch in the fourth century. For the moment let it suffice to conclude that nothing argues against a late elevation of the patriarchate, and therefore it is reasonable to set the conferral of the title very close to the evidence that we have for it.

Such an elevation is certainly possible in Julian's time, perhaps as compensation for the loss of the patriarchal tax, in connection with the building of the Temple, or more generally in the context of the emperor's religious policy. It is also possible that the rank was conferred under Theodosius; he may have been interested in a strong, central and also more easily controlled representative of his Jewish subjects; or it may have been in recognition of the Jewish leadership's cautious response to Julian's enticements. Another possibility is an elevation of the patriarchate in stages, for example the conferral of the title *clarissimus* by Julian and of the highest rank of *illustris* under Theodosius. It is of course not impossible that the title was conferred earlier, but the complete lack of any evidence makes this not very likely.[17] If the official title

---

[16] L. I. Levine, 'The Jewish Patriarch', 685.
[17] E.g. R. Syme, 'Ipse ille Patriarcha', 124, suggests a conferral of the rank under Julian or even Theodosius; M. Avi-Yonah, *Jews*, 195 and 206 n. 32, presents conferral under Julian as a fact. By contrast, K. Strobel, 'Jüdisches Patriarchat', 65f., 74–7 thinks it a possibility that Jehuda ha-Nasi was already raised to the rank of senator and received the title *clarissimus*, arguing from structural parallels between the patriarchate and the priestly dynasty of Emesa and the ruling family of Palmyra.

was indeed only conferred under Theodosius I, the description of the patriarch as *lamprotatos* in the Hammath Tiberias mosaic would have to be understood as an informal one.

2. Power and Political Influence

The titles of rank granted to the patriarchs by the emperors were not simply decorations entailing no political power. Rather, they expressed the fact that the Roman government recognized the patriarch as the leader of Judaism and supported him. The legal support of the patriarch's position within Judaism also gave him a significant degree of influence in the outside world.

From the point of view of the legislature two aspects of the patriarch's position within Judaism were of particular interest (the third, i.e. ordering the finances of the patriarchate, will be treated later). Firstly, the law required recognition by the patriarch if anyone wished to be exempted from curial duties as a Jewish minister of religion. In Constantine's law CTh XVI.8.2, dated 330, those in the service of the patriarch represented only one of several categories of persons who were exempt from certain duties; but CTh XVI.8.13, dated 397, states clearly: Only those who are subject to the power of the illustrious patriarch enjoy privileges, as religious officials, corresponding to those of the Christian clergy. Thus the government had a strong interest in a central leadership of the Jewish congregations. Since the time of Jehuda ha-Nasi, the patriarchs had increasingly endeavoured to exercise their influence when local Jewish leaders were appointed (presidents of congregations, synagogues, the staffing of the Jewish courts);[18] but in the late third century they had encountered increasing criticism on the part of the rabbis. In view of the attempts of leading rabbis to become ever more independent of the patriarchs, such backing from the state could only be welcomed by the latter.[19]

---

[18] On this development, see M. Jacobs, *Die Institution*, 171–90; C. Hezser, *Rabbinic Movement*, 79–93, 186–224.

[19] See B.-Z. Rosenfeld, 'The Crisis of the Patriarchate in Eretz-Israel in the Fourth Century' (Hebrew), *Zion* 53 (1988), 239–57, who sees the estrangement between patriarchs and rabbis as the principal cause of the crisis of the patriarchate, down to its abolition. It is a fact that there was an increasing coolness, but the patriarchate appears hardly to have suffered by it – contrary to Rosenfeld's view.

Secondly, the law recognized the patriarch as the final court of appeal in the Jewish administration of justice. These judicial powers of the patriarch also go back at least to the beginning of the third century, but had again been questioned in some Jewish circles. A rescript of Diocletian's dating from 293 should probably be understood in this context. The text is addressed to a certain Judah, without title or description of office, who should probably be understood as the Jewish patriarch Jehudah III:[20] 'A consensus of laymen cannot make a judge of someone who presides over no court; and whatever such a person decrees does not carry the authority of a case come to judgement' (CJust 3.13.3).

During the weakening of the patriarchate some rabbis had also made themselves independent in the matter of ordination, which represented an important condition for exercising judiciary power within Judaism – among other things, it protected them from claims arising from miscarriages of justice.[21] Perhaps the patriarch himself turned to the government as a consequence and asked for support. Diocletian, who had an interest in a centralized administration, was glad to publish a rescript accordingly. This forced the rabbis to reach an agreement with the patriarch and find a compromise.[22] In both cases, the question of ordination and of the administration of justice, the patriarch's traditional position of leadership at the head of his court had thus been secured by the authority of the state.

The ruling of the Codex Theodosianus regarding the exemption of Jewish religious officials from curial duties was entirely in line with this rescript of Diocletian, and CTh XVI.8.8, dated 17 April 392, is even more so:

---

[20] See A. M. Rabello, 'On the Relations', 160–2; id., 'The Legal Condition', 733–5. Arguments against this interpretation may be found in G. Alon, *Jews, Judaism and the Classical World*, 433–5; M. Jacobs, *Die Institution*, 272–4, thinks a Jewish addressee is doubtful; the text treats 'not a question of internal Jewish law, but of Roman law in general' (274).

[21] For the difficulties associated with the usual view of ordination, see M. Jacobs, *Die Institution*, 171–90, and especially C. Hezser, *Rabbinic Movement*, 79–93. In the sphere of the administration of justice we should probably assume that judges appointed by the patriarch had the stronger legal position, despite the variety of daily practice.

[22] Thus A. M. Rabello, 'On the Relations', 163–6; L. I. Levine, 'The Jewish Patriarch', 682–5. The latter also points to the relationship between R. Abbahu of Caesarea and the court of the Roman governor as a sign of the weakness of the patriarch of the time.

According to Jewish complaints, despite protests on the part of the leaders of their law, people whom they have excluded according to their own wishes are being received back into their religious community on the authority of judges. We command that this injustice be removed altogether. A zealous group within this religion may not obtain the possibility of unmerited readmittance [*reconciliatio*], either by the power of judges, or by scheming to obtain a rescript, if their leaders are against it, who definitely have the power to decide in matters of their religion, according to the judgement of the noble and illustrious patriarchs.

If a Jewish judge appointed by the patriarch excommunicates someone from the Jewish congregation, this person may not appeal to a secular court, and it may not intervene in the affair.

CTh II.1.10, dated 3 February 398, largely abolished Jewish legal independence in non-religious matters. 'Jews who live according to the universal Roman law, in cases that have to do not with their beliefs, but rather with jurisdiction, laws and legal requirements, must have recourse to the courts in the usual way, and pursue and defend all court cases according to Roman law; in short, they must be subject to our laws ...' But even this law retained the option that in civil cases, if both parties agreed, any Jew or the patriarch might be chosen as arbitrator. Then there was nothing to prevent the verdict being accepted as public law. The provincial judges were obliged to enforce these verdicts like those of official arbitrators. Thus the use of Jewish judges was entirely voluntary, but nevertheless the Jewish system of justice remained a legally recognized option, even over and above purely religious law.

In practice, however, the patriarch appears not even to have been bound by this given framework. Apparently his prestige was sufficiently great for even Christians to call on him as an arbitrator, or to let him judge in disputes they had with Jews; for the normal course of public law was extremely expensive and could take many years. CTh XVI.8.22, dated 415, seeks to counter this. Gamaliel, who had been disciplined for various offences, 'has no power to give judgement among Christians; and if there is a dispute between them and Jews, let it be judged by the provincial governor.' The wording of the text suggests that the law was meant as a punishment aimed at Gamaliel, not as a ruling on principle intended to be permanently and generally in force. Gamaliel was not deprived of the power to adjudicate in internal Jewish matters.

However, this last law already belongs to the final phase of the patriarchate. Only a few years earlier public legislation expressly protected the patriarch, as shown by CTh XVI.8.11, dated 396 and addressed to the *Comes Orientis*: 'If anyone should dare to make defamatory remarks about the patriarch in public, let him be punished.' And CTh XVI.8.15, as late as 404, states: 'All the privileges, which Our father of blessed memory and earlier rulers have accorded to the honourable (*spectabilis*) patriarchs or those whom they have set over the others, remain in force.'

Thus until well after the year 400 the Jewish patriarch was an extremely influential personage with considerable power, distinguished by the conferral of state privileges and the highest titles of rank. Various evidence clearly shows that this had an effect even beyond the Jewish community. In the main these are letters of Libanius, the great rhetorician from Antioch, who corresponded with the Jewish patriarch on several occasions.[23]

Libanius' *Letter* 1105 to the patriarch is of particular interest:

> As long as Hilarius is in a bad way, he and I both mourn. None of all this ought to have happened, nor should all the talk in the cities about what occurred. But since he has become involved in it by misfortune, which caused a man of understanding to make a mistake – for if you had nothing to reproach him with, you would not have behaved towards him as you did, since you shrink from harming anyone and are rather accustomed to doing good – act now as Achilles did to Telephus: heal by your gentleness what was done in anger, and cause all to say that you have rebuilt the first house among us that fell, causing much damage.

The Hilarius mentioned in the letter was governor of Palestine. Apparently he was involved in some difficulty – unfortunately Libanius is too refined to offer more than hints in his letter. The Jewish patriarch, who ranked higher than the governor, was affected by it and apparently had obtained the governor's dismissal, if not legal proceedings against him. In Libanius'

---

[23] See M. Schwabe, 'The Letters'. For the texts with translation and notes: M. Stern, *Greek and Latin Authors* II, 589ff.

opinion, only the intercession of the patriarch could now reverse the fortunes of the governor who had fallen so low.

This story may remind us of a letter of Jerome's from around 390: 'Recently the emperor Theodosius had condemned to death the governor Hesychius, who was a bitter enemy of the patriarch Gamaliel, because he had incited a notary and forced an entry into his [the patriarch's] papers.'[24]

Thus towards the end of the fourth century the patriarch was so influential that he could even assert himself against the Roman governor. This also explains why Libanius repeatedly addressed letters of recommendation to him. *Letter* 973 represents such a letter of recommendation, which introduces Philippianus to the patriarch, who came to Palestine in 390 in the suite of the governor Siburius, a pagan; towards the end the letter also mentions what a good opinion the governor has of the patriarch. In *Letter* 974, Libanius recommends to the patriarch the jurist Euthymius, who is short of cash: 'after the goddess of luck, both you and the governor are in a position [to change that], you even more than the governor'. *Letter* 1084 is written in favour of a certain Theophilus, who is in Palestine for a legal matter. A letter to his pupil Priscio, whom Libanius also approaches on Theophilus' behalf, reveals that Theophilus is a pagan from Palestine (*Letter* 1085). A further letter of Libanius' (*Letter* 917) intervenes with the patriarch in favour of a certain Ammonilla. The fact that this type of relationship between the patriarch and Libanius was not one-sided is shown by *Letter* 914 from the year 388. Here the rhetorician is answering an intervention on the part of the patriarch concerning an injustice done to Jews. Libanius assures him that he has not been influenced by the opposing side.

The fact that Libanius also writes to the patriarch on internal Jewish matters is significant for the relationship at least of Diaspora Jews to their highest representative in the Roman empire. We refer below (p. 247) to *Letter* 1097, which urges that the Antiochene Jew Themnestos should not have to leave his home town any more, in connection with the patriarchal tax. *Letter* 1251 to Priscianus, the governor of Palestine, is extremely interesting: In the Jewish community at Antioch people were extremely uneasy because they feared that a president of the

---

[24] Jerome, *ep.* 57.3 (CSEL 54, 506).

congregation who had been deposed because of his tyrannical behaviour might take over the leadership of the community again. The Jews were of the opinion that this was happening by order of the patriarch,[25] because the governor wanted it so, but they could not prove it. Libanius apologises to the governor for passing on this mere supposition on the part of the excited crowd, and does not add a direct plea; apparently he believes he has already attained his goal by passing on the information. If this interpretation of the letter is correct, it follows not only that the patriarch had the power to appoint the president of a large Diaspora congregation like Antioch; but in addition, the round-about way chosen by the Jewish citizens who were outraged by the impending decision, and who asked Libanius to write to the governor of Palestine so that the patriarch should revoke a decision taken because of the governor's wishes, reveals a network of relationships which would never have been guessed at without this letter. At least, in a case where people believed that the patriarch had come to a decision by arrangement with the Roman authorities, they thought it reasonable to ask a pagan to intervene with the authorities instead of turning directly to the patriarch.

The above shows clearly enough that in the fourth century the patriarch moved in the highest circles; he was simply the highest-ranking man in Palestine. It is surely no exaggeration when L. I. Levine writes that the authority of the patriarch in the fourth century even exceeded that of the Hasmonaeans and the Herodian rulers in some respects.[26] Thus the often-repeated assertion that the position of the Jews deteriorated significantly in the fourth century is at least untrue of their highest authority.

The fact that the patriarch's exposed position and his influence could make him the target of attack and ridicule is shown by CTh XVI.8.11, dated 396, which threatens punishment for insulting

---

[25] The text does not explicitly mention the patriarch, but rather the *archōn tōn archontōn*, 'leader of leaders'. But this can scarcely mean the president of the council of the Antioch congregation, since then the involvement of the governor of Palestine would make no sense. Thus also M. Stern, *Greek and Latin Authors* II, 599, following M. Schwabe, 'A New Document'. He dates the letter (p. 108) to 364. M. Jacobs, *Die Institution*, 270, again argues in favour of referring the letter to the president of the Jewish congregation in Antioch. On pp. 259–73 he is in general more cautious and prepared to regard the Jewish patriarch as the addressee of at least some of the letters mentioned here.

[26] L. I. Levine, 'The Jewish Patriarch', 651.

the patriarch. The nature of such derogatory remarks about the patriarch may be shown by a curious passage in the *Historia Augusta*, which was of course written about this time. In *Quadr. tyr.* 8.1–4, the following statement is attributed to the emperor Hadrian:

> In general I have experienced Egypt ... as thoughtless, fickle and following after every rumour. Those who worship Serapis are Christians there, and there are worshippers of Serapis who describe themselves as bishops of Christ. There is no *Jewish president of the synagogue* there, no Samaritan and no Christian priest who is not an astrologer, a bird-diviner, a fortune-teller. The *Patriarch himself*, if he comes to Egypt, is forced by the one to worship Serapis, by the other to worship Christ.

The passage should not be taken to refer to the Christian patriarch of Alexandria, as has occasionally been thought; rather it speaks of a foreign dignitary, who is apparently neither a Hellenist nor a Christian, as the last sentence quoted suggests. It must therefore be the Jewish patriarch, presumably Gamaliel V, who is the object of the author's ridicule.[27] However, it is doubtful whether the patriarch was ever able to travel to Egypt, if only because of his rank.[28] His usual method of communication with the Diaspora was certainly by means of his messengers, the *apostoloi*. W. Schmid prefers not to exclude entirely the possibility that the patriarch travelled to the Diaspora. He takes the text, not as expressing a 'violent threat to the patriarch by the Christian mob or that of the religion of Serapis',[29] but the constraint of the political situation. This forces the patriarch to show consideration both for the Christian imperial state and its creed, and for paganism, which had revived under Julian. Thus Schmid translates the text as follows: 'Even that patriarch, if he comes to Egypt, is

---

[27] R. Syme, 'Ipse ille Patriarcha', 128, on the *Historia Augusta*'s attitude to the Jews: 'The HA's attitude to Jews was apparently neither unified nor particularly malevolent; rather fun and curious behaviour than any prejudice regarding religion, race and nationality.' On the dating of the Historia Augusta see also M. Stern, *Greek and Latin Authors* II, 612ff., on the passage quoted 639f.

[28] R. Syme, 'Ipse ille Patriarcha', 127 n. 45: 'The Roman government would not have been pleased to see a *vir illustris* intervening in Egypt.'

[29] W. Schmid, 'Die Koexistenz', 172.

forced one the one hand to show reverence to Serapis, and on the other to Christ.'[30]

We should hardly assume the existence of an actual event on which these remarks were based. More likely they simply intend to characterize Egyptian fickleness by asserting that even the Jewish patriarch would be forced to make concessions towards Christianity and paganism, although the Jews cling so stubbornly to their religion. Thus the text serves primarily as evidence for the fame of the patriarch far beyond the borders of Palestine, and for his uncompromising attitude regarding religious questions.

The fame of Gamaliel, who is presumably meant here, even outside the Jewish world, may also be seen from a medical work written about 400: 'The patriarch Gamaliel has recently proved by experiment a unique remedy for the spleen.'[31]

3. Messengers and Patriarchal Tax

The letter of Hadrian in the *Historia Augusta*, after the passage quoted above (8.6f.), speaks of the Egyptian population as follows: 'Their only god is money. The Christians worship it, the Jews do the same and so do all peoples.' Because of the context and the previous mention of the patriarch, W. Schmid sees here a reference to the patriarchal tax: the background is the polemic within Judaism against the levying of the 'crown money' (*aurum coronarium*) by the patriarch, the comment in the *Historia Augusta* being that in fact all are equally rapacious, since the Christians are mentioned first.[32] It is doubtful whether this intention may rightly be attributed to the text, even though the patriarch is mentioned shortly beforehand. After all, the Jews are mentioned here in general, between Christians and all peoples. However, the subject of the patriarchal tax and the polemic against it is certainly an important one.

When the patriarchate was recognized by the Roman state, the institution's finances must also have been regulated in some way. Among other things this probably involved conferring the leasehold of state lands on the patriarchal house, as is mentioned

---

[30] W. Schmid, 'Die Koexistenz', 174.
[31] Marcellus, *De medicina* XXIII.77, *Corpus Medicorum Latinorum* V, ed. M. Niedermann, Leipzig-Berlin 1916, 185.
[32] W. Schmid, 'Die Koexistenz', 176f.

several times in rabbinic texts.[33] We also know of trading activity by the patriarchal house as early as the third century, and also of the sale of judiciary and community posts. Doubtless there were efforts from an early date to set the institution of the patriarchate on a sound financial footing by means of donations from the Jewish population and perhaps also regular contributions from the congregation. J. Juster takes the earliest mentions of messengers of the patriarchs to imply the introduction of a patriarchal tax (*aurum coronarium*) as a Roman privilege as early as the second century.[34] However, the appointment of messengers does not necessarily imply the levying of a regular tax for the patriarch, even though fourth- to fifth-century texts often connect the two. The levying of a patriarchal tax as a Roman privilege is not likely before Jehuda ha-Nasi, around 200. It is also possible that this internal Jewish tax only arose later, for example in connection with the dropping of the *fiscus Iudaicus*, probably in the period of inflation in the third century. Certainly our only evidence for the levying of a tax for the patriarchate is from the fourth century, and then only in the Diaspora.

The level and form of collection of the patriarchal tax are as unknown as its origins. Juster describes the patriarchal tax as a 'fixed yearly contribution', which he deduces from the name and the expression *anniversarius canon*, used in CTh XVI.8.29, dating from 429. However, voluntary contributions are more likely, and according to that law the Roman authorities needed to make inquiries to discover their amount; this would presumably not have been necessary in the case of a fixed tax. Juster's assumption of additional contributions in the form of tithes and firstfruits relies on the story of Count Joseph in Epiphanius. However, since such agricultural donations were in any case prescribed by a law that was only in force in Palestine, and even there fell into oblivion after the destruction of the Temple, Epiphanius' information (expressed in words taken from the Bible) is of no use to us.

In fact the story of Count Joseph,[35] who was sent as a messenger (*apostolos*) to Cilicia and there levied 'tithes and firstfruits' from

---

[33] However, M. Jacobs, *Die Institution*, 144–6, is right to stress that it is doubtful whether the principal proof text, jSheb 6.1.36 d, may rightly be used as a direct historical record. Nevertheless, there should be no doubt of the fact that the patriarchs possessed extensive estates.
[34] J. Juster, *Les juifs* I, 385.
[35] Epiphanius, *Panarion* 30.11 (GCS 25, 346).

the Jews in each city, is the earliest evidence for the fact that the Palestinian patriarchate looked for financial support from the Diaspora. Despite Epiphanius' anachronistic form of expression, the fact that the patriarch sent out messengers for the sake of financing his office, among other things, should not be doubted. However, the primary task of the messengers was generally to maintain the connections between the patriarch and the Diaspora. Eusebius also mentions the 'apostles' in this general sense: 'Even now it is customary among the Jews to call those men apostles who bring the circulars from their leaders.'[36]

In his *Letter* 1097, Libanius writes to 'the patriarchs' in the interests of a certain Theomnestus, who seems to have been such a messenger. The fact that Libanius here addresses 'the patriarchs' in the plural, whereas he usually addresses the patriarch directly, whom he knows personally, may perhaps have to do with a change in the patriarchate, whose new occupant he does not yet know personally; but perhaps he is simply addressing the patriarchal court as an institution, in which the patriarch is responsible for the appointment of messengers together with his Sanhedrin. In any event, Theomnestus has asked his friend Libanius for this letter to the patriarchate, because at his age he does not wish to travel any more. He would like to stay in Antioch; however, if this is not possible, he would at least like to return to his home in Antioch as soon as possible. Libanius gives no details about this man's duties, but again it is striking that a high-ranking Jew should ask the pagan Libanius to intervene on his behalf with the patriarchal court.

The first direct mention of the patriarchal tax is contained in the letter of the Emperor Julian, whose authenticity is somewhat in doubt. After assuring the Jews that he has protected them from unjust tax demands and has thrown incriminating taxation lists into the fire with his own hands, Julian writes: 'And since I wish you to flourish still more I have admonished Brother Iulos, the most honourable patriarch: let the messenger tax [*apostolē*] which apparently exists among you be forbidden, and let no-one from henceforth have the power to oppress the masses of your people with the collection of such levies.'

This is the only passage where the tax levied by the patriarch is explicitly described as a 'messenger tax'. Does Julian mean to

---

[36] Eusebius, *Comm. Isa.* 18.1f. (GCS 119).

describe it as unjust oppression (*adikein*)? Or does this expression refer more generally to the previously mentioned unjust tax burdens of the Jews? It fits Julian's policies that he means to abolish the patriarchal tax along with excessive state burdens. At the same time, this would attack and weaken the independent position of the patriarch, which again would fit well with his project to rebuild the Temple.

Those authors who regard the letter of Julian as a Jewish forgery from around 400 often see this passage as reflecting the internal Jewish polemic against the levying of the patriarchal tax; the passage already quoted from the *Historia Augusta* has been interpreted in the same way. Naturally Julian could just as easily have made use of such polemic, which could certainly have existed in parts of Diaspora Judaism, for his own ends.

It is certainly possible, but not necessary, that in a number of passages where the Church Fathers speak of the avarice of the Jewish leaders, they are gleefully making use of internal Jewish complaints. They may simply be expressing envy at the wealth of the patriarch. John Chrysostom is of the opinion that it cannot be lack of money that prevents the Jews from rebuilding the Temple: 'Does not the patriarch gather together the contributions of all from everywhere, and possess immeasurable treasures?'[37] Elsewhere he says, 'Do not speak to me of these patriarchs, these grocers, these shopkeepers, who are filled with all kinds of wrong!'[38] Palladius picks up the subject in his work about John Chrysostom, in connection with the internal church polemic on the sale of ecclesiastical honours by the patriarch of Alexandria: 'It is said that the shameful and wrongfully so entitled patriarch of the Jews changes the presidents of the synagogue yearly or every other year, in order to raise money' – the Christian patriarch is emulating this example.[39] Finally there is Jerome, who describes the leaders of the Jews as 'inventive in greed and ostentation'.[40]

The first mention of the patriarchal tax in law comes in an intervention against it on the part of the state. CTh XVI.8.14, dated 11 April 399, was published in Milan and addressed to the *Praefectus praetorio* for Italy, Messala:

[37] John Chrysostom, *Contra Iudaeos et Gentiles* 16 (PG 48, 835).
[38] John Chrysostom, *Adversus Iudaeos* 6.5 (PG 48, 911).
[39] Palladius, *Dialogus de vita S. Ioannis Chrysostomi* 15 (PG 47, 51).
[40] Jerome, *Comm. Isa.* II.5.18f. (CC 73, 76).

It is [the expression] of an unworthy superstition that the presidents of the synagogue or elders of the Jews or those who call themselves apostles, and are sent out at certain times by the patriarch to demand gold and silver, and to bring him the sums demanded and levied from the individual synagogues. Therefore let everything which has already been collected – as we trust, having regard to time – be faithfully transferred to our state treasury. Moreover we decree that nothing may be sent to the above-mentioned person. Therefore let the peoples of the Jews know that we have abolished the practice of such exploitation. As for those who have been sent out by this depopulator of the Jews for the business of this levy, if they are handed over to the judges, let them be judged as those who have offended against our laws.

Remarkable in this law are some word-for-word parallels with Julian's letter on the same subject, and in particular the aggressive and insulting tone. It may again take up internal Jewish polemic, but this is difficult to prove. It probably should be understood in the context of the dispute between Honorius and Arcadius, as a fiscal harassment of the eastern part of the empire, but not as a primarily anti-Jewish measure. The intention is simply to avoid the draining of money into the opposing part of the empire. The fact that a special law was passed seems to indicate that considerable sums of money were involved.

Only five years later, when the relationship between the two imperial brothers had improved again, the law was revoked: 'Recently we ordered that that which is customarily paid to the patriarchs by the Jews of these districts should no longer be paid to them. Now however we take back this earlier order and let all know that, according to the privileges accorded by earlier emperors, we have granted the Jews permission, in our goodness, to send [money again]' (CTh XVI.8.17, dated 25 April 404).

4. The Calendar Privilege

From the very beginning of this institution, an important duty of the patriarch's messengers was to deliver the dates of the festal calendar to the congregations of the Diaspora. This was made necessary by the custom of making the observation of the new moon in Israel an indispensable precondition for determining the beginning of the month, and even more so by the repeated necessity of bringing the Jewish lunar year into line with the solar year by the addition of intercalary months, since most Jewish festivals are agricultural festivals bound up with the seasons.

The religious calendar was probably originally determined in the Temple, for which it was of the first importance. Later, as the leader of Judaism the patriarch made it his privilege to determine the yearly calendar of feasts together with the court that he presided over and appointed.[41] This privilege represented an excellent means of binding the Diaspora congregations to the central leadership in Palestine. For this reason the patriarchs clung to it tenaciously, even when the mathematical and astronomical skills of the Jewish population, in particular the rabbinate, would long since have allowed a fixed calendar to be calculated.

The patriarch is said only to have renounced his privilege, under pressure from the Christians, in the fourth century. For, in connection with the Christian Quartodeciman controversy, in order to deter the (majority of) Christians who continued to celebrate Easter together with the Jews on the 14th Nisan and not on a Sunday, 'the patriarch residing at Tiberias was forbidden to fix beforehand the date of Passover'.[42] Since the patriarch realized that resistance was useless in this case, he gave up his calendar privilege and proclaimed a fixed calendar.

The representation of the zodiac in the mosaic of the Hammath Tiberias synagogue is said to commemorate this act, being a calendar picture. For the zodiac together with the seasons was 'an accepted artistic device that also served as a kind of calendar in conjunction with the appropriate priestly courses listed on the walls'.[43] Jewish tradition gives the year 358 as the date for the introduction of a fixed calendar by the patriarch Hillel II. However, M. Dothan, who dates the Hammath Tiberias mosaics to the last decades of the third or the first quarter of the fourth century, thinks it possible that Hillel II introduced the

---

[41] See L. I. Levine, 'The Jewish Patriarch', 669–71; H. Zucker, *Studien*, 167–9. M. Jacobs, *Die Institution*, 195–205, seems to me to be too sceptical on this point. A central authority was probably indispensable for practical reasons in this particular case, even though individual rabbis did not always accept it.

[42] M. Avi-Yonah, *Jews*, 166.

[43] M. Dothan, *Hammath Tiberias* 68; cf. 48f.

fixed calendar early in his term of office, possibly between 320 and 330, which would correspond with the period of building of this layer of the synagogue.[44] We have already considered the extent to which unfounded hypotheses are involved in the dating of the synagogue mosaic, in connection with the use of the expression *lamprotatos* for the patriarch in the mosaic (pp. 231ff.). If a Jewish historical tradition is now being used to interpret the zodiac, but only at the cost of altering the traditional date, this must necessarily arouse suspicion.

There is scarcely any genuine evidence even for the original tradition. Usually reference is made[45] to a passage in the Talmud, which first quotes as an early tradition (Baraita), concerning the year with an intercalary month, that in urgent cases the intercalary month might be added immediately after New Year, but that at all events it must be the month of Adar, the last month in the Jewish calendar. The Talmud then comments on the text as follows:

> Is that the case?! [The message] was sent to Raba: A couple was coming from Raqqat [= Tiberias] and an eagle seized them; in their hands were things made of what is manufactured in Luz – and what is that? Purple [for the ceremonial thread]. Through [God's] mercy and their own merit they came away safely. And the descendants of Nahshon's loins wanted to determine a representative, but the Edomite did not permit them. But the men of the congregation came together and determined a representative in the month in which Aaron the priest died [the month of Ab]. (Sanh 12 a)

Thus this precedent would contradict the earlier tradition, according to which the intercalary month must always be the month of Adar. In order to smooth over the contradiction, the Talmud adds this Aramaic commentary to the text: 'They determined it but did not make it known.' There then follows the explanation of the word 'representative' for the month from 1 Kgs 4:7: Solomon had twelve 'representatives' who each had to supply the king for a month.

---

[44] M. Dothan, *Hammath Tiberias*, 49, 52.
[45] Thus H. Graetz, *Geschichte* IV, 395; he is followed e.g. by M. Avi-Yonah, *Jews*, 166.

The text describes in riddling form difficulties which the Roman government, here described as eagle or Edomite, made in the time of Raba for Jewish messengers (who died in 352 according to tradition), who were travelling on religious business (purple thread as ceremonial thread); it also mentions that the government wished to prevent the insertion of an intercalary month.

S. Lieberman interpreted the hindering of the calendar messengers in Sanh 12 a in the context of the Christian Easter controversy.[46] He refers to Epiphanius, according to whom the *Diataxis Apostolōn*, which was widely known in Mesopotamia, says: 'You make no calculations, but make it (Easter) when your brothers of the circumcision keep it. Celebrate it together with them ... And if they err, let it not concern you.'[47] In order to prevent this practice steps were taken against the proclamation of the Jewish festival calendar. The Jewish patriarch was aware that this did not represent an attack on Jewish tradition, and that he had no hope of asserting himself in what was ultimately a private Christian matter; therefore he introduced a fixed calendar.

Despite the plausible appearance of this hypothesis, the proof affords some difficulties. For in the entirety of rabbinic literature there is not a single clear reference to this event, which would have brought about a significant change. H. Graetz sees jEr III.9.21 c as evidence for the fixed calendar: 'R. Jose sent them [the people of Alexandria] a letter: "Although they [Venetian printing: we] have written to you the lists of the festivals (*sidre mo'adot*), do not change the custom of your fathers of blessed memory".' That is, despite the fixed calendar they are not to give up the second feast day which was prescribed for the Diaspora, in order to guarantee the keeping of the correct day in any event, despite the uncertainty of transmitting the information.[48] However, there is no reason why this text should refer to a fixed calendar and not simply to the usual yearly list of the festivals.

The first explicit evidence for the fixing of the calendar by Hillel II comes from a work on the calendar by Abraham bar Hiyya from 1122.[49] He speaks of differences of opinion in

---

[46] S. Lieberman, 'Palestine', 333f.
[47] Epiphanius, *Panarion* 70.10 (GCS 31, 243).
[48] H. Graetz, *Geschichte* IV, 552f., n. 58.
[49] Abraham bar Hiyya, *Sefer ha-Ibbur* III.7, ed. H. Filipowski, London 1851, 97. A version of the text of this passage, corrected with reference to three MSS, is

calculating the years since the creation of the world, and refers to a response by Hai Gaon, who treated this question extensively. In that text Hai Gaon stresses that the method of calculating the calendar that was current in his own day was not handed down from the time of the first human being. Moses taught Israel the basic principles of calculating calendars, but at the same time gave the order that as long as a Sanhedrin existed they should stay with tradition, and move the festivals forwards or backwards if for example the state of vegetation demanded it. However, from an early date people calculated cycles, while altering them according to their need, 'until the days of Hillel b. R. Jehuda in the year 670 of the Seleucid calendar [358/359 CE]. From that year on [festivals] were no longer moved forward or backward, but the order was retained that then existed; for thereby the end of the calculations of earlier people had come.'

This information raises some difficulties. Sherira Gaon, the father of the Hai Gaon quoted by Abraham bar Hiyya, wrote a letter on the same subject in the year 994/995, which was found in the Cairo Genizah. It is possible that this letter is the text to which Abraham bar Hiyya refers. If Hai, as head of the rabbinic court (*Ab Beth Din*) at his father's academy, signed the response together with him, it would be entirely understandable that the text was later attributed to him, in view of the often abbreviated form of quotation. It is also possible that Hai is quoting an earlier letter (from 991/992) to the Jews of Egypt on the same subject, which is mentioned in the Genizah letter. Certainly this text does not mention Hillel II at all.

A comparison between the Genizah text and the quotation in Abraham bar Hiyya led J. Mann to the conclusion that the sentence about Hillel II, together with the passage to which it belongs, represents a commentary on the text of the response by Abraham bar Hiyya, and not part of the original text.[50] If this

---

offered by M. M. Kasher, *Torah Shelemah* XIII, 24, and also H. Z. Taubes, *Otzar ha-Geonim le Massekhet Sanhedrin*, Jerusalem 1966, 92.

[50] J. Mann, *Gaonic Studies. HUC Jubilee Volume*, Cincinnati 1925, 223–62, 239; the text of the response, 241–8. M. M. Kasher, *Torah Shelemah* XIII, 24, n. 3, strongly rejects this hypothesis of Mann's. In particular, the change in the text from 'we' to 'I', which Mann regards as the beginning of the interpolated commentary, is not present in the MSS; and Abraham bar Hiyya particularly stresses at the beginning of the response that it is not necessary for him to add anything.

assumption were correct, it would mean that the tradition about the reform of the calendar could only be proved from 1122.

Of course this does not mean that this statement is an invention by Abraham bar Hiyya. The dating of the patriarch according to the Seleucid calendar speaks against that; it was not usual in Spain and is correct as far as we know. Hillel II was otherwise of practically no importance in Jewish tradition and remained almost unknown.

But even if Abraham bar Hiyya is correct in his reference to Hai Gaon, who lived not long before him, or otherwise has access to Gaonic traditions – the fact remains that the extant Jewish texts were silent for centuries about an event that must have had the greatest significance for the Jewish religion. Where did Hai Gaon get his knowledge of this tradition? Saadya Gaon treated the question of the calendar extensively – although his *Sefer ha-Mo'adim* is extant only in fragmentary form – but he apparently did not mention this tradition. Later authors such as Maimonides, who also dealt with the calendar, also fail to mention the introduction of the fixed calendar in the fourth century.

However, Maimonides does appear to offer indirect evidence for an alteration in the practice of the calendar at this time. He says that the determination of the beginning of the month by a sighting of the new moon, and the insertion of an intercalary month, could be done only by the Sanhedrin in the land of Israel or by a court of ordained scholars appointed by the Sanhedrin, for practical reasons. If there was no Sanhedrin there, then the present-day custom of calculation must be followed.

> And when did Israel begin to calculate according to this calculation? Since the end of the scholars of the Gemara, in the time when Israel was laid waste and no fixed court remained there. But in the days of the scholars of the Mishnah and also in the days of the scholars of the Gemara down to the days of Abaya and Raba, people relied on the determination [of the calendar] in the land of Israel.[51]

Abaya and Raba, who died according to tradition in 339 and 352, are mentioned as belonging to the final period of the traditional determination of the calendar, which matches the time given by Abraham bar Hiyya. However, Rambam's additional information –

---

[51] Maimonides, *Mishne Tora, Hilkhot Qiddush ha-Hodesh* V.1–3.

the end of the Gemara and of a fixed rabbinic court in Palestine – would point to a later date. As in other cases, Maimonides has no precise historical ideas. However, if he had been aware of the tradition about a fixed calendar introduced by Hillel II, he would certainly have expressed himself with greater precision.

Although the silence of centuries is significant, even more so is the fact that even in the Gaonic period there was no uniformity in matters of the calendar. This is not the place in which to give a detailed description of the development of the fixed calendar, but a few facts should suffice.[52]

Firstly, the Samaritans' customs with regard to the calendar are of interest. Like the Jewish calendar, they follow a nineteen-year cycle, the Metonic cycle introduced in Athens in 432 BCE which reconciles the solar and lunar calendars. Its exact application remains to this day the privilege of the high-priestly family, which publishes the calendar twice a year.[53] The Samaritans speak of the secret of the calendar being handed down from Adam, to whom God revealed it; however, the chain of tradition does not correspond with the rabbinic one given in Pirqe Rabbi Eliezer 8. Does the fact of a shared cycle indicate a long-distant common calendar tradition? It would be possible, since there would scarcely have been any mutual borrowings between Jews and Samaritans on such important points at a later date. Another possibility is that each independently arrived at a solution to their problem, using the widely-known Metonic cycle as an example.

After their separation from the main branch of Judaism, the Karaites wished to have nothing more to do with a calendar determined by calculation. They returned to determining the new moon on the basis of observation, and also included the intercalary month according to the ripening of the barley in Palestine.

---

[52] The work of C. J. Bornstein, 'Mahaloqet Rab Saadya Gaon u-Ben Meir', *Festschrift* for N. Sokolow, Warsaw 1904, 19-189; id., 'Dibre yeme ha-ibbur', *HaTequfa* 16 (1922f.), 237–92, is fundamental. See also E. Mahler, *Handbuch*, but his description ends with Hillel II.

[53] On this, see S. Powels, *Der Kalender der Samaritaner anhand des Kitab Hisab As-Sinin und anderer Handschriften*, Berlin/New York 1977, 27–54. The Jewish and Samaritan calendars have in common the fact that there are seven years with intercalary months in the nineteen-year cycle, but not which years those are. The Samaritan calendar has adopted many details from the Arabs, which means that the possibility of an early, shared calendar tradition for Jews and Samaritans must remain an hypothesis which is difficult to prove.

This fact suggests at least that the fixed calendar was not yet an unquestioned practice in the eighth century.[54]

If this assumption is correct, it would only be logical if the Karaite example found followers within the wider world of Judaism, and criticism became more widespread in calendar matters. The calendar was fixed in its general outline; but even in Gaonic times a number of questions to do with its practical application were not yet settled. In particular the ancient custom that Yom Kippur might fall neither on a Friday nor a Sunday, and other similar traditions, required additional rules that were not fixed.

A letter of the exilarch (David ben Jehuda?) from 835 shows that Babylonian Judaism still relied entirely on Palestine in calendar matters. At that time the question was whether the months of Marheshvan and Chislev were to be reckoned as defective (29 days) or full (30 days). Palestine decided on the former option, since there the new moon of the month of Nisan was already visible on a Tuesday, and the beginning of the month could not be delayed until the following Thursday. The exilarch ends with the following general remarks: 'We always rely on them [the Palestinian leaders], so that Israel may not be split into groups. And I and the heads of the academies, the Rabbis and all Israel, we keep to the calendar which has been sent out from the scholars [of Palestine].'[55]

However, Israel's pre-eminence in calendar matters appears later to have been ignored. In the year 921/922 there was a great dispute when the Palestinian Gaon Aaron ben Meir – or perhaps his father was still Gaon at that time and Aaron was his representative for calendar matters – made use of his right to proclaim the

---

[54] See Z. Ankori, *Karaites in Byzantium, The Formative Years 970-1100*, New York 1959, 292–353; L. J. Weinberger, 'On the Provenance of Benjamin b. Samuel Qustani', *JQR* 68 (1977f.), 46–60. According to the Karaites, R. Isaac Nappacha introduced the calculated calendar, apparently meaning not the Palestinian scholar of the third century but a later Babylonian rabbi (Ankori 350 n. 138). The Rabbinic reply to the Karaite polemic that the calendar was a late invention consisted in tracing the calendar back to the time of Adam. See also S. Lieberman, *Shkiin*, Jerusalem ²1970, 19f., on evidence for a connection between Gamaliel and the introduction of the calendar. These various texts at least show clearly that by Gaonic times there were no longer any clear memories of the introduction of a fixed, calculated calendar.

[55] Text in J. Mann, *The Jews in Egypt and in Palestine under the Fatimid Caliphs*, New York 1970 (reprinted from 1920–22) II, 41f.; also I, 52f.

calendar and apparently ruled against the opinions of the Babylonian Jews. Saadya heard of ben Meir's calendar ruling in Aleppo, and in his polemical work *Sefer ha-Mo'adim* he presented, sharply and extremely aggressively, the Babylonian point of view. Fragments of this work have become known from the Cairo Genizah.[56] The details of the controversy are immaterial for our purposes; what is important is the fact that, even at this date, a uniform fixed calendar, which would have solved all the problems and been recognized by all, was still unknown.

It remains an open question when the fixed calendar was introduced in its present form. Neither do we know when and where the tradition originated according to which the patriarch Hillel II reformed the calendar. It is of course possible that there were indeed attempts at a reform of the calendar during his time. However, this is impossible to verify, and thus an explanation involving Christian difficulties with the controversy surrounding the date of Easter is a doubtful one.

The few facts known to us from the later history of the Jewish calendar suggest that in late Talmudic or early Gaonic times, when Babylon increasingly took over the leadership from Palestinian Judaism, which was growing weaker, the Babylonian Jews became increasingly independent of Palestine for the purposes of calculating the calendar. The basic principles of such calculation went back to a much earlier period. Only in disputed cases, such as in the year 835, were the Palestinian leaders acknowledged to have the right to decide. Apparently in the course of their fight against the Karaites, who returned to older traditions in calendar matters as in other things, the Babylonian leaders then made themselves completely independent on this point. In this context, Ben Meir's attempt to revive old Palestinian privileges was doomed to failure.[57]

To conclude: the interpretation of the Hammath Tiberias zodiac mosaic as a calendar picture commemorating the introduction of the fixed calendar by Hillel II is therefore untenable. It is neither possible to make use of the date of the introduction

---

[56] S. Poznanski, 'Ben Meir and the Origin of the Jewish Calendar', *JQR* 10 (1898), 152–61; E. Fleischer, 'Literary Documents Concerning the History of the Gaonate in Eretz Israel' (Hebrew), *Zion* 49 (1983f.), 375–400, offers a new fragment (pp. 375–85), for literature see ibid.

[57] Thus more or less S. Poznanski, 158f. See also H. Malter, *Saadia Gaon. His Life and Works*, Philadelphia 1921, 69–88.

of the fixed calendar as a point from which to determine the date of the mosaic, nor, conversely, by dating the mosaic early to bring forward the traditional time of the proclamation of the calendar. We must look for a different reason for the introduction of the zodiac to synagogue art. Most likely, in our context, are cultic traditions that gave great prominence to the sun and stars, even in early Israelite times. Because of the Christianization of the Roman empire, the subject lost its pagan associations, and thus also the taboo belonging to it as far as Judaism was concerned. In view of the cultural openness of significant sections of Palestinian Jewish society in the fourth century, even the pictorial representation of the sun-god surrounded by the zodiac would no longer seem offensive. It only became so again in the fifth century: when the synagogue was rebuilt there was no longer any use for this picture, and it was covered by a new mosaic floor.[58]

5. The Patriarchate and Hellenistic Culture

Although the Hammath Tiberias mosaic is of no use for determining the calendar question, the existence of the zodiac on the floor of this synagogue may certainly be regarded as evidence for cultural openness within the patriarchate's sphere of influence. In such close proximity to the patriarch's residence we may definitely assume his influence, as the mention of Severus as one of the donors also suggests. Hammath Tiberias is one of the earliest examples of the use of figure representation in synagogue mosaics. Also striking is the purely Hellenistic model for the picture, which stands in sharp contrast to the later zodiac mosaic of Beth Alpha.

The synagogue's mosaic inscription describes Severus as 'protégé' (*threptos*) of the illustrious patriarchs. M. Dothan contrasts this expression with *mathētēs*, as a student of halakhah

---

[58] An extensive treatment of the subject is J. Maier, 'Die Sonne im religiösen Denken des antiken Judentums', *ANRW* II 19/1, Berlin/New York 1979, 346–412; G. Stemberger, 'Die Bedeutung des Tierkreises auf Mosaikfußböden spätantiker Synagogen', *Kairos* 17 (1975), 23–56 (today I would be more cautious in formulating the details of interpretation); G. Foerster, 'Representations of the Zodiac in Ancient Synagogues and their Iconographic Sources' (Hebrew), *EI* 18 (1985), 380–91; H.-P. Stähli, *Solare Elemente im Jahweglauben des Alten Testaments*, Göttingen 1985.

would probably have been described; in such a case we would also expect a mention in rabbinic sources. As a *threptos*, by contrast, 'he would have belonged to an almost anonymous group referred to in rabbinic sources only as *di bei nsi'ah* or *'ilin d'nsi'ta*, i.e. the people of the House of the Patriarch' (thus jAZ III.1.42 c in connection with R. Jose, i.e. also from our period). With reference to Sota 49 b, Dothan mentions the large groups of young men who lived in the house of the patriarch and were educated there, and concludes for Severus' case: 'His cultural background – the Greek education he received at the court of the Patriarch – was a sufficient ground for pride to warrant mention in two of our Greek inscriptions.'[59]

It would be extremely interesting for our purposes if the assertion that there was a Greek school at the fourth-century patriarchal court were correct. Unfortunately it goes beyond what we are able to prove. Firstly, the definition of the Greek word *threptos* in this sense is debatable: its primary meaning is the slave who has grown up in the house, then more generally a foster-child (for example, a Greek who grew up in Egypt is once described as a *threptos* of the Nile). The expression can hardly mean more than a close relationship with the patriarch or his court (note the plural); that is what Severus is proud of. Secondly, the Talmudic text that is supposed to prove the existence of a Greek school at the patriarchal court is concerned with Rabban Gamaliel, around 100. The Greek school which the text attests for this early period at the court of the patriarch need not necessarily have still existed more than two hundred years later. But even if this were so, it probably was only an elementary school; for the patriarch was forced to send his own son away to study, as follow from Libanius' *Letter* 1098, who writes to the patriarch:

> Your son has arrived. He was already able to learn, since he shared in me already before he saw me, thanks to Argeios' eloquence. Thus nothing more beautiful was waiting for him. But perhaps it was advantageous that he saw so many cities, as Odysseus did. I beg you therefore to show understanding for his running away, not to be angry with him nor to embarrass him. For that could make him sad, which – as we see – is an obstacle even to those who strive mightily for eloquence.

[59] M. Dothan, *Hammath Tiberias*, 57.

The classification of this text in the collection of Libanius' letters presents some difficulties, which however most scholars take to be ultimately solvable. The addressee is most likely to be the Jewish patriarch, Gamaliel.[60] His son had already attended a non-Jewish school under Argeios, a pupil of Libanius, probably in Caesarea or Beirut. He was supposed to complete his education under the great rhetorician Libanius himself, but he soon ran away from him. It appears that problems with the education of the sons of the patriarchs were not uncommon. This is attested by the story of Count Joseph, among others, according to which the dying patriarch entrusted his son, who was still a minor, to Joseph; but the son preferred to hang about the baths at Gadara and chase girls there.[61] Without dwelling on the details, a connection is clearly indicated between the son of the patriarch, his friends, and the Hellenistic spa of Gadara, which can scarcely be dismissed as a malicious invention.

The fact that often very young men entered upon the office of patriarch after it had become hereditary is positively a commonplace of patristic literature. Already, in his commentary on Isaiah 3:4 – 'I will make boys their princes, and babes shall rule over them' – Eusebius relates it to the Jewish patriarchs: 'When one sees the so-called patriarchs among the Jews, who are youths indeed, not only with regard to the youthfulness of the body, but spiritually immature and unformed in mind', then one knows of what the prophecy spoke.[62] Jerome, dependent on Eusebius, comments on the same verse as follows: 'When we see the patriarchs of the Jews, who are youths or even boys, effeminate and pleasure-seeking, then we see the prophecy fulfilled.'[63] A passage from the *Catechetical Lectures* of Cyril of Jerusalem probably also belongs in this context. He interprets Gen. 49:10 – 'The sceptre shall not depart from Judah, nor the ruler's staff from between his feet, until he comes to whom it belongs' as follows: 'The ending of Jewish rule indicated the coming of Christ. If they were not now under the rule of the Romans, Christ would not yet have come. If they still possessed anyone from the tribe of Judah or

---

[60] See M. Schwabe, 'The Letters of Libanius', 102–4. M. Stern, *Greek and Latin Authors* II, 596, also offers the arguments against this attribution, and for him the matter remains doubtful.
[61] Epiphanius, *Panarion* 30.7 (GCS 25, 342).
[62] Eusebius, *Comm. Isa.* 3.4 (GCS 23).
[63] Jerome, *Comm. Isa.* II.3.4 (CC 73, 49).

David, the expected one would not yet have come. For I am ashamed to mention their more recent history regarding those men who are now called patriarchs among them, what their origin is and who their mothers are. I will leave that to those who know.'[64] In other words, for Cyril the position of the patriarch does not seem to contradict the assumption that the rule has departed from Judah, which he interprets as a sign of the arrival of Christ.

M. Avi-Yonah sees jMeg III.2.74 a also in this context.[65] R. Jirmejah tells Judan Nesiah in a letter: 'Hate your friends and love your enemies', that is, he is to leave the friends of his youth. But chronological difficulties stand in the way of such an interpretation, since Jehuda III was probably much older than Jirmejah.[66] In consequence, the passage, which has no context attached, is probably to be understood in a more general sense and has nothing to do with the problems of education discussed above.

The letters of Libanius to the patriarch Gamaliel, mentioned above, complete the picture of the Hellenistic culture pursued at the court of the patriarchs. In itself the fact that the rhetorician repeatedly addresses the patriarch in the course of his extensive correspondence shows clearly that he presupposes a shared degree of education, and that the patriarch is known and recognized outside the Jewish world. The letters often refer to Greek mythology, presupposing a corresponding education on the part of the patriarch. He is expected to understand passing allusions to Homer, and it is taken for granted that the mention of Greek gods does not upset him. The patriarchal house, and surely also wider circles among the Jewish communities of the east, must have felt quite at home in the society and culture of the Roman empire.

6. The End of the Patriarchate

Thus a far-reaching degree of cultural assimilation to its Hellenistic surroundings, a very high standing and extensive

---

[64] Cyril of Jerusalem, *Catechetical Lectures* 12.17 (PG 33, 745).
[65] M. Avi-Yonah, *Jews*, 167.
[66] Even the traditional date for Jehuda III in the fourth Amoraic generation, in office between 300 and 330, would suggest that he was older than Jirmejah. The date suggested by L. I. Levine, 'The Jewish Patriarch', 688, who estimates the period of office of Jehuda Nesia as *ca.* 275–305, would further increase the chronological difficulty.

political influence, coupled with a certain distance towards rabbinic circles, all characterize the picture of the patriarchate that emerges from the statements of the non-Jewish texts and the silence of rabbinic literature. However, CTh XVI.8.14, dated 399 (see p. 248f.) disturbs the harmonious picture. The tenor of the law is of scarcely credible aggression towards an officially highly respected minority representative within the Roman empire. If the suggestion of internal Jewish polemic against the patriarchal tax is correct, then persons near the emperor Honorius could have understood this as a signal that not every representative of the Jews set any great store by the traditional form of Jewish self-government. As has already been said, however, the law is really only to be understood in the context of Honorius' dispute with his brother, and thus was revoked again not long after its publication.

Honorius' action represented a warning signal. Nevertheless, CTh XVI.8.22, dated 20 October 415, comes like an unexpected thunderbolt:

> Because Gamaliel believed he could transgress laws (*delinquere*) with impunity the higher he was placed because of the splendour of his honours, let your illustrious authority know [meaning the *Praefectus praetorio* Aurelianus, to whom the law is addressed]: Our imperial majesty has given order to the illustrious *Magister officiorum* that he is to be stripped of the privileges of an honorary prefect, so that he finds himself in the rank in which he was before he was awarded the prefecture.

Thus the patriarch is stripped of his honorary prefecture and reduced to his previous rank (*spectabilis?*) by way of punishment, because he felt himself to be above the law. Conscious of his elevated position, he apparently overstepped the bounds of the possibilities open to him. The continuing text of the law shows which offences he is accused of: he may no longer build synagogues (see pp. 156f.), adjudicate in legal cases between Jews and Christians (p. 240), he may not convert Christian or generally non-Jewish slaves, and may not possess Christian slaves at all (p. 38).

As we have already seen, the archaeological findings clearly show that the Jews (of Palestine) never respected the prohibition of building new synagogues. The laws regarding circumcision and the keeping of slaves were also unworkable in practice, as the many repetitions of such rulings even after 415 make clear. It is all the more surprising that now the emperor is suddenly taking such drastic measures against the Jewish patriarch; the same accusations could surely have been brought against him at an earlier time. The most likely conclusion is that someone intervened accordingly in Constantinople. A number of people are possible candidates for this: the bishop of Jerusalem, perhaps also the bishop of Caesarea, who was also metropolitan of the ecclesiastical province of Palestine, or perhaps a bishop who wished to settle in Tiberias itself, where there was already a Christian monastery at this period. The governor of Palestine may also have been offended by the proud behaviour of the patriarch, who outranked him; finally, one of the ladies of the imperial family, such as Pulcheria, who were also interested in Palestine, would be a possible candidate. Unfortunately we cannot advance beyond such speculations.

This time the attack on the patriarch seems to have passed off without serious consequences. He was simply demoted and reminded to observe existing laws. However, the fact that he is simply named without the addition of any honorifics whatsoever is a bad omen. Indeed, the next information we have about the patriarchate is already the notice of its fall. CTh XVI.8.29, dated 30 May 429, is addressed to the *Comes sacrarum largitionum*, one of the finance ministers of the Byzantine administration, and simply regulates the fiscal remains of the once powerful institution:

> The leaders of the Jews (*primates*) who are appointed in the sanhedrins of the two Palestines, or dwell in other provinces, are to be forced to yield up whatever they have received as tribute (*sub titulo pensionis*) after the departure (*post excessum*) of the patriarch. In future however, at their own risk, a yearly fixed sum (*anniversarius canon*) is to be demanded from all synagogues, under pressure from the financial administration, equivalent to what the patriarchs once demanded under the title of crown money. Strive diligently to discover how much that is; and let that which used to be brought to the patriarch from the western districts also be delivered to Our treasury.

Therefore the patriarchate must have become extinct between

415 and 429. Its end is often dated to 415.[67] However, this by no means follows from the text of the law, and there is no other evidence. But the fact is certainly of interest that, only two weeks after the law of 20 October 415, CTh XVI.9.3, dated 6 November, is addressed not to the patriarch, but to 'Master (*didascalus*) Annas and the elders of the Jews'. The law's content is even more striking, because it contradicts that addressed to Gamaliel:

> We give order that Jewish masters may own Christian slaves without fear of slander, on condition that they permit them to retain their own religion. Therefore the provincial judges are to check the reliability of their information, and are to suppress the insolence of those who believe they can wrongly accuse them [the Jews] by opportune applications ...

CTh XVI.8.23, dated 24 September 416, is also addressed to Annas and the elders of the Jews. This law is concerned with the fact that Jews have become Christians, not for religious reasons, but 'in order to avoid criminal proceedings and because of various necessities'. They are to be permitted to return to their own law, and the provincial judges (i.e. governors) are to be informed accordingly.

Both cases involve laws which are to be in force in more than one province. It would be interesting to know what position Annas held within Judaism at this time. Was he at the head of an internal Jewish administration covering more than one province? Was he the representative of the Jews in the western Roman empire (both laws were promulgated at Ravenna)? Or was he simply the speaker for a number of local Jewish congregations, who had been entrusted by them with the petition to the government and was therefore also mentioned in the reply? Unfortunately we have no information whatever as to whether a form of organization existed in the western Empire that embraced several Jewish congregations, nor what form it might

---

[67] For example, *PLRE* II only counts Gamaliel until 415; A. M. Rabello, 'The Legal Condition', 714, n. 212 (also 'On the Relations', 167, n. 110) writes that Gamaliel was deposed in 415 and that the office of patriarch also disappeared in the years that followed. But 429 (thus e.g. J. Maier, *Geschichte des Judentums im Altertum*, Darmstadt 1981, 133) also cannot be proved and is unlikely; for the law assumes that money in place of the patriarchal tax has been accumulating in the congregations for some considerable time already.

have taken. However, these laws are not to be taken as evidence that the patriarchate had already been replaced by regional organs of Jewish self-government. Perhaps the laws were only of interest in the west, or were published in conscious contrast to the regulations in the eastern Empire.

Recently Y. Dan has attempted to date the end of the patriarchate with greater precision, starting from a note in the *Chronicle* of Marcellinus for the year 418.[68] The text, which is very defective, is concerned with Count Plinta, who is said to have died in a revolt in Palestine. However, the same text mentions Plinta later as one of the consuls for 419. His appointment has in the past been regarded as a reward for suppressing that revolt. In Dan's opinion the revolt of 418, if it was a Jewish revolt, could be taken in connection with the abolition of the patriarchate, which should then be set before 420. But the text seems far too isolated, and also too unclear, to support the assertion that there was such a Jewish revolt in Palestine in 418. This in turn destroys the basis for the hypothesis that the patriarchate was abolished in connection with the revolt.

The expression *post excessum patriarcharum* in CTh XVI.8.29 suggests that the patriarch was not suspended from his post, but that the direct line of the patriarchal family had died out, and that there were no direct male heirs. A parallel to client kings has often been drawn in this context. It was an ancient Roman practice to install these in areas that for various reasons could only with difficulty be brought under direct Roman rule; for them inheritance was possible only in the direct line. If there was no son to inherit, the Roman government could either install another relative or, if the situation permitted it, itself take over direct rule. For various reasons this is a very problematic analogy.[69] However, the case of the Jewish patriarchal dynasty appears to have been similar at least as regards the law of succession.[70] The Jews had been peaceful for so long now that the

---

[68] Y. Dan, 'The Leadership of the Jewish Community In Eretz Yisrael in the Fifth and Sixth Centuries' (Hebrew), *8th WCJS* II, Jerusalem 1982, Hebrew section 23–8.

[69] See K. Strobel, 'Jüdisches Patriarchat'; M. Jacobs, *Die Institution*, 250f., 303. The main arguments against the analogy are that the comparable examples of client kings are much earlier, and also that the patriarchs never possessed territorial sovereignty or the right to mint coinage.

[70] The opinion of M. Jacobs, *Die Institution*, 351, that it is unlikely 'that the internal Jewish office of *nasi*, whose core character was religious, stood in need of Roman accreditation', i.e. that it was an internal Jewish decision not

Romans believed that they could master them without a buffer in the form of a large degree of autonomy.

For the moment at least, certain forms of Jewish self-government were still permitted,[71] perhaps even new ones introduced, i.e. the sanhedrins of the two Palestinian provinces. The province of *Palaestina tertia*, which of course already existed at this period, is not mentioned in the law, probably because the number of Jewish inhabitants was too low. Thus the sanhedrins mentioned were those of Galilee and Judaea, the former of which certainly resided at the previous patriarchal seat of Tiberias. We know nothing of the latter – perhaps it resided in Caesarea. Primates in other provinces are also mentioned. It is a possibility that the government hoped to weaken Judaism by fragmenting its internal self-government; but here, as on so many other points, the evidence is lacking.

In the following period there is no mention of such representatives of the Jews in the various provinces; thus this form of organization appears not to have lasted long, and seems not to have been accepted by the Jews. The fact that the new primates did not have control over the money provided by the Jewish community, which rather had to be delivered to the imperial tax office, shows the government's lack of interest in such a form of self-government. It appears, therefore, to have been a temporary measure, or to have been regarded as a concession to the Jews. Real influence on the further development of Judaism, especially Palestinian or rabbinically orientated Judaism, seems only to have been exercised by the Sanhedrin (but did this continue to exist as such any longer?) or the rabbinic school in Tiberias.

At the close of the chapter let us mention briefly the succession of patriarchs after 300. Firstly, here is the list put together by H. Graetz[72] and adopted almost universally: Jehuda III 300–330;

> to appoint a new patriarch, appears to me to be contradicted by the development of the patriarchate evidenced in the laws of the CTh. Furthermore, the special status of the Jews extended far beyond the 'religious' sphere in the modern sense.

[71] M. Schwabe, 'A New Document', 120, deduces from Libanius' *Letter* 1251 that the Jewish self-government presupposed in CTh XVI.8.29 existed as early as 364; the contentious *archōn* of Antioch perhaps had the position of a 'minor patriarch'. M. Jacobs, *Die Institution* 306–8, is of the opinion that the sanhedrins of the two Palestines mentioned in the law had already existed previously. There is no evidence for this, however.

[72] H. Graetz, *Geschichte* IV, 556–8.

Hillel II 330–365; Gamaliel V 365–385; Jehuda IV 385–400; Gamaliel VI ('the Last') 400–425. Naturally the dates given for the individual patriarchs are merely guidelines; and the list as a whole is very uncertain because of the extremely defective sources. Rabbinic literature mentions no patriarch by name after Jehuda III Nesia, unless jBer III.1.6 a, where R. Mana refuses to take part in the funeral of Nehorai, the sister of Jehuda Nesia, refers to Jehuda IV Nesia.[73] However, since this refers to the patriarch's surviving sister, this would probably bring us into conflict with the dates given by Graetz; we should rather think of a sister who survived Jehuda III by many years. L. I. Levine suggests the interpolation after Jehuda III Nesia, whom he dates to about 275–305, of an additional Gamaliel (whom he calls Gamaliel V). This Gamaliel is supposed to have reigned from 305 to 320.[74]

The only source for a list of the patriarchs is the *Seder Tannaim ve-Amoraim* from the ninth century, which names after Jehuda III Hillel, Gamaliel, Jehuda and Gamaliel.[75] However, the individual MSS differ markedly from one another, so that the editor offers the following suggested order: Jehuda Nesia, Gamaliel, the brothers Jehuda and Hillel (sons of R. Gamaliel), Gamaliel, Jehuda Nesia, Gamaliel 'the Last'.[76]

The only possibility of verifying this list, which is late and extant in different forms, is that offered by non-Jewish mentions of individual patriarchs. Epiphanius says, in the story of Count Joseph, that the patriarch of the time was called Hillel and his son Jehuda; but he admits his uncertainty on this point. It is normally assumed that he accidentally reversed the order. The emperor Julian writes to the patriarch Hillel (even if the letter is spurious, the chronological attribution should be correct); in addition we have the late information that this Hillel (II) reformed the calendar in 358. The addressee of Libanius' letters in the years 388–392 remains nameless; however, we may probably assume that there was no change in the office holder during this time. Jerome mentions the patriarch Gamaliel in *Letter* 57 around 395, and Marcellus' medical work, around 400, and CTh XVI.8.22 of 415, also name Gamaliel. It is not clear whether these various

---

[73] Thus S. S. Miller, *Studies*, 119.
[74] L. I. Levine, 'The Jewish Patriarch', 688.
[75] K. Kahan (ed.), *Seder Tannaim ve-Amoraim*, Frankfurt 1935, § 2 b. 3 a.
[76] K. Kahan (ed.), *Seder Tannaim ve-Amoraim*, 20–2.

mentions refer to the same Gamaliel; if so, he must have had a very long period in office, beginning before 390 and end after 415. This is of course not impossible, but difficulties would then arise from the fact that in the laws of 392–397 the patriarch is *illustris*, but in 404 he is only *spectabilis*, whereas Gamaliel was again *illustris* when he was demoted in 415. This is probably most easily explained with a change of incumbent (see p. 235). However, since a son does not normally receive his father's name (unless he dies before the child's birth), a further patriarch would have to be postulated if we are to assume two Gamaliels, and there are no grounds at all for this.[77]

A solution of the difficulties in establishing a list of patriarchs cannot be attempted here, if only because of the lack of reliable sources. However, even to have pointed out the difficulties and the complete lack of foundation of the traditional list is not unimportant.

---

[77] M. Schwabe, 'The Letters', 104–6, has attempted to prove the existence of two different Gamaliels, of whom the earlier was the recipient of Libanius' letters.

X

The Rabbinate

The Judaism of the period described here is usually reckoned as belonging to 'rabbinic' Judaism. This implies that the rabbinate set the pattern at that time. But what importance did it really have in the Jewish society of Palestine? The extant Jewish reports from this period, in so far as they are literary, are exclusively the product of the rabbinic group. We should be in danger of overemphasizing these literary reports and taking them at face value, if it were not for the existence of the archaeological finds which indicate caution and suggest that we read the rabbinic texts critically.

Let us begin from a simple fact: Based on the rabbinic writings, it is possible to attribute approximately one hundred and fifty names of rabbis to the fourth and fifth Amoraic generation, that is, to the teachers of our period. Other rabbis doubtless also existed at that time who are not mentioned, and many names cannot be located chronologically since they appear only once and without context. In such a count there are also many possible sources of error; for example it is likely that similar names sometimes refer to one and the same person. But two or three times the number mentioned should probably suffice to include those rabbis of whom not even a single sentence was thought worthy of record. Even if we estimate such a number, we could not assume that more than perhaps one hundred rabbis were active in Palestine at any one time. If we then take into account the fact that large numbers of them lived in the centres of Tiberias, Caesarea and Sepphoris, possibly also Lydda, it becomes clear that only a few Jewish village congregations, if any, had their own rabbi.[1]

---

[1] C. Hezser, *Rabbinic Movement*, 171–84, is right to stress the decentralization of the rabbinic movement; but most of her evidence comes from an earlier

What is more, the Jewish inscriptions of this period that have so far been discovered practically ignore the Talmudic rabbis. The analysis of all the Jewish inscriptions from the first six centuries shows that in them a number of men are titled Rabbi; but it is almost never possible to identify these with rabbis known to us from rabbinic literature. Neither does it ever follow from the inscription that the title Rabbi is more than a common title of honour. Thus the people mentioned need not necessarily have been rabbis in the sense intended in the rabbinic writings, men who after years of studying Jewish tradition and of discipleship under an older master were then recognized as independent masters of tradition.[2] Even if a funerary inscription from Qasrin in the Golan Heights, which mentions a R. Abun, were indeed to refer to the R. Abun mentioned in the rabbinic writings, who died around the middle of the fourth century, it makes little difference to the generally negative picture.[3]

But perhaps something about the spread of rabbinic ideals can be gleaned from the places of origin of the rabbis. Most of them naturally come from the rabbinic centres named earlier, Tiberias, Sepphoris and Caesarea. But one or two have the epithet 'Daroma' or similar, that is, they come from the south, in other words generally from Lydda or its environs. Some come from Jaffa, others from Tyre and Sidon, cities with which the Jews of Galilee maintained a close relationship, as we have seen; others from the country east of the Jordan (Bosra, Edrei). Yet others still come from Babylon, but the other countries of the Diaspora are

---

period. It is of course correct that rabbis living in isolated locations were less likely to be quoted in the texts, and therefore that the rabbinic writings do not offer a representative picture of reality.

[2] S. J. D. Cohen, 'Epigraphical Rabbis', *JQR* 72 (1981f.), 1–17, is perhaps overly sceptical regarding the Beth Shearim inscriptions; but this makes little difference to his overall conclusions. C. Hezser, *Rabbinic Movement*, 119–23, rightly criticizes some of the criteria by which Cohen differentiates the rabbis in the inscriptions, and takes them too to be fundamentally Torah scholars who have disciples. But then again she also sees differences between the two groups.

[3] The identification of R. Abun from the Qasrin funerary inscription is argued by D. Urman, 'Jewish Inscriptions', 542–4; id. in Urman and Flesher (eds.), *Ancient Synagogues* II, 478–81. However, his argumentation is somewhat circular, when he first attributes the gravestone to the older of the two Abuns mentioned in the Talmud with no further epithet, and then dates the stone accordingly.

hardly represented in the Palestinian rabbinate of the period. One rabbi is described as a Cappadocian, another as an Alexandrian, while R. Zemina at least spent some time in Rome. In Jewish inscriptions from the Diaspora from the pre-Islamic period, the title rabbi occurs only occasionally, and is probably always intended in the general sense and does not mean a Talmudic rabbi. This confirms the impression that at this period the rabbinate was still an almost exclusively Palestinian (and Babylonian) institution. Even Annas the *didaskalos*, to whom two laws of the Codex Theodosianus, promulgated in Ravenna, are addressed, was not necessarily a rabbi in the Talmudic sense.

A further striking fact is that no rabbi of this period is named after a town in the Tetrakomia, the heartland of Jewish settlement in Galilee, unless R. Eleazar bar Merom is named after Meiron.[4] It is probably not sufficient to assume that this area was the natural place for recruiting the new generation of rabbis, and therefore did not appear in their names. We must also take into account the fact that many of the rabbis mentioned were themselves the sons or fathers of rabbis. The hereditary principle was therefore already strong, and a rabbinic caste grew up because of it. This means that the number of families involved in the rabbinic movement is even smaller than the already small number of names of rabbis would lead us to expect. This must surely have consequences for the probable spread of influence of the rabbinate.

1. The Rabbinic Schools

There is evidence for rabbinic schools in our period only in three or four places, in Tiberias, Sepphoris, Caesarea and possibly Lydda. By far the most important of these centres was Tiberias. The city had been the seat of the patriarch since the late third century, and of his school probably even earlier, which was originally led by R. Jochanan bar Nappacha, who died in 279 according to tradition. In view of this concentration of the rabbinate in Tiberias, it is astonishing that not a single piece of epigraphic evidence for the title Rabbi comes from Tiberias or its environs. To my knowledge rabbis from Tiberias are never

---

[4] The rabbi's name is extant in various forms; see W. Bacher, *Die Agada* III, 698.

mentioned either in Libanius' letters to the patriarch or in contemporary patristic texts. Only in the literature written by themselves are they constantly the centre of attention. This may be a coincidence, but is nevertheless remarkable.

Rabbinic texts repeatedly mention the [great] house of study (*sidra rabba*) in Tiberias (e.g. jSanh X.1.28 a); perhaps it is the same as the double portico (*diplē stoa*: MidrPs 93.8.B. 416) to which R. Haggai was wont to go. It is said of R. Abun that he had new gates made for the great house of study. In response, R. Mana is said simply to have quoted Hos. 8:14 by way of criticism: 'Israel has forgotten his Creator and built great palaces' (jSheq V.6.49 b). The house of study was probably the official patriarchal school, although the patriarch is never mentioned in this context.[5] If R. Huna is described as *Safra de-sidra* (jKil III.1.28 c; jShab IX.2.12 a), that is probably his official function in the work of teaching in Tiberias, alongside that of the head of the school. This title does not reveal whether he was officially responsible for Biblical teaching, i.e. whether he was the school's exegete (jKil is concerned with the orthography of a word in Isa. 61:11), or perhaps was only in charge of a primary school associated with the rabbinic school.

The most important representatives of the school of Tiberias in our period were R. Jirmejah, who had immigrated from Babylon and taught at the same time as R. Acha from Lydda and R. Haggai. Jirmejah's pupils were Jonah and Jose, who were the leading scholars in Tiberias in the middle of the fourth century, also R. Hizkiyyah and R. Zera the Younger. R. Jonathan was the most prominent among Haggai's pupils, and Acha's most important pupil was R. Huna, mentioned above.

On looking through the names of the rabbis who worked in Tiberias in the fourth century, we see that a number of prominent people did not come from there, but from abroad. The attraction of the city lay in its great tradition (although that of the other centres was no less), but particularly in the fact that the seat of the patriarch was here, who together with his council claimed the privilege of ordaining rabbis and of appointing them to offices.[6]

---

[5] C. Hezser, *Rabbinic Movement*, 197–200, therefore denies the existence of a patriarchal school, preferring to assume the existence of a number of non-institutionalized groups of disciples around individual rabbis in Tiberias.

[6] The question of ordination and the difference between this and the appointment to an office is in need of a thorough new treatment. See M.

As we have seen, the position of a religious official subordinate to the patriarch was also necessary as far as the Roman law was concerned, at least in the late fourth century, for exemption from curial duties.

The fact that the rabbis hardly criticized the patriarchate any more in the fourth century is clearly due to its legal recognition. The criticism of the patriarchate's appointment practice that was voiced at the end of the century came not from Tiberias, but Caesarea (jBik III.3.65 d, Jacob of Kefar Neburaya and others). In Tiberias, and perhaps in the rabbinate in general, a *modus vivendi* must have been reached between rabbinate and patriarchate. As has been mentioned, the rabbis had to cooperate with it in the matter of the calendar (jEr III.9.21 c; Sanh 12 a). It is likely that there were other rabbinic teachers with their disciples in Tiberias as well as the patriarchal school, and that not all of them were organized in the same school; the same holds for the other centres.[7]

The school of Sepphoris was older than that of Tiberias. It had been the school of the patriarchate before that of Tiberias and retained its importance. One R. Hanina of Sepphoris is said to have ceded his office there (as a rabbinic teacher or judge, or in a congregational post?) to R. Mana (jPes VI.1.33 a), who was probably a son of R. Jose of Tiberias.[8] Possibly R. Mana (= Mani) moved to Sepphoris because of a disagreement between himself and the patriarch in Tiberias. Certainly Taan 23 b mentions people belonging to the patriarchal house who cause R. Mana great difficulty when they ride through Sepphoris. Only a prayer by R. Mana at his father's grave rids him of these molestations. Similar tensions may be attested by another passage, according to which R. Mana refuses to take part in the burial of Nehorai, the sister of Jehuda Nesia (jBer III.1.6 a).

If the text locates the burial of the patriarch's sister in

Jacobs, *Die Institution*, 171–90; much more sceptical is C. Hezser, *Rabbinic Movement*, 79–93; 424–9, according to whom there was no *semikha* in Amoraic Palestine, but the patriarch was able to bind rabbis to himself by means of appointments.

[7] See C. Hezser, *Rabbinic Movement*, 195–214, who rightly stresses the fact that individual schools centred on personalities and lacked institutional character.

[8] This identification raises difficulties, since R. Jose is not listed as a priest, whereas the Palestinian Talmud appears to presuppose this in R. Mana's case: S. S. Miller, *Studies*, 119, n. 328.

Sepphoris (and perhaps also the preceding passage about the burial of Jehuda Nesia himself), this would constitute evidence for continuing ties between the patriarchal house and that city, even after the patriarchate had moved to Tiberias.

The fact should also be mentioned that apparently many priestly families lived in Sepphoris at this period, which occasioned corresponding halakhic discussions, and probably promoted interest in handing down the *Tetragrammaton*, the most sacred name of God (jJoma III.7.40 d). One R. Abdima from Sepphoris, a contemporary of R. Mana, is mentioned several times in the tradition.

We are relatively well informed about the rabbinic schools of Caesarea. Their members are repeatedly quoted in the Palestinian Talmud collectively as the 'Rabbis of Caesarea', as it were as a closed corporation or guild.[9] The beginnings of Caesarea as a rabbinic centre go back to R. Hoshaya in the early third century; around the turn of the fourth century it blossomed for a second time, when R. Abbahu (who died around 309) was its most important representative. At that time the rabbis of Caesarea were in regular contact with their Babylonian colleagues, some of whom studied in Caesarea. In the later course of the fourth century we have no more evidence for such close ties with Babylon. However, Caesarea was still highly regarded with teachers such as Abbahu's son R. Zera, R. Isaac b. Eleazar II, R. Zeriqan, R. Hizkiyya and others.

We have almost no knowledge of the work of the rabbis of Caesarea in the second half of the fourth century; but it is likely that the rabbinic schools of the provincial capital continued to be active into the fifth century. Life at the seat of the provincial government probably involved special responsibilities for the local rabbinate, just as the cosmopolitan character of the city, by contrast to the largely Jewish centres of Tiberias and Sepphoris, must have shaped the character of the rabbinic schools.[10]

Lydda, the fourth rabbinic centre under discussion, had already passed its heyday in the period we are considering. However, it still produced a number of eminent rabbis, in particular R. Jehuda ben Pazzi and R. Acha. A teacher of Jerome's

---

[9] However, the word 'guild' should not be understood to mean a fixed organization, as C. Hezser, *Rabbinic Movement*, 182–4, rightly stresses; she herself prefers the sociological expression 'opinion cluster'.

[10] L. I. Levine, *Caesarea under Roman Rule*, 86–106.

(not necessarily a rabbi) also came from this city, which did not enjoy the best of reputations among some rabbis, since its inhabitants were thought to be proud and insufficiently familiar with the Torah (thus R. Jirmejah in jSanh I.2.18 c). The city also had a reputation for poverty. Z. Frankel's opinion that this southern centre of rabbinic tradition perished in the revolt against Gallus around 352 cannot be proved in any way, even if we do not hear much about southern rabbis in the late fourth century. They simply did not belong to the centre of literary activity of the rabbis who at this period were occupied with editing the Palestinian Talmud.

2. The Rabbis' Position and Duties

The rabbinic writings could give the impression that, immediately after the destruction of the Temple in 70 CE, the rabbis took over the leadership of the Jewish people, and were universally recognized in this position both within Judaism and very quickly also on the part of the Roman government. E. Schürer's opinion is typical: 'The Pharisees and the rabbis entered into the heritage of the Sadducees and priests. They were excellently prepared for this role, for they had been pressing for leadership during the last two centuries. Now, at one stroke, they acquired sole supremacy, ... These scholars who in such fashion cultivated Israel's greatest good, now constituted, more exclusively and unrestrictedly than ever before, the nation's supreme authority.'[11]

However, a close analysis of the rabbinic texts reveals the extent of the gap between wish and reality. The beginnings of the rabbinic movement are romanticized with hindsight, and situations that were the result of slow growth are projected back into the 'prehistory' of the movement in order to withdraw present circumstances beyond the reach of criticism because 'they had always been so'.

In the decisive centuries, being a rabbi was never seen as a job, but as a way of life. Learning the Torah was a holy act in itself that

---

[11] E. Schürer, *Geschichte des jüdischen Volkes im Zeitalter Jesu Christi* I, Leipzig 1901 (reprinted Hildesheim 1964), 656f. The thoroughly revised English edition of this standard work, by G. Vermes, F. Millar and M. Black (Edinburgh 1973, I 524f.) retains this passage unchanged.

was practised within the group of disciples and also was put into practice in one's own life. But it was not related to earning one's living by leading a community or synagogue, or in the Jewish courts. The rabbis initially formed a closed caste, whose influence on the normal Jewish life of Palestine was a matter of spiritual influence and not official functions. Only from the third century did the rabbis, in the service of the patriarch who now had official recognition, increasingly take on responsible community positions or office at the patriarch's court. For a rabbi, public influence was largely tied to recognition by the patriarch, who attempted to enforce as his own privilege the right to appoint to a number of posts ('ordination'). Although an individual rabbi might be able to gain authority and recognition in certain circles independently of the patriarch, being associated with him was extremely helpful for advancement in rabbinic society. This was the only way a rabbi might expect to be accepted into the inner circle of Jewish leadership, or to take part in the patriarch's rabbinic court, which retained the prerogative of determining the religious calendar and also represented the highest court of appeal in Jewish law in all other matters. This institution is often taken to be the direct successor of the high council of the Temple period; but in reality the patriarch's *consilium* only attained a central, publicly recognized importance in the course of centuries. After the end of the patriarchate it was able to take over its leadership role, probably together with the rabbinic school in Tiberias.

For a long time the rabbis resisted taking on public duties, according to the rule of Abot IV.5 that the Torah may not be used as a spade to earn one's living with. Many rabbis also regarded work in the public administration of the community as inferior and despised ordinary schoolteachers as uneducated, as well as the popular preachers of the synagogue. This partly had to do with the fact that in the Jewish communities older leadership structures of landowning nobles survived for a long time and could not be avoided even by the patriarch. Only in the third century did the rabbinate make significant attempts to gain a footing in the leadership of the community, in the synagogue's liturgy and preaching, and in school-teaching.

(a) The position of the rabbi in the synagogue

The situation of a later period particularly connects the rabbi with the synagogue and its worship. But in the early rabbinic period many rabbis were of the opinion that the synagogue was less honourable than the house of study, and that study should not be interrupted for the sake of the community worship in the synagogue, but rather that prayers in the house of study were to be preferred. For a long time the synagogues did not form part of the direct sphere of influence of the rabbinate, which is confirmed by the extant synagogue inscriptions, which ignore the rabbis, as has already been mentioned. A further striking fact is that there are no indications in rabbinic literature for most of our synagogue finds, and conversely there is as yet no archaeological proof for the existence of most of the synagogues mentioned in rabbinic texts. Thus there is only a small degree of overlap between the synagogues whose existence is confirmed by archaeology and those mentioned in literature.

The powerlessness of rabbis in the synagogues is clearly shown in jAZ III.3.42 d: 'In the days of R. Jochanan people began to paint the walls with pictures, and he did not prevent them.' A fragment of text from the Genizah, now in Leningrad, continues: 'In the days of R. Abun people began to lay mosaic pictures, and he did not prevent them.' It is a generalized statement, but is at least true of the synagogues as well, as the archaeological evidence makes clear. This is explicitly said in the Targum Pseudo-Jonathan on Lev. 26:1, which adds the following sentence to the Biblical prohibition of images: 'But you may lay a floor decorated with representations and pictures in your holy places, but not in order to prostrate yourselves [in worship] before it.'

In the course of the third century the rabbis' attitude to the synagogue became increasingly positive, and their attempts to gain influence multiplied, as has been mentioned. This is shown in a number of sayings of rabbis on the importance of the synagogue in jBer V.1.8 d – 9 a, where also R. Jochanan's saying that people should pray in a place suitable for prayer is immediately taken to refer to the synagogue, although another saying is also attributed to Jochanan, according to which whoever prays at home is as if they were surrounded by an iron wall (so concentrated and protected). For the rabbis of the following generation it was already a matter of course that the synagogue was *the* place of prayer.

jBer IX.1.12 d already attributes to R. Jochanan and R. Jonathan attempts to standardize prayers. They 'went into certain towns of the south in order to bring peace. They came into a town and heard the prayer leader saying "The great, heroic, terrible, mighty and paramount God". And they silenced him. They said to him: You have no right to add anything to the expressions that the scholars have determined in the blessings.' It is likely that the two rabbis from Tiberias were not simply travelling in their capacity as rabbis, but on an official mission from the patriarch who was attempting to exercise his control over the synagogues of the country.

A conclusion that may be drawn with certainty from this text is the fact that local forms of prayer deviated from the rabbinic standard. This did not change significantly in the following centuries. jBer V.4.9 c is typical: R. Acha and R. Jehuda ben Pazzi are sitting in the synagogue and hear a prayer leader leave out a blessing in the Eighteen Benedictions. They do not intervene, but first need to enquire of R. Simon what the correct response should have been. R. Levi bar Hita, in Caesarea, hears the people pray the Shema in Greek (presumably in the synagogue) and wishes to enforce its recitation in Hebrew; but R. Jose, hearing of it, permits the prayer in Greek if people are unable to recite it in Hebrew (jSota VII.1.21 a). Neither is there uniformity in the practice of reading the Bible: in LevR 3.6 (M.69) R. Hananiah b. Acha only hears in the synagogue which reading will be read. Throughout jBer offers evidence for the rabbis' interest in the liturgy of the synagogue and in the Bible readings for the festivals. But this does not imply that they were also in a position to enforce their opinions, but only that they attempted to do so and abandoned their earlier reserve towards the synagogue.[12]

Occasionally the rabbis were able to assume special rights in the synagogue. For example, jMeg III.4.74 a reports of R. Berechia that in the synagogue of Beth Shean he rebuked a man who washed his hands and feet in the basin there. On the next day he did it himself, and the man he had rebuked confronted him saying, 'Rabbi, is it permitted for you and forbidden for me?' In reply the rabbi quoted R. Jehoshua ben Levi: 'The synagogues and houses of study belong to the scholars and their teachers.'

As their regard for the synagogue increased the rabbis began to

---

[12] See C. Hezser, *Rabbinic Movement*, 214–24.

preach in the synagogue services. For example, R. Berechia preaches in an unnamed synagogue, and ends his lecture by calling for donations for a Babylonian immigrant (LevR 32.7, M. 752f.). R. Jirmeja preaches in Tiberias in the council synagogue (jTaan I.2.64 a). The rabbis of Caesarea appear to have had a particularly close relationship with the synagogue. A number of them work in the 'synagogue of the revolt', for example, R. Isaac ben Eleazar in the fourth century (jBik III.3.65 d).[13] However, we should not automatically assume that a sermon was preached in a synagogue every time a rabbi is said to have 'preached' or 'interpreted', unless it is expressly stated, although many such passages should doubtless be located in a synagogue. For example, a sermon (or lecture) by R. Jona is mentioned, at the entrance to the house of the patriarch, i.e. probably in the open air (Shab 155 b). The sermons on the occasion of the public fasts for rain may also have taken place in the open air (e.g. jTaan II.1.65 b, R. Berechia and R. Haggai; Lev R 3.6, M. 69, R. Hananiah bar Acha).

The rabbis appear to have had an influence on the Jewish population in general as regards the matter of public fasts. For example, jTaan mentions several fasts ordered by the rabbis (e.g. III.4.66 d, R. Acha). The patriarchs are to take part as well, as R. Helbo says to Judan the patriarch. But this appears to have been unsuccessful, since a quote from R. Jose follows, saying that the fasts of his time are no longer proper fasts, since the patriarchate does not take part in them (II.1.65 a). Elsewhere R. Jacob bar Acha tells teachers what they are to answer women who ask them on which days fasting is permitted (II.13.66 a). Thus this is an area of religious life which the Jewish population had apparently entrusted to the rabbis.

However, a sermon of R. Hanan of Sepphoris shows how little the rabbis were able to influence the people with their ideas, even in what were for them the simplest questions of prayer. He applies Song 2:2, 'like a lily among brambles', to the one who as the only one of ten men in the synagogue is able to recite the prayer before the Shema, and who is able to say the blessing over the bride and groom at a wedding or the blessing over the mourners at a death (LevR 23.4, M.530f.). Thus even such simple and common forms of prayer as these are apparently unknown to most people.

---

[13] See L. I. Levine, *Caesarea under Roman Rule*, 102.

(b) Rabbis in the leadership of the community and in the courts[14]

The Palestinian Talmud presupposes that rabbis have certain rights of decision-making in the Jewish communities. The cases it discusses largely have to do with theoretical discussions of religious law, but practical decisions by rabbis are also cited; they are often mentioned in passing as a matter of course in order to illustrate a theoretical discussion. There is no reason to doubt such statements in principle, although we ought not to generalize from the picture offered by the Talmud. Naturally the influence of the rabbis was greater at the seat of the patriarch in Tiberias, or in Sepphoris where he had previously resided, than in the ordinary Jewish villages, for example, where the old-established ruling classes continued to lead the communities. And even in the rabbinic centres, the rabbis had to put up with competition from the dignitaries appointed by the patriarchs, as the polemic in jBik III.3.65 d clearly shows.

jPea VIII.7.21 a tells of R. Haggai and R. Jose (cf. jSheq V.2.48 d) that they appointed *Parnassim*, people concerned with public welfare or generally with leadership in the community. This probably happened on the patriarch's instructions, since they taught in his school. The *Parnassim* appointed by R. Jose in Kafra had to be persuaded to take on this duty. The fact that it was no easy task to find people for such posts is also shown by LevR 25.1 (M. 568f.). Here R. Huna recommends as penance, in the case of a serious sin that cannot be punished by an earthly court, to double the customary amount of religious study; but anyone who has studied neither the Bible nor the Mishnah is to put himself forward as *Parnas* or treasurer for the poor box.

Rabbis who were active in the courts, if they were not simply called on as adjudicators, were apparently also appointed by the patriarch, if only on the strength of their ordination in general. They were undoubtedly able to implement their rulings, if necessary against resistance on the part of those concerned. This follows from jKet VII.9.31 d, for example, according to which

---

[14] See especially G. Alon, *Jews, Judaism and the Classical World*, 374–432; J. Neusner, *Judaism in Society*, 115–97; L. I. Levine, *The Rabbinic Class in Roman Palestine in Late Antiquity*, Jerusalem 1989, 162–85; C. Hezser, *Rabbinic Movement*, 353–404.

R. Jirmeja forced a man to divorce his wife. In jKet I.2.25 b R. Hanina ruled on the payment of the sum owed to a woman from her marriage contract, and brought in R. Mana to sign the document. jKet XI.1.34 d is concerned with a question of inheritance, jKet IX.10.33 b with regulating the debts of an absent person. Further such examples could easily be found.

It is an interesting fact that the examples from the Talmud often also quote cases in which a rabbi sits in judgement on a case together with men who are not rabbis: for example jBB III.3.14 a, R. Huna together with Hilqiyya bar Tobi and Hiyya bar Rab. Despite all their polemic against non-ordained judges, and despite occasional calls not to sit in judgement together with such people, the rabbis are forced to reconcile themselves to the existing situation.

Decisions affecting large groups in the Jewish community are also attributed to rabbis, as we have already seen in connection with the revolt against Gallus: R. Jonah and R. Jose permit the supplying of Roman troops with bread even on the sabbath, in the days of Ursicinus. R. Mani does the same for Proclus' troops in Sepphoris (jSanh III.6.21 b). This is a religious ruling in the strict sense. In another case, which has also been briefly mentioned, we have a ruling on civil law: 'In the days of R. Mani a *numerus* [a Roman unit of troops] was in Sepphoris, and their [the inhabitants'] sons were pawned by them [or seized by the soldiers]. When the time came for them to leave, R. Mani published a proclamation according to R. Immi's ruling [that in emergencies even houses which are rented out may be sold]. He said: It is not that I agree with him, but in the interests of the people of Sepphoris [I have ruled thus] so that their sons are not lost for ever' (jPes IV.9.31 b). Apparently it was necessary to find the money for exemption from military service (*aurum tironicum*).[15] If R. Mani's ruling had not been supported by a corresponding authority, one would have expected a flood of court cases brought by the tenants affected by the ruling. Thus we may probably deduce from this episode that individual rabbis, at least, had the authority to decide even such comparatively far-reaching questions.

According to the Talmud, individual rabbis also ruled on questions of religious law even beyond their own place of work.

---

[15] On this passage see S. S. Miller, *Studies*, 43f.; S. Lieberman, 'Palestine', 353.

There are a number of examples for Tyre in particular. For example, R. Jassa ruled in Tyre on whether or not certain containers were permitted (as R. Jirmea had done previously in the Golan Heights: jAZ II.4.41 c). In Tyre R. Ba and R. La considered a question about whether fruit was permitted in connection with the sabbath year (jShebi II.6.33 d). Also of interest is a question addressed by R. Tanchum bar Papa from Alexandria to R. Jose on two matters of marriage law (jQid III.14.64 d). Cases like these do not necessarily prove that the rabbis had powers that extended beyond their own province; rather they were consulted for their legal opinion as recognized scholars. In each case it would be necessary to discover how many Jews in Tyre even thought of themselves as belonging to the rabbinic form of Judaism. Apparently the rabbis' authority was not entirely secure there, not even by those who cared about such religious questions.

This may be seen from anecdotes about Jacob, a man from Kefar Neburaya. He did not have the title Rabbi, but was consulted in Tyre on halakhic matters, on which he decided in each case according to his understanding of the Bible. In one case the question was whether the son of a Gentile woman and a Jewish man might be circumcised on the sabbath, in another whether a fish needed to be ritually slaughtered. In both cases Jacob got into conflict with R. Haggai, who appealed to the traditional understanding of the law (GenR 7.2, Th-A 50–52; the first case also jJeb II.6.4 a = jQid III.14.64 d). We have already encountered the same Jacob in Caesarea as an opponent of the practice of giving certain appointments for payment (jBik III.3.65 d). Some have attempted to call this Jacob a Jewish Christian,[16] but there is no reason to do so.

Although many details remain extremely unclear as regards the actual influence of the rabbis on Jewish community life and courts of law in the fourth century, nevertheless the fundamental tendency of the evidence we have may be summarized as follows, quoting J. Neusner:

> The Talmud portrays the rabbi as an effective authority over Israel. Yet details of the portrait time and again contradict its main lines. The rabbi was part of the administration of a man who stood at the margins of the

---

[16] E.g. W. Bacher, *Die Agada* III, 711.

rabbinical estate, one foot in, the other out. The sage was further limited in his power by popular will and consensus, by established custom, and by other sorts of Jewish Big Men. ... On the one side, the rabbi could make some practical decisions. On the other, he competed for authority over Israel with the patriarch and with local village heads. And, in general, no Jew decided much.[17]

3. The Rabbis and their Non-Jewish Surroundings

This is not the place for even a short description of the religious and spiritual ideas of the rabbis in the fourth century; it would also be extremely difficult to separate the spiritual developments of this period from those of the preceding century. Only two closely related topics will be mentioned briefly, which may usefully throw a new light on the history of the period under review. What relationship did the rabbis have with their Roman rulers, and how did they react to the fact that their surroundings had become Christianized? Can we detect changes in comparison with the time when the opponents of Judaism were still paganism and a pagan government?

As regards their attitude to the government, we have already mentioned the reserved and pragmatic behaviour of the rabbis in connection with the revolt against Gallus and Julian's project of rebuilding the Temple. They sought for a way to coexist with the government, as long as no fundamental religious interests were touched upon, as apparently never happened in our period. Of course this statement can only be made with the reservation that the editors who were responsible for the writings that we have naturally also filtered their material. But if the resulting picture diverged too strongly from reality, we might expect to find corrections in the course of history or from non-Jewish sources, and this is not the case.

The rabbinic writings show that the rabbis by no means lived in a sealed world, rather that they stood in daily contact with the Roman world and its administration. The Greek and Latin borrowings in the rabbinic texts show a certain degree of knowledge of the general administration of their time, that is,

[17] J. Neusner, *Judaism in Society*, 196.

also of the reforms introduced since the beginning of the fourth century and of the new titles of administrative rank. In particular, the expressions taken over as borrowings from the legal vocabulary are very informative.[18]

Such concrete information as we have refers primarily to the process of law. Among other things, the insidious manner of questioning the accused in court is described (thus R. Hanina b. Isaac, GenR 37.2, Th-A 345; anonymously 63.10, Th-A 693), also the process of law from the accusation via torture to the execution (R. Berechia in PRK 24, M.357f.). The successive courts of appeal from the *Dux* to the provincial governor (*eparchos*) to the *Magister militum* (*stratēlatēs*) are mentioned (R. Jehuda b. R. Simon in GenR 49.9, Th-A 510f.).[19] A favourite subject is the corruptibility of officials (R. Acha in SongR 7.9), also complaints about taxes, as for example when R. Isaac b. R. Zera speaks of the greed of Esau (PRK 6, M.115). The trade tax (*chrysargyron*), only introduced by Constantine, is also already mentioned (jBQ III.1.3 c).

The transition from Latin to Greek, even for the language of public administration, is apparently reflected in R. Jehuda b. R. Simon's polemic that it is shameful for Rome that it does not sign its documents in its own language. R. Hanina bar Adda counters in protest that this is indeed the case (EsthR 4.12). The polemic against Rome's dependence on the culture of Greece is nothing new in rabbinic texts, it is simply continued. For example, R. Huna says in GenR 16.4 (Th-A 148) that Greece was ahead of the wicked empire (Rome) in three things: in seafaring (on another reading: in customs or laws), in painting and in language. Earlier in the same passage it is said that all kingdoms (i.e. including Rome) are named after Assyria, because they enrich themselves at Israel's expense (*mitasherot*). R. Jose adds a pun of his own to that of R. Huna, this time on the name of Nineveh: All empires adorned themselves at Israel's expense.

---

[18] See D. Sperber, *A Dictionary of Greek and Latin Legal Terms in Rabbinic Literature*, Bar Ilan 1984. For titles of administrative rank see e.g. LevR 28.6, in a sermon on the Book of Esther attributed to R. Levi, where it is said that Haman used to appoint the *comes pantōn* (according to the Parisian MS; according to others *comes privatarum*), the *comes calator* and (according to the printed editions) the *magister palatii* (M. 665).

[19] The immediately following words of R. Jehuda apparently refer to the division of the empire in the fourth century: 'When you (God) wished to judge your world, you gave it into the hands of two like Remus and Romulus. If one of them wishes to do something, the other prevents him.'

In MidrPs 14.1 (B. 57 a) R. Jehuda expounds in the name of Samuel that the fool (*nabal*) mentioned in Ps. 14:1, who believes that there is no God, is Esau (= Rome), which has filled the whole world with corpses (*nebelot*). R. Huna then limits the pun as follows: 'because it filled the land with the corpses of the Israelites'. But this clearly has to do with historical memories, not contemporary experience (despite Jerome's assertion that thousands died in the revolt against Gallus). For we hear of almost no concrete complaints of oppressive measures on the part of the government in their own time. In jMQ III.1.81 d we are told that there was distress in the days of Jirmeja, and W. Bacher understands the expression '‛aqa' as an oppressive government edict,[20] but the continuation of the passage makes it clear that simply financial difficulties are meant, perhaps a tax claim that has fallen due or similar; for R. Jirmeja reacts by sending a message to R. Jacob b. R. Bun and asking him for a silver lampstand, which he indignantly refuses (apparently claiming a rabbi's immunity from taxes). Neither can we find anything more concrete in the story about R. Isaac b. Eleazar: he attempts in vain to bury a bone on the beach at Caesarea, it continually reappears. The rabbi sees a sign from God in this. 'After a few days a government messenger (*veredarius*) passed by. It [the bone] rolled between his feet, he stumbled over it and fell, killing himself. People came and searched him and found that he was carrying negative information [literally: bad letters] against the Jews of Caesarea' (LevR 22.4, M. 506; GenR 10.7, Th-A 81f. and elsewhere).

Despite all the (generally traditional) complaints about their subjection to the foreign Roman rule, the rabbis are not prepared to exercise active resistance. As earlier generations had also taught, the masters of the fourth century pin all their hopes on salvation brought about directly by God at the end of time. Until then, one can only observe with resignation, like R. Nahman in GenR 6.3 (Th-A 42f.): Rome follows the solar calendar and Israel the lunar calendar. As the sun only rules by day, so Rome only rules in this world; the moon, however, rules by night and day, so Israel will rule in this world and the next. 'As long as the light of the great [heavenly lamp] is there, the light of the small one is not

---

[20] W. Bacher, *Die Agada* III, 101. M. Sokoloff, *A Dictionary of Jewish Palestinian Aramaic*, Ramat Gan 1990, 415: 'trouble, distress, adversity'.

apparent. But once the light of Esau has gone down, the light of Jacob will be apparent. That is the meaning of the Bible passage "Arise, shine" (Isa. 60:1).'

But the coming of this time is not to be forced, as R. Helbo deduces from Song 2:7 in SongR 2.18: 'Four oaths are contained here. [God] made Israel swear that it will not revolt against the kingdoms, that it will not push the coming of the end, that it will not reveal its secrets to the peoples of the world and that it will not go up [all together] like a wall from the Diaspora [to the land of Israel].' Then R. Judan combines the text, ['Do not stir up or awaken love until it is ready'] with Gen 25.28 ['But Isaac loved Esau'] and arrives at the interpretation that they must wait 'until the pleasure of the old man [Isaac] has been fulfilled', until his blessing on Esau [= Rome] has been fulfilled. But R. Berechia interprets 'love' as meaning God's love to Israel, although he too thinks that this love cannot be awakened before time, but all must be left to God.

Statements about the government occasionally show by their terminology that they reflect their time, but otherwise do not differ from earlier statements. At least on the surface there is no noticeable reaction to a state that has now become Christian. This is not altered by pointing to individual statements of rabbis, for which we now have the first – or at least more – evidence.

In this connection rabbinic texts are often quoted according to which other peoples claim to be Israel. Several times in rabbinic literature the parable is used in this sense in which wheat, straw and chaff argue for which of them the field is sown; the decision will only come at harvest time. Just so the peoples of the world will say, 'We are Israel and for our sake was the world created', but Israel answers, 'Wait until the coming of the day of the Lord, blessed be He; then we will know for whom the world was created.' R. Abun, to whom this parable is attributed (GenR 83.5, Th-A 1000f.; SongR 7.7 on 7.3), gives the following explanation for the fact that the majority of the Torah is not written, but transmitted orally (jPea II.6.17 a = jHag I.8.76 d). In this way a differentiation is possible between Israel and the peoples of the world. The latter are also able to produce the book with the written Torah, but they do not possess the oral Torah.

J. Heinemann thinks it possible that the parable of the wheat field could also be directed against Samaritan claims.[21] But in

---

[21] J. Heinemann, *Aggadah and its Development* (Hebrew), Jerusalem 1974, 230 n. 4. But for him too the principal target is Christianity.

view of the plural – 'the peoples of the world' – this is unlikely. It certainly seems reasonable to interpret this text as a reaction to Christian claims, although this interpretation cannot be fully proved.[22]

The same is true of R. Hiyya bar Luliani's statement, concluding from Zeph. 3:9 that the Noachids, i.e. the peoples who follow only God's covenant with Noah (Gen. 9) and not the whole Torah, will one day take all the commandments upon themselves, but in the end will again return to worshipping idols (deduced from Ps. 2:3). This statement refers too closely to the Biblical passage to permit the conclusion that the rabbis recognized that the non-Jewish world they were surrounded by had turned towards a more Biblical form of religion (jAZ II.1.40 c).

The same is also true of the statement in jNed III.12f., 38 a, attributed to R. Acha in the name of R. Huna (perhaps more correctly the reverse):

> The wicked Esau will shroud himself in his prayer shawl and will sit with the just in the garden of Eden for the future. But the Holy One, blessed be He, will pull him away and lead him out. What is the scriptural proof? 'Though you soar aloft like the eagle, though your nest is set among the stars, from there I will bring you down, says the Lord' [Obad. 4]. 'Stars' means nothing else but 'just men', as it is said: 'Those who lead many to righteousness [shall shine] like the stars for ever and ever' [Dan. 12:3].

A reference to Rome having now become Christian is likely here too, but the motif that Rome thinks of itself as 'just' is too old for such an interpretation of the text to be absolutely conclusive.[23]

No single rabbinic statement, taken by itself, can be understood as an indisputably proven reaction to Christianity as the new power. The fact that the Palestinian Talmud (and equally the contemporary Midrashim) does not see any necessity for distinguishing clearly between Christianity and paganism is interpreted by J. Neusner as follows: 'Not to know that people revering the

---

[22] J. Maier, *Jüdische Auseinandersetzung*, 194, whose conclusion is probably too negative in view of his methodological principle only to assume what may strictly be proved. To what extent may not even an accumulation of certain statements, which taken individually might also be understood differently, be seen as at least a strong indication of Jewish reactions to Christianity?

[23] See J. Maier, *Jüdische Auseinandersetzung*, 263 n. 643, against earlier literature.

same ancient Scriptures that Israel held sacred now ruled in Rome, not to acknowledge that paganism in its gross form had given way to a religion speaking about Israel and claiming to constitute a piece of Israel – that seems to me a deliberate act of self-delusion ...'[24]

Was this really the case? This would presuppose that the rabbis recognized the change and nevertheless did not want to admit it. But perhaps their own view of themselves meant that the transition from paganism (which had long ceased to be the gross polytheism of earlier times) to Christianity was not so significant as to warrant a reaction different from that against the earlier paganism. We should also take into account the fact that rabbinic thought was very much bound by tradition, and also the defensive attitude towards everything non-Jewish that had been practised over centuries. This attitude afforded protection, but also hindered agility of mind, nuancing and differentiation. All of this is difficult for us to comprehend today.

Thus J. Maier's more restrained words are probably better: he asks to what extent, from a Jewish, rabbinic point of view, the continuity between the pagan and Christian Roman empire was the centre of attention, so much so that specifically Christian issues could not be heard as such. But then he attempts the following explanation:

> This may have had to do with the kind of Christianity that they generally encountered, but the fundamental reason was an idea that continued to be influential, the division of humanity into two camps, Israel and the 'peoples of the world', and the fact that they reckoned with four world empires, as in Daniel. The confrontation with 'Rome' (Esau/Edom), the fourth and final world empire, formed contemporary consciousness of salvation theology to such

---

[24] J. Neusner, 'The Experience of the City', 51. But in his book *Judaism and Christianity in the Age of Constantine: History, Messiah, Israel and the Initial Confrontation*, Chicago 1987, Neusner then demonstrates how the fourth-century rabbis on the one hand did not enter into direct dialogue with the Christian theologians, but on the other were forced to reconsider subjects such as the goal of history, the role of the Messiah and the question of the true people of God. The simultaneous importance of these three subjects for Church Fathers and rabbis alike can only be understood, according to Neusner, as a reaction to the altered political situation.

an extent that no particular attention was paid to the religion of this world power for a long time.[25]

The fact that Roman law in the Codex Theodosianus often lumps together heretics, Jews and pagans in a single law as a common enemy, also shows us this thinking in two camps on the opposing, Christian side.

4. The Rabbinic Writings

We know only from their own writings what has so far been said about the rabbis. However, we should not simply use these texts as a quarry from which to pick out those individual statements that seem interesting to us. They should also be taken as a whole into our picture of contemporary Judaism. The Palestinian Talmud, Genesis Rabba, Leviticus Rabba and Lamentations Rabba, but probably also Song of Solomon Rabba, Ruth Rabba and Pesiqta de Rab Kahana are products of the century described here, and so also evidence for it. Although the material contained in these writings partly goes farther back in time, they found their characteristic expression in the fourth century and their final form in the early fifth century.

Why was it precisely now, roughly contemporarily with the end of the patriarchate and the promulgation of the Codex Theodosianus, that the urge arose to edit the collected traditions, to bring them into a fixed form and close them? If we were able to answer this question we would probably know more about the rabbis' understanding of their own time and history than we can deduce from the individual statements. But unfortunately there is little we can say with certainty on this point, and we must rely on conjectures and hypotheses.

We are most likely to find indications in the Palestinian Talmud. It no more contains direct statements than any other rabbinic work as to who wrote it when and to what end. But from the names of the rabbis named in the Talmud we may conclude that only a date after 400 is possible. The lack of references to any later situation also makes it unlikely that the date is much later. The authors, or rather editors, should be sought in rabbinic

---

[25] J. Maier, *Jüdische Auseinandersetzung*, 206.

circles, since the text was clearly written as literature for those of whom it constantly speaks.

In its layout the Talmud is a commentary on the Mishnah, the religious law of the rabbis which was edited around 200. But of course the text is not only interested in theoretical discussions of how the law of the Mishnah forms a unity with that of the Bible and is augmented by additional traditions that were not included. In the constant discussions of how this law is to be applied in the practice of the present day, the Talmud naturally contains references to contemporary events. However, it is striking how few concrete events that can be verified from non-rabbinic sources were recorded in the Talmud. No emperor is mentioned after Diocletian, unless it is Julian in jNed III.2.37 d; but the reading of the name is completely uncertain. Thus the only figure of the 'profane history' of the fourth century that remains is Ursicinus, Gallus' general.

The fourth-century colouring in the Palestinian Talmud therefore does not arise from the mention of historical persons and events, but from the language of daily life, amd the titles, institutions, offices and bureaucratic procedures mentioned which stamped the Roman empire and its administration after Constantine. Otherwise, the feeling of a significant historical distance from the authorities of the Mishnah only arises from the maturity of rabbinc thought processes that has now developed, and in particular from the chains of tradition that are repeatedly mentioned, by means of which specific statements are followed back across generations of rabbis. There no longer appears to be any concern with the events of world history.

J. Neusner understands the fact that the Palestinian Talmud is useless for any reconstruction of the facts of history to signify that the editors were indifferent to contemporary events: 'A document so reticent about events in its own day clearly wishes to claim that it be read as if composed in a vacuum ... What we learn is about people unable to cope except through massive efforts at feigning indifference.'[26]

Was the rabbis' attitude to their own day really that of 'not even ignoring' it? Certainly they separated themselves as far as possible from their non-Jewish surroundings. They attempted to retain their own rhythm of life, in the knowledge that there would be no

---

[26] J. Neusner, *Judaism in Society*, 15f.

more significant changes within history before the end of the 'fourth empire', the world powers, should come and the kingdom of God should begin. This attitude brought a pronounced quietism, a timelessness and sense of being untouched by history, although it is not possible to describe this attitude as consciously ignoring, or as pretending that nothing had changed. It was also encouraged by the basic text on which the rabbis were working: for the Mishnah too is only peripherally concerned with the events of its own time, and is meant rather as an expression of the eternal, divinely willed order of the world. Thus the work of the rabbis stood from the beginning under the aspect of eternity.

But how was the Palestinian Talmud actually compiled and edited? Because of the many long repetitions in the text, but also the fact that there are no commentaries on many tractates of the Mishnah, it has occasionally been said that the text was never edited in the strict sense; rather that the rabbis simply put together existing blocks of material without altering them. But this hypothesis is untenable. Rather, the repetitions are an expansive form of reference to parallel passages, whereby the entire surroundings of a quotation were quoted as well in order not to take it out of context. The fact that tractates are missing can be explained on other grounds. It is very likely that in the rabbinic schools, where the Mishnah soon came to be the principal subject-matter, the text of the Mishnah was first tested for its compatibility with Biblical tradition and with other Tannaitic teachings. In the course of time increasingly extensive commentaries came into existence on the various chapters and tractates of the Mishnah. These were supplemented and revised by means of exchange between the different schools, and finally received their definitive form in a comprehensive revision by the rabbis of Tiberias, who were responsible for the final editing.

But the Talmud text was not edited in Tiberias in its entirety. The tractate Neziqin with its three 'gates' (Baba Qamma, Baba Metsia, Baba Batra), which treats of property law and law of damages, was perhaps edited in Caesarea. This inference is drawn from the rabbis mentioned in this tractate, the large number of examples set in Caesarea, and also from its language, which has a particularly large number of Greek borrowings.[27] S. Lieberman's

---

[27] Locating the edition of the tractate in Caesarea is likely to a certain degree, but cannot be directly proved. C. Hezser, *Form, Function and Historical*

opinion, voiced in the same context, poses rather more difficulties. He says that this tractate was also written earlier than the rest of the Palestinian Talmud, around 350, which would explain its rudimentary character in comparison with the rest of the Palestinian Talmud.[28]

J. Neusner understood the Palestinian Talmud's indifference towards contemporary history as a deliberate self-deception, as mentioned above. This is an attitude which the editors would not have been able to maintain if the Talmud had been edited in a cosmopolitan centre. But this is precisely the case with Neziqin, and nevertheless Neziqin is no different from the rest of the Palestinian Talmud in this respect. Neusner is of the opinion that it is hardly possible, in the case of Neziqin, to judge how the rabbis of Caesarea reacted to the surroundings in which they lived their lives, because this tractate contains too little non-legal material.[29]

However, does not this explanation miss the real point? Why did the rabbis of Caesarea restrict their work to such a degree, why did they not engage with their surroundings? The subject-matter of Neziqin would have permitted it; and it would surely have been welcomed by the supposed addressees of the work, the Jewish judges of Caesarea who were inexperienced in Halakhah. Another difficult question is why a Jewish rabbinic school living in a largely non-Jewish city did not take on the tractate Aboda Zara, 'idol worship'. The matters treated in it were particularly burning questions for the Jews of Caesarea. Here too, there are more questions than answers.

The greatest difficulty in assessing the Palestinian Talmud lies in the matter of the missing tractates, in particular the entire order of Qodashim and almost the entire order of Toharot (with the exception of three chapters of the tractate Nidda

---

Significance of the Rabbinic Story in Yerushalmi Neziqin, Tübingen 1993, 405, rightly states with regard to the criteria which are brought forward in favour of Caesarea: 'Although none of these phenomena points toward Caesarea exclusively, Caesarea remains a possible location for the redaction of the y. Bavot'.

[28] S. Lieberman, *The Talmud of Caesarea* (Hebrew), Jerusalem 1931; id., *Siphre Zutta (The Midrash of Lydda) II. The Talmud of Caesarea* (Hebrew), New York 1969. G. A. Wewers, *Probleme der Bavot-Traktate*, 289ff., raises a number of criticisms of Lieberman's hypotheses.

[29] J. Neusner, 'The Experience of the City', 51.

on the uncleanness of menstruating women). The occasionally suggested hypothesis is untenable, that there once existed a Palestinian commentary on these two orders, which was lost in the course of time. The other theory, that the historical circumstances prevented the completion of the Palestinian Talmud, initially sounds plausible. But it raises the question of why work was not continued as soon as the situation had improved.

As far as the contents are concerned, it could be argued that the order of Qodashim on the Temple service was not commentated because the Temple no longer existed, and the treatment of the subject in the Mishnah (partly also in Sifra and other midrashim) appeared to suffice for its expected restoration. However, we would then at least have expected a commentary on the tractate Chullin for the practical application of the food laws. As regards the purity laws in Toharot, the practical impossiblity of applying a large proportion of these laws could also have been the reason for including nothing in the Talmud except the tractate on menstruating women, which was of practical importance. However, these remain conjectures, and do not exclude the possibility that external circumstances were also partly responsible for the fact that the editors of the Palestinian Talmud were so brief, by comparison with their Babylonian counterparts, and left out extensive areas of the Mishnah.

The classic answer to our question is the 'catastrophe theory': the unfavourable situation, the increasing pressure from the Christian government and finally the fall of the patriarchate led the masters of the school of Tiberias to bring their traditional knowledge, accumulated over centuries, into an ordered form, and thus to hand it down to coming generations.

In its extreme form this theory has largely been discredited today. However, it would be an equally wrong and unhistorical way of thinking to neglect the actual historical situation altogether. The present study has shown that in the first century of Christian rule, the Jews of Palestine by no means did as badly as is often asserted. The flowering of the patriarchate in the final decades of its existence, and the legal and state support for the central leadership of Judaism in the Roman empire, cannot have failed to influence the situation of the rabbinic school in Tiberias also. The resources arising from the patriarchal tax and other sources must also have secured a sufficient financial basis for the rabbinic academy. On the other hand, the patriarchate's state-supported monopoly on the appointment of Jewish religious officials in the broadest sense must also have raised the requirements of training and demanded a text as a point of reference equal to that of the Mishnah at the time of Jehuda ha-Nasi. Apparently this is what the rabbis of Tiberias attempted to realize in the form of the Palestinian Talmud.

Therefore the starting-point for this undertaking by the rabbis of Tiberias was rather positive than otherwise. The fall of the patriarchate before 429, or even its reprimanding in 415, may have contributed to the work being brought to a hurried conclusion, because the continued existence of the school of Tiberias appeared to be in danger. Another aspect which should perhaps be taken into account for the historical understanding of the Palestinian Talmud is the fact that the autonomy of the Jewish courts was largely abolished in 398. A Western Jew reacted to this by writing the *Collatio legum Mosaicarum et Romanarum*, in order to show that there was a high degree of correspondence between Biblical and Roman law, and therefore no reason to suspend the autonomy of the Jewish courts.[30] The law of 398 may have been the occasion for the rabbis of Tiberias to bring their work to a premature conclusion, since it was now only of limited practical use in a court of law. However, it could also have helped to give the work a more inward-looking and largely theoretical orientation than had perhaps originally been planned. However, if the Palestinian Talmud is to be dated rather later, then a certain, as it were atmospheric, connection with the preliminary work for the Codex Theodosianus, which was commissioned in 429, should perhaps not be entirely excluded. These remain hypotheses, but also food for thought when considering the Palestinian Talmud in its historical context.

As has already been mentioned, at this time the rabbis not only completed the Palestinian Talmud, but also composed a number of midrashim. Genesis Rabba and Leviticus Rabba are closely connected with the Palestinian Talmud. Not only do the same names of rabbis and the same language connect these writings, but they also have a large number of passages in common. But the individual parallel passages are difficult to assess. Generally a

---

[30] Some authors continue to argue in favour of a Christian author for the *Collatio*. For the present state of the discussion see L. V. Rutgers, *The Jews in Late Ancient Rome*, Leiden 1995, 210–59.

fairly complicated pattern of relationships between the writings is assumed, for example that the editors of the Palestinian Talmud had an early form of Genesis or Leviticus Rabba at their disposal, but that for the final form of these midrashim their authors used the final form of the Palestinian Talmud. A similar pattern may be assumed in the case of Lamentations and Ruth Rabba. Finally, the Pesiqta de Rab Kahana should be mentioned here, a collection of sermons for feast days and special sabbaths. This is very closely related to Leviticus Rabba, so that occasionally even a common author for the two works has been suggested. A number of other midrashim were probably written soon after these fundamental works.[31]

It is no longer possible to assess more exactly the literary relationships of these works. But the closeness of their relationship is clear, which is also visible in a pronounced tendency to a common formulaic language. G. A. Wewers stresses: 'The very great number of formulaic expressions and their identical application in different writings of the tradition point either to an extreme degree of standardization or a very tightly circumscribed historical location.'[32]

In fact the short period of time in which these works were written, and the limited circle of rabbis who are possible authors, are probably the decisive factor for explaining their extensive interconnection. If the rabbis of this period wrote a work that was primarily, though not exclusively, one of religious law, i.e. the Palestinian Talmud, and at the same time Biblical commentaries, indeed books of sermons on Biblical texts in the case of Leviticus Rabba and Pesiqta de Rab Kahana, this shows the breadth of their interests and also their endeavours to gain influence over synagogue preaching.

G. Scholem conjectured that a number of Jewish mystical writings 'appear to have been edited in the fifth and sixth centuries', and that 'there can be no reasonable doubt that the atmosphere of these writings is in harmony with contemporary political and social conditions'. 'It was', he says, 'the depressing conditions of the period, the beginning of the era of persecution by the Church

---

[31] For details on the rabbinic writings, see G. Stemberger, *Introduction to the Talmud and Midrash*, 2nd ed., Edinburgh 1996.
[32] G. A. Wewers, *Probleme der Bavot-Traktate*, 324.

since the fourth century' that diverted the gaze of these mystics away from the realm of history and towards the higher world of the divine throne chariot.[33]

Our study has shown that the situation of this period was by no means so negative for the Jewish population that we might comprehend the beginning of a new mystical movement in this context. Newer publications have also shown that Scholem generally dates these mystical texts much too early, and that the circles which produced the Hekhalot literature rather belong to post-Talmudic times.[34]

However, even without such dubious attributions of Jewish writings to the period here under consideration and to the circle of rabbis of the late fourth and early fifth centuries, sufficient certain writings remain for us to describe this period as the most productive literary period of the Palestinian rabbinate since the edition of the Mishnah around 200 (and of the Tosefta and the halakhic midrashim not long afterwards). It is hardly possible to regard this positive explosion of literary creativity as simply the reaction to the warnings of a coming storm, an attempt to bring the harvest into the barns in time, in order to transmit to coming generations and more peaceful days the intellectual legacy of the time. The anonymous editors of the rabbinic writings of this period were not mere collectors, but also creative men, and the inheritors of the rabbinic tradition of Palestine were able to continue working for centuries on the basis which they had produced. Although the abolition of the patriarchate and the sometimes increasing pressure of Christianity may have given their work a particular note of urgency, nevertheless it cannot be understood in its entirety as simply a reaction to the troubles of the time.

Like the synagogue buildings of the period, the literary production of the Palestinian rabbinate in the early fifth century, does not show a hectic nervousness before their fall, but a vitality and optimism that had not been seen for a long time. The fact that, by the will of the Roman legislature, after the end of the patriarchate the regional Jewish sanhedrins were to be the official representatives of Judaism, which probably means principally the

---

[33] G. G. Scholem, *Major Trends in Jewish Mysticism*, 3rd ed., London, 1955, 44, 73.
[34] See the stimulating study by P. Schäfer, *Gershom Scholem Reconsidered (The Twelfth Sacks Lecture)*, Oxford 1986.

rabbinic schools with their most important representatives, also shows the public recognition of the power of the rabbinate. Although this externally-imposed order did not endure and was ultimately unsuccessful, yet nevertheless the school of Tiberias and its head succeeded the patriarchate in its position of leadership in many matters, for the next few centuries.

Prospect

In the course of this study we have shown that fourth-century Palestinian Judaism, despite the fact that it was forced to accept certain limitations and was put on the defensive by the advance of Christianity, nevertheless maintained its position extraordinarily well against the overwhelming might of Christianity. In these final pages a synopsis of these results will be attempted, as also a presentation of what prospects for the future lay ahead for Palestinian Judaism in the early fifth century. The two main emphases of the study, the Christian legislation regarding Jews from the Codex Theodosianus and the relationship between Jews and Christians in Palestine, will continue to be the focus of attention.

1. The Codex Theodosianus and Political Reality

Until now we have discussed the laws of the Christian emperors regarding Jews in their respective thematic contexts. This has necessarily meant that the overall pattern of development of this legislation has been somewhat neglected, and it is to this we now turn.

Approximately fifty laws concerning Jews are extant from the period between Constantine and Theodosius II (the number is not exact, since a few laws in the Codex Theodosianus are separated into thematic units, or occasionally duplicated). Only ten of these laws come from the time before Theodosius I, that is, the greater half of the period in question. Twenty laws each were promulgated in the reigns of Theodosius I or Arcadius and Honorius, in the years 383–404, and in the reign of Theodosius II, between 408 and 429. Theodosius' *novella* 3 of 438 then summarizes a number of important laws.

Thus, simply from the point of view of the number of laws, Judaism occupied much more of the attention of the legislature after Christianity was declared the state religion in the year 380, than had been the case in the first decades of Christian rule in the

Roman empire. What consequences did this have for the actual situation of the Jews? M. Avi-Yonah's title for the chapter in which he discusses this question is as follows: 'The great assault on the Jews and Judaism, 363–439'.[1] Can one really say this, and if so, did this great attack actually succeed?

An overview of the relevant laws shows that they are not based on any planned, future-orientated policy concerning the Jews on the part of the Christian emperors. Rather, particular events and the intervention of individuals led to the promulgation of laws. These were often regionally and temporally limited in their application, as is clearly shown by the large number of repetitions and contradictions of laws on the same subject. Therefore it is important in each individual case also to take into account the place where a law was promulgated and the name of the addressee. Many texts were of no importance from the outset as far as Palestine is concerned, and only came into force here after the promulgation of the Codex Theodosianus (which still has no bearing on their practical enforcement).

Some basic themes of the legislation, from Constantine onwards, are: the protection of Jewish converts to Christianity against attacks by their former co-religionists – a practical application of the freedom of religion proclaimed by Constantine, the prohibition of Jews' circumcising their Christian slaves (perhaps continuing earlier Roman laws on circumcision, but certainly also intended as protection for Christians); and on the other hand the exemption of Jewish religious officials from the duties of the *curia*, the city council.

Strikingly, the majority of the laws regarding conversion were published in the west of the empire; apparently the problem was more urgent there than in the east. A direct link to Palestine cannot be proved, nor can it be inferred from the contemporary literary evidence. Conversions of Jews to Christianity were principally a problem of the Diaspora.

But even in the Diaspora, conversions were not a one-way phenomenon. This follows from CTh XVI.8.7, dated 353, according to which a Christian who converts to Judaism forfeits his property to the state treasury. Thirty years later, the emperor Gratian again had to comment on the matter. In CTh XVI.7.3, promulgated on 21 May 383 in Padua, he threatens punishment

---

[1] M. Avi-Yonah, *Jews*, 208.

for those who 'neglect the dignity of the Christian religion and name, and allow themselves to be stained by the Jewish contagion'.[2] Also published in the west, in Ravenna, is CTh XVI.8.19, dated 1 April 409, against the sect of the 'worshippers of heaven', a North African group who kept the Jewish law. These people 'dare to misuse the faith so much that they force certain Christians to take on the abominable and ugly name of Jews'. They are to be admonished, 'so that persons who are initiated into the Christian mysteries may not be forced to accept a perversion which is Jewish and foreign to the Roman empire, after they have become Christians ... It is more serious than death and more cruel than murder if someone from the Christian faith is stained with Jewish unbelief.' Thus the problem of the Judaizers was also a live issue in the west of the empire; a few years earlier it had led John Chrysostom to deliver his sermons against the Jews.

On the other hand, CTh IX.45.2, promulgated by Arcadius in Constantinople in 397, speaks of Jews who seek refuge in Christianity for non-religious reasons, and who may only be admitted after their debts have been paid or their innocence proved. In other words, it was recognized that an enforced favouring of Christianity ran the risk of only attracting suspect persons. CTh XVI.8.23, as late as 416 (Ravenna) permits converts to return to Judaism if their motives were not religious. Thus the laws on conversion show Christianity, despite now being the state religion, rather on the defensive than otherwise, and not at all sure of itself.

As regards slaves, Constantine limited himself to prohibiting the circumcision of non-Jews (CTh XVI.9.1). In 339 Constantius went further (CTh XVI.9.2) by making simply the purchase of non-Jewish slaves by Jews a punishable offence. This order could not be implemented in practice, as is shown by two laws published later in the western Empire. CTh III.1.5, dated 22 September 384 (the copy sent to Rhegium was incorporated in the Codex), rules more precisely:

No Jew, whoever he may be, may buy a Christian slave nor

---

[2] E. Demougeot, 'L'Empereur Honorius et la politique antijuive', *Hommages à L. Herrmann*, Brussels 1960, 277–91, 277, refers the text to Jews who had converted to Christianity and then apostatized again; but the text does not mention this.

infect a former Christian with Jewish rites. If a public enquiry establishes that this has occurred, the slaves must be taken away and their owner must suffer a suitable punishment for the crime. Let it be added that if slaves who are still Christians are found in a Jewish household, or such as have become Jews from being Christians, they are to be bought out of slavery by the Christians at a suitable price.

Contrary to Constantius' law, the Jewish owner is here promised compensation. How inconsistent the legislation was is also shown by the fact that CTh XVI.8.22, dated 415, ruled that any Christian slaves in Gamaliel's possession should become the property of the church, while only a few months later Honorius in Ravenna permitted the possession of Christian slaves (CTh XVI.9.3).

In the east the matter was taken up again by CTh XVI.9.4, dated 10 April 417: 'A Jew may neither buy a Christian slave nor obtain one as a present'; if he nevertheless does so, he loses his possession, and the slave who reported the fact is set free as a reward. However, the slaves whom the Jew already owns, although they are Christians, and those whom he obtains now or in the future as an inheritance or as security, he is permitted to keep, as long as 'he neither against their will nor with their agreement mingles them with the obscenity of his own sect'. Although the language is insulting to Jews, the law nevertheless permits them to possess Christian slaves under certain conditions. The tone of CTh XVI.9.5, dated 9 April 423, is even harsher: '... for we think it an injustice that highly devout slaves should be stained by the lordship of most godless buyers'.[3] However, in its content the law offers nothing new and simply documents the ineffectiveness of previous edicts.

The fundamental intention of the laws that prohibit Jews from owning Christian slaves is plainly to protect the Christian religion; any economic motives are secondary at best. However, the message increasingly comes across that Jewish rule over Christians is generally to be rejected.

CTh IX.7.5, dated 14 March 388, is aimed against mixed marriages between Jews and Christians. The law, promulgated by

---

[3] H. Langenfeld, *Christianisierungspolitik*, 97ff., notes that this law was published on the Monday of Holy Week and should be seen as a kind of Easter edict, addressed primarily to the clergy and the faithful, which also determines the strongly anti-Jewish language.

Theodosius I in Thessaloniki, equates a mixed marriage between Jews and Christians with the crime of adultery, presumably for religious reasons: 'Let no Jew take a Christian woman to wife, and let no Christian enter into marriage with a Jewess.' For a tradition-conscious Jew it was self-evident that he would only marry a non-Jewish woman after she had converted to Judaism; thus the subjects of this law were probably to be found on the fringes of Judaism, particularly in the Diaspora. Palestinian Judaism, which was increasingly coming under the influence of the rabbinate, was hardly affected by it.

In the early fifth century, the Christians apparently became more sensitive towards some Jewish customs in certain districts, and the Jews probably also became more aggressive as the dispute intensified. This is documented by CTh XVI.8.18, dated 29 May 408 and published in Constantinople, according to which the provincial governors are to forbid the Jews to burn a kind of cross (Haman's gibbet) at Purim in memory of earlier events, 'despising the Christian faith and with a blasphemous attitude ... They are not to involve the sign of our faith in their jokes, but may retain their rites without despising the Christian law. However, they will without doubt lose what has been permitted until now, if they do not refrain from what is forbidden.'

A few months later, Honorius has cause to write a law in Ravenna for Donatus, the proconsul of Africa (CTh XVI.5.44, dated 24 November 408). For 'the new and unprecedented audacity of the Donatists, heretics and Jews has made clear that they intend to bring the sacraments of the Christian faith into confusion'. He is to proceed with severity against this infectious plague. This is the fierce and lengthy battle of the Catholic church against the African Donatists, with whom the Jews are lumped together. Shortly afterwards (CTh XVI.5.46, dated 15 January 409, Ravenna) the Donatists are named in a sweeping statement together with all heretics, the Jews and also the pagans. All of these should not believe that the laws passed against them in the past are no longer valid. But apparently this was precisely the case, as is shown by the following threats against negligent judges and officials. The church was here clearly on the defensive.

CTh XV.5.5, promulgated on 1 February 425 in Constantinople, is also primarily concerned with internal Christian interests. It forbids theatre and circus performances in all cities on Sundays and Christian festivals, so that the Christians may devote themselves entirely to worship. With a passing shot against Jews and pagans, it adds: 'Although some people are still trapped in the madness of Jewish godlessness or in the error of foolish paganism, they are to know that there are times for prayer and other times for pleasures.' Jews who observed the traditions had nothing to do with circus and theatre; the attack on them is of a piece with the spiteful rhetoric of many laws at this time. It is noticeable that such spiteful language against Jews is particularly evident in those laws that defend Christian interests, i.e. which probably originated in ecclesiastical circles or with officials who sided with the church. Although the sometimes anti-Jewish tone doubtless seemed threatening, it scarcely had any consequences for the day-to-day life of the Jews. From the Jewish point of view, the laws on slavery and conversions, which of course interfered with the law of inheritance, among other things, were more disturbing. However, we do not know of any consequences for the Jewish communities in Palestine.

The laws mentioned so far fundamentally aimed at separating the Christian community from the Jewish, in Christianity's interests. As far as the Christians were concerned they attempted to safeguard the present situation; the barrier was to be permeable from the Jewish to the Christian side, but not the reverse.

However, a second large complex of laws dealt with the Jews directly, their privileges, their self-government, their freedom of worship and religion. Since the time of Constantine the only laws in this context related to the question of *curia* duties (beginning with CTh XVI.8.3, dated 321); these have been extensively discussed earlier. These exemptions are clearly modelled on the regulations for the Christian clergy (CTh XVI.8.2, 4, dated 330 and 331; explicitly so XII.1.99 and XVI.8.13, dated 383 and 397 respectively). It was natural that Jews who were not exempt from the *curia* were held to their duties (CTh XII.1.158, dated 398, for southern Italy; XII.1.165, dated 399, for universal application). It should be stressed that all these laws are couched in sober, neutral legal language, and that several of them contain a recognition of regular forms of Jewish self-government.

Internal Jewish self-government was strengthened as early as Constantine's law CTh XVI.8.2, dated 330, exempting Jewish religious officials from *curia* duties only if they are subject to the patriarch and the elders. As for the patriarchate, it has already been pointed out that its official status reached its zenith in laws from 392. Apart from the special case of CTh XVI.8.14 (Milan 399), which abuses the patriarch, the language of the laws is neutral to reverential. The limitation of the internal Jewish jurisdiction to religious matters and adjudication (CTh II.1.10, dated 398) should not be understood as an anti-Jewish measure, but belongs in the government's attempts to standardize the legal system. It should be stressed that as late as 396, a law addressed to the Jews by Arcadius (CTh XVI.8.10, dated 27 February 396) awards them and their leaders the sole right of determining market prices: 'For it is just to leave to each their own business.' Any interference by outsiders is threatened with punishment. And CTh XVI.8.20 and VIII.8.8 (both Ravenna, 26 July 412) still determine that Jews may not be commanded to appear in court or any other office on the Sabbath. The serious intervention in internal Jewish organization only came with the abolition of the patriarchate between 415 and 429.

The legislature expressly recognized synagogues as religious buildings (Trier, CTh VII.8.2, dated 373?). From 393, laws protecting these became necessary, and CTh XVI.8.21, dated 418?, from Illyria, for the first time also contained a warning to the Jews not to become overconfident, relying on their legal protection. CTh XVI.8.25, dated 423, brought a clear deterioration of the Jews' situation, in favour of Christians who had committed attacks on synagogues. If their interests appeared to demand it, the Christians no longer had to return the synagogues, but could offer other properties by way of replacement. They could also keep objects taken from the synagogues if they offered financial compensation. Threats of punishment against Christians are no longer mentioned, but the Jews were forbidden to build new synagogues. XVI.8.26, published only a short while later, abuses the Jews before confirming the legal protection for synagogues, and then threatens them with punishment if they dare to circumcise non-Jews.

Thus the year 423 was clearly a low point for the Jews. Since the legislature only protected them half-heartedly after repeated Christian attacks on their synagogues, and forbade the building of new synagogues, its assurances that 'the religious denomination of the Jews is forbidden by no law' (CTh XVI.8.9, dated 393), and that 'the Jews are to keep to their own ceremonies'

(CTh XVI.8.13, dated 397), were at least temporarily robbed of their force.

A development which was to have serious consequences for the Jews began with their gradual exclusion from the civil service. By 22 April 404, Honorius had already excluded Jews and Samaritans from service as *agentes in rebus* (intelligence service), in CTh XVI.8.16. CTh XVI.8.24, published by Honorius on 10 March 418 in Ravenna, attempted a more comprehensive ruling:

> Those who live according to the Jewish superstition are forbidden to enter the imperial service [*militia*] in future. Thus whoever has already taken the oath of service in the intelligence service or with the Palatini is hereby permitted to finish his service and pursue the legal career to its end, and we will ignore this fact, without showing favour. However, in future it shall not be permitted, although we shall overlook it for the present in the case of a few persons. As regards those who are bound to the perversity of that people and who are proved to have [nevertheless] attempted to enter the armed services, we order explicitly that they must return their belts of office. Any previous merits will not avail. We will certainly not deny the freedom to practise as lawyers to any Jews who have completed the relevant course of study. We also permit them to enjoy the honour of the duties [*munera*] of the *curia*, which are theirs by right of birth and the splendour of their family. This must suffice for them; therefore they are not to regard the prohibition of imperial service [*militia*] as discrimination.

The permission to continue serving on the *curia* must have seemed like mockery in view of the burdens associated with it.

The *Constitutiones Sirmondianae*, a collection of church laws, contains a law of Valentinian, published on 9 July 425 in Aquileia and addressed to the *Praefectus praetorio* for Gaul. It expands this exclusion from certain occupations and gives it a Christian justification. After forbidding Manichees and all other heretics to stay in cities, it says: 'Jews and pagans are also refused permission to represent cases at law or to belong to the imperial service. We do not wish persons who belong to the Christian religion to serve such people, so that they may not exchange the venerable religion for the sect, because of the occasion offered by their masters' (CSirm 6).

Although this legislation was to have such serious consequences for the further development of the Jews' legal position in Christian countries, it must be stressed that all the laws mentioned here were published in the western empire and primarily addressed a specific problem of the western Diaspora, before they were taken up into the Codex Theodosianus. We do not know how many Jews were affected by these rulings. But we can hardly be wrong to assume that they were of little importance for the Jewish heartland of Palestine. A Jewish gravestone from Jaffa, whose title shows it to belong to the fourth century, names one Tanchum, son of Simon, as a *centenarius* (equal to the earlier *centurio*) of the frontier troops.[4] Another grave inscription, from Beth Shearim, mentions a man who was the father of R. Paregorios and of the *Palatinus* Julian;[5] thus Julian was an imperial tax official. Finally, we encountered a lawyer in the synagogue inscriptions. However, such Jewish officials or soldiers in Palestine were surely a tiny minority. For religious reasons alone, a career in the civil service must have remained exceptional. At most, work as a lawyer could have seemed worth pursuing in the interests of one's own community.

The third *novella* of Theodosius, dated 31 January 438, summarizes a number of anti-Jewish rulings of the preceding years, but does not therefore represent a systematic definition of Theodosius' Jewish policy. Rather, the text gives the impression of being a solemn programmatic pronouncement on the occasion of the emperor's thirtieth regnal anniversary. The preamble would fit this understanding, in which he describes concern for the true religion as one of the principal interests of his reign, and (aged 37!) announces his intention of handing down the experience of his long life as an eternal law for posterity.

Who would not, the text goes on to say, in view of the wonderful order of nature, ask after the creator of such a work? 'The Jews, whose senses are blinded, the Samaritans, pagans and the other kinds of heretical monsters dare to do this.' The fact that the accusation, at least in such a generalized form, is incorrect as regards Jews and Samaritans does not worry the emperor. He concludes from it as an eternal law: Jews and Samaritans may not

---

[4] *CIJ* II, 132 (No. 920). See S. Applebaum, 'Jews and Service in the Roman Army', *Roman Frontier Studies*, Tel Aviv 1967, 182.
[5] Text in M. Schwabe and B. Lifshitz, *Beth Sche'arim* II, Jerusalem 1967, No. 61.

obtain dignities or honours, nor an office in civic administration, not even the function of defender of the city. Whoever is at enmity with the highest majesty and the Roman laws cannot appear as the avenger of these laws. It would be an insult to the faith if such people could pronounce verdicts against Christians, and even against bishops. Furthermore, Theodosius forbids the construction of new synagogues, and only synagogues that are in imminent danger of collapse may be restored. Whoever entices a Christian, whether slave or free, to join another religion, is threatened with capital punishment and loss of property. Whoever has gained an office under false pretences is to lose the honour, whoever has built a synagogue is to know 'that he has built to the advantage of the Catholic church'. Honours gained under false pretences are without effect, and building work on a synagogue that is not simply repair work entails a penalty of fifty pounds of gold; in addition, the building is confiscated. Finally, the *novella* orders that members of any religious community whatsoever continue to be obliged to take on the burdens of the *curia* and also the duties of a court usher (*cohortalinus*), in the public interest, and are not exempt. The only qualification is that clerks (*adparitores*) are only permitted to execute the judgement of the court in private cases, and that they are not permitted to serve as prison overseers, so that they may not be in charge of Christian prisoners. Finally, the text mentions further regulations for pagans and heretics.

The *novella*, which is formulated in a highly rhetorical style full of repetitions, represents the strictest, most comprehensive attack of any emperor against all non-Catholics. It not only abuses them, but prevents them from taking up any posts in the civil service, except where the duties are such that anyone would gladly avoid them. It also ghettoizes the non-Catholic groups by completely forbidding conversion to them, and further limits freedom of religion by prohibiting the building of new synagogues.

However, the question remains to what extent the *novella* was effective in practice. We return here to the text of CTh XVI.5.46, dated 409, quoted earlier, according to which Jews are not to think that earlier laws were no longer valid, and which threatens Roman civil servants with punishment if they do not apply the laws, or are careless in doing so. As A. H. M. Jones emphasizes, we assume too readily that Roman citizens obeyed the laws:

My own impression is that many, if not most, laws were intermittently and sporadically enforced, and that their chief evidential value is to prove that the abuses which they were intended to remove were known to the central government. The laws, in my view, are clues to the difficulties of the empire, and records of the aspirations of the government and not its achievement.

Elsewhere, Jones writes: 'Except for their exclusion from the public service and the bar the Jews thus incurred no serious civil disabilities until the reign of Justin.' Despite the increasing pressure of public opinion, the government remained relatively tolerant towards the Jews.[6]

A general answer to the question of the consequences of these laws in daily life, especially of the third *novella*, is not possible. The necessary evidence is not available. With some caution, we may perhaps maintain that the exclusions from professions were the most effective, as is also attested by a number of passages in the Church Fathers from this period. It was more difficult to oversee the prohibitions of possessing Christian slaves and of converting to Judaism. The church is likely to have been principally concerned with this, and to have denounced possible transgressions to the authorities. As regards the construction of new synagogues, we may state with certainty that this prohibition was observed in Palestine for a short time at most, and that in the following centuries very many new synagogues were built. Altogether, the Jews of the Diaspora were probably more affected by the legislation than the Jewish community of Palestine. This was principally affected by the abolition of the patriarchate, but was apparently able to maintain its unity even without it.

Avi-Yonah's assertion that from 383 the Roman state mounted an all-out attack on Judaism is clearly not correct in this sweeping form. Even after the law against Gamaliel of 415 there are still laws that represent improvements on earlier edicts, for example CTh XVI.9.3,4, dated 415 or 417, which permits Jews to own Christian slaves in certain circumstances, and also XVI.8.23, dated 416, permiting Jewish converts to return to Judaism in certain circumstances. The barring of certain professions for Jews from 404 was probably limited to the western empire, and became

---

[6] Jones, *LRE* VIII and 948.

effective in the eastern empire also only with the promulgation of the Codex Theodosianus and with the third *novella* in 438. Certainly the laws protecting synagogues, from 393, show that the Jewish communities were increasingly subject to attacks from the Christian mob and the church. But as yet the legislature is firmly on the side of law and order.

As regards the eastern empire, the laws show a worsening of the general atmosphere for Jews only in the years 423–425, under the *Praefectus praetorio* Asclepiodotus, although he was still denounced as too friendly towards the Jews by fanatical Christians. A further low was reached in the year 438 with the third *novella*. But even the promulgation of the Codex Theodosianus did not mean the legal situation was now completely uniform. This is attested, for example, by the contradictory rulings on the matter of Christian slaves of Jewish owners which were included side by side in the collection of laws and thus offered the authorities a certain amount of room to manoeuvre. Otherwise it would not have been necessary to publish laws repeatedly in the following decades on questions which in theory were already covered in law.

2. Barsauma: Pressure from Anti-Jewish Fanatics?

The laws of 423 protecting synagogues are sometimes regarded as a reaction to the riots of the fanatical monks belonging to the Mesopotamian abbot Barsauma. Equally, the anti-Jewish rulings of the third *novella* are occasionally put down to events in Jerusalem in 438; here too this Syrian monk is said to have been at the centre. Thus we shall now consider the story of Barsauma, since it may illustrate the pressure exerted by fanatical monks on the Christian legislation regarding the Jews, at a decisive moment.

Until the beginning of this century we knew almost nothing about the Mesopotamian monk Barsauma. All that was known was his participation in the 'Robber Council' of Ephesus in 449 and the Council of Chalcedon two years later. Then F. Nau published, in several sections, excerpts from the Syriac biography of Barsauma, which also appears to offer important insights into the history of Palestine in the early fifth century, as F. Nau pointed out in a later study.[7] The full text of the biography has still not been published.

---

[7] F. Nau, *Revue de l'Orient Chrétien* 18 (1913) 272–6; 379–89; 19 (1914) 113–34; 278–89, offers a summary of the text; id., 'Deux épisodes'.

Barsauma (not to be confused with Barsauma of Nisibis, who was a Nestorian; our Barsauma was a Monophysite) is said to have been born near Samosata and to have become a monk at an early age. Around 400 he went on pilgrimage to Jerusalem for the first time, when a large number of pagans still lived in Palestine, and when the Jews and Samaritans persecuted the Christians. In the years 419–422, he is then said to have marched to Jerusalem with forty monks, and further to the Sinai desert, and on the way to have destroyed temples and synagogues. The Syriac text gives a detailed description of the destruction of the synagogue of Rabbat Moab east of the Jordan, which is said to have been comparable to the Temple of Solomon in its size and splendour. The laws protecting synagogues, which were published in letters addressed to the *Praefectus praetorio* Asclepiodotus and which also protected the pagan temples, were in Nau's opinion a reaction to the attacks of these fanatical monks. According to Nau, Asclepiodotus, who was an uncle of the empress Eudokia (according to the *Life* of Simeon Stylites), and probably still a pagan, was behind these laws favourable to Jews and pagans, together with the empress, who was not baptized until 421.[8]

Barsauma, together with a hundred brothers, is said to have travelled again to Palestine in 438. Travelling by sea via Cyprus, the monks probably landed at Caesarea and then went on to Jerusalem via Sebaste. At Eudokia's request, the two met, and the Augusta exchanged a valuable veil for the ascetic's coat. At that time Eudokia permitted the Jews, who had petitioned her, to pray at the site of the Temple in Jerusalem. Thereupon 'the priests and leaders of Galilee' addressed a letter to the people of the Jews: 'Know that the time of the dispersion of our people has come to an end, and that the day of the reuniting of our tribes has come. For see, the kings of the Romans have ordered that our city of Jerusalem is to be returned to us. Hurry to come to Jerusalem for the feast of Tabernacles, since our kingdom will be restored in Jerusalem.'

Meanwhile, Barsauma had come to Jerusalem again with his monks, startled by the rumours. On the first day of the feast of Tabernacles he entered the city secretly and remained hidden in a monastery. But one or two of his monks went to the Temple square to see the pinnacles of the Temple, and there saw the Jews

---

[8] F. Nau, 'Deux épisodes', 192f. On Asclepiodotus, see also *PLRE* II, 160.

lamenting. The two groups clashed and there were a number of persons killed among the Jews. Then the Jews, accompanied by Romans, went to Eudokia, who was at Bethlehem. In response to their charges, eighteen monks were arrested, but judgement was left to the governor, who had been summoned from Caesarea. But Barsauma succeeded in obtaining the release of his monks, since the bodies of the Jews showed no wounds, so that they must have died a natural death.

Nau's historical reconstruction sets Barsauma's third visit to Jerusalem at the beginning of 438, and the fourth visit in October of the same year. Then at the end of the year Eudokia was back in Constantinople, and her report led to the anti-Jewish third *novella* of Theodosius, which accordingly should be dated to January 439, instead of 438.[9]

The Syriac biography of Barsauma offers no dates. F. Nau has inferred them by comparison with a number of sources, e.g. the Codex Theodosianus with its laws of 423 protecting synagogues, the statements about Eudokia's journey to the Holy Land and the Syriac biography of Simeon Stylites. However, a number of problems arise. Not only does he unnecessarily transfer Simeon's intervention against the imperial protection of the synagogues to the year 438 (instead of the usual date of 423); but there is no proof that Asclepiodotus was in Antioch when the empress gained that city's goodwill on her journey to Jerusalem, nor that he ordered compensation to be given for the destruction of a synagogue during her stay there. Rather, the *Life* of Simeon probably refers to Asclepiodotus (as Consul Asclepiades) only because of the laws of 423 connected with his name, on account of which he was exaggeratedly described as sympathizing with pagans and Jews (despite the insulting language of these laws against the Jews!) and as an enemy of Christians.

As regards the dating of the third *novella*, there are various reasons for giving the year 439: there is manuscript evidence for it, also the fact that a date in January 438 would make it hard to understand why it was not incorporated in the Codex, which was promulgated later. However, neither is a conclusive argument, which is why Th. Mommsen retained 438 in his edition of the text.

---

[9] F. Nau, 'Deux épisodes', 205f.; he is followed, e.g., by E. Demougeot, 'La politique antijuive de Théodose II', *Akten des XI. internationalen Byzantinisten-kongresses München 1958*, Munich 1960, 95–100, 97f.

It is not necessary to understand the *novella* as a reaction to the reports of Eudokia, already returned from her pilgrimage. Nor is a circular argument permissible, concluding from the hypothesis that the text reacts to Eudokia's report that it must have a later date.

Fitting two journeys to Jerusalem by Barsauma into the same year 438 also raises difficulties, although it would not be wholly impossible for both journeys to take place in this short interval. Therefore M. Avi-Yonah dates Barsauma's fourth journey to the period of Eudocia's exile to Jerusalem from 443. The letter of the Jewish leaders of Galilee to the Jews of the Diaspora, quoted in the *Life* of Barsauma, is in his opinion 'undoubtedly spurious, but it reflects the Jewish feelings at that time. The only practical result of such hopes was that Jews were now allowed to visit Jerusalem (perhaps even to settle there). This permission remained in force even after the anti-Jewish excesses instigated by the monk Bar-Sauma.'[10] Equally, K. G. Holum dates these events to the first years of the empress' exile. Her permission for Jews to pray in the Temple square was greeted with enthusiasm in the Diaspora, 'and many of the pious Jews made their way to the Holy City. Eudocia had created a Zionist movement and an explosive situation.'[11]

Although it is possible to find evidence for Jewish messianic expectations around 440, it would be going too far to make use of the Barsauma story in this context. E. Honigmann's brief analysis of the text has shown sufficiently clearly that it is of no use for historical purposes. According to him, the text was written around the middle of the sixth century, and thus cannot be the report of a pupil of Barsauma, i.e. of an eyewitness, as F. Nau had suggested. A large proportion of the content is legendary, although the text does reveal some knowledge of contemporary history and geography. Since neither the *Life* of Peter the Iberian nor the *Plerophoria* of John Rufus mentions the deeds of this first hero of the Monophysites in Jerusalem, Honigmann prefers to see in the present description rather a version of the events of 516–518, which are told by Cyril of Scythopolis in his *Vita Sabbae*.[12]

---

[10] M. Avi-Yonah, *Jews*, 224.
[11] K. G. Holum, *Theodosian Empresses. Women and Imperial Dominion in Late Antiquity*, Berkeley 1982, 217.
[12] E. Honigmann, *Le couvent de Barsauma et le patriarcat jacobite d'Antioche et de Syrie*, Louvain 1954 (cover: 1967), 6–23. Also sceptical is A. Baumstark, *Geschichte der syrischen Literatur*, Bonn 1922 (repr. Berlin 1968), 180.

Unfortunately, the publication of the complete text and a thorough analysis of it in the context of Syriac Christian literature remains to be accomplished; without doubt it would bring to light a number of stylizations and clichés in the dispute between the Syrian church and Judaism. Until such an analysis is available, any historical interpretation of the text should be handled with great caution, even though the anti-Jewish elements of this monastic legend fit very well with our other knowledge of the attitude of monks to Judaism at this period, in particular of the uneducated monks of Syria and Egypt. Another reservation should also be mentioned here. W. Cramer thinks it a fact that in the east theological conflicts even ended with the destruction of churches and synagogues, but describes reports of such events as 'unreliable hagiographical legends ... in which such stories belong to the *Genus litterarium*, so that nothing can be learned from them for the individual, concrete case in question. In any case, such mutual destruction of churches is also reported for internal Christian disputes, and is therefore not only typical of the quarrels between Christians and Jews.'[13]

S. Safrai, speaking of a hatred of Jews which was stirred up in particular by Church Fathers and monks, and of the attacks by fanatics against the Jews and their institutions, goes on to say: 'The case of the monk Barsauma of Nisibis, who roamed over Palestine with a band of followers in the years 419–422 and razed synagogues, was only an instance that had many parallels in the Diaspora'.[14] But there is not sufficient evidence for this. There is still a pervasive danger in Jewish historiography of accepting too uncritically as a fact anything that can support a history of Jewish suffering, although the opposite danger of being too quick to play down traces of anti-Semitism in history cannot be denied.

3. The Effects of a Century of Christian Rule?

As the result of our survey we may note that the Jewish population of Palestine did not suffer to the extent that is often stated during the first century of Christian rule. Certainly, in the course of time

---

[13] W. Cramer in K. H. Rengstorf and S. von. Kortzfleisch (eds.), *Kirche und Synagoge* I, Stuttgart 1968, 209 n. 78.

[14] S. Safrai in H. H. Ben-Sasson (ed.), *A History of the Jewish People*, London 1976, 349.

the Christian pressure increased, even in Palestine. But, by contrast to the Diaspora, we cannot prove any destruction of synagogues by fanatical Christians. Neither do we have any evidence for forcible baptisms at this period in the Holy Land, by contrast to Minorca, for example, where on the arrival of the relics of St. Stephen there were anti-Jewish riots and forcible baptisms.[15]

Finally, there was probably no change for the worse in the share of Jews in the population of Palestine, despite the fact that Jerome writes: 'Compared with their previous numbers, scarcely one-tenth of them remains.'[16] Which period of comparison does he refer to, and how does he justify his opinion? S. W. Baron believes that, despite the exaggeration even in respect of Palestine, which this statement is primarily concerned with, it nevertheless reflects 'the enormous shrinkage in Jewish manpower throughout the empire'.[17] But is not Jerome here proceeding from exegetical motives, rather than actual observation? For the synagogue excavations in Palestine show that the Jewish population by no means shrank in the fifth to sixth centuries, but rather expanded, and certainly maintained its economical position.

Naturally Palestinian Judaism was restricted by the advance of Christianity, which gradually attained the majority in the country. But the Jews were still in a position to share in the general prosperity of the country; for specifically at this period, when it became the place of Eudokia's exile, Palestine remained an important spiritual centre of the empire, and also profited by this economically. Eudokia's repetition of Helena's pilgrimage gave new impetus to the institution of pilgrimage, and Jerusalem's elevation to be a patriarchate in its own right, which occurred shortly afterwards, freed it from the spiritual domination of Alexandria or Antioch. Although many laws were now in place that shielded Christianity from Judaism and for this reason limited the career prospects of Jews, yet the situation of Jews in the Roman empire, and Palestine in particular, continued to be characterized by the principle incorporated in the Codex Theodosianus: *The Jewish religion is forbidden by no law.*

---

[15] Cf. G. Stemberger, 'Zwangstaufen von Juden im 4.-7. Jahrhundert. Mythos oder Wirklichkeit?', in C. Thoma et al. (eds.), *Judentum – Ausblicke und Einsichten* (*Festschrift* Kurt Schubert), Frankfurt 1993, 81–114.

[16] Jerome, *Comm. Isa.* 6.11–13 (CC 73, 94).

[17] S. W. Baron, *A Social and Religious History of the Jews* II, New York ²1952, 210.

Thus the history of the first Christian century in Palestine was certainly not always easy and pleasant for the Jewish population, but neither is there any occasion to write a history of sorrow and suffering. The Jewish tradition proved itself to be stronger and more full of life than people often gave it credit for, both at the time and later.

Bibliography

This bibliography only comprises titles occurring several times, which are cited in abbreviated form in the footnotes. All other titles are to be found in the footnotes with full bibliographical information.

Abel, F.-M., *Géographie de la Palestine*, 2 vols., Paris ³1967.
Adler, M., 'The Emperor Julian and the Jews', *JQR* 5 (1893), 591–651.
Alon, G., *The Jews in Their Land in the Talmudic Age* II, Jerusalem 1984.
——, *Jews, Judaism and the Classical World*, Jerusalem 1977.
Avigad, N., *Discovering Jerusalem*, Oxford 1984.
Avi-Yonah, M., *The Jews of Palestine: A Political History from the Bar Kokhba War to the Arab Conquest*, Oxford 1976.
——, 'The Economics of Byzantine Palestine', *IEJ* 8 (1958), 39–51.
Bachrach, B. S., 'The Jewish Community of the Later Roman Empire as Seen in the *Codex Theodosianus*', in J. Neusner, E. S. Frerichs (eds.), *'To See Ourselves as Others See Us': Christians, Jews, 'Others' in Late Antiquity*, Atlanta 1985, 399–421.
Bacher, W., *Die Agada der palästinensischen Amoräer* III, Strasbourg 1899 (repr. Hildesheim 1965).
Bagatti, B., *Alle origini della chiesa. I: Le comunità giudeo-cristiane, II: Le comunità gentilo-cristiane*, Vatican 1981–2.
Baras, Z., Safrai, S., Tsafrir, Y., Stern, M. (eds.), *Eretz Israel from the Destruction of the Second Temple to the Muslim Conquest* (Hebrew), I, Jerusalem 1982.
Ben-Dov, M., *The Dig at the Temple Mount* (Hebrew), Jerusalem 1982.
Bieberstein, K., Bloedhorn, H., *Jerusalem. Grundzüge der Baugeschichte vom Chalkolithikum bis zur Frühzeit der osmanischen Herrschaft*, 3 vols., Wiesbaden 1994.
Bonfils, G. de, *Gli schiavi degli ebrei nella legislazione del IV secolo. Storia di un divieto*, Bari 1992.
Bowersock, G. W., *Julian the Apostate*, London 1978.
Bowman, J., *Samaritanische Probleme*, Stuttgart 1967.
Brock, S. P., 'The Rebuilding of the Temple under Julian. A New Source', *PEQ* 108 (1976), 103–7.
——, 'A Letter Attributed to Cyril of Jerusalem on the Rebuilding of the Temple', *BSOAS* 40 (1977), 267–86.
Broshi, M., 'The Population of Western Palestine in the Roman-Byzantine Period', *BASOR* 236 (1979), 1–10.
Browning, R., *The Emperor Julian*, Berkeley 1976.
Chiat, M. J. S., *Handbook of Synagogue Architecture*, Chico 1982.

Cohen, J., 'Roman Imperial Policy Toward the Jews from Constantine Until the End of the Palestinian Patriarchate', *Byzantine Studies* 3 (1976), 1–29.
Cohen, J. M., *A Samaritan Chronicle*, Leiden 1981.
Corbo, V., *Il Santo Sepolcro di Gerusalemme*, 3 vols., Jerusalem 1982.
——, *Cafarnao I: Gli edifici della città*, Jerusalem 1975.
Coüasnon, C., *The Church of the Holy Sepulchre in Jerusalem*, London 1974.
Crown, A. D. (ed.), *The Samaritans*, Tübingen 1989.
Crown, A. D., Pummer, R., Tal, A. (eds.), *A Companion to Samaritan Studies*, Tübingen 1993.
Crowfoot, J. W., *Early Churches in Palestine*, London 1941 (repr. Munich 1980).
Dan, Y., *The City in Eretz-Israel During the Late Roman and Byzantine Periods* (Hebrew), Jerusalem 1984.
——, 'Palaestina Salutaris (Tertia) and its Capital', *IEJ* 32 (1982), 134–7.
Donner, H., *Pilgerfahrt ins Heilige Land: Die ältesten Berichte christlicher Palästinapilger (4.-7. Jahrhundert)*, Stuttgart 1979.
Dothan, M., *Hammath Tiberias. Early Synagogues and the Hellenistic and Roman Remains*, Jerusalem 1983.
Dubnow, S., *Weltgeschichte des jüdischen Volkes* III, Berlin 1926.
Esbroeck, M. van, 'Jean II de Jérusalem et les cultes de S. Etienne, de la Sainte-Sion et de la croix', *Analecta Bollandiana* 102 (1984), 99–134.
Frankel, Z., 'Der Aufstand in Palästina zur Zeit des Gallus', *MGWJ* 16 (1867), 143–51.
Fuks, G., *Scythopolis – A Greek City in Eretz-Israel* (Hebrew), Jerusalem 1983.
Geiger, J., 'The Last Jewish Revolt Against Rome: A Reconsideration', *Scripta Classica Israelica* 5 (1979f.), 250–7.
Geva, H., 'The Camp of the Tenth Legion in Jerusalem: An Archaeological Reconsideration', *IEJ* 34 (1984), 239–54.
Goodblatt, D., *The Monarchic Principle. Studies in Jewish Self-Government in Antiquity*, Tübingen 1994.
Graetz, H., *Geschichte der Juden* IV, Leipzig ^{4}1908.
Gregg, R. C., Urman, D., *Jews, Pagans and Christians in the Golan Heights. Greek and Other Inscriptions of the Roman and Byzantine Eras*, Atlanta 1997.
Hachlili, R., *Ancient Jewish Art and Archaeology in the Land of Israel*, Leiden 1988.
Hachlili, R., (ed.), *Ancient Synagogues in Israel*, Oxford 1989.
Hezser, C., *The Social Structure of the Rabbinic Movement in Roman Palestine*, Tübingen 1997.
Hüttenmeister, F., *Die antiken Synagogen in Israel I: Die judischen Synagogen, Gerichtshöfe und Lehrhäuser*, Wiesbaden 1977.
Hunt, E. D., *Holy Land Pilgrimage in the Later Roman Empire AD 312–460*, Oxford 1982.

Jacobs, M., *Die Institution des jüdischen Patriarchen*, Tübingen 1995.
Jeremias, J., *Heiligengräber in Jesu Umwelt*, Göttingen 1958.
Jones, A. H. M., *The Later Roman Empire*, Oxford 1964.
Juster, J., *Les juifs dans l'empire romain*, 2 vols., Paris 1914.
Kasher, M. M., *Torah Shelemah* XIII, New York ²1954.
Kippenberg, H. G., *Garizim und Synagoge*, Berlin 1971.
Klein, S., *Sefer ha-jischub* I, Jerusalem 1939.
Langenfeld, H., *Christianisierungspolitik und Sklavengesetzgebung der römischen Kaiser von Konstantin bis Theodosius II*, Bonn 1977.
Levine, L. I., *Caesarea under Roman Rule*, Leiden 1975.
———, 'The Jewish Patriarch (Nasi) in Third Century Palestine, *ANRW* II 19/2, Berlin 1979, 649–88
Lewy, Y.(H.), 'Julian the Apostate and the Building of the Temple', *The Jerusalem Cathedra* 3 (1983), 70–96 (a complete version in *Zion* 6, 1940f., 1–32, Hebrew).
Lieberman, S., 'Palestine in the Third and Fourth Centuries', *JQR* 36 (1945f.), 329–70; 37 (1946f.), 31–54 (repr. in id., *Texts and Studies*, New York 1974, 112–77).
Lifshitz, B., *Donateurs et fondateurs dans les synagogues juives*, Paris 1967.
Limor, O., 'Christian Tradition – Jewish Authority' (Hebrew), *Cathedra* 80 (1996), 31–62.
Linder, A., 'The Roman Imperial Government and the Jews under Constantine' (Hebrew), *Tarbiz* 44 (1974f.), 95–143.
———, *The Jews in Roman Imperial Legislation*, Detroit/Jerusalem 1987.
Loffreda, S., 'The Late Chronology of the Synagogue at Capernaum', *IEJ* 23 (1973), 37–42.
Lucas, L., *Zur Geschichte der Juden im vierten Jahrhundert*, Berlin 1910.
MacDonald, J., *The Theology of the Samaritans*, London 1964.
Mahler, E., *Handbuch der jüdischen Chronologie*, Frankfurt 1916 (repr. Hildesheim 1967).
Maier, J., *Jüdische Auseinandersetzung mit dem Christentum in der Antike*, Darmstadt 1982.
Manns, F., Aliata, E. (eds.), *Early Christianity in Context: Festschrift for E. Testa*, Jerusalem 1993.
Mantel, H., *Studies in the History of the Sanhedrin*, Cambridge, Mass. 1961.
Maraval, P., *Lieux saints et pèlerinages d'Orient. Histoire et Géographie. Des origines à la conquête arabe*, Paris 1985.
Mayerson, P., 'The City of Elusa in the Literary Sources of the Fourth–Sixth Centuries', *IEJ* 33 (1983), 247–53.
Mazar, B., (with the co-operation of G. Cornfeld), *Der Berg des Herrn. Neue Ausgrabungen in Jerusalem*, Bergisch Gladbach 1979.
Meyers, E. M., Strange, J. F., Meyers, C. L., *Excavations at Ancient Meiron, Upper Galilee, Israel, 1971–72, 1974–75, 1977*, Cambridge, MA 1981.
Miller, S. S., *Studies in the History and Traditions of Sepphoris*, Leiden 1984.
Montgomery, J. A., *The Samaritans*, Philadelphia 1907 (repr. 1968).

Nathanson, B. G., *The Fourth Century Jewish 'Revolt' During the Reign of Gallus*, doctoral dissertation Duke University, Durham, NC 1981.

Nau, F., 'Deux épisodes de l'histoire juive sous Théodose II (423 et 438) d'après la vie de Barsauma le Syrien', *REJ* (1927), 184–206.

Naveh, J., *On Stone and Mosaic. The Aramaic and Hebrew Inscriptions from Ancient Synagogues* (Hebrew), Jerusalem 1978.

Neusner, J., *Judaism in Society. The Evidence of the Yerushalmi*, Chicago 1983.

——, 'The Experience of the City in Late Antique Judaism', W. S. Green (ed.), *Approaches to Ancient Judaism* V, Atlanta 1985, 37–52.

Noethlichs, K. L., *Die gesetzgeberischen Maßnahmen der christlichen Kaiser des vierten Jahrhunderts gegen Häretiker, Heiden und Juden*, doctoral dissertation Cologne 1971.

Parkes, J., *The Conflict of the Church and the Synagogue*, London 1934 (repr. New York 1974).

Pharr, C., *The Theodosian Code and Novels, and the Sirmondian Constitutions*, Princeton 1952.

Phillips, C. R., 'Julian's Rebuilding of the Temple. A sociological analysis of religious competition', *SBLSP* 2 (1979), 167–72.

Rabello, A. M., 'On the Relations between Diocletian and the Jews', *JJS* 35 (1984), 147–67.

——, 'The Legal Condition of the Jews in the Roman Empire', *ANRW* II 13, Berlin/New York (1980), 662–762.

Reeg, G., *Die antiken Synagogen in Israel II: Die samaritanischen Synagogen*, Wiesbaden 1977.

Roth-Gerson, L., *The Greek Inscriptions from the Synagogues in Eretz-Israel*, Jerusalem 1987.

Russell, K. W., 'The Earthquake Chronology of Palestine and Northwest Arabia from the 2nd through the mid-8th Century A.D.', *BASOR* 260 (1985), 37–59.

Safrai, Z., *Gebulot we-Schelton be-Eretz Israel be-Tequfat ha-Mischna we-haTalmud*, Tel Aviv 1980.

Schäfer, P., 'Der Aufstand gegen Gallus Caesar', *Tradition and Re-Interpretation in Jewish and Early Christian Literature. Essays in Honour of J. C. H. Lebram*, Leiden 1986, 184–201.

Schmid, W., 'Die Koexistenz von Serapiskult und Christentum im Hadriansbrief bei Vopiscus (Quadr. tyr. 8)', *Bonner Historia Augusta-Colloquium 1964/1965*, Bonn 1966, 153–84.

Schwabe, M., 'The Letters of Libanius to the Patriarch of Palestine' (Hebrew), *Tarbiz* 1.2 (1930), 85–110.

——, 'A New Document Relating to the History of the Jews in the 4th Century C. E., Libanius ep. 1251 (F)' (Hebrew), *Tarbiz* 1.3 (1930), 107–21.

——, 'Chapters on Hellenistic Palestine at the Time of the Redaction of

Talmud Yerushalmi. I: The Hellenistic High Priest in the Days of Julian the Apostate' (Hebrew), *Tarbiz* 5 (1933f.), 358–69.

Schwemer, A. M., *Studien zu den frühjüdischen Prophetenlegenden. Vitae Prophetarum*, 2 vols., Tübingen 1995–6.

Simon, M., *Verus Israel*, Paris ²1964 (repr. 1983).

———, *Recherches d'Histoire Judéo-Chrétienne*, Paris 1962.

Smallwood, E. M., *The Jews under Roman Rule*, Leiden 1976.

Sperber, D., *Roman Palestine 200-400 – Money and Prices*, Ramat Gan 1974.

———, *Roman Palestine 200–400. The Land. Crisis and Change in Agrarian Society as Reflected in Rabbinic Sources*, Ramat Gan 1978.

Stern, M., *Greek and Latin Authors on Jews and Judaism*, 3 vols., Jerusalem 1974–84.

Strobel, K., 'Jüdisches Patriarchat, Rabbinentum und Priesterdynastie von Emesa: Historische Phänomene innerhalb des Imperium Romanum der Kaiserzeit', *Ktema* 14 (1989, published 1993), 39–77.

Syme, R., 'Ipse ille Patriarcha', *Bonner Historia Augusta Colloquium Bonn 1966/7*, Bonn 1968, 119–30.

Testa, E., *Il Simbolismo dei Giudeo-Cristiani*, Jerusalem 1962.

———, *I graffitti della Casa di S. Pietro (Cafarnao IV)*, Jerusalem 1972.

———, *The Faith of the Mother Church*, Jerusalem 1992.

Urman, D., 'Jewish Inscriptions of the Mishna and Talmud Period from Kazrin in the Golan' (Hebrew), *Tarbiz* 53 (1983f.), 513–45.

Urman D., Flesher, P. V. M. (eds.), *Ancient Synagogues. Historical Analysis and Archaeological Discovery*, 2 vols., Leiden 1995.

Vogt, J., *Kaiser Julian und das Judentum*, Leipzig 1939.

Walker, P. W. L., *Holy City, Holy Places? Christian Attitudes to Jerusalem and the Holy Land in the Fourth Century*, Oxford 1990.

Wewers, G. A., *Probleme der Bavot-Traktate. Ein redaktionskritischer und theologischer Beitrag zum Talmud Yerushalmi*, Tübingen 1984.

Wilken, R. L., *John Chrysosostom and the Jews. Rhetoric and Reality in the Late Fourth Century*, Berkeley 1983.

Wilkinson, J., 'Christian Pilgrims in Jerusalem During the Byzantine Period', *PEQ* 108 (1976), 75–101.

Zucker, *Studien zur jüdischen Selbstverwaltung im Altertum*, Berlin 1936.

Index of Passages Cited

1 Rabbinic writings

(a) Mishnah

Abot	IV.5	276
Jad	IV.6	107

(b) Tosefta

Ed	I.3	177
Pes	II.3	218
Qid	V.14	177

(c) Palestinian Talmud

AZ	I.2.39 c	176, 221
	I.5.39 d	65
	II.1.40 c	287
	II.4.41 c	287
	III.1.42 c	32, 259
	III.3.42 d	277
	III.13.43 b	31
	IV.4.43 d	31
	V.4.44 d	24, 218–21
BB	III.3.14 a	281
Ber	II.4.4 d–5 a	20
	II.8.5 c	32
	III.1.6 a	267, 273
	V.1.8 d–9 a	277
	V.1.9 a	136, 167
	V.4.9 c	278
	IX.1.12 d	278
Betsa	I.6.60 c	166f.
Bik	III.3.65 d	273, 279, 280, 282
BQ	III.1.3 c	284
Hag	I.8.76 d	286
Demai	II.1.22 c	19
Er	III.9.21 c	252, 273
Hor	III.9.48 c	14 n. 16, 32
Jeb	II.6.4 a	282
	VII.3.9 d	218
	XVI.2.15 c	166
Joma	III.7.40 d	274
	IV.4.41 d	173
Ket	I.2.25 b	281
	VII.8.31 c	176
	VII.9.31 d	280
	IX.10.33 b	281
	XI.1.34 d	281
Kil	III.1.28 c	272
Meg	III.1.73 d	139
	III.1.74 a	166
	III.2.74 a	261
	III.4.74 a	278
MQ	II.3.81 b	30
	III.1.81 d	285
MSh	V.2.56 a	207
	V.8.56 d	177
Ned	III.2.37 d	290
	III.12f. 38 a	287
Pea	I.1.16 a	32
	II.6.17 a	286
	VIII.7.21 a	280
Pes	IV.1.30 c	32
	IV.9.31 b	175, 281
	VI.1.33 a	273

Qid	III.14.64 d	282		7.2	282
	IV.1.65 d	218		10.7	285
Sanh	I.2.18 c	275		16.4	284
	III.6.21 b	166f., 281		31.16	166
	X.1.28 a	272		37.2	284
Shab	VI.8 a	136		43.6	98
	IX.2.12 a	272		49.9	284
	XII.3.13 c	32		63.10	284
Shebi	II.6.33 d	282		76.6	30
	IV.2.35 a	166		79.7	42
	IX.2.38 d	15		81.3	219
Sheq	V.2.48 d	280		83.5	286
	V.6.49 b	272		99.12	91
	VII.2.50 c	31	LamR	1.11	191
Sota	VII.1.21 a	278	QohR	9.8	207 n. 62
	IX.3.23 c	166	LevR	3.6	278f.
Taan	I.2.64 a	31, 279		22.4	285
	II.1.65 a	207, 279		23.4	279
	II. 1.65 a–b	14		25.1	280
	II.1.65 b	279		28.6	284 n. 18
	II.13.66 a	279		32.7	279
	III.4.66 d	279	MidrPs	5.6	46
	III.6.66 d	177		14.1	285
				18.36	207
				93.8	272

(d) Babylonian Talmud

			PesR	8	163
			PRK	2	16
Ber	28 b	93		6	284
Joma	69 a	167		24	284
Sanh	12 a	251, 273	SongR	2.5	13
Shab	155 b	279		2.18	286
Sota	49 b	259		7.7	286
Taan	23 b	273		7.9	284

(e) Midrashim   **2 Legal sources**

DtnR	1.7	174	CTh	I.4.2	35
EsthR	4.12	284		II.1.10	23, 240, 304
ExR	31.17	15			
GenR	6.3	285		III.1.55	200f.

Index of Passages Cited

IV.13.7	30	XVI.8.12	155
V.17.1	16	XVI.8.13	34, 235, 238, 303, 305
VII.8.2	154, 304		
VII.20.3–4	19		
VIII.8.8	304	XVI.8.14	248, 262, 304
IX.7.5	301		
IX.17.7	106	XVI.8.15	235, 241
IX.45.2	80, 300	XVI.8.16	137 n. 35, 226, 305
X.10.10	186		
X.20.8	176, 180	XVI.8.17	249
XII.1.55	33	XVI.8.18	302
XII.1.56	33	XVI.8.19	300
XII.1.99	33, 303	XVI.8.20	155, 304
XII.1.158	35, 303	XVI.8.21	155, 304
XII.1.165	35, 303	XVI.8.22	39, 156, 158, 235, 240, 262, 267, 301
XIII.5.18	226		
XV.5.5	302		
XVI.2.1.2	33		
XVI.2.3	33	XVI.8.23	264, 300, 308
XVI.2.5	27 n. 8		
XVI.5.44	302	XVI.8.24	137 n. 35, 305
XVI.5.46	302, 307		
XVI.7.3	299	XVI.8.25	156, 304
XVI.8.1	26, 36, 43f., 80, 170 n. 22, 235	XVI.8.26	157, 304
		XVI.8.27	156, 157
		XVI.8.28	80, 226
		XVI.8.29	246, 263, 265, 266 n. 71
XVI.8.2	27, 34 n. 23, 235, 238, 303		
		XVI.9.1	37, 300
XVI.8.3	26, 303	XVI.9.2	38, 39, 178f., 300
XVI.8.4	28, 303		
XVI.8.5	37	XVI.9.3	264, 301, 308
XVI.8.6	178f.		
XVI.8.7	181, 299	XVI.9.4	301, 308
XVI.8.8	235, 239	XVI.9.5	301
XVI.8.9	155, 156, 304	XVI.10.2–6	187
		XVI.10.7	196
XVI.8.10	304	XVI.10.10ff.	196
XVI.8.11	235, 241, 243	XVI.10.16	196
		XVI.10.21	196

XVI.10.22	198	CJust	1.8.1	68
XVI.10.25	196		1.9.7	23
Nov. 3	136, 158,		1.9.18	137 n. 23
	226, 306f.,		3.13.3	239
	309, 311f.		11.51.1	16

Const. Sirmond.
    4   38
    6   305

Index of Names and Subjects

Acco 65, 164, 165
Aelia Capitolina *see* Jerusalem
Alma 129
Ambrose 57, 155, 158, 194, 196, 202, 211 n. 70, 215
Ammianus Marcellinus 4, 16, 86, 169, 171, 173, 175, 184, 193, 202, 205, 211 and n. 70, 212, 215
Anaia 150f.
Arbel 141
Arcadius 33, 106, 149, 155, 298, 300, 304
Arians 74 and n. 73
army, military 10–12, 24, 32, 175, 183, 191, 281, 305
Ashdod 50
Ashkelon 9, 11, 16, 20, 50, 152, 191, 193f.
Augustine 114
Aurelius Victor 10, 162, 169, 171, 172, 174, 181, 183

Baba Rabba 222–9
Barʿam 129
Bethel 49, 70, 90, 103
Beth Gubrin (Eleutheropolis) 10, 50, 90, 104, 112, 113, 115, 122, 150, 152, 159, 193
Bethlehem 4, 42, 64, 83, 88, 94, 102, 104, 116, 119, 162
Beth Shean (Scythopolis) 9, 16, 18, 50, 72, 73, 74, 89, 97, 117, 139, 144, 159, 165, 175, 176, 177f., 180f., 190, 193, 228, 278
Beth Shearim 133–5, 159, 182, 234
Bordeaux Pilgrim 4, 7, 40–2, 52, 55, 57, 62, 64, 88–95, 101, 170 n. 20

Caesarea 4, 6, 9, 16, 18, 19, 20, 49, 62, 89, 138, 152, 159, 167, 176, 188, 191, 193, 221, 229, 260, 263, 266, 269f., 271, 273, 274, 278, 279, 282, 291, 292, 310, 311
calendar 5, 208, 236f., 249–58, 255 n. 53, 256 n. 54, 273, 276
Cana 103, 138
Capernaum 69, 73, 75, 103, 122, 126, 141, 143–8, 159, 183
Cassius Dio 54
Chariton 115
Chorazin 141–3, 147, 159, 183
Christians, Christianization 18f., 48–85, 287–9
churches 48–71, 82–85, 104, 191, 198
circumcision 23, 24, 35–40, 157, 181, 199, 221, 262, 282
city council *see curia*
Constantine 1, 9, 13, 15, 18, 25–47, 51, 55, 56–67, 71, 74, 80, 84, 86, 134, 145, 161, 170 n. 39, 186f., 202, 206, 213, 225, 235f., 238, 298, 299, 300
Constantius 30, 38, 47, 67, 72, 74, 134, 145, 162, 169,

Constantius (*cont.*)
170 and n. 22, 174, 175, 178 and n. 39, 180, 181, 184, 185, 187, 213, 236, 300f.
conversion 24, 25, 35–40, 60, 72, 80f., 179, 181, 213, 264, 299f., 307
Count (title) 73 and n. 70, 136
Count Joseph 36, 71–81, 246, 260, 276
curia (city council) 24, 26–35, 43, 45, 238, 239, 303, 305, 307
Cyril of Jerusalem 4, 14, 41, 42, 55, 62, 78, 81, 87 n. 7, 192, 198, 203, 206, 213, 214, 260f.

Dalton 129
Diocaesarea *see* Sepphoris
Diocletian 6f., 9, 10, 13f., 15f., 18, 23, 24 and n. 3, 49, 60, 86, 137, 142, 148, 176, 218, 220, 221, 236, 239, 290
Diospolis *see* Lydda
Dor 69, 70 n. 65, 82
Dora 189

Egeria 4, 57, 68, 78, 88, 95–100, 101, 108, 118
Ed-Dikke 131
Eilat (Aila) 7, 10f., 50, 52
El-Khirbe 227
Eleutheropolis *see* Beth Gubrin
Elijah 89, 94, 97, 100, 101, 103
Elusa 7, 189f., 191, 193
En Gedi 20, 70, 150
En Nashut 132
Ephrem the Syrian 202, 205, 209, 212

Epiphanius 4, 36, 41, 48, 70 and n. 72, 71–6, 79, 99, 115, 116, 136, 138, 219, 229, 246f., 252, 267
Eshtemo'a 150
Eudokia 84 and n. 99, 210, 310–12, 314
Eudoxia 70, 84, 197
Eusebius 4, 7, 10, 11, 18, 20, 38, 39, 40f., 42, 43, 49, 53, 55, 56, 59 and n. 38, 60, 62, 63, 64, 67, 68, 70, 72, 79 and n. 88, 80, 82, 83, 86, 90, 94, 97, 99, 102, 116, 141f., 150, 189, 195, 198, 229, 247, 260
Eustochium 84, 101, 116, 118
Euthymius 116f.
Evron 70
Expositio totius mundi 16, 176, 178, 193

fiscus Judaicus 25, 200, 246

Gadara 50, 72, 260
Gallus (revolt against) 3, 126, 134, 143, 147, 153, 161–84, 185, 225, 275, 281, 283
Gamaliel the Elder 108–11
Gamaliel (Patriarch) 110, 156, 158, 240f., 242, 244, 245, 256 n. 54, 260, 261f., 264, 267f., 268 n. 77, 301, 308
Gaza 9, 11, 16, 18, 50, 51, 59, 65, 67, 70, 71, 82f., 104, 115, 118, 190, 193f., 197f., 229
Gerizim 89, 219, 220, 222, 223, 225 and n. 14, 227, 228
Golan 9, 20, 30, 132f., 282
Goliath 89f.
Gratian 33, 34, 299
Gregory of Nazianzus 194,

Index of Names and Subjects

202, 204, 205, 209, 211 and n. 70, 212f., 215
Gregory of Nyssa 118
Gush Halav 125, 126, 128f., 130

Hammath Tiberias 145, 148f., 231–8, 250f., 257f.
Hebron 89, 102, 150
Helena 57, 58, 59, 64, 86, 142, 314
Hezekiah 93, 94
Hilarion 115, 117, 120, 189
Hillel II 250–8, 267
Historia Augusta 24, 244, 245, 248
Honorius 149, 155, 262, 301, 302, 305
Horvat Ammudim 138
Horvat Rimmon 151

Jacob's Well 70, 90, 103
Jaffa 101, 270
Jafia' 138
Jericho 11, 17, 50, 69, 89, 94, 97, 102, 115, 159, 193
Jerome 4, 10, 41 n. 38, 42, 55, 56, 57, 58, 64, 67, 68, 70, 71 n. 66, 75 n. 74, 78, 80, 87, 88, 90, 93, 96, 99, 100, 101–5, 103 n. 42, 106, 114, 116, 118, 119, 120, 141f., 150, 162, 163, 170, 181, 182f., 184, 189, 190, 201, 216, 242, 248, 260, 267, 274, 285, 314
Jerusalem (Aelia Capitolina) 4, 6, 10, 11, 18, 40–3, 36, 50, 51–64, 68, 78f., 82, 83, 87, 88–95, 97, 98f., 100, 102, 109f., 119f., 163–5, 193, 201–17, 309–13

Jewish Christians 2, 59, 71–81, 89, 94, 100, 109–13, 138, 282
Job 89, 94, 96, 97, 100, 108
John Chrysostom 4, 46 and n. 55, 54, 78, 96, 161, 175, 185, 197, 202–4, 211 n. 70, 215, 248, 300
John of Jerusalem 59, 102, 109, 112, 114, 117
Judiciary 22f., 238–41, 294, 303f.
Julian 3, 4, 33, 54, 55, 115, 126, 148, 162, 185–216, 225, 234f., 244, 247, 248, 249, 267, 283, 290
Juvenal of Jerusalem 50, 117

Kabul 50 and n. 6
Kafr Fahma 227
Kafr Misr 138
Kephar Selemia 109
Khirbet Marus 129
Khirbet Samara 217
Khirbet Shema' 126f.
Kokhab ha-Jarden 141

Lactantius 6, 25
Libanius 4, 7, 187f., 191, 192, 193, 196, 241–3, 247, 259–61, 267
Licinius 1, 25, 41
Lydda (Diospolis) 16, 18, 20, 30, 50, 89, 101, 112, 162, 164f., 176, 181f., 182 n. 46, 193, 269f., 274

Macarius of Jerusalem 18, 58, 59f., 65
Machpelah 43, 107

Magen 69 and n. 63
Mampsis 69 and n. 64
Mamre 65, 82, 102, 104, 190
Ma'on 151
Ma'oz Hayyim 139 n. 44, 140
Mark the Deacon 71 n. 67, 82, 84, 190, 197
Marriage law 23, 218
Meiron 122–8, 129, 130, 143, 183, 271
Melania the Elder and Younger 84, 116
Melchizedek 97, 98–100
Melito of Sardis 57
Micah 104, 113
Midrashim 3, 294f.
Milan, Edict of 1, 25, 185
mixed marriages 179, 218, 301f.
monks 96, 97, 108, 115–19, 309–13

Nablus 227
Nabratein 127, 129f., 183
Nahum 104
Nave 20, 167, 168
Nazareth 9, 70, 73, 75, 77, 103, 135
Neapolis 9, 16, 50, 89, 99, 176, 177, 178, 193, 219f.
Nicaea, Council of 1, 18, 43, 49f., 59
Nissana 69
Notitia Dignitatum 10f., 175

Oboda 69
Origen 35, 55 n. 23, 116

pagans, paganism 18, 56, 62f., 65, 67, 82, 121, 186–98, 221, 310

Paneas 15, 99, 105, 195
Patriarch(ate) 2, 4, 22, 28, 34, 36, 45, 72, 133, 134, 135, 141, 148, 149, 156, 160, 166, 173, 200, 202, 203, 208, 230–68, 233 n. 9, 239 n. 22, 243 n. 25, 272f., 276, 278, 279, 280, 293f., 303
Patricius 162, 173
Paula 84, 88, 101–5, 116, 118, 142
Paulinus of Nola 58, 113, 120
Paulus, *Sentences* of 22, 24, 35, 36, 37
Peter the Deacon 96
Petra 7, 10
Philostorgius 195, 213
Poim(e)nia 68, 84, 181
Porphyrius of Gaza 59, 70, 117, 198

Qasrin 132 and n. 25, 270
Qedesh 190
Qedumim 218 n. 4

Rabbis 28, 31f., 65, 111, 167, 171f., 208f., 230f., 238f., 262, 269–97
Rehov 139f.
Rehovot 69 n. 64
Rufinus of Aquileia 58, 95, 116, 192, 195, 206, 209, 213

Safed 20, 129
Safsaf 128
Salem 98f.
Samaritans 19, 20, 21, 24, 35, 73, 89, 98, 100 n. 37, 103, 106, 113, 121, 136 and n. 33, 137 n. 35, 163, 178, 193, 217–29, 226 n. 16, 228 n. 21,

Index of Names and Subjects

255 and n. 53, 286f., 305, 306, 310
Samuel 106, 113
Scythopolis *see* Beth Shean
Sebaste 50, 70, 103, 195
Sedima 97f.
Sepphoris (Diocaesarea) 9, 18, 20, 22, 30, 32, 71, 73, 75, 76, 77, 122, 135f., 162f., 164, 167, 168, 169, 173f., 178, 182 and n. 47, 184, 190, 234, 269f., 271, 273f., 279f., 281
Shave Zion 70
Slaves 24 n. 4, 36–40, 177, 178, 179, 262, 300f., 309
Socrates 58, 64, 162f., 181, 182f., 204, 206, 213
Solomon 91, 94
Sozomen 58, 59, 67, 81, 108 n. 58, 112, 162, 182, 190, 194, 198 n. 39, 200
Stephen 105, 106, 108–12
Subeita 69
Sumaqa 153, 159
Susiya 151
synagogues 20, 28, 29, 40f., 85, 91, 93, 121–60, 213, 216, 222, 226–9, 262, 276, 277–9, 296, 304, 307, 308, 309, 310

Tabgha 68, 70
Talmud (Palest.) 2, 3, 274, 275, 289–95
Tell Shalem (Tell er Radgha) 98
Temple (Jerusalem) 42f., 51, 53f., 91f., 93, 94, 124, 201–16, 223f., 225, 248, 293, 310
Teqoa 125, 126f., 128, 130
Tetrakomia 10, 30, 50, 123–33, 183, 271
textile industry 16, 173f., 176–81
Theodoret of Cyrrhus 182, 194, 213, 215
Theodosius I 68, 186, 196, 237, 238, 242, 298, 302
Theodosius II 1, 157, 197, 298, 306f., 311
Theophanes 163
Tiberias 18, 20, 22, 30, 31f., 71, 72, 117, 122, 123, 141 and n. 48, 142, 159, 162, 164f., 168, 176, 178, 181, 263, 266, 269f., 271f., 278, 280, 281, 291, 294, 297
Tyre 85, 123, 128, 136, 173f., 176, 270

Ursicinus 4, 166f., 167 n. 15, 168 n. 16, 171, 172, 173, 182 n. 46, 184, 282, 290

Valens 182, 188

Zebulon 50 and n. 6
Zechariah 92f., 112f.
Zoar 20, 208
Zur Natan 227

Index of Authors

(excluding purely bibliographical remarks in the footnotes)

Adan-Bayewitz, D. 123 n. 5
Adler, M. 211 and n. 70
Alon, G. 20 n. 29
Amit, D. 143 n. 59, 151 nn. 73, 75
Ariel, D. T. 132 n. 24
Avigad, N. 53, 129 n. 18
Avi-Yonah, M. 4f., 17, 19, 36 n. 26, 42, 45, 46, 77 n. 81, 84 n. 99, 88 n. 10, 105, 119, 141 n. 48, 145, 153 n. 79, 161, 164, 167 n. 15, 169 n. 17, 170 n. 22, 174, 175 n. 33, 176, 178, 182, 186, 207 n. 61, 208, 214, 216, 219, 237 n. 17, 261, 299, 308, 312
Ayalon, E. 227 n. 18

Bacher, W. 207, 285
Bachrach, B. S. 173 n. 27, 179, 182 n. 47
Bagatti, B. 54 n. 21, 73 n. 72, 77, 138
Barag, D. 150
Baron, S. W. 314
Ben-Dov, M. 51f., 54
Bieberstein, K. 55 n. 23
Binns, J. 115 n. 78
Biran, A. 130 n. 19
Blockley, R. C. 169 n. 18
Bloedhorn, H. 55 n. 23, 144 n. 60, 231 n. 3, 232 n. 5
Bonfils, G. de 35 n. 25, 37 n. 27, 39 n. 31, 178 n. 39
Borgehammer, S. 57 n. 32

Bowersock, G. W. 214f., and n. 78
Bowman, J. 222 n. 11
Bradbury, S. 112 n. 69
Braude, W. 164, 165
Brock, S. 203, 206, 214 n. 77
Broshi, M. 17, 141 n. 48
Büchler, A. 32 n. 21
Bull, R. J. 225 n. 14

Chen, D. 138 n. 41
Cohen, J. M. 217, 222 and n. 10, 220 n. 7
Corbo, V. 61, 75, 144, 148
Cramer, W. 313
Crowfoot, J. W. 82
Crown, A. D. 224 n. 12

Dan, Y. 265
Dar, S. 154 n. 80
Dauphin, C. M. 70 n. 65, 82 n. 95, 133 n. 26
Demougeot, E. 300 n. 2
Donner, H. 41, 88, 92 n. 17, 94f., 96, 101, 108, 121
Dothan, M. 148f., 232 n. 7, 233 n. 9, 236 and n. 14, 250, 258
Drijvers, J. W. 57 n. 32
Dubnow, S. 165, 172

Esbroeck, M. van 79 n. 89, 110 n. 60, 112

Fischer, M. 144 n. 60

Index of Authors

Flesher, P. V. M. 122 n. 3
Foerster, G. 124 n. 6, 190 n. 16
Frankel, Z. 166 n. 13, 167 n. 15, 173, 182 n. 46, 275
Frey, J.-B. 231, 233 and n. 9

Geiger, J. 167 n. 15, 169 n. 17, 173 n. 29, 174 n. 31, 210 n. 69
Geva, H. 51f.
Gibson, S. 55 n. 23
Goodblat, D. 230 n. 1
Goodman, M. 124
Goranson, S. C. 71 n. 68
Graetz, H. 161, 164, 170, 171, 184, 252, 266
Green, J. 98 n. 31
Gregg, R. C. 131 n. 22, 133 n. 26
Gregoire, H. 197 n. 37

Hachlili, R. 122 n. 3, 138 n. 39, 140 n. 47
Hall, B. 224 n. 12
Heinemann, J. 286 and n. 21
Hengel, M. 231 n. 3
Hezser, C. 238 n. 18, 239 n. 21, 269 n. 1, 270 n. 2, 272 n. 5, 273 nn. 6, 7, 274 n. 9, 278 n. 12, 280 n. 14, 291 n. 27
Hirschfeld, Y. 115 n. 78
Holum, K. G. 312
Honigmann, E. 312
Horbury, W. 153 n. 79
Hunt, E. D. 106, 110

Ilan, Z. 129 n. 18, 130 n. 20, 141 n. 50, 151 nn. 73, 75
Irshai, O. 40 n. 36
Isaac, B. 11 n. 11, 175 n. 33

Jacobs, M. 28 n.10, 230 n. 1, 232 n. 5, 233 n. 9, 238 n. 18, 239 nn. 20, 21, 243 n. 25, 246 n. 33, 250 n. 41, 265 nn. 69, 70, 266 n. 71, 272 n. 6
Jacoby, R. 129 n. 17
Jeremias, J. 107 n. 53
Jones, A. H. M. 176, 187 n. 5, 191 n. 17, 307f.
Juster, J. 23 n. 1, 246

Kasher, M. M. 253 and nn. 49, 50
Kippenberg, H.-G. 219 n. 6, 225 n. 14
Klein, S. 20 n. 29, 88 and n. 9, 90 n. 13, 104
Kloner, A. 152 n. 76
Kugener, M.-A. 197 n. 37

Langenfeld, H. 37, 39, 301 n. 3
Levine, L. I. 237, 239 n. 22, 243, 261 n. 66, 267
Lewy, Y. (H.) 200 n. 45
Liebermann, S. 27, 47, 125, 161, 167 n. 14, 169 n. 17, 175, 207 n. 62, 252, 291f.
Lifshitz, B. 136 and n. 31, 232, 233
Limor, O. 58 n. 37, 110 n. 61
Linder, A. 23 n. 6, 27 n. 8, 29, 59 n. 38, 137 nn. 33, 35, 155 n. 82, 235 n. 13
Loffreda, S. 141f., 144, 145 and n. 62, 147
Longstaff, T. R. W. 182 n. 47
Lorenz, R. 74 n. 73
Lucas, L. 74 n. 73
Luria, B. Z. 161 n. 1

Macdonald, J. 217, 226 n. 15

Mader, E. 82
Magen, Y. 189 n. 11, 218 n. 4, 224 n. 14, 225 n. 17, 228 n. 19
Maier, J. 262 n. 67, 287 n. 22, 288
Mann, J. 253 and n. 50
Ma'oz, Z. U. 131 and n. 22, 132 and nn. 24, 25, 133 n. 26, 183 n. 48
Maraval, P. 97 n. 27, 108, 118 n. 82
Mayerson, P. 9 n. 4
Mazar, B. 53, 209, 211
Meshorer, Y. 142
Meyers, E. 123 and n. 5, 124, 125, 126 and n. 13, 128 and n. 16, 129 and n. 19, 131
Mintzker, Y. 154 n. 80
Mittmann, S. 110 n. 62
Mommsen, Th. 155 n. 82, 311
Montgomery, J. A. 222 n. 9, 226 n. 16

Nathanson, B. G. 46 n. 55, 181 n. 44, 182f., 183 n. 48
Nau, F. 309, 311, 312
Nauerth, C. 90 n. 12
Naveh, J. 138 n. 41
Negev, A. 69 and n. 64, 196 n. 35
Netzer, E. 135 n. 30, 181 n. 45, 236 n. 14
Neusner, J. 1 n. 1, 282, 287, 288 n. 24, 290, 292
Noethlichs, K. L. 178 n. 39, 179 n. 42
Noy, D. 233 nn. 8, 9

Onn, A. 138 n. 40

Oudenrijn, M.-A. van den 111 n. 64

Parkes, J. 1
Patrich, J. 115 n. 78
Pritz, R. A. 80 n. 91

Rabello, A. M. 24 n. 4, 264 n. 67
Reeg, G. 228
Rosenfeld, B.-Z. 238 n. 19
Roth-Gerson, L. 136 n. 31, 152 n. 77
Rubin, Z. 59 n. 38
Russell, K. W. 126 n. 12, 134 n. 28
Rutgers, L. V. 294 n. 30

Safrai, S. 313
Safrai, Z. 17 n. 25, 20, 85 n. 101
Schäfer, P. 168 nn. 16, 17, 173 n. 29
Schmid, W. 244, 245
Scholem, G. 296
Schürer, E. 275
Schwabe, M. 136 and n. 31, 188, 266 n. 71
Schwemmer, A. M. 94 n. 20, 107 n. 53, 113 nn. 70, 71
Seaver, J. 173 n. 28
Segni, L. di 98 n. 31, 153 n. 79, 190 n. 16, 228 n. 20
Shahîd, I. 11 n. 12, 116 n. 79, 117 n. 80
Shoham, Y. 130 n. 20
Simon, M. 100 n. 37
Slouschz, N. 148
Sokoloff, M. 285 n. 20
Sperber, D. 16
Stemberger, G. 42 n. 45, 112 n. 69, 295 n. 31, 314 n. 15

Stenhouse, P. 217 n. 1, 224 n. 12
Stern, M. 54, 243 n. 25, 260 n. 60
Strobel, K. 237 n. 17, 265 n. 69
Strange, J. F. 125, 128 n. 16, 182 n. 47
Sussman, V. 229 n. 26
Syme, R. 237 n. 17, 244 nn. 27, 28

Taylor, J. E. 55 n. 23, 65 n. 53, 68 n. 60, 76 n. 76, 77 n. 84
Testa, E. 76 and n. 77, 80 n. 90
Thornton, T. C. G. 71 n. 68
Trombley, F. R. 187 n. 5
Tsafrir, Y. 68 n. 60, 69 n. 64, 75 n. 74, 98 n. 31, 144 n. 60, 190 n. 16, 229 n. 23
Tzaferis, V. 68 n. 60, 69 n. 63, 140 n. 46, 147 and n. 64

Urman, D. 131 and nn. 22, 23, 132 n. 25, 133 n. 26, 183 n. 48, 270 n. 3

Vitto, F. 134 n. 29
Vogt, J. 205 n. 56

Walker, P. W. L. 57 n. 33, 63 n. 48, 64 nn. 51, 52
Weiss, Z. 77 n. 81, 135 n. 30, 149 n. 70, 181 n. 45, 236 n. 14
Welten, P. 65 n. 53
Wewers, G. A. 31, 292 n. 28, 295
Wilken, R. L. 47, 78 n. 87
Wilkinson, J. 41, 55 n. 23, 56, 88, 95, 105

Yeivin, Z. 141, 142 and nn. 54, 55, 147, 150 n. 72, 151 n. 74

Zori, N. 139